THE RISE OF MODERN EUROPE

A SURVEY OF EUROPEAN HISTORY
IN ITS POLITICAL, ECONOMIC, AND CULTURAL ASPECTS
FROM THE END OF THE MIDDLE AGES
TO THE PRESENT

EDITED BY

WILLIAM L. LANGER

THE RISE OF MODERN EUROPE

Edited by WILLIAM L. LANGER

THE AGE OF THE

BAROQUE

1610–1660

BY

CARL J. FRIEDRICH

ILLUSTRATED

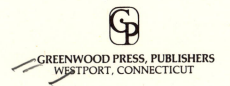

GREENWOOD PRESS, PUBLISHERS
WESTPORT, CONNECTICUT

Library of Congress Cataloging in Publication Data

Friedrich, Carl J. (Carl Joachim), 1901–
    The age of the baroque, 1610–1660.

    Reprint. Originally published: 1st ed. New York :
Harper, c1952. (The Rise of modern Europe)
    Bibliography: p.
    Includes index.
    1. Europe—History—17th century. I. Title.
II. Series: Rise of modern Europe.
D246.F74 1983   940.2'4   83–10736
ISBN 0-313-24079-5 (lib. bdg.)

Reprinted in 1983 by Greenwood Press
A division of Congressional Information Service
88 Post Road West, Westport, Connecticut 06881

Printed in the United States of America

10 9 8 7 6 5 4 3 2 1

To

HANS EBERHARD FRIEDRICH
Historian, poet, friend

TABLE OF CONTENTS

ILLUSTRATIONS

The illustrations, grouped in a separate section, will be found following page 112

INTRODUCTION

OUR age of specialization produces an almost incredible amount of monographic research in all fields of human knowledge. So great is the mass of this material that even the professional scholar cannot keep abreast of the contributions in anything but a restricted part of his general subject. In all branches of learning the need for intelligent synthesis is now more urgent than ever before, and this need is felt by the layman even more acutely than by the scholar. He cannot hope to read the products of microscopic research or to keep up with the changing interpretations of experts, unless new knowledge and new viewpoints are made accessible to him by those who make it their business to be informed and who are competent to speak with authority.

These volumes, published under the general title of *The Rise of Modern Europe,* are designed primarily to give the general reader and student a reliable survey of European history written by experts in various branches of that vast subject. In consonance with the current broad conception of the scope of history, they attempt to go beyond a merely political-military narrative, and to lay stress upon social, economic, religious, scientific and artistic developments. The minutely detailed, chronological approach is to some extent sacrificed in the effort to emphasize the dominant factors and to set forth their interrelationships. At the same time the division of European history into national histories has been abandoned and wherever possible attention has been focused upon larger forces common to the whole of European civilization. These are the broad lines on which this history as a whole has been laid out. The individual volumes are integral parts of the larger scheme, but they are intended also to stand as independent units, each the work of a scholar well qualified to treat the period covered by his book. Each volume contains about fifty illustrations selected from the mass of contemporary pictorial material. All noncontemporary illustrations have been excluded on principle. The bibliographical note appended to each volume is designed to facilitate further study of special aspects touched upon in the text. In general every effort has been made to give the reader a clear idea of the main movements in European history, to embody the monographic contributions of research workers, and to present the material in a forceful and vivid manner.

It is altogether natural that the period of the Thirty Years' War and the English Civil Wars, the period of such eminent and colorful personalities as Richelieu, Gustavus Adolphus, Wallenstein and Cromwell, should have attracted the interest of many of the great historians. Yet most of the historical writing on the period, even the most noteworthy, has been rather narrowly conceived in national terms. In the spirit of the nineteenth century it has been focused rather strictly on political and military events. Even the deep religious conflicts have generally been reduced to political concepts. Professor Friedrich, in contrast, has approached the subject from a broad European standpoint and has attempted to view the developments of this highly dynamic age as expressions of a prevalent state of mind—that of the baroque. This approach has enabled him to relate to each other many of the major features of the period—the internal and the external, the political, religious, artistic and scientific—and to demonstrate the interplay of forces in different countries and under apparently widely varying conditions. This has led him to expound rather unorthodox views about the political theories of James I and Charles I and about many other dominant issues of the time. His book is a stimulating contribution to the understanding of one of the most dramatic and fateful phases of European development.

WILLIAM L. LANGER

PREFACE

"THE last thing one settles in writing a book is what one should put in first," Pascal wisely remarked in one of his *Pensées*. He might have added that quite often one never settles it at all. This study, which has occupied a good part of the last twenty years, will never, could never, be really finished. The interrelation between politics and all the other manifestations of man's vegetative and creative life is so multiform, so rich in unexplored vistas, even for a limited period, that all one can do is to "close the books" at some reasonable point and bid one's conclusions farewell as one submits them to the indulgent critical examination of one's fellows in the pursuit of learning. The first half of the seventeenth century is one of the richest and most fully explored of western Europe's history. No two generations ever produced a richer harvest of towering individuals, and it has therefore justly been called the "age of giants." These giants created in their image the great Leviathan, as Hobbes, one of the greatest, called the state or commonwealth in striking symbolism.

This their most lasting creation had long been in process of formation. Its origins reach back to classical antiquity through the long ages of medieval corporate life and law. But in its modern incarnation it was a *novum* just as much as modern science, its intellectual counterpart. For it proposed to live a "life eternal without benefit of clergy." Power was and has remained its dynamic essence; justice, liberty, culture its incidental product, often perverted, in theory and practice, into instruments of its "restless search for power after power unto death." When we say the state "emerged," we mean that by 1660 it was there for all to see and for none to doubt, whereas in 1610 older institutional patterns like the empire, papacy, estates and free cities were still alive and active rivals.

Why should one link this emergence of the modern state to the baroque? Because it is my firm belief that men express through their works of art, their creations of beauty, what they have experienced and have thought to be true. Style is a mysterious quality, true only if spontaneous and spontaneous only if a projection of genuine feeling and true experience. Style convinces by its unique individuality. It cannot be "proven." To him who would deny the existence of a baroque style one can only answer with Goethe: *"Wenn ihr's nicht fühlt, ihr werdet's nie erjagen."* It is customary at this point to speak of "intuition." But this romantic category seems to me less suited than "sympathy" for describing the process by which a beholder becomes aware of, and eventually participates in, experiencing a certain style. The basic Greek concept, so well preserved in the German *"Mitleiden,"* that is to say the agony of sharing in the suffering that accompanies the birth of anything alive, genuine and true, seems to me to come closer to what it takes to understand a style.

If my feeble effort should help the reader to enter upon the high adventure of such vicarious experience, of such sharing of what two of the most remarkable generations of European man felt and forged, I shall be content. For it is the great privilege of the historian to try to conjure up such dramas of the past. And I may add that in my view the smallest detail may be as striking as the most universally recognized "historical event." Poet and scientist, artist and scholar must be blended somehow to give us convincing history. The varied individual destinies which interweave to form the carpet of history may or may not form patterns suitable for generalization. They do exhibit great and coherent unities of style, and the most expressive artist of the style of a period offers us, it seems to me, the most meaningful key to an interpretation of his time. The reason is simple: he knew the deepest creative impulses of his time. "When we see a natural style, we are astonished and delighted; for we expected to see an author, and we find a man." This penetrating observation of Pascal offers a clue: beyond the individual artist we find humanity.

During the long years of work on this study, help has been received from many quarters, from fellow scholars, students and assistants. It seems impossible to record them all. First of all, I should like to acknowledge my great debt for their many helpful courtesies to the staffs of the several Harvard Libraries, especially Widener, of the Concord Public Library, and last but not least of the Fogg Museum. Their patience proved inexhaustible. Many other libraries both here and abroad also helped. In the early days sound assistance and encouragement were provided by Roger Dow, Jr., now of the State Department, who developed bibliography and drew some of the maps. In more recent years, the fine scholarship of William F. Church helped me with Chapter Seven, and that of Charles Blitzer with Chapter Nine. To my son Paul William I am grateful for giving me many helpful hints in regard to Chapter Eight, which falls within his chosen field. The crucial issues of the more recent discussions of baroque as a style were opened up for me by two friends at Harvard, Wilhelm Köhler, professor of Fine Arts, and the late Karl Vietor, professor of Germanic Languages and Literatures. The first four chapters were read and the sections on the arts most helpfully criticized by Jacob Rosenberg, professor of Fine Arts, who also helped me greatly in the selection of paintings. More stimulating to me than he probably realizes were the suggestions I received from George Sarton early and late on the subject of philosophy and science. Hajo Holborn read and wisely commented upon Chapter Six. I might well wish that I were as learned as these and other friends who are specialists in the fields involved. But there is one nonspecialist who deserves gratitude above all; Lenore P. Friedrich. She read the proofs and prepared the index. What is more, she endured the antics of the scholar lost in thought, listened to the readings of drafts into the small hours, and kept my perspective on many items large and small for twenty years. As unbaroque as most truly English folks, she has taught me how to tell much that is imponderable in the story of the baroque age, how it lived and created its unique blend of medieval and Renaissance ways.

CARL J. FRIEDRICH

Chapter One

THE PATTERN OF POLITICS AND ECONOMICS

I. EUROPE IN 1610: THE SETTING

. . . the increase of any estate must be upon the Foreigner . . . (for whatsoever is somewhere gotten is somewhere else lost) . . .   —BACON

IT IS proverbially easy in retrospect to be wiser about events than were the contemporaries. For example, it now seems perfectly clear that nothing but the establishment of the modern state system could have been expected in 1610. Yet at the time, many thoughtful men were very uncertain. The activists of the Counter Reformation were, in fact, determined to re-establish the lost unity of Christendom, if necessary by force. Yet modern states had certainly been in the making over a long period; in England and France, in Sweden and Spain princes of superior ability had been developing effective bureaucracies, the core of modern government. "No great institution begins at a definite moment. It must be the result of long preparation and its leading features must be to some extent anticipated before any birthday may be selected."[1] Such a great institution—and is not the modern state the greatest of them all?—"emerges" rather than being born, and what is meant by "emergence" is the process by which during a given period its outlines become visible to all, like a whale coming to the surface of the sea. In the period when Thomas Hobbes could discourse upon the great Leviathan and when John Lilburne could cry out in anguish against this trend[2] the modern state may therefore be said to have emerged. It happened in these fifty years between 1610 and 1660. In 1610 the ancient Empire still seemed the focal point of Europe's order, politically. The Gunpowder Plot in England and the murder of Henry IV in France had just highlighted the aggressive potential of

[1] G. N. Clark, *The Seventeenth Century* (1929), 34, makes this observation with reference to joint stock companies. His admirably lucid and comprehensive discussion of the economic developments during the seventeenth century is, together with Eli Heckscher's *Mercantilism* (1931; English edition, 1935), the best general introduction to mercantilism.

[2] John Lilburne, *Jonah's Cry Out of the Whale's Belly* (1647), is a moving indictment of the state's threat to individual liberty in the day of the emergent dictatorship of Cromwell.

the expanding forces of the Counter Reformation; England seemed on the road to princely rule no less than the continent, in fact somewhat further advanced; and the papacy under Paul V was earnestly at work to restore the temporal power of the Holy See, skillfully seconded by the Order of the Society of Jesus. The great Bellarmine had vindicated the Pope's unique position as *arbiter mundi Christiani,* by his doctrine of the indirect power of the Pope in temporal matters. James I, in combating this doctrine, was more modern than he knew. "Jesuits are nothing but Puritan-Papists," he exclaimed.[3]

In 1660 all this was gone. The Empire had become an adjunct of the house of Hapsburg's Austrian dominions, while all other German princes, large and small, were "sovereign," notably the elector of Brandenburg whose impending challenge to Sweden foreshadowed the Prussian career. France was clearly and incontestably a modern, national state, absolute in its sway as the *Roi Soleil* took over the reins in the following year. If Mazarin had dreamed of securing the ancient imperial throne for his king, it was the last gasp of a moribund world of ideas. Dead also was the Counter Reformation and its ambition for reuniting Christianity, and Saint Peter's successors had ceased to be a major factor in Europe's great politics. At the same time, modern constitutionalism had crystallized in England as the permanent legacy of a long revolutionary struggle upon which the more moderate elements could all unite. This issue, to be sure, was not finally settled till 1688 when the English "people's" right to settle their own constitution was finally vindicated.

The contrast is not so striking, perhaps, in the economic as in the political field. For the growing forces of capitalism extended their sway throughout the period, as they had done before and continued to do thereafter. But whereas in 1610 the old leadership of Germany, Italy and to some extent Spain was still pretty generally acknowledged, and Venice and Augsburg, Genoa, Nürnberg and Cologne and many of the other great trading cities of the preceding age remained centers of European commerce, finance and industry, by 1660 all these had moved into the background. The economic leadership of three modern *nations,* organized as states, had taken their place. England, the Netherlands (United Provinces) and France were universally regarded as the focal points of European economic life. The joint stock company, though well under way in 1610, was by 1660 becoming the pacemaker of economic progress, while mer-

---

[3] Bellarmine, *De Romano Pontifice* (1610), Bk. V, Chs. 1–8. C. H. McIlwain, *The Political Thought of James I* (1918), Introduction.

cantilism had achieved pretty universal acceptance as the sound policy of increasing "the wealth of nations." [4]

The revolution of political and economic thought and action is all symbolized in the word and concept of the "state." While in 1606 Knolles could still translate Bodin's famous six books on the "republic" as a work dealing with the problems of "commonwealth," in England as on the continent it was the state that was acknowledged in 1660 to be the triumphant form of political organization. When Samuel Pufendorf, disguised as Monzambano, described the remnants of the empire as a monstrosity,[5] he was applying the standards of "reason of state." It was the impossibility of locating sovereignty in this putrefying remnant of the medieval empire which so aroused the brilliant young lawyer-statesman.

Perhaps most revealing is the fact that at the end of our period the first beginnings were being made of ascertaining the basic data of national life, and this new science was given, characteristically, the name of statistics.[6] Men concerned with these matters of state were likewise called "statists" in this period. All thought of public life revolved, in short, around the idea of the state. But before we consider in greater detail the institutional and theoretical ramifications of this development, it may prove helpful to sketch the basic economic data, such as population, commerce and industry, and to outline the doctrine of mercantilism which provided the framework of ideas in terms of which they were directed.

II. POPULATION

It was not until after 1660 that the full significance of vital statistics was appreciated by those who concerned themselves with the new national states. Hence, in spite of the great stress laid by the mercantilists upon the interrelation between population and general prosperity, our knowledge in matters of population is inferential, rather than based upon statistical data in the modern sense. There are some exceptions, but in general the statements of these problems remained nonquantitative throughout the

[4] For this see below, pp. 12 ff.

[5] Severini de Monzambano, *De Statu Imperii Germanici ad Laelium fratrem liber* (1666); cf. the interesting comments in Pütter's *Literatur des Teutschen Staatsrechts* (1776), I, 234 ff.

[6] To be sure, the importance of detailed statistical knowledge with regard to cities had been clearly recognized in the later Italian renaissance. On this point, I must dissent from Clark who seems to overlook these precedents, so brilliantly portrayed by Jacob Burckhardt in *Die Kultur der Renaissance in Italien,* translated as *The Civilization of the Renaissance in Italy* by S. C. G. Middlemore (1878).

fifty years here under review.[7] Such writers as Hippolitus a Collibus and
Botero,[8] in describing the growth of cities, expounded the view that more
hands brought more riches, and more riches more hands. But while such
scholars were fertile in describing and explaining the process of population growth, they were singularly unprecise about the numerical facts.
The many descriptive accounts of countries and cities, like the famous
Matthaeus Merian's *Topographia Germaniae* (1642), did not give any
definite information about the population of these cities, though there
were occasional remarks containing a hint: 11,000 died of the plague at
Augsburg in 1642, and in the following year another fourth—so presumably Augsburg had about 45,000 inhabitants. By exploring all such
available hints and inferences, scholars like Beloch have computed comparative figures. Still they remain largely guesswork. The Empire had
perhaps twenty million inhabitants, France sixteen, Italy thirteen, Spain
and Portugal ten, England and Wales four and a half, Poland more than
three, Scotland and Ireland two, the Dutch republic two and a half, the
Scandinavian kingdoms over two.[9] But the Empire and Italy were, of
course, broken up into many principalities. Since there were about five
and a half million inhabitants in the Hapsburg lands proper within the
Empire, one can see, by adding this amount to Spain and Portugal, that
Europe was divided into two almost equal great powers, France with
sixteen million and Hapsburg with fifteen and a half; around these
tension poles were grouped in shifting agglomerations the numerous
smaller principalities, ranging from a few hundred thousand, like Denmark, to the five million of England.

Europe at this time was still overwhelmingly rural and agricultural.
There were no more than thirteen or fourteen cities with over 100,000
inhabitants. These cities were essentially of two types: the great trading
centers, like Antwerp, and the capitals of the large countries, like London,

[7] Cf. for most carefully developed estimates Beloch, "Die Bevölkerung Europas zur Zeit
der Renaissance," *Zeitschrift für Sozialwissenschaft*, III, 765 ff. Miss C. V. Wedgwood, in
her book on the *Thirty Years' War*, expresses herself as so discouraged about statistics of the
period that she simply recites contemporary accounts in all their extravagance.

[8] *Incrementa Urbium sive de Causis magnitudinis urbium liber Unus* (1600) by H. a
Collibus is a compilation of reasons without quantitative specification; the same is true of
Botero's *Delle Cause della grandezza delle città* (1588; English translations 1606 and 1635),
although it anticipates Malthus in its discussion of the limits of urban growth in which a
quantitative factor is implied, though not empirically developed.

[9] How extreme are the variations in estimates, can be seen from such contrasts as France
5–20, Italy 3–13, Poland 3–11. The population estimates for Russia are even more uncertain; they vary from 5 to 15 million for 1600.

Paris and Vienna. While the former were still crowded within walls and moats, symbols of medieval defensive strength, the capital cities of the princes, great and small, were beginning to sprawl all over the pacified countryside. At the same time, what economic historians have called the "metropolitan economy," while far advanced in England by 1610, was becoming universal by 1660. As the greater part of England had become the economic hinterland of London, its center of commerce and capital resources, the same happened in regard to Paris, Vienna and other capital cities. The expanding economic life brought rapid growth to such metropolises. In many ways the "heart" of the emergent modern state, these capital cities soon outstripped the older mercantile centers, like Venice and Antwerp.[10]

While there occurred these shifts in population, the over-all growth was not very considerable. In fact, Clark and others have argued for a relative stability of populations. After giving the comparative figures for a few leading states between 1600 and 1700,[11] he observes that if additions to territory could be discounted, these increases would seem less, but "the whole is little better than guess-work."

III. COMMERCE AND FINANCE

As already indicated, trade routes underwent a steady change during the first half of the seventeenth century. The United Provinces forged ahead against Spain, while Britain grew strong enough under the Protectorate to challenge the Dutch successfully in the first national trade war of modern history. Meanwhile the financing of these ever-widening commercial activities likewise passed from Italian and German into Dutch and British hands. The shift in trade was connected with the opening of new ocean routes, which brought a great increase in volume rather than a basic change in the character of international trade. There were added, however, some important new commodities, especially tobacco and potatoes.

[10] However, Paris and London belonged even in medieval times among the largest cities, the former having perhaps 100,000, the latter 35–40,000. Most cities were then not over 10,000.

	1600	1700
[11] France	16	19
Spain	8	6
Austria	5½	7½
England	4½	5½
Netherlands ...	2½	2½

These figures are taken from Beloch, op. cit., it appears.

Sombart has asserted that "the modern state emerged from the silver mines of Mexico and Peru and the gold mines of Brazil"; [12] while this may be considered an exaggeration, the great influx of precious metals undoubtedly played a significant role, and occasionally the capture of treasure fleets vitally affected the course of events, as will be described in later chapters.

Besides this overseas trade, there was of course a great deal of exchange trade going on throughout Europe. Various countries and regions specialized in different products, both basic and manufactured. From the Mediterranean came wines, oil, and fruits; from England and Spain, wool; from France and Portugal, Poland and Salzburg, salt; from Sweden and Spain, iron and other minerals; from Germany and the Low Countries, textiles, which France also exported; while England exported lead and tin. There was also a considerable trade in bread grains. The Netherlands, crowding over two millions into a small and to some extent barren land, had to import these grains, as did Norway. Much grain came from the Baltic countries, but France also was an exporter, at times to Italy and Spain. This inter-European trade, while important, did not match the trade in precious metals and spice from the "Indies," from Asia and Africa and America. Both were closely interrelated in the hands of the great merchants who carried on this work.

The seventeenth century is, of course, the heyday of the trading companies, merchant adventurers and the like. The difference between them and the merchants of Italy, Germany and the Low Countries may, however, be easily overstated. The work of the Fuggers and Welsers of Augsburg, for example, while built around the nucleus of a family, was carried on by many other members of the firm who acquired partnership through participation in the capital and work of these houses. The existence of shares or joint stock also seems to have been a common characteristic. The main point of divergence—and it is an important one in the light of the general statist trend of the age—is the fact that the new joint stock companies were chartered by a monarch in the name of the state. Thus the East India Company, perhaps the greatest of them all, had been so chartered in 1600, and the Dutch East India Company in 1602. They were followed by the Hamburg Company, chartered in 1611, which all but

[12] Werner Sombart, *Der Moderne Kapitalismus* (1922, fifth edition), 366. Sombart adds to this often-quoted remark the broader reflection: "To put it another way: '[There was] as much state as silver (later gold)!' Of course only in the sense of a conditioning: without such a rich production of precious metals as occurred since the discovery of America the modern princely state would not have developed so rapidly and generally."

monopolized continental trade; presumably its annual commerce with Germany and the Low Countries during the reign of James I was about £1,000,000.[13] It was followed in 1613 by the Russia Company, also an offshoot of the merchant adventurers which had been started in the middle of the sixteenth century. Finally, the Levant Company had received a charter in 1592 when it was formed as an amalgamation of the Turkey and Venice companies. Dutch activity closely rivaled these British enterprises, for the success of which James I had such a tender regard. Indeed it is not perhaps too much to say that for the prosperity of these enterprises James made peace with Spain one of the cornerstones of his foreign policy—a policy which had far-reaching consequences.[14] The French in turn joined the fray. In vain did Henry IV try to force the Dutch to yield him a share in their East India Company. When they remained adamant, he set about to start his own, in 1604, but it failed. It was later to be followed by a somewhat more successful attempt on the part of Richelieu and Mazarin (1626, 1642), who also started a number of additional companies. Other countries, such as Sweden and Brandenburg, were even less successful.[15]

While these commercial organizations were getting under way, backed as they were by the rising national states, it stands to reason that the older patterns disintegrated. In the beginning of our period, we find such houses as the Welsers still engaged in very aggressive enterprises. By linking themselves with the Spanish monarchy, these merchants not only handled what to the "noble Spaniard" appeared too sordid a business, but the Welsers in the sixteenth century even operated a virtually autonomous colonial state of their own in South America, as did the Jesuits in their famous state of Paraguay throughout most of the seventeenth. But these merchants could not successfully compete with the rising metropolitan economies and their militarily powerful backers. The great days of the Hanse were already over; by 1629 only Lübeck, Hamburg and Bremen remained important Hanse cities, while the Dutch and the Swedes fought over their inheritance.

That the masters of the great territorial states, like France and England, should seek to free themselves of "foreign" dependence, such as their financing by Florentine and German bankers, is rather natural. But sim-

---

[13] W. B. Duffield, "Chartered Companies" in Eleventh *Encyclopedia Britannica*.
[14] See below, pp. 131, 274.
[15] The far-reaching consequences of the special companies organized for North America will, because they became settling rather than trading enterprises, be treated elsewhere. See below, Chapter Five, pp. 154 ff., 286 ff.

ilar considerations also impelled commercial and industrial enterprises to prefer domestic capital resources. Thus the rise of industry and commerce was accompanied by the development of banks.

In the early part of the century, the financial traditions of the "Age of the Fuggers," following the "Age of the Medicis," were still very potent.[16] The ever-increasing need for funds to carry on the wars had obliged the princes to go to these early capitalists and bankers for help. But in our period, these requirements became so large that the shrinking resources of houses like the Fuggers were no longer able to meet them.[17] What happened in our period was that the state itself became the source of credit, rather than the financial houses who had hitherto loaned funds. "War became an industry of the State. The only credit adequate to carry it on was the credit of the states, or more exactly the great lending states, round which were grouped fringes of smaller, poorer, subsidized or borrowing states, the clients of the great allies who financed their armies for them." [18] This development will become particularly vivid later in the course of the story of the Thirty Years' War. In a certain sense, it can be said that Richelieu conquered the German polity by dint of his grasp of the new finances. Richelieu has often been criticized for his financial administration, because the debts of France rose, but it is equally true that he had a clear appreciation of the credit resources of a great state.[19] Olivárez, his Spanish rival, failed to do so. Likewise Mazarin did not carry through Richelieu's conceptions, and the state went bankrupt in 1648—an event which had quite a bit to do with the outbreak of the Fronde (see below).

The one really sound state, from a financial standpoint, was the Netherlands. Here, in a merchants' oligarchy, the state dealt directly with the lenders. Besides, the Bank of Amsterdam, founded in 1609 and following the Italian patterns, provided a remarkably steady management for the currency resources of the country. Throughout our period, this great bank was the financial center of northern Europe.[20]

The Bank of Amsterdam also developed a thriving exchange which, while much concerned with the trade in various goods, also started the

---

[16] Cf. R. Ehrenberg, *Das Zeitalter der Fugger* (1896), Vol. II.

[17] It should be noted that the Fuggers, distrustful of the lasting value of money obligations in an age of rising prices, had steadily immobilized their resources by acquiring great landed estates and titles which handicapped them, of course, in their banking operations.

[18] Clark, *op. cit.*, 42.

[19] See Henri Hauser, *La Pensée et l'Action Économiques du Cardinal de Richelieu* (1944).

[20] Ernest Baasch, *Holländische Wirtschaftsgeschichte* (1927). Note also the famous discussion in Adam Smith, *An Inquiry into the Nature and Causes of the Wealth of Nations*, Bk. IV, Ch. III, Pt. I, 443–52.

trade in the stock of joint stock companies. London followed suit later; in both cases the development of these exchanges became a mighty factor in the expansion of the capital market and an extension of the credit system, both public and private. It is challenging to reflect upon the interrelationship between these thriving business marts and the "golden age" of Dutch art and culture. Even if no facile causal relationship may readily be constructed in line with the economic interpretation of history, there appears to be a striking coincidence in economic and cultural creativity, as in Italy earlier.

The other important bank founded in our period was that of Hamburg (1619). Like its Dutch sister, it encountered occasional difficulties, by going beyond its deposit and exchange function, and engaging in loans to the government. But on the whole it was remarkably successful.

IV. INDUSTRY AND AGRICULTURE

It may seem strange to link industry and agriculture, since it has been customary, in view of the industrial revolution, to treat these two realms of economic activity as strictly antithetical. But in the period here under consideration, both appeared so closely bound up with each other as the country's productive base, that they were often treated together by writers in the mercantilist tradition. Not to anticipate the discussion of their views,[21] I should merely want to draw attention to the fact that in the seventeenth century industry had not yet acquired the specialized meaning of a later age.

Production increased slowly, but steadily, throughout the period from 1610–1660, in the advancing nations, while in Germany and Spain it fell off quite markedly. A slow extension of the factory system took place; for it must not be supposed that the factory had to await the machine; since times immemorial, especially in antiquity, large numbers of workers had been gathered in one place of productive effort. Not only in textiles, but in numerous other lines, the "spirit of capitalism" made itself felt in the setting up of larger industrial establishments. Printing works, sawmills, sugar refineries, breweries, distilleries, soap-boiling and candle-making works, tanneries, various chemical and dyestuff works, as well as the finishing processes in the textile field, like dyeing and fulling, were among those which profited from large-scale organization.[22] The same is true, of course, of mining and the ensuing metal-working tasks, like smelting. We

---

[21] See below, pp. 12 ff.
[22] Clark, *op. cit.*, 65 ff.

find the Fuggers and Welsers, as well as other great merchants, engaged in financing these enterprises—clear indication of the interrelation between commerce and industry. But as the century wore on, ever-greater efforts were made to free industrial production from these commercial controls. Princes, like James I and Charles I, were ready to assist such enterprises by the grant of charters of monopoly. Richelieu was similarly ready to stimulate industrial production by royal support. On the other hand, these "monopolistic" policies not only aroused fierce opposition, and often bitter resistance, but also encouraged an unsound exploitative conduct of the businesses themselves.

While these larger production units were being organized, we find little organization of the employees serving in these enterprises. Nor was the law favorable to such undertakings until much later. Occasional outbursts of violence occurred, especially on the part of journeymen and apprentices; they were vigorously suppressed. They were viewed in the light of re-bellions, especially in all those cases where the state's authority was involved through charters, or the grant of privileges and capital support. Here and there we find the state inclined to shape policy in accordance with the medieval tradition of fair play within the guilds and corporations, so as to give everyone a "living." But such paternalism often conflicted with the main objective of mercantilist statesmen: to increase the state's revenue and power.[23]

It is curious how relatively limited a role inventions and innovations played in the industrial advance during this period. There were some minor improvements, and generally speaking localized patterns of in-dustrial production spread to wide areas. But there was nothing like an "industrial revolution." Science, as we shall see, was indeed making some of its most basic discoveries, and within the limited circle of its devotees there was great enthusiasm for its eventual utility. But as yet science was too "basic," too philosophical and abstract to be of much value to those who were engaged in making the necessaries and luxuries of life for gain. Such inventions as ruby glass, etched glass, fire hoses and the like, surely are not very impressive; certainly nothing like the printing press of the fifteenth, or the guns of the sixteenth century. Not infrequently, the innovations which an ingenious inventor had made available, like the ribbon loom, were actually forbidden by the authorities, as depriving men of their living, being a "devilishe invention." So advanced a nation as the

23 See below, p. 13.

Dutch repeatedly restricted its use during our period. Finally the desire of the authorities to develop manufactures took the form of forbidding the export of particular raw materials; thus England throughout the period maintained strict laws against the export of wool.

It is, of course, impossible to enter the vast field of industrial locations even on a selective basis. A few instances must suffice. Leiden and Haarlem were the wool manufacturing centers in the Netherlands. France's woolen centers were Rouen and Amiens, while Lyons, Tours and Nîmes specialized in silk. The chief center for cotton textiles was Holland, although after the middle of the century England surpassed it.

There is one kind of industry which is necessarily localized, and that is mining. For iron, the Erzberg in Styria, the Erz Gebirge between Saxony and Bohemia, and Sweden were most important.[24] Coal was as yet little used, but a number of the locations since become famous seem to have been operating at this period or before, notably Yorkshire, Saxony, Silesia, and the Ruhr. Many metals other than iron were mined in the Erz Gebirge (hence its name: Ore Mountains), such as silver, which was mined also in Spain and in the Tyrol. Tin and copper likewise came from this territory, as well as from Cornwall and Sweden. Finally we might mention the mercury mines of Almadén in Spain, the richest in the world to this day.

Agriculture, like mining, is based upon the given fact of a country's soil and climate. But the variations are relative, not absolute. Great setbacks to agricultural production were caused by the wars of this period and its attendant devastations; in Spain, in France, and more especially in Germany, whole villages were abandoned and the soil allowed to lie fallow for many years. England was not similarly afflicted, and perhaps the steady growth of her population may in part be related to this preservation of agricultural production. Certain specific improvements spread in our period and helped to increase the productivity of agricultural lands, such as fertilizers and fallow crops. Sir John Norden in his *Surveyor's Dialogue* (1607) urged the introduction of clover as a fallow and feed crop; similarly Sir Richard Weston's *Discourse on Husbandry in Brabant and Flanders* (1645) advocated the introduction of clover.

In line with such improvements, there was considerable interest in the science of botany and botanical gardens became the fashion throughout Europe. Following the earlier example of Padua and Leiden, among

[24] For this and the following see Werner Sombart, *op. cit.,* 532 ff., and the literature cited there.

others, the *Jardin des Plantes* was started in Paris which to this day preserves its formalized baroque layout. Other such gardens were started in Strassburg (1620), Upsala (1627), Jena (1629), and Oxford (1632).

To the extent that meats, as well as woolens and hides, were recognized as important sources of national wealth, definite efforts were made to improve agricultural stock. A number of the important breeds of cattle and sheep seem to have come into being in this period, although the data are not reliable enough to be specific. Although as yet far removed from modern genetics, there was practical appreciation of the importance of breeding and better, sounder methods of selection seem to have been developed, or to have spread from one part of Europe to another.

V. MERCANTILISM AS A SYSTEM OF POWER

All these varied activities were encompassed within the set of economic and political doctrines which became known as mercantilism. As the name suggests, by mercantilism is understood a welter of ideas about how to organize commerce; commerce however was very broadly interpreted to mean economic activity in general. There has been a great deal of controversy about the true meaning of mercantilism, as there were many arguments among those who expounded mercantilist ideas. If one wants to call it a system at all, it certainly was full of divergencies, if not contradictions. There were variations in successive periods, and there were considerable differences between different nations. But the central idea of mercantilism is quite distinct: it was the assignment to the state of the central role in shaping economic well-being. The state in this context is understood as a secular organization with practical and expedient rather than moral objectives. In a sense, mercantilism is at least as much a political as it is an economic theory. Indeed, it may be called the most comprehensive theory of the modern state, as it was emerging in this period.[25]

It has been claimed that mercantilism was in a sense merely the extension of the medieval system under which "the government of each separate town controlled the enrichment of that town as a whole."[26] Such a statement involves a misunderstanding of the essence of the modern state, organized for the acquisition of power. This search for "power after power unto death" (Hobbes) is entirely alien to the medieval notion of "an

---

[25] Philip W. Buck, *The Politics of Mercantilism* (1942). Also Eli Heckscher, *Mercantilism*, Vol. II, P. I, "Mercantilism as a System of Power."

[26] Clark, *op. cit.*, 22.

adequate living," which in any case was transcended by the higher moral purpose of man's religious loyalties. If mercantilists strove to increase the wealth of a nation—and there can be no quarrel on that—they did it primarily, if not exclusively, for the purpose of providing the sinews of war and conquest. As Colbert was eventually to put it in a famous letter: "Trade is the source of public finance, and public finance is the vital nerve of war." And victory in war was seen in turn to be the basis for aggrandizement and power.

With that ultimate power objective clearly in one's mind, one can say that "national wealth through the regulation and protection of commerce" was the mercantilist credo. This regulation and protection of commerce was superimposed by an authoritarian bureaucracy, idealized as the state, as contrasted with the autonomous and self-governing guilds of the Middle Ages. So early an act as the Elizabethan Statute of Artificers (1563) clearly shows the trend which was to triumph in the period between 1610 and 1660 in the policies of men like Richelieu, Wallenstein, Gustavus Adolphus and Cromwell. For this is the striking thing about mercantilism, that no matter how deeply divided politically, all the top-ranking leaders of this period were practitioners of mercantilist policy, and much of their success flowed from their superior handling and radical application of these policies. The active governmental concern with every department of economic life is a recurrent theme of the period. The state was made into the ever-alert guardian of the nation's entire economic life. If an economy was to prosper, it could do so only by the exertions of a "creative state"—a theme which has been resumed in our time. What intensified these efforts was the notion that the gain of one was necessarily the loss of another. In Bacon's words: "The increase of any estate must be upon the foreigner, for whatsoever is somewhere gotten is somewhere lost"; hence, at the height of mercantilism, after the middle of the seventeenth century, the trade wars are starting with the English-Dutch war during the Protectorate.[27] Mercantilism is what one might call "cash box thinking" and indeed the mercantilists became unduly preoccupied with the gathering of "treasure," more especially gold and silver.

Early mercantilism had found one of its most clear-cut expressions in John Hales's *Discourse of the Common Weal of this Realm of England* (1581); it was more fully developed in Thomas Mun's *England's Treasure by Foreign Trade* (written in the late 1620's, but not published till 1664).

[27] See below, pp. 308-9.

Both writers objected to the medieval idea of restraining trade in order to prevent local scarcities, and urged the expansion of trade as the only sound road to national wealth. The same idea was most succinctly put by Richelieu in his *Testament Politique* in the section dealing with the problem "concerning trade as dependent upon dominion over the seas," but it likewise animates his general discussion of "sea power" (*puissance sur mer*). Clearly recognizing the key importance which colonies had for the Spanish crown and the consequent determination of the Spaniards to be strong at sea, he urged France *"pas d'y être faible."* The success of the Spanish monarchy in this field had indeed been a mainstay of its rising power in the preceding age. Time and again victory on the battlefield had gone to the Spaniards on account of the professional armies they had been able to develop with the silver and gold brought from the Indies. Colonial enterprise of this early, predatory nature redounded to the advantage of kings, not only in their conflicts with other princes, but likewise in those with their subjects. What would have happened to the parliamentary party in England if Charles I could have drawn upon a store of silver and gold as vast as Philip II had tapped when he reduced the estates of Castile? Having witnessed the decisive effect of gold upon the fate of governments, it is understandable that mercantilist writers should have concentrated upon how to acquire gold or its equivalents as the prince's main concern. That the emphasis shifted from the physical capture of gold and other treasures to the development of trade is perhaps the most significant achievement of the mercantilist thinkers. Mercantilism came to foster many remarkable innovations to enlarge the government's resources; [28] none more so than the modern state itself.

VI. THE STATE VERSUS THE ESTATES

None of these economic doctrines are really comprehensible unless they are viewed against the background of political thought about the state itself. Such political theory in turn calls for a brief sketch of the institutional evolution which it sought to rationalize and for which it set the frame. To understand the disintegration of the government with estates

[28] In his *Testament Politique*, Richelieu wrote: " *A peine les armées combattent—elles une foi en un an, mais il faut qu'elles vivent tous les jours, et qu'elles subsistent avec ordre. . . . Il se trouve en l'histoire beaucoup plus d'armées péries faute de pain et de police que par l'effort des armées ennemies."* Cf. also Eli Heckscher, *Mercantilism, passim,* for numerous examples. Jacob Viner's criticism is not supported by the evidence as I see it; cf. his "Power versus Plenty as Objectives of Foreign Policy in the Seventeenth and Eighteenth Centuries," in *World Politics,* I, 1 ff.

without including the economic revolution resulting from colonial enter-prise is surely impossible. But to understand the economic doctrines of mercantilism without a grasp of the political thought of rising absolu-tism, of state and sovereignty, is equally out of the question. Advanced thought was absolutist thought, and it was mercantilist thought. It was thought which revolved around the central idea that men have the power to mold their social environment by appropriate legislation and policy.

These ideas had a common root in the notion of "reason of state." Set forth by G. Botero (1540–1617) in a famous book *Della Ragion di Stato* (1589), the idea captured the imagination of the early baroque age. Dis-tilled from the Renaissance like a Jesuit church, it has been said, "reason of state," *"raison d'état"* or *"ragione di stato,"* was the universal subject of discussion among politically interested men, especially in Italy. Following Botero, a large body of writing on reason of state was put forward in Italy,[29] baroque in spirit and structure, of which perhaps the most re-markable is T. Boccalini's *Ragguagli di Parnaso* (1612–13), in which various writers and actors of the political scene are brought before Apollo's court to be judged for their doctrines and deeds, foremost among them, of course, Machiavelli.

The way in which reason was, in this literature, reinterpreted as mean-ing the rational means for the accomplishment of metarational ends illustrates the shift from ethics to politics, or rather the blending of the two through the skillful rationalization of means. It had been no accident that a Counter Reformation Jesuit, G. Botero, had popularized the term. In a deeper sense, the very doctrine of the Jesuit Order (see below) might be called a doctrine of "reason of church." Such effort at rationalizing the means required for the success of the papacy in pursuing the goals of the Counter Reformation would necessarily, in its search for adequate secular support, seek to mobilize the "state" as a means toward this end, and to justify its deeds of coercion and violence when directed toward the victory of sound doctrine. It was characteristic of this entire literature that a dis-tinction was being drawn between a good and a bad reason of state, depending upon what ends it was put to. This is a distinction which would have provoked the scorn of Machiavelli's frankly pagan and blandly pragmatic mind. But to these baroque minds it was as natural as the curves with which their artists dissolved the stately harmony of renais-

[29] See the brilliant study by G. Ferrari, *Corso sugli scrittori politici d'Italia* (1862), and F. Meinecke, *Die Idee der Staatsraison* (1924), Chs. III–V, who suggested the comparison with a Jesuit church, p. 83.

sance forms. Hence they argued: "The reason of state is a necessary violation [*eccesso*] of the common law for the end of public utility." [30] Linked to this idea of a special means-end rationality directed toward the public utility is, as can be seen from this definition, the notion of particular necessities occasioned by a state's peculiar interests. Hence a doctrine about the "necessities" of particular states sprang up out of the arguments over reason of state. The concrete manifestations of this doctrine we shall encounter in the chapters which describe the policy of men like Richelieu, Wallenstein and Gustavus Adolphus.

But one's comprehension of the problem would be most inadequate, if he assumed that all thought and action followed one persistent trend. The illustrious names of Grotius, Richelieu, Hobbes, Cromwell, Spinoza, Gustavus Adolphus and the great elector of Brandenburg all represent the dominant and victorious trend—victorious, that is, in 1660. But in 1610 and for many years thereafter there were other men who struggled to resist and these too had their champions in speech and writing. Most important among these opposing trends was the one which endeavored to uphold the cause of the representative estates. Opinions here ranged all the way from feudal reaction to democratic dreams. Nor were these forces uniformly unsuccessful. There were regions in which they did not succumb to the rising absolutism, notably England. The British Isles, then more inaccessible from the continent than America is today, under the Tudors had seen a greater measure of effective monarchical absolutism than any other country. Indeed, what happened on the continent in the period from 1610 to 1660 had been anticipated in England under the Tudor dynasty. Their absolutism had offered escape from the devastating civil war of the Roses; the absolutism of seventeenth-century Europe seemed likewise to hold the promise of an escape from the horrors of the civil wars of religion. It has often been remarked that James I and Charles I, the much criticized Stuart kings, were not so much striving to set up a type of government previously unknown in England, as struggling to maintain the royal prerogative as established by the Tudors. While this is true enough, such comparisons neglect the fact that the rule of Henry VIII and Elizabeth rested securely upon royal ministers of outstanding ability, more especially the two Cecils. What the Stuarts forgot was that royal favorites were no tenable substitute for such skillful councilors.

[30] Pietro A. Canonhiero, *Dell'introduzione alla politica, all ragion di stato . . . Libri X* (1614): "*La ragione di stato è un necessario eccesso del guire commune per fine di publica utilità.*"

It cannot be denied that theorists as well as practitioners in this period talked about monarchy as if it were the Aristotelian rule of one. Yet who ruled in France, Richelieu or Louis XIII? This combination, so typical of the age, really constituted a partnership, for neither king nor minister could rule without the other. In the Aristotelian sense, there really ruled only one monocrat between 1610 and 1660, and that was Oliver Cromwell. Yet he was most reluctant to acknowledge it; it was a revolutionary idea. The Protector, as he eventually allowed himself to be called, realized that nothing could make so evident the illegitimate origin of his government as his assumption of the title of a king or sovereign. Of course, there were kings, like Henry IV and Gustavus Adolphus, who closely approached his despotic rule. But the great French king had his Sully, the Swede his Oxenstierna.

What is more, behind these famous builders of the modern state stood the army, and the bureaucracy, the nameless hundreds and thousands of faithful servants of the king and crown who in these decades emerge as the core of modern government. It is this closely knit and increasingly efficient hierarchy of officials, modeled after the pattern of the priesthood of the Holy Church, which wrapped itself into the mysterious and awe-inspiring cloak of the "state"—to this day capitalized in French as *"État."* It was in the days of Richelieu that this impersonal state emerged.

To the modern mind the word *state* has become so all-embracing in its connotations, so thoroughly permeated with the ideas of sovereignty and independence that it is difficult to recapture the thought and feeling of an age in which the employment of the word as signifying unity was a startling, novel concept. Prior to this period it had always been the plural "estates." The English language obscures the connection which in French is still patent, between *"L'État"* and *"les États."* The state emerges as the unitary, singular estate from the multitude of estates which had characterized the medieval constitutional order. There had been the several estates of the king, the nobility, the clergy and the commons united in parliament —to illustrate by the English example. Numerous variations in detail do not alter the fundamental outline; even the rich complexity of the estates of the Holy Roman Empire in central Europe followed the general pattern. To be sure, within its highly organized institutional structure there were estates within estates, so that the elector of Brandenburg, himself a member of the electoral estate of the Empire, faced in his own realm several bodies of estates composed of the territorial nobility and towns. During the second half of the sixteenth century these local estates had been gaining ground in many territories, and as we shall see, the fatal cataclysm of the Thirty Years' War originated in a conflict between the estates of Bohemia and their prince. These developments show clearly a disintegration of the medieval order, an irreconcilable dualism which in England manifested itself in the novel idea that parliament was a thing separate and apart from the king. "In the later Middle Ages there had everywhere grown up a new type of institution . . . the system of estates." [31] The estates' assemblies occupied different positions in different places, but almost all of them operated under a system of government rather similar to that of England. To be sure, there were no estates in Italy. And in Spain, the Cortes had been crushed in Castile, if not in Aragon, during the sixteenth century, while in France the estates were on the vanishing point at the beginning of the seventeenth century, the last one being held in 1618. But elsewhere they were holding their own or even challenging the crown in the impending struggle for supremacy.

The system in its typical form was a joint or mixed government by a prince, himself considered an estate, and the other estates. The division of competence was not very clearly defined; it oscillated between prince and estates according to the circumstances. Such a prince would be hereditary in fact, but his taking office was conditional upon an oath of office administered by or in the presence of the representatives of the other estates. Who were these other estates? No general answer can be given. They might consist of the clergy, the nobility, the squirearchy, the municipalities and the peasants. But either the clergy or the nobility were occasionally, and the peasants usually, lacking, and after the Reformation the clergy disappeared in many of the Protestant territories. There were then, usually, two estates, the nobility, including the squirearchy, and the cities. The noblemen appeared in person, whereas the cities were represented by the mayor and members of the town council and town assembly; these together constituted the estates assembly or diet (*Landtag*). One territorial state, if composed of several territories, often had a corresponding number of diets whose main effort was directed toward the maintenance of local custom and local interest. Often they attempted to prevent the prince from spending the taxes collected in one province (*Landschaft*) anywhere else. These diets met when convened by the prince, once a year or oftener. They presented complaints and petitions, voted taxes,

---

[31] G. N. Clark thus begins his illuminating essay on comparative constitutional history in his *op. cit.* My own discussion was published as an essay in a memorial volume for Alfred Weber, entitled *Synopsis* (1948).

consented to important laws and so on. The estates treated in separate houses (*curiae*) and while the majority decided within each house, unanimity was usually required between the houses. From the sixteenth century onward the diet, or even its separate houses, often employed a legal adviser or syndic who often acquired considerable importance. Moreover they often kept a separate exchequer and developed their own tax-gathering bureaucracy. From all this it may seem as if the estates were nothing but a collection of various interests. But from the very beginning there was a tendency to consider them the representatives of the whole community, though this view expressed a hope rather than a reality. It is easy, however, to overstate the contrast with later conditions, for neither in the time of Burke nor today are representative assemblies *in reality* composed of men (and women) devoting themselves, in lofty disdain of their local electorate, to the common interest.

The real contrast lies in the fact that these estates were looked upon as apart and separate from the lord or prince. Hence, government *with* estates, not *by* estates, expresses best the dualistic nature of this system and indicates why the German expression *Ständestaat* is very misleading. Both princes and estates had their sphere of competency, often overlapping and ill-defined, but nevertheless thought of as distinct and settled in terms of an agreement. This agreement was often called *tractatus* or treaty, thus expressing the fact that the two authorities were looked upon as distinct entities. This dualism had three aspects. First there was homage and the oath of allegiance. The formulas which were used indicate the contractual nature of the relation between prince and estates. The duty to swear this oath was conditional upon the prince's swearing also to fulfill certain obligations. Similarly only part of the finances were in the hands of the prince, broadly speaking the *domanium*.[32] The other part, including all income from special taxes, was kept more or less securely under the control of the estates' assembly. As a result, there were two exchequers and two financial administrations in many of the governments with estates. What is more striking, even in military affairs a separate organization was built up under the direction of the estates, giving the estates their own army like Cromwell's Model Army. Finally, the estates carried on their own negotiations with foreign princes and the estates of other countries.

[32] This word is here used loosely to comprise the income from the *regalia,* including the mint and customs, as well as the income from the older *Bede,* a regular tax. See von Below, *Territorium und Stadt* (1900), 124 and 251. There has been a good deal of controversy over the *Ständestaat* among German scholars, notably Friedrich Tezner, Felix Rachfahl and others.

It is only natural that this system, controversial in its day, should have elicited conflicting interpretations. There are two schools of thought; one has taken the Thirty Years' War as the turning point in the history of the estates. The other has insisted that the estates were doomed anyway once the idea of sovereignty, of monarchical or royal supremacy, as expressed in the doctrine of the *"jura regalia et majestatis"* early in the seventeenth century, had reduced them to the state of dependent corporations. It is easy to see how such a view might be supported from a number of countries and territories; certainly in Castile, the "heart" of Spain, estates had been eclipsed before 1600, and they had likewise been practically dispensed with in Bavaria and the Palatinate. In Sweden Charles IX had had Erik Sparre decapitated in 1598 for his claims on behalf of parliament, while in England the parliament had become a willing tool in the hands of Tudor "absolutism." There can be no doubt that once the unifying potentialities of medieval Christianity had been destroyed by the Reformation, the dualistic constitutionalism of a "government with estates" faced issues which were apt to render the collaboration of the divided powers precarious. As the religious issues injected themselves, the struggle for supremacy became more intense. As far as the center of Europe was concerned, the religious peace of Augsburg had attempted to straddle this issue for the Empire by leaving the decision to each "estate." But that merely transferred the struggle from the imperial estates to each of the territories. They, like the emerging national states outside the Empire, came to fight it out by force of arms.

That is the setting within which the first half of the seventeenth century witnessed the emergence of the modern state. Throughout the wars of the period, with the single exception of England, estates proved to be inefficient in war and a hindrance to its effective prosecution by the monarch. So wherever possible, the princes sought to discard their assemblies altogether. The *États Généraux,* as we have said, never met again after 1618. In many of the German territories estates also disappeared. James I's efforts to dispense with parliament are well known. But there were exceptions. Of these, the British parliament's assertion of supremacy after 1640 is the most important and best-known. But likewise in Sweden the death of Gustavus Adolphus in 1632 enabled the estates to reassert themselves and eventually in the eighteenth century to acquire supremacy. In the county of Frisia, Johannes Althusius' sphere of activity, the estates and particularly the city of Emden continued to claim the ancient dual share in the government. Althusius may be called the outstanding theorist of this system of government with estates and will be further discussed below. Finally in Poland, where the aristocracy had been especially strong, the landowning nobles became dominant and the estates triumphed.

In short, the period of the Thirty Years' War brought to a head the conflict implied in the dualism between princes and estates. The system was the heritage of an age united through a common faith. The medieval constitutionalism was built upon a division of power between prince and estates and as such had rested upon the unity of faith which now was gone. Everywhere the claimants for a "true Christian religion" were entrenching themselves in the estates' assemblies, ripping wide-open the older constitutional order. Everywhere the conflict between princes and estates was also a conflict between Catholic and Protestant, between Calvinist, Lutheran and Nonconformist. It is a curious fact that in some ways the political implications of this conflict found their most extraordinary spokesman in King James I of England. He, more than any one else, represented the theoretical claims of the emergent state as personalized in the divine right of kings.[33]

James I is usually spoken of as a theorist. With all due respect to his learning, it might be better to call him an illusionist. At any rate, in his day he was a radical. He proposed to push the doctrines of royal supremacy, of caesaropapism, which lay implicit in Luther's ideas, to their logical extreme. There was no sphere, religious or other, which James admitted to be free from the supreme authority of the king. His ideas, supported by much theological learning, were destined to come to full fruition in the elaborate structure of Thomas Hobbes's political system. In 1603 James mounted the throne of England; in 1651 Hobbes's main work, the *Leviathan,* appeared in print. During the intervening fifty years European political thought had been largely secularized. The true significance of Hobbes lies not so much in his rational justification of despotism as in his attempt to construct an authoritarian system without biblical underpinnings. We find the same secularizing trend in the camp of the constitutionalists: between 1603 and 1690, from Johannes Althusius to John Locke, constitutionalism became secularized. The sovereignty of the people acting through elected popular representatives constitutes the central political idea of these two writers, but whereas Althusius is much concerned with the evidence Holy Writ has to offer in support of this

---

[33] See, for James, Charles H. McIlwain's *The Political Thought of James I* (1918), Introduction.

tenet, Locke almost exclusively relies upon general philosophical argumentation.

VII. THE LAW OF NATURE AND THE LAWS OF NATURE: ALTHUSIUS AND GROTIUS

It has justly been remarked that it is more important, if one wishes to comprehend an age, to identify the ideas which men have in common than to follow their controversies. Political thought is no exception to the rule. Two ideas, besides that of the state, occupied men's thought in the first half of the seventeenth century. One was the idea of natural law as a superior norm now that the state and its magistrates were increasingly accepted as ultimate arbiters of human, man-made law. The other was the problem of who was "sovereign" and what sovereignty included. The prevalent medieval view had been that law was fixed, and if not immutable, then at any rate changing slowly, almost imperceptibly. Statutory enactments were seen as "interpreting" or making manifest a law which was believed to be already there.

The solution of the first of these problems was complicated by the new impetus to discover the regularities according to which the universe functions. The scientific impulse of the age was focused upon the discovery of laws of nature. Hence every political system worthy of the name in this period was concerned with the law of nature. The Stoic elements of the humanist revival had mingled with the traditional notions of Christian writers to create a setting for this all-embracing preoccupation with natural law. Melanchthon, Hooker, and the Spanish jurists immediately come to mind as outstanding representatives of this trend. Indeed, Hooker's panegyric on the law can be taken as symbolic of the time:

Of Law there can be no less acknowledged, than that her seat is in the bosom of God, her voice the harmony of the world: all things in heaven and earth do her homage, the very least as feeling her care, and the greatest as not exempted from her power: both Angels and men and creatures of what condition soever, though each in different sort and manner, yet all with uniform consent, admiring her as the mother of their peace and joy.

Hence absolutist and constitutionalist writers undertook to prove their contentions as logical deductions from the law of nature. What was this law of nature? The age was none too sure about its substance. It vacillated between the older classical conception of the law of nature as a collection of just norms, and the new notion of the laws of nature as describing the regular course of nature. The former are exemplified by rules of conduct like the famous triad of the Corpus Juris: *"Honeste vivere, neminem laedere, suum cuique tribuere"* (To live rightly, to hurt no one, to give to everyone his own), while the scientific laws of nature seemed most awe-inspiring when regulating the motion of the heavenly bodies. Just norms had been learned by study of the Bible and by reason, while the scientific laws of nature were being discovered by observation and experiment.[34] The political thought of the period was inclined to have recourse to both methods; indeed for many thinkers the difference was obscured, if not obliterated, by the fact that God, the law-giver of the universe, was the author of both sets of regulations.

Intrinsically, the new scientific passion was remote from the controversies of politics. So prominent an exponent as Bacon contributed little to political theory, in spite of a lifetime spent in political activity. Descartes was likewise not prominent in the annals of political thought. It is only with Hobbes and Spinoza that a broad union of the two aspects was achieved. And yet, ever since Machiavelli's bold challenges, political speculation was inclined to buttress itself by some species of realism, some endeavor to prove the coincidence of facts and theory. The thoroughly Calvinist political system of Johannes Althusius, which first appeared in 1603, was animated throughout by an earnest desire to show that the doctrines therein set forth were more nearly in keeping with history and reality than the views which the author combatted. In typically Calvinist fashion the law of nature was held to be identical with the Ten Commandments, implemented by the Christian doctrine of love. Yet Althusius undertook to show that commonwealths had in fact been operated in accordance with these laws. Whenever they had not, they had come to grief. In short, the sanction for the norm came through the threat of destruction. The norm was rooted in the facts of nature. Tyranny is real, but it is bad, not only because it is wicked but also because it does not work.

When Althusius came to write his *Politica,* the estates in many German territories, as well as in the Reich were groping for a position of supremacy. In juristic circles the Bodinian doctrine of sovereignty, heralding the need for one ultimate legislative authority in each well-governed realm, was gaining rapidly.[35] Althusius, by applying the co-operative,

---

[34] See Chapter Four.

[35] Bodin himself had attributed sovereignty to the Reich's estates. In England, a distinct claim for parliamentary sovereignty, as against highest power for the king in parliament, was put forward only in 1630. Cf. C. H. McIlwain, *The High Court of Parliament and*

associational principle and by linking it with the Aristotelian doctrine of the sociability of man, constructed a theory of the estates' assemblies as the representatives of a federally united people who exercise the sovereignty which is an attribute of the organized community in its entirety. By proclaiming the majesty of the people he vindicated supremacy in the government for the estates. "Taking the side of the estates in general, and of the third estate in particular as strongly as he did, Althusius' volume seems to have created an immediate sensation among those who were struggling to broaden the power of the Estates." [36] It seemed at the time the winning side in Germany. In many territories, such as Brandenburg, the estates were triumphing over their territorial lords.

But there was a peculiar contradiction implicit in the situation, and Althusius' own life illustrates it. When he first wrote the *Politica* he was a councilor of Count John of Nassau, a member of the imperial estates which were asserting themselves against the weak Rudolf II (1556–1612), though John, his lord, did not recognize any estates in his own realm. But a year later when Althusius became the syndic of the city of Emden, he found himself the advocate of territorial estates in the county of Frisia. The confusion of the situation is well reflected in this transition; for Althusius there was justification in both positions as the count of Nassau had been Calvinist, and so were the estates of Frisia. What was more, the neighboring United Provinces were a living model of the government by rather than with estates. Here the estates general most certainly claimed supremacy and looked upon the regents, the princes of Nassau, as magistrates appointed to carry on the executive work. In the United Provinces, moreover, Althusius' Calvinism was quite acceptable as a foundation for his political philosophy. Although this was not true elsewhere, it is clear that the Calvinist position made such a system possible.

Unhappily the Dutch constitution suffered from uncertainties which made it inadequate once the question of sovereignty was raised. One of the most prominent victims of the constitutional conflict was Hugo Grotius, who throughout his famous discussion of sovereignty argued against the orthodox Calvinist view of the Dutch constitution, and hence against Althusius. Grotius, deeply inspired with the freer spirit of Arminianism and sick of the theological dogmatism of the time, under-

---

its Supremacy (1910). In Sweden Erik Sparre, the friend of Hotman, in *Lex-Rex-Grex* had likewise raised the banner of estates' supremacy, but paid for it with his life. Cf. Erland Hjärne, *Fran Vasatiden till Frihetstiden* (1929).

[36] See my *Johannes Althusius' Politica Methodice Digesta* (1932), Introduction, p. xxix.

took to found the law of nature upon human reason and reason alone. Such reason he would distill in prevalent humanist fashion from the writings of the ancients, especially Cicero and the Stoics. No theological doctrine, he held, was essential for the comprehension of reason. Thus war, which had gradually deteriorated during the religious wars into the most barbarous slaughter, which took no heed of the rights of civilians at all, was once more made subject to certain general rules, obligatory upon Catholic, Protestant, and Mohammedan alike. Gustavus Adolphus as well as Richelieu thoroughly agreed with Grotius' views and made considerable efforts to put them into practice. Rules of conduct binding all men were henceforth acknowledged by the best minds of the age, apart from all theology and ecclesiastical controversy. It is true, of course, that similar views had been expounded long before Grotius by the great Spanish jurist of the sixteenth century. But their idea rested upon Catholic dogma rather than philosophy, and hence they were unacceptable to half of Europe as popish "gibberish."

VIII. STATE AND SOVEREIGNTY

It is fascinating to see how these common and yet conflicting ideas on natural law reflected themselves in a similar body of thought on sovereignty and state absolutism. For Althusius and Grotius, like Hobbes and Spinoza, were all convinced that there must be a sovereign authority, a supreme ruler, in any commonwealth worthy of the name. Here once more the preoccupation with law intruded itself. For as God had given the laws to the cosmos, so the sovereign ruler must give laws to the state. Order, in other words, presupposing laws, cannot prevail where there is no law-giving organ or body. There seems never to have been any dissenting voice, either from absolutist or constitutionalist, to the tenet that the most important function in the state is the legislative function. Yet, the most striking institutional development of the period was undoubtedly the establishment of central administration. In the mind of the seventeenth century, these central administrative staffs had as their most important function to make the law "conducive to a well ordered polity." It is highly significant that even John Locke never dreamed of claiming this legislative function for "the legislature." On the contrary, its very importance required the full participation of the king and his administrative staff. Thus, sovereignty is vindicated as the law-making authority and was admitted to be bound by natural law, whether exercised by monarch or popular representatives or both.

How could such awful, Godlike power of giving laws to men ever be legitimately acquired? The answer to this portentous question produced the greatest amount of controversy in the seventeenth century. Bodin, who was the first to stress the power of making laws as the main aspect of sovereignty, had been inclined to recognize not only the restricting limits imposed by natural law, as pointed out above, but also those of certain "constitutional" laws, or *leges imperii,* like the Salic law of succession. He maintained that the sovereign's position rested upon these *leges imperii.* But such a purely historical, inductive foundation ran counter to the logical passion of the age. In short, there must be a law according to which sovereign power is established. This law the seventeenth century found in contract. It seems startling to a modern mind that in this age of strident absolutism the core of governmental authority was time and again attributed to a contract between individual human beings. Indeed, no element in the political thought of the period is so alien to us in its essence as these controversies over the nature of contracts supposed to lie at the base of the sovereign authority; no part of their thought smacks to us so much of purely antiquarian interest. And yet, so strange a preoccupation must have had some ground. Was it merely as a reaction to the bitter realization of absolute power as a fact that men felt the need of justifying it? Or were there antecedent notions of a like character which survived in this speculation? Or was the contract a symbol of peculiar force at that time? There is some truth in affirming each of these statements. The contractual recognition of governmental authority was, as we have noted, an ingrained element of medieval constitutionalism. Princes on their accession to the throne were wont to swear an oath before an assembly of popular representatives to rule according to the established laws and privileges of the realm. In much of the monarchomachical literature these feudal remnants had been enlarged upon by writers who were associated with groups determined to resist the encroachments of rising royal absolutism. The Catholic Church in its efforts to keep the secular power within bounds had always insisted upon these legal limitations.

But what was so potent an argument in the armory of the opponents of absolutism could, Hobbes showed, be molded into a tool for the support of this very absolutism. What if the subjects themselves had made a contract amongst themselves to submit altogether to such a sovereign? Their fear of violent death, so imminent in the state of nature, would surely predispose them toward such a step. Unhappily, by the very logic of his argument Hobbes was compelled to admit that physical violence against the subjects, and a failure on the part of the sovereign to provide peace and security made the destruction of such a sovereign a practical certainty. No more was needed, nor ever claimed, by the opposite side. Indeed, a writer like Althusius never went so far as to admit the right of the individual to offer resistance to violence. It was all up to the legitimate representatives, the estates, to do so. In the view of Althusius, such action was not the consequence of the individuals' natural right, but rather of the breach of contract between the ruler and the estates—the ephors, as he called them, following Calvin. For him, and for those who wrote in the same vein, sovereignty is therefore not based upon contract, but rests upon natural law. The people and its representatives have it, and can never lose it; it is theirs by nature and hence inalienable. To Grotius, the absolutist, this doctrine seemed most objectionable. He urged in turn that the people could, and evidently often had, transferred the sovereign power by contract, explicit, tacit or implied. In support of this contention he adduced some rather peculiar historical examples, and further sought to buttress the argument by suggesting conquest as the origin of legitimate government. There could be no gainsaying the fact, but how it helps the logic of his argument is hard to perceive. In considering Grotius' reflections, one ought to remember that the estates of the United Netherlands had some decades previously intended to confer the sovereignty upon William the Silent, and had after his death offered it to the king of France and to the queen of England. It was hard for a legal mind like Grotius' to agree to the proposition that such a thing could not be done, when evidently it might have come to pass. But he failed to perceive the deeper issue in which the sovereign power presented itself as absolute and unlimited. For any contract always hinges for its enforcement upon some third power which is apart from and above the mutually contracting parties. This third power had been the Holy Church in medieval constitutionalism. It was Hobbes' genius to detect this basic flaw and to seek an escape by admitting a contract solely between the subjects to be governed. What difficulties he fell into by so doing we must now explore.

IX. THOMAS HOBBES: PHILOSOPHER OF POWER

Hobbes was the philosopher of power par excellence. He more than any other man penetrated to the very core of his age's enthusiasm and rationalized it in sweeping, overwhelming generalizations. Hobbes' is the most secular view of the all-powerful state as a system of ordering the universe of human life. Humanist and scholar, rather than man of affairs, Hobbes throughout his life was convinced that absolute monarchy was the best form of government. But the inclination to contrast him with those with whom he took issue in rationalizing such government has led people to assume that he was further apart from them than was actually the case. The absolute monarch, the ruler, is by reason, according to Hobbes, bound to observe the laws of nature. Nor are these laws of nature so very different from those of Grotius or Althusius. They are general moral norms derived from Stoic and Christian tradition. But Hobbes attempted two things which constitute radical departures. On the one hand he tried to give an existential significance to these rules of natural law, even while he elaborated them. And somewhat contradictorily he also made them entirely dependent upon the sovereign's will and enforcement. What he seems to say is this: These so-called natural laws are either true laws of nature, i.e., generalizations based upon observed matters of fact, in which case they will always be enforced; or they are merely normative judgments, in which case they will only be enforced to the extent that the sovereign chooses to put his power behind them. Insofar as natural law possesses the quality of existential laws of nature, Hobbes undertook to derive them from his basic conception of human nature. Thus "a law of nature" (*lex naturalis*) is a precept, or general rule, found out by reason by which a man is forbidden to do that which is destructive of his life, or takes away the means of preserving the same, and to omit that by which he thinks he may be best preserved." [37] Hobbes insisted that law and right must be clearly distinguished, because law binds, and hence the two differ as much as obligation and liberty. Hence his first law of nature is that "every man ought to endeavor peace, as far as he has hopes of obtaining it; and when he cannot obtain it, that he may seek and use, all helps and advantages of war." The "ought" in his statement is not, presumably, a moral norm, but a prudential rule, flowing from a true generalization. Characteristically, and in keeping with the entire discussion of the several "laws of nature," Hobbes concludes his argument with the following observation: "These dictates of right reason men used to call by the name of laws; but improperly: for they are but conclusions, or theorems concerning what conduces to the conservation and defense of themselves; whereas law, properly, is the word of him that by right has command over others."

[37] *Leviathan*, XIV, spelling modernized.

The Copernican revolution which Hobbes brought about in the view of the law of nature was based upon his ambitious theory of the nature of man, which made him the founder, in a sense, of psychology. His mechanistic psychology, which is built upon the notion that men's actions are determined by passions restrained by the fear of violent death, enabled him to interpret the law of nature as a system of rules of prudence, dictated by reason, to be sure, but not the higher reason founded on faith. Rather these rules of prudence are calculated to aid man in his struggle for survival and self-enjoyment. Hobbes' mechanistic psychology had the further effect, however, of convincing him that there was no chance for these rules of prudence to prevail outside the organized commonwealth. Indeed, the evidence in support of his view seemed to him so overwhelming that he concluded that men above all else will seek to escape from the dreadful conditions of "the state of nature in which there is no place for industry; no culture of the Earth, no Navigation, nor use of the commodities that may be imported by the Sea; no commodious Building; . . . no Arts; no Letters; no Society; and in which there is worst of all, continual fear and danger of violent death; and the life of man, solitary, poor, nasty, brutish, and short." Here speaks the student of Thucydides' *History of the Peloponnesian Wars,* the observer of the religious wars in Europe, the contemporary of the civil war in England. But what Hobbes forgot was that most men do not share his views on human nature, and hence would not enter into a contract dictated by its implications. For all its bitter pessimism, Hobbes' political philosophy is not realistic in taking man in his relation to government as he actually presents himself. Instead, Hobbes identifies himself with mankind—not an uncommon failing amongst philosophers.

What Hobbes, the English closet philosopher, had begun, Baruch Spinoza, the Dutch Jew and closet philosopher, completed. Whereas Hobbes' system still recognized a natural law with moral connotations, even though diluted through utilitarian calculations, Spinoza radically asserts the completely naturalistic tenet that might makes right. "The big fishes devour the little fishes by natural right." This debonair sentence written around 1660 states with sweeping skepticism what was the actual practice of politics as pursued by Richelieu, Mazarin, the Hapsburgs, the Hohenzollerns. Theoretically, these ideas found striking expression in the work of a man like Samuel Pufendorf (1632-94), whose main work belongs to a subsequent period.

In England, on the contrary, Hobbes was not only anathema to the revolutionaries, whether Presbyterian or sectaries, but he also aroused the deep concern of the Anglican clergy after the Restoration. Charles II found himself obliged to silence him, although he liked him very much personally and greatly enjoyed his conversation. And while the obvious objections were on religious grounds, there was also the deep-seated and ineradicable distrust of the great anticonstitutionalist. This sense of dislike for the cynical candor of the philosopher of fear is related to the basic polarity of baroque feeling.[38]

But among this entire group of thinkers, natural law retained its distinctly normative tinge. From a more optimistic psychology and a more kindly view of the state of nature, these thinkers derived tenets of natural law which do not seem to require enforcement by the government. Reason as against passion and self-seeking, is allowed a concomitant place in the make-up of man. There can be no doubt that in Locke we perceive the dawn of the day of the heavenly city of the eighteenth-century philosophers. But the faith in reason was not as yet unbounded. Throughout the seventeenth century, and particularly up to 1660, the conviction persisted of man's inherent wickedness, which only the church or the state can mitigate and restrain. Nor should it be forgotten that the deep distrust of rulers, characteristic of the parliamentary and populist literature throughout the age, is itself an expression of that pessimistic view of man. It was for the eighteenth century "to put their faith in tyrants" and expect universal welfare from the enlightened benevolence of otherwise unrestrained despots. By 1660 it had only come to pass that men would maintain a right to revolution, or to stay with Spinoza's figure of speech, "Many little fish devour a big fish by divine right too." Spinoza himself threw out some suggestions along this line.

X. ENGLISH CONSTITUTIONAL IDEAS: MILTON AND HARRINGTON

The countercurrent of political thought which developed in the course of the English revolution has rather inaccurately been designated as "English democratic ideas." For the prevailing tone of these writings was constitutionalist, rather than democratic. To be sure, there were democratic strands, like that of the Levelers and Diggers,[39] but the prevailing mood was that of constitutionalism. At first this mood manifested itself in

[38] See below, Chapter Two.
[39] See below, Chapter Nine.

the form of a reassertion of traditional elements. The parliamentary opposition to Stuart pretensions, grouped around men like Sir Edward Coke and Sir John Eliot, was bent upon what they conceived to be the re-establishment of the "ancient rights of Englishmen," or as the Petition of Rights (1628) would have it, the "liberties" embodied in the frequently re-enacted great charters from Magna Charta onward. Custom and statute, the solemn acts of kings in parliament, were held by these men to safeguard the Englishman against arbitary search and seizure, against the yielding of taxes and the like, against imprisonment and the rendering of oaths. These arguments from what was asserted to be "law" received their strength and evidential value, however, from theoretical views which were slowly crystallizing among Englishmen, and not only Englishmen. But whereas efforts, such as those of Althusius and Sparre, to modernize medieval constitutional ideas and fit them into the developing ideas of state, government and power, fell upon barren ground elsewhere, they proved fertile in England and Scotland. At first reinforced by Calvinist theology, as in Samuel Rutherford, they soon were liberated from this dependence and became fully secular. Samuel Rutherford (1600–1661), a Presbyterian divine, expounded in his *Lex Rex* (1644) a pattern of ideas largely reminiscent of Althusius. But his thought lacked the systematic foundation; instead he addressed himself more fully to the concrete problems of "parliamentary" institutions. Rejecting the idea that kings derive their authority directly from God, Rutherford had little hesitation in asserting that "the Estates taken collectively do represent the people both in respect of office and of persons . . . and a legislative power is more in the Estates." Then reiterating the hoary doctrine that the "law" is above the king, he pointed out that "because no law, in its letter, has force . . . if the law, or King, be destructive to the people, they are to be abolished." The king, he held, is not the final interpreter of this law, but the estates. We have here a clear juxtaposition of king and estates, and an assertion of the supremacy of the latter. It is the position fought for by the Presbyterians in the revolutionary civil war, and vindicated when the parliamentary army beheaded the king, albeit contrary to the Presbyterian party's view.

It was essential for the constitutionalist position to shed this theological garb. Milton, Prynne, and Harrington all contributed to this development some important ingredients. William Prynne (1600–1699) in his widely read *Sovereign Power of Parliaments* (1643) expressly applied the new doctrine of sovereignty to his political thought and vindicated it for the

English parliament. Parliament was, according to him, above the king. Appealing to the law of nature, Prynne broke with the legalistic tradition of the earlier constitutionalists, like Coke. A monarchist, he made decidedly less use of the theological aspect of the matter. Even more outspokenly anticlerical was John Selden (1584-1654), whom Grotius called "the glory of England." In his celebrated *Table Talk* he would even withdraw the matter of religion from the clergy—he was an Erastian through and through. To him, the people as a whole are the true sovereigns, and kings "all individual." "A king is a thing men have made for their own sakes," he proclaimed. But for this reason to call him a "democrat" is quite far off the mark; [40] he was a constitutionalist. He would consult the contract between prince and estates "to know what obedience is due to the prince."

But that the rights of the people, of the individual human being, might also be placed into jeopardy by its representatives, was soon to become apparent through the oppressive policies of the Long Parliament. One of the most telling blows against this new "absolutism" and denial of the essential core of constitutionalism—effective regularized restraint upon government—was struck by John Milton in his *Areopagitica*. This work, published in 1644, first clearly vindicated the right to freedom of opinion, and more especially of the press. Its ringing phrases have been quoted again and again, and in some respects state the modern western view in definitive terms. "For if we be sure we are in the right, and do not hold the truth guiltily . . . what can be more fair, than when a man judicious, learned and of a conscience, for aught we know as good as theirs that taught us what we know, shall . . . openly, by writing, publish to the world what his opinion is, what his reasons, and wherefore that which is now thought cannot be sound." The confident expectation that truth will prevail, if given a fair chance, is at once the glory and the limit of this central constitutional tenet.

Such ideas must not be taken as equivalent to toleration. Milton readily excluded "papists" and other enemies of freedom from his plan for basic rights. A revolutionary age is not a tolerant one; the period in which the key ideas of modern constitutionalism were shaped in response to the challenge of the absolutist claims of the partisans of the state in terms of sovereignty was full of violence. But Milton—whether in his *Defence of the People of England* (1649), in which he sought to justify the beheading

[40] This is done in G. P. Gooch and H. J. Laski, *English Democratic Ideas in the Seventeenth Century* (second edition, 1927).

of the "tyrant," King Charles I, or in his *The Ready and Easy Way to Establish a Commonwealth* (1660), his last desperate plea not to relapse into the "old vassalage under kings" but instead to establish a highly aristocratic political order—was the dramatic voice of constitutionalism in its secular, humanist form whereunder the all-powerful secular state is carefully patterned, like a modern machine, in such a way that the principle of balance keeps the power from running amok.

Less effective and well-known, but in some respects more penetrating and certainly fully as keen about the constitutionalist analysis and organization of power, was James Harrington (1611–77). A scholar in the best sense, Harrington like Hobbes was hesitant to line himself up with the parties of the revolutionary age. A republican at heart, he was yet a friend of King Charles I. Proponent of a specific constitutionalist program in 1660, he was nevertheless the author of a great utopia, an imaginary commonwealth which he delineated in his main work, *Oceana* (1656).[41] More clearly than any other writer of the period, Harrington recognized the determining influence of economic and class conditions upon the constitutional order. Basing his analysis upon Aristotelian and Machiavellian elements, enriched by much observation and study, Harrington went beyond the power analysis of other writers, including Hobbes, and arrived at conclusions which closely resemble what a Richelieu had set down as the sum total of his political experience. Thus in *Oceana* we find the following statement:

As Leviathan said of the Law that without the (Public) Sword it is but Paper; so he might have thought of this Sword, that without a Hand it is but cold Iron. The Hand which holds this Sword is the Militia of a Nation. . . . But an Army is a Beast that has a great belly and must be fed; wherefore this will come to what Pastures you have, and what Pastures you have will come to the balance of Property, without which the public Sword is but a name or mere spit-frog.[42]

Hobbes would, of course, have replied: "Sure. But who determines the balance of property? The sovereign who has the unlimited power to do so." It is an endless argument. Historically speaking, Harrington had nevertheless the better of the argument. For what his analysis showed was

[41] I should like to acknowledge the detailed knowledge of Harrington's views which I owe to the work of Mr. Charles Blitzer, who is completing a study on Harrington's political thought.
[42] *Oceana* (ed. by Toland, 1700), 41.

that the control of the land had passed into the hands of the middle class; hence the middle class was in the ascendant and would shape the future. If there could be any doubt on this score in 1610, no such doubt could reasonably be entertained in 1660. Whether the continent would go the same way remained to be seen. Bourgeois strivings surely were associated with the policy of Richelieu and Mazarin, of the Dutch Republic and the scientific advance. An intense individualism, such as breathed in the work of Hobbes and Descartes, no less than in that of Milton and Harrington, had produced the problem of how one might comprehend the togetherness of human society; the social bond and the contractual theories had been the answer, as they had been in classical antiquity.

XI. THE BOURGEOIS ELEMENT

Contract is an idea intimately linked with the life and work of the trading middle classes; it is a symbol of the shop. Hence it was well suited to serve as an idea of great potency in the circles in which political thought was being secularized throughout this age. It is noteworthy that the four leading thinkers whom we have mainly considered here were all commoners. Althusius was a typical product of the German guild spirit as it prevailed in many of the free towns. Grotius was prominently associated with the commercial aristocracy of Holland's thriving city culture. Hobbes, while living most of his life in the company of the great landowning aristocracy of England, was nevertheless through his masters in intimate touch with the incipient growth of mercantile development in London and overseas. Spinoza once more belongs to the city culture of Holland.[43]

These writers were members of the bourgeoisie, of the capitalist middle class which in this period occupied, politically speaking, a varying position. Where the town economy had securely established itself in its own right, as in Holland and the free German cities, the burgher was on the side of the estates until civil and religious war threatened his security. But once emergencies of a serious sort arose, he shifted his allegiance to monarchism, particularly if monarchical government seemed to hold out a promise

[43] The bourgeois aspect of Hobbes' political thought is skillfully laid bare in Leo Strauss's *The Political Philosophy of Thomas Hobbes* (1936). The general point is central to H. J. Laski's *The Rise of Liberalism—The Philosophy of a Business Civilization* (1936), especially Chapter II, which deals with the seventeenth century; but Laski overstates the point, in Marxist fashion, and "liberalism" is not the right term to designate the political thought of the seventeenth century, when the bourgeoisie of France and other countries was clearly absolutist, as was Hobbes.

of checking the pretensions of the feudal aristocracy. Hobbes was particularly violent in his sentiment against the so-called "aristocratical virtues," which seemed to him mainly a seeking after vainglory. At the end of the period this alliance between bourgeoisie and monarchy was nearly universal throughout Europe. Only in England the course of civil wars made patent a different situation. At any rate, all these writers were ready to advocate a strengthening of mercantile and industrial development; all claimed riches as one of the primary objects of political activity; and while mercantilism was only in its infancy, there were suggestions of a distinctly mercantilist slant throughout the political literature of the period.

It was undoubtedly a part of this bourgeois spirit of the newer political thought, secularized and urban in its orientation, that it tended to eliminate the church from any role in the political sphere. Spinoza and Hobbes were frankly and outspokenly antiecclesiastical. Grotius was by his very destiny Erastian to the core; for had not the misfortunes of the party of which he was so conspicuous a member one of their primary roots in its leader's determined insistence upon the supremacy of state over church? Had Oldenbarneveld, this leader, not aroused the ire of the orthodox Calvinist clergy by seeking the appointment of the Arminian Vorstius to a theological chair in the University of Leiden? And even Althusius, though himself an orthodox Calvinist and a bitter opponent of Arminianism because of its softening of the doctrine of predestination, was fairly explicit in claiming the superiority of the state over the church. For him, however, the problem did not appear so serious, since in a community of orthodox Calvinists governed according to popular will, no serious conflict was apt to arise. Yet this was precisely the condition under which the constitutional crisis arose which cost Oldenbarneveld his life. For, as the event showed, even Calvinists could disagree amongst themselves, and it was then again a question of who should decide. Perhaps Althusius had a vision of the situation under modern constitutionalism, where Oldenbarneveld, if popularly rejected, would have resigned his post into other hands. Such conflicts had at that time to be solved by shedding blood. But as the history of the Protectorate was to prove later, Cromwell was not destined to be any more successful than the Dutch estates in fostering the cause of "toleration by agreement." Cromwell had the army at his disposal with which to purge parliament and disperse the popular majority.

While these leading writers were all inclined toward the secular authority, there were powerful voices raised in this period on behalf of theocracy, or as it should more properly be called, hierocracy: the rule by priests. The claims advanced by Jesuits on behalf of the papacy and the claims of radical Calvinists coincided in demanding that the secular rulers be subject to ecclesiastical authority in the final analysis. Probably the greatest controversy of the entire seventeenth century was stirred up in the very beginning by James I's great Jesuit antagonist, Cardinal Bellarmine, whose views brought down upon him the wrath of innumerable writers, both lay and ecclesiastical. His brilliant exposition of the papal claims, while inherently an anachronism, was at the same time the culmination of the Counter Reformation. The period from 1610 to 1660 witnessed a continual decline of this body of doctrine. Even in strictly Catholic countries, "Gallican" ideas, which were to find an impressive, if somewhat pompous theorist in J. B. de Bossuet (1627–1704), gained the ascendancy. These views merely put the stamp of theoretical approval upon the political practices of Richelieu and his successors. It was inevitable that the smaller princes should follow the example. The house of Hapsburg, on the other hand, although viewed with apprehension by such men as Urban VIII (Pope 1623–42), remained the acknowledged protector of ultramontane ideas. But no theorist of European stature arose to defend this sort of interpretation as of universal significance. Men were too deeply convinced of the realities of "reason of state" of the *arcana imperii* as manifest in the states' interests, to be willing to believe again that any universal, all-embracing pattern of interests could be found to unite the warring states in a genuine Christian community of faith. If the Hapsburgs sponsored such outmoded ideas, they surely did so, thoughtful men reflected in the middle of the seventeenth century, because such a pretense suited their particular "reason of state." Nor was such an idea compatible with the bourgeois notions of a mercantilist age. Competition was increasingly vigorous, and occasional voices began to applaud it not only as the lifeblood of trade, but as good in itself.

XII. CONCLUSION

The rapid sketch which we have given of the variegated patterns of political and economic thought and institutions reveals an underlying common core. This core is the new sense of power, the power of man to shape his own society, his own destiny. This sense of power was, in some of the key thinkers and actors of the age, Promethean in its limitless striving. Who is to say whether the modern state emerged in this period because some of its most striking representatives were filled with this sense of power, or whether they were filled with this sense of power because the modern state emerged? In any case it is clear that the two developments were closely linked and that they molded the climate of opinion, the *Weltgefühl* and *Weltanschauung,* the fundamental outlook and feeling of man in the seventeenth century. From it stems, as indeed it was shaped by it, the style which has come to be known as baroque. It was a style in which Renaissance elements of revived forms of classical antiquity were molded into a new and specifically western form. The essential characteristics of this new style in its varied manifestations in literature, art and thought must be more fully explored before the extraordinary stage can be seen upon which the gigantic dramas of the Thirty Years' War, Richelieu's building of modern absolutism, and the English revolution were to be enacted. It is a stage the like of which western civilization had not seen before or since.

Chapter Two

BAROQUE IN LIFE AND LETTERS

LIKE the term "gothic," baroque originated as an expression of esthetic opprobrium. Of uncertain linguistic origin,[1] this expression was a favorite in the late eighteenth century with art critics like Winckelmann; they used it to describe works of art and architecture which did not meet the standards they believed to have eternal validity as "classic" forms of true beauty. Indeed, this tradition has been so persistent in English-speaking countries ever since the renaissance that the idea of the baroque as a distinct style has remained rather unfamiliar until recently.[2]

At the same time, every traveler is on intimate terms with many of the glorious creations which are commonly considered "baroque": the great castles of the continental capitals, the imposing canvases of Rubens and Rembrandt, of Velasquez and van Dyck, the statuary of Bernini and of the royal porcelain manufactures of Sèvres, Dresden and Royal Bavarian. Last, but not least, who has not been fascinated by the colorful spectacle of the Italian opera?

It is far easier, unfortunately, to name such great achievements of the seventeenth century than clearly to mark off in time or effectively to characterize the common features of so vast an array of grandiose creations. Is it to be wondered at that baroque style has given rise to extended controversies? Those who dislike it have laid stress upon its ebullient, ornate, often heavy qualities. Others, contrasting it with the renaissance, have dwelt upon its dynamic character, its predilection for curves, its avoidance of clear outline or distinct contrast, its preoccupation with expressing inner states of the mind, of feelings, personality and *Stimmung*. The clamor of nationalist prejudices has been added by those

---

[1] The most probable derivation is that which links baroque to the scholastic term *baroco,* a designation for one of the more complicated figures of formal logic. Thus it would be associated with the humanist dislike for scholasticism, and would mean "intricate," "perverse," and "eccentric."

[2] Characteristically, the word *baroque* does not occur in the index of G. N. Clark's *The Seventeenth Century* (1929), though some passing references are found in the text.

38

who have claimed it as distinctively and peculiarly Italian or Spanish or German, again as un-English or as un-French. For a long time it was customary to contrast it with French classicism, but now French "classicism" is held by leading interpreters to be characteristically baroque. Even the Slavic soul has been entered as a contestant for the honor of having produced it. All these views are narrow-minded and partial; baroque art was European in scope and transcended all national boundaries. Like all other great styles it possessed national variations. But each nation contributed to it its specific share in different spheres of life, art, and letters.

The origins of baroque architecture are now commonly traced to Rome and other Italian cities. If that view is correct, baroque considerably antedated the seventeenth century. Among its earliest examples were churches built by the Jesuits, such as Il Gesù in Rome.[3] What can be said with some hope of general agreement is that the baroque style clearly emerged as a European form of art, of letters and of life in the course of the decades after 1600. It is impossible to enter here upon the complicated and highly controversial issues raised by the weak and affected productions of the period of transition, from undoubted renaissance to equally evident baroque. Anyone with eyes to see can perceive the difference between Dürer and Holbein on the one hand, Rubens and Rembrandt on the other. The contrast between Raphael and Velasquez is equally striking. But as elsewhere in life the changes were gradual, the startling achievements of the Renaissance were followed by a period of groping and subtleties, and there are those who would have us recognize a unique style separating renaissance from baroque, the style of mannerism (*Manierismus*). Whatever the ultimate conclusions on this debatable point, there seems to be no likelihood that mannerism will ever appear as a style of such general significance as romanesque, gothic, renaissance or baroque.

The baroque style, then, can be seen roughly to extend from the middle of the sixteenth to the middle of the eighteenth century, with its culmination point somewhere about 1660. Like all styles, it had no uniform set of traits, but can better be described in analogy to two magnetic poles operating within a common field of ideas and feelings.[4] This common field of feeling was focused on movement, intensity, tension, force.

---

[3] Cf. Alois Riegl, *Die Entstehung der Barockkunst in Rom* (1923).

[4] This approach is suggested by R. Kautzsch, "*Kunstgeschichte als Geistesgeschichte*," *Belvedere*, Vol. VII (1925), 6–15. While intended as a *Miszelle* to Dvorak's volume by the same title, he expresses serious doubts about an "*einheitlicher Stilbegriff*."

Baroque art found its richest fulfillment in the castle and the opera, two creations for the completion of which many arts have to be worked into a harmonious whole. Castle and opera are manifold units. In architecture baroque produced the richly ornamented façade, the sweep of magnificent staircases, the ornamental garden as a setting of the castle and a foreground of a distant view. In painting baroque reveled in the effects of light and shadow, employed the intermediate shades of many-hued grays, browns and greens, explored the subtleties of individuality in nature through the portrayal of landscape and of the human face. Theater and the drama, more especially the heroic tragedy, seemed peculiarly adapted to the baroque spirit in the field of letters; but fairy tale, knightly novel and ornate lyrics were peculiar baroque creations along with the extravagant comedy. Throughout, baroque developed the art of effective characterization, either of individuals or of types, but more particularly the latter. First Spain and then France took the lead. Finally in music the expressive depicting of emotional states and sentiments reached a high level, first in the solo parts of opera and oratorio singers, soon afterward in the varying combinations of stringed instruments, finally in gigantic combinations of human voices and instrumental music, both in the oratorio and in the opera.

Where did this new style come from? Since it molded all spheres of life and art, a profound revolution of the spirit is clearly manifest through it. It has been argued that this revolution must have been the Counter Reformation—the Catholic Reformation. In this simple form, describing baroque art as the direct expression of the spirit of the Counter Reformation, the argument can scarcely be maintained. There are too many contradictions involved. The Catholic Reformation, as most strikingly represented by the ascetic Pope, Pius V (1565-72), brought a revival of medieval religiosity. Indeed, the popes of that period and their clergy went so far as to outlaw nudity, establish rules for the use of secular melodies in composition, decree the Index of forbidden books. Baroque art, on the other hand, was worldly or at least deeply immersed in naturalism, grossly sensuous, for example in the canvases of Rubens, often celebrating the heroic ideal of antiquity. Nor was the connection in time a very close one. To be sure, the origins of Italian baroque fall into the period of the Counter Reformation after 1550.[5] But in the period when baroque culminated, the spirit of the Counter Reformation was pretty

[5] Those who would include Michelangelo—and they are many—would have to go even further back; cf. A. E. Brinckmann, *Die Barockskulptur* [c. 1919].

nearly dead. Under the reign of Urban VIII and his successors the papacy had returned to a strong interest in secular concerns. What is more, many of the finest flowers of the baroque style, particularly in painting and music, were the creation of Protestant people who can scarcely be imagined moved by the spirit of the Counter Reformation. The baroque style is, however, in part animated by ideas and feelings which the Reformation and Counter Reformation had ushered in. The violent clash of religion and politics, of church and state, expressed itself in new forms of political thought. The amoral paganism of a Machiavelli gave way to the tortuous rationalizing of writers like Botero and Hobbes, who constructed a moral "justification" for doing what was necessary. For Machiavelli it had been enough that it was necessary; for later moralists the necessity had to be wrapped into the sugar-coating of "divine right" and "contract." As contrasted with the debonair worldliness of the Renaissance, reflected in the luminous harmony of the paintings of Raphael, baroque was tormented by doubts, shot through with conflicts and tension. Not a happy and unreflective pleasure of the senses, but gross sensuality alternating with pangs of conscience become the dominant note. The baroque age was torn between extremes. The worldliness and *Sinnenfreude* of the renaissance turned to coarse materialism and carnal debauch, while the philosophical and scholarly inquiries of humanism led to skepticism and scientific discovery. On the other hand the religious protest against renaissance and humanism, which Reformation and Counter Reformation share, intensified otherworldly beliefs. The revival of religion strengthened a fierce moral fanaticism often culminating in arid dogmatism and intolerant persecution, in superstition and violence. Since the Counter Reformation constituted an essential ingredient of these conflicting attitudes, it undoubtedly contributed its share to the ideas and feelings which animated the baroque artist.

Another school has held that the dominant impulse for the baroque style originated in the life of the monarchical courts under absolutism. This view is based upon the well-known patronage which the princes of seventeenth-century Europe bestowed upon the art of the time. Indeed, a good many princes took a very direct personal interest in these matters. Nor can there be any question that some of the most characteristic creations of the baroque style were courtly: the sumptuous castle set within a vast layout of artificially created parks and gardens. Likewise the opera first made its appearance as part of lavish court festivals, such as the marriage of Henry IV of France and Marie de'Medici in 1604. Yet therefore to make baroque *the* art of monarchical absolutism is again going too far. One cannot link the feelings of baroque simply to the particular political structure of absolutist monarchy. For there are enough signs pointing in other directions. The beginnings of baroque style in architecture are to be found, as has already been remarked, in ecclesiastical Rome and especially in certain Jesuit churches.[6] What is more, many of the most beautiful structures reared in the baroque period were ecclesiastical: churches, cloisters, and abbeys. Nor is this all. Apart from court and church, there was the rich bourgeoisie not only in these absolute monarchies, but in England, Holland, Venice and the rest. They built beautiful town houses, bought the canvases of painters, and freely supported the new musical forms of opera, oratorio and symphony. In Holland even the artisans and simple folk shared in the general enthusiasm. Such artists as Rembrandt, Nicolas Poussin and Claude Lorrain were indifferent, if not actually hostile, to court life. The extremes of mysticism and rationalism which divided religious feeling in this period[7] were reflected in baroque style. Sometimes these contrasts occurred in the work of the same artist. Compare Champaigne's Louis XIII with his portrayal of the two nuns of Port Royal. More often they divided different artists whom one may contrast in their emphasis; Rubens and Rembrandt, Bernini and Algardi are famous examples. In any case the stage and the church, with their plays and oratorios, while fostered by the princes, were the common possession of all, and not the exclusive privilege of the few; they perhaps most significantly expressed the spirit of the age.

These general remarks about baroque would not be complete without some explicit comment on "national" aspects of this style. It would really be more appropriate to speak of "regional" variations; for while some regional peculiarities were national, as in England, France and Spain, others like Roman as contrasted with Venetian, Hapsburg as contrasted with Saxon or Rhineland baroque, were not fully integrated into a national style. Baroque in the Austrian lands of the Hapsburgs bore a greater kinship to Spanish baroque than to North German forms. An attempt adequately to characterize the several national and regional variations would be difficult; indeed to this day historians of art are seriously at odds concerning important features of these contrasts. The

[6] The common contention that Jesuit architecture is identical with baroque architecture throughout this period has been disproved with much learning by Joseph Braun, S.J., in a number of works.

[7] See Chapter Four.

situation is complicated by the fanning out of Italian, Flemish and other artists and musicians all over Europe; it often becomes very difficult to decide whether they were influencing or being assimilated. Nor was this cosmopolitan wandering entirely one-sided: Poussin spent most of his life in Rome, the German poet Opitz went to Poland, Descartes to the Netherlands, Grotius to France. Baroque was a European way of feeling and thinking, of experiencing the world and man and creating works of art and letters in the image of these *Erlebnisse*. Yet, regional variations there were, and they were strongest where the national life was most nearly integrated. Thus the baroque of Spain was the most extreme in its contrasts and tensions, so that some have felt it to be the *most* baroque. In France, greater restraint and an emphasis on classical themes obscured for a long time the essentially baroque quality of Corneille, Pascal and Descartes, if not of Poussin and Claude Lorrain. In England, the revolutionary implications of Protestantism, so long held in check by the skill and power of the Tudors, and the long-range effects which link the Puritans with modern liberalism, hid from many the sway of baroque feeling in letters and art in the England of the Stuarts and their court. The extraordinary flowering of German literature in the "classic" age of Kant, Goethe, and Schiller who, inspired by Lessing, fought the baroque heritage in letters, art and life with a neohumanist enthusiasm for classical antiquity, prevented appreciation of the extraordinary achievements of that preceding age; in any case much of the finest baroque in these regions was created in the generations following our period. Typically, Heinrich Schütz' memory was virtually blotted out by the towering achievements of Handel and Bach. Yet his musical creations were superb in their depth and novelty. The same may be said even more emphatically of the Slavic world; the Czechs, the Poles and the Russians responded with truly baroque violence to the artistic possibilities of this style, especially in architecture. Indeed, it may be said that baroque is *the* European art form most nearly commensurate with the depth of feeling and the extravagance of conduct expressive of the Slavic spirit. But most of the Slavic baroque belongs to the generations after 1660.

II. THE COMMON GROUND: THE RESTLESS SEARCH FOR POWER

Perhaps all styles are less unified than is usually assumed by those who write and talk about them. Regional and period styles on closer inspection seem often to contain mutually exclusive aspects and traits. Of no style is this more true than of the baroque. It is in any case a highly polarized style, and startling combinations have been constructed to account for this multicolored, manifold, glittering quality. There certainly is no agreement among scholars as to any one dominant theme, unless it be that there is no such theme. However, the original negative attitude of the postbaroque neoclassicism as represented by Jacob Burckhardt's interpretation of the Renaissance has now been supplanted by a more understanding view—a view which recognizes that the unquestioned achievements of the baroque age, represented by such names as Velasquez, Rembrandt and Corneille, ought to be considered along with baroque's undoubted extravagances. In recent years, some writers have gone to the opposite extreme; Oswald Spengler has suggested that baroque is in fact the fulfillment of the "Faustian soul" of western man.[8] Without accepting such an exaggerated view, one can today safely consider baroque to have been one of the four or five most universally significant forms of expression of occidental culture. Baroque sought to give literary and artistic expression to an age which was intoxicated with the power of man; in some ways this explains perhaps its fascination with the impossible. Hausenstein has put it neatly: "Baroque means the unthinkable: the river with two mouths."[9]

At the height of the baroque, architects, sculptors, painters, poets and musicians strove to accomplish the impossible in *all* directions. Hence materialism vied with spiritualism, radical naturalism with extreme formalism, the most terrifying realism with the most precious illusionism. Metaphysical poetry sought to probe into ultimate mysteries, while voluptuous and lascivious erotic poetry violated all canons of good taste. Here are some typical, concrete *"sujets"* of baroque artistic endeavor: monarchs, cardinals and princesses, devout nuns and praying saints competed with beggars, miscreants and cripples in the canvases of Velasquez, Rubens, Rembrandt and his fellow Dutchmen; highly ornamented altars decorated in gold contrast with severe church exteriors, colorful and dramatic murals with geometrically rigid gardens. Such an age, excited beyond measure by the potentialities of man, might well through some of its representatives establish the foundations of modern science, while through others it would persecute superstitious old women as witches; for both presume an exaggerated belief in the power of man to

---

[8] Oswald Spengler, *Der Untergang des Abendlandes,* I, 342 ff., e.g., and *passim.*

[9] Willi Hausenstein, *Vom Geist des Barock* (1924). I am reminded of that matchless cartoon in *The New Yorker* showing the tracks of a skier, one track on each side of a tree trunk, with the skier unconcernedly going on. That is baroque.

think and to do as with heightened powers he confronts a mysterious, exciting world. God by his limitless will orders the universe; Satan by a comparable effort seeks to disturb this order. The fascination which Satan seems to have had for Milton has often been remarked upon; it was born of the admiration for the kind of strength that will challenge rather than be subordinated. The statesmen of this age made a cult of power and of its adornments: the vast spectacle, the impenetrable intrigue, the grue-some murder. Power has always been *one* of man's dominant ends, and the search for it one of his great passions. But probably no age allowed this passion to become so all-engulfing, unless it be our own, in many ways so strangely akin to the baroque. Hence Thomas Hobbes, self-styled "child of fear," in his uncompromising adulation of power, coined perhaps the age's most revealing phrase: "So that in the first place, I put for a generall inclination of all mankind, a perpetuall and restlesse desire of Power, after Power, that ceaseth only in Death." To him, all passions were in the last analysis reducible to that dominant passion for power, "for Riches, Knowledge and Honour are but severall sorts of Power." [10]

The same sense of power inspired Milton as he faced the cosmic strug-gle of good and evil, of God and Satan. In confronting the Son of Man with Satan the Tempter, Milton created a scene which "is one of the high moments of Milton's art, an English masterpiece of the baroque, analogous to great Italian painting." [11] There was in Milton, more per-haps than in any other poet of his time, a deep sense of the dynamic spiritual potential of language; he "did not merely use language: he carved it, shaped it with the vigor of a baroque architect, and piled it up until it became a monument of words in marble." A sense of power calls in the artist for the capacity to portray, to dramatize tension; that is the quintessence of baroque.

III. PERSONAL BEHAVIOR

Of all those peculiarities of personal behavior by which an age or nation is seen as it were "naked to the watchful eye," the wig is probably the most revealing symbol of the baroque. Its origin is by legend at-tributed to Louis XIII who, it is said, wished to hide his baldness. It was in fact a vivid expression of that desire to push things to the extreme and to cultivate the theatrical exaggeration of reality. In the first gen-

[10] *Leviathan*, Chs. VIII, X, XI.
[11] James H. Hanford, *John Milton, Englishman* (1949), 211. The subsequent quotation is from Louis Untermeyer's comment in *A Treasury of Great Poems* (1942), 460.

eration of the seventeenth century hair became longer, beards more flowing and dramatic. As the century progressed, beards and mustaches became smaller, eventually vanished; for they hide the face, instead of setting it off as does a wig.

Costumes were very stately and elaborate, except where strong moral convictions led to startling simplifications; the Puritans and the fellowship of Port Royal achieved a highly dramatic effect by their monklike uniformity, as did individuals like Father Joseph. Ladies' fashions were similarly elaborate and often bordered on the disguise. The passion of the age for "dressing up" in weird attire made even the exalted, such as the king of Spain, indulge in occasional "masques."

The sense of "face" was as highly developed as ever in the Orient, and men went to great lengths to avenge any infringement of their honor. Honor became the most sought-after sign of power, and the endless quarreling and dueling took such a toll of the aristocracy in countries like France that the government felt compelled to take vigorous measures to combat it. Corneille's drama was preoccupied with the portrayal of clashes of honor, and the same theme dominated the stage of Spain, England and Germany.

At the same time, gross sensuality engulfed both high and low. The excesses in eating and drinking, while probably most extreme at the courts of Germany, were a universal habit, taking the subtler forms of elaborate gourmanderie in Italy and France. Associated with these lusts of the palate were violent sexual debauchery, both male and female. Again, there was a contrasting fanatical enthusiasm for chastity which may be considered a perverted form of sexuality. The cloisters of Spain and France, circles like the Port Royal, and the notorious Puritanical extremities were as characteristic of the age as the libidinous and licentious court circles of Britain, France and Spain, Italy and Germany. Figures like Simplicius Simplicissimus show that the common folk were as prepared to glory in the exhibitionism of sexual swagger as the aristocracy. Yet, in contrast to the renaissance and to later periods, there was a displayful enthusiasm for the passions as such, and an unprecedented sense for the drama of the stuggle between these passions and the rational mind, heightening their role by ordained efforts to control them.

If one asks oneself, what was the baroque's view of man, he finds a view closely linked to these aspects of personal behavior. The stress was on action, personal success, constant combat and the resulting heightening of the sense of self. The ceremonial of social contact was related to dignity and gravity; it has been argued that even the Cartesian formula, *"Cogito, ergo sum,"* expressed this self-centered activism; for through the process of thought the ego is here held to be manifest.[12] Therefore, baroque man emphasized having rather than being something, and the passions were believed central to man's essence: Descartes, Hobbes, Pascal, Spinoza all philosophized in terms of the passions and their great power over human destiny; these baroque philosophers sought to explore and understand them; hence the beginning of psychology in this generation. At the same time, man struggling passionately and willfully to master his fate was yet seen as fate's helpless victim. The meteoric rise and the cataclysmic fall of favorites, conquering heroes, royal concubines, were highly symbolic of the baroque. Buckingham and Olivárez, Gustavus Adolphus and Wallenstein, Father Joseph and Sor Maria, the duchess of Chevreuse and the dowager queen, these and ever so many others crowded the baroque period as so many tragic characters, storming heaven, plunging into damnation, crying out: "I shall yet force my fate." It is almost as if baroque man had insisted that the final consummation of man's most striking exhibition of the never-ending quest for power was a violent death, or at least banishment, exile, oblivion.

IV. POETRY AND LITERATURE

(a) England

Milton's Satan was perhaps as striking a portrayal of baroque man as the age created:

> . . . aspiring
> To set himself in glory above his peers,
> He trusted to have equalled the Most High,
> If he opposed, and, with ambitious aim
> Against the throne and monarchy of God,
> Raised impious war in Heaven, and battle proud,
> With vain attempt.[13]

Yet, one must try to imagine Milton (1608–74) together with Corneille (1606–84) and Calderón (1601–87), Joost van de Vondel (1587–1679), Martin Opitz (1597–1639) and Andreas Gryphius (1616–64), Paul Gerhardt (1607–76), Grimmelshausen (1618–76), and Pascal (1623–62), to

---

[12] Willi Flemming, "Die Auffassung des Menschen im 17. Jahrhundert," *Deutsche Vierteljahrschrift für Literatur und Geistesgeschichte* (1928), VI, 403 ff.
[13] *Paradise Lost,* I.

appreciate the fullness of his baroque stature. *Paradise Lost* was the Protestant response to the challenge of the Italian *dramma di musica* as Milton had experienced it on his Italian journey.[14] It also sounded the counterpoint to the entire dramatic poetry of the renaissance, but more especially of Shakespeare and Spenser. Protestant Christianity, so to speak, extended in him its hand to medieval Christianity as celebrated by Dante. The *Divine Comedy* was the true inspiration of Milton, as St. Augustine and St. Thomas had been of Luther, Calvin and their followers.

In all these writers renaissance elements were present to some extent, but basically that was true of all baroque forms: they sought to combine somehow the formal perfection of the preceding age with the sense of the working of supernatural powers, within and beyond man. Deeply metaphysical, the baroque poets and writers strained to the utmost their powers of formal art to capture the sense of these dynamic forces. Hence they reveled in movement, in colorful and violent contrasts, often piling up descriptive adjectives and exclamatory nouns. A tremendous power of imagination was at work in these dramas, epics, and great chorales. True children of the century of rational intelligence, these writers celebrated self-esteem and gravity, pomp and heroic pathos, as expressive of secular and religious passions. Tension and struggle were everywhere. Resurgent Catholicism, ardent, devout, fanatical, and subtle; stalwart Protestantism, convinced, moral, ruthless, and self-righteous, fought each other in a long-drawn-out contest to an eventual stalemate. Similarly monarchical absolutism and representative constitutionalism won here, lost there, either of them now aggressive and revolutionary, now defensive and conservative, now rational and sober, now deeply felt and emotional. Poets and writers carried both to extremes of formal self-expression.

The language in all of them is highly ornate. Rigorous forms are maintained at the cost of an artificiality which to modern ears is often highly irritating. The great passions which pulsate beneath this formal structure bring forth strange flowers which obscure the view like ice-ferns on the window in deep winter. The description Milton gives of the procession of evil spirits leagued with Satan abounds in such baroque word-painting. Tortuous similes were beloved by all these writers, as were classical allusions. But their most urgent concern was the depicting of human passions, seen as proliferations of supernatural powers rather than in the

[14] See below for the opera of 1639, pp. 86–7.

strictly human terms familiar to the renaissance and humanism. The lines here were not sharp, however, and the shift of emphasis must not be taken as a complete antithesis. Some of Shakespeare's great dramas, notably *Othello, Macbeth,* and *King Lear,* have a distinctly baroque flavor, as do his late plays, especially the idyllic romances, *The Winter's Tale* and *The Tempest.* While the last two open our period, the preceding three belong to the first decade of the seventeenth century. There is no reason why Shakespeare, hypersensitive as he was, should not have turned toward baroque and its supernatural concerns. Surely the first three tragedies are Promethean in their portrayal of human beings who, drunk with power, attempt the superhuman, and when beaten down by avenging higher forces yet maintain their human dignity, their share of power. In fact, *King Lear* is the most baroque of the three; the closing lines of the dying king were never surpassed in expressive pathos by Corneille, Calderón or Milton. As Lear looks upon the dead Cornelia, he cries:

> No, no, no life:
> Why should a dog, a horse, a rat, have life,
> And thou no breath at all? O, thou wilt come no more,
> Never, never, never, never, never!

We have here that piling up of words which became so grotesque in writers like Gryphius. In Shakespeare we witness the turning to violent expressiveness, and the contrasting lyricism of a dream world. Truly, by bridging the gap, Shakespeare earned Ben Jonson's celebrated epitaph:

> Triumph, my Britain, thou hast one to show,
> To whom all scenes of Europe homage owe,
> He was not of an age, but for all time!

This was said in 1616, when Jonson himself had already done his best work; for his most appreciated plays are, by general consent, *Volpone* (1605) and *The Alchemist* (1610). Yet Ben Jonson continued in general favor and became poet laureate of England. King James greatly liked the blunt and vigorous Ben who, until his death, occupied the center of the stage of literary England. His work too showed increasingly baroque features. The numerous masques and antimasques were distinctly baroque in feeling. There was a mixture of the elegant with the grotesque, the elevated with the tedious, and a pervading lyricism, supported by music such as later enchanted Milton, written by such men as N. Lanier and

William and Henry Lawes.[15] This genre of writing, combining poetry of great delicacy with contrasting songs of coarse vulgarity, was much in vogue in France and Spain, as well as Italy. Out of it developed the opera. It is impossible to convey its spirit by short quotations, but perhaps the opening lines of two of Ben Jonson's more famous works will give a vague idea. "The Vision of Delight" (1619-20) has Delight enter with the train of fairy-like attendants, and say:

> Let your shows be new and strange,
> Let them oft and sweetly vary,
> Let them haste so to their change,
> As the seers may not tarry. . . .

By contrast, "Pleasure Reconciled to Virtue," truly a baroque theme, starts lustily:

> Room! Make room for the Bouncing Belly!
> First father of sauce, and deviser of jelly,
> Prime master of arts, and the giver of wit,
> That found out the excellent engine, the spit. . . .

(b) Spain

It was not England, but Spain, which experienced the baroque most intensely as the genuine form of its literary genius. The Spanish outburst of creativity in this period remains one of the marvels of the age, as startling as painting in the Netherlands, or politics in France and England.

Like Shakespeare in England, Cervantes (1547-1615) outgrew the renaissance. In keeping with the anticlassical temper of Spain's national impulses and traditions, Cervantes in his celebrated *Don Quixote* (1605 and 1615) created an immortal figure which is as baroque as the laughter it elicits is humanist—not of an age, but for all time. If it is the fulfillment of the Renaissance in its humane mockery at medieval knightly ideals, it is also the opening of the gates to new and more deeply felt passions. For the baroque is Spain's true form and fulfillment. Góngora (1561-1627), the subtle lyricist, Lope de Vega (1562-1635), the torrential creator of nearly a thousand dramas, epics, lyrics and sacred plays, Molina (1571-1648), the priest who wrote impudent comedies and devout sacred plays of deep wisdom, finally Calderón (1600-1681), the great

---

[15] See below Manfred F. Bukofzer, *Music in the Baroque Era* (1947), Ch. VI.

dramatist—they truly constitute the flowering of the Spanish genius in literature. The dynamic tensions of the baroque, its antithesis between idealistic, ardent spirituality and earthy, passionate sensuality find a deep response in Spain's native inclinations. The exaggerated formalism and the search for subtle and complex ornamentation go hand in hand with poignant naturalism and erotic intensity. Góngora, who founded the "*estilo culto*" or cultivated style [16] carried the classicist enthusiasm of humanism to baroque lengths of preciousness.

The theater provided the most characteristic literary form in Spain. If the world is a stage, the stage is also the world. The theater was by no means an appendage of the court; indeed, in courtly Spain the king and queen could not publicly attend the theater, but had to do so clandestinely. With men and women strictly separated, the stage was so arranged in a public square that the more elevated noblemen and ladies could watch from windows in the houses looking down upon the square, while others were seated in front of the stage. Playwrighting was not a very lucrative activity; even those who were enormously successful like Lope de Vega and Calderón achieved only moderate wealth. In *Keep Your Own Secret* (*Nadie fie su secreto*) Calderón tells us: "Your women are like new plays, which self-complacent authors offer at some eight hundred royals each, but which when once they are tried, you purchase dear eight hundred for a royal." Perhaps this has something to do with the incredible productivity of the Spanish playwrights of this period. It certainly contrasts strangely with the universal enthusiasm of court, nobles and common folk for these dramatic productions. In any case, few fields of baroque life display the sense of limitless activity, of a feeling of power to accomplish the impossible more strikingly than the Spanish stage, with its thousands upon thousands of plays. Lope de Vega, credited alone with nearly a thousand plays, himself claimed when he was sixty-nine to have written over fifteen hundred. Some of these he completed in twenty-four hours. Tirso de Molina presumably did four hundred, Calderón nearly five hundred. Not all of these survive, but we have about four hundred of Lope, about one hundred of Molina, over a hundred of Calderón. It is a productivity comparable only to that of Bach and Handel later.

These Spanish dramas and sacred plays were quite simple in basic structure. The best ones, like Lope's *La dama boba* (*Lady Dunce*), *El*

---

[16] Elisha Kent Kane, *Góngorism and the Golden Age: A Study of Exuberance and Unrestraint in the Arts* (1928).

ausente en el lugar (*The Absent in the Village*),[17] Molina's *Seducer of Sevilla* and *Don Gil of the Green Trousers,* and Calderón's *The Constant Prince, Life Is a Dream,* and *The Mayor of Zalamea* move swiftly from action to action in terms of conflicts that highlight the typical Spanish values, especially honor in all its variants. Thus the mayor in the last-named play will submit to royal authority on all matters except honor:

Don Lope: Know you not, you are bound by your allegiance to submit?
Crespo: To all cost of property, yes; but of honor, no, no, no! My goods and my chattels, ay, and my life—are the king's; but my honor is my soul's, and that is—God Almighty's!
Don Lope: Fore God, there's some truth in what you say.[18]

This sentiment was not always maintained. Lope de Vega had a poor Spanish officer sacrifice his honor to the king's service with the words:

> Service to King Philip's duty
> If it ruins my honor
> It will be re-established by him.[19]

The political attitudes of the great Spanish writers, Cervantes, Lope de Vega, Calderón and the rest were those of intense patriotism, with full acceptance of the monarchy. This does not mean that they approved the excesses of absolutism; far from it. But these excesses were treated as emanations of a mysterious, divinely ordained order of things. Lope, indeed, treated the same prince now as a tyrannical monster, now as a just and graceful ruler, as for example Don Juan of Portugal in *The Duke of Viseo* and *The Perfect Prince,* respectively. To try to explain this contrast in some such terms as that "the highest power of the state, the absolute king, was beyond good and evil and above the moral standard," [20] is very wrong. How could Philip III and Philip IV have leveled the bitter accusations against themselves, blaming all Spain's misfortunes on their own personal wickedness, if they had been "beyond good and evil" à la Neitzsche? No, absolutism meant a heightening of monarchical responsibility. After all, was not Mariana a Spaniard? The

---

[17] Cf. Rudolph Schevill, *The Dramatic Art of Lope de Vega* (1918).
[18] Translated by Fitzgerald.
[19] *Pobreza no es vileza* (Poverty Is Not Vileness), Great Academy Edition, Vol. XII (1626). Cf. Karl Vossler, *Lope de Vega und sein Zeitalter* (1932).
[20] Vossler, *op. cit.,* 235. Generally, Vossler's political interpretation is inadequate, compared to his esthetic insight.

contrast in Lope's interpretation is partly to be understood in terms of his lighthearted indifference to historical evidence, and partly in terms of his truly baroque willingness to look at men from varying angles, as reflected in many mirrors, so to speak. Just as a profile may be beautiful and a full view homely, so a ruler may appear evil and tyrannical when seen in relation to individuals close to him, and just and wise when considered in relation to the people or in some other perspective.

In Spain the prevailing view was that all kinds of crimes committed for honor's sake were a duty in this world and a sin before God. All the dramatists of this period strove to show the conflict between worldly and divine rules of honor in all their variations and potentialities. Here perhaps more than in any field of dramatic events the specific baroque relation to the world of reality occurs which has been called "illusionism" and which the Spanish poets pushed to extreme lengths.[21] That life is a dream, expressed not only Calderón's view, but also Lope's, while Quevedo exclaimed that life is a comedy or show: *No olvides, es comedia nuestra vida, y teatro de farsa el mundo todo."* (Don't forget: our life is a comedy, and the whole world a comic theater." [22] Shakespeare, in his late, baroque stage lets Macbeth sound the same note:

> Life's but a walking shadow, a poor player
> That struts and frets his hour upon the stage,
> And then is heard no more; it is a tale
> Told by an idiot, full of sound and fury,
> Signifying nothing.

This sense of life as an illusion is even deeper in *The Tempest* (1611):

> We are such stuff
> As dreams are made of, and our little life
> Is rounded with a sleep.

The basis of this sense of the illusory quality of observed reality was a deeply felt religiosity and more specifically a renewed belief in the transcendence of God as the true reality. All human activities were vanity compared with this higher being. This very tendency to look upon human life as outward, deceptive appearance enabled baroque writers to treat it in a playful manner ideally adapted to dramatization. It called, so to speak, for a heightening and dramatization. "From its own nothing-

---

[21] L. Pfandl, *Geschichte der Spanischen Nationalliteratur in ihrer Blütezeit* (1929); Elisha Kent Kane *op. cit.*

[22] Vossler, *op. cit.*, 220.

ness life flees upon the stage, and people flock to it to get intoxicated by it." [23]

In keeping with this new overpowering sense of the vanity of all human activities, Lope de Vega and Calderón both entered holy orders in middle age, Lope about 1641, at the age of fifty-two, Calderón at fifty-one. Both also had volunteered for and served in the military service of the king of Spain in their younger years, thus testifying by their very lives to the two great loyalties of the Spaniard. Of the two, Calderón, the nobleman of ancient lineage, appears to have been more seriously involved and more deeply affected: indeed for more than a decade he refused to write any plays. Only considerably after 1660 did he, at the king's urgent insistence, resume his writing and then mostly in the form of Corpus Christi plays (*autos sacramentales*).

In many ways the most remarkable work of Lope de Vega, comparable in some ways to Goethe's *Poetry and Truth,* was his *Dorotea.* He started it in his youth, as he says, "in those days when I rushed from my studies to the standards of the illustrious duke of Medina Sidonia"—1588 or thereabouts. But he did not complete it until 1632, and most of it belongs to this period:

> A late-born of my muse, Dorotea
> The most beloved of my children, I can say,
> The last of my creative power,
> It still seeks th' light,
> And by the grace of the good count of mist
> Guzman, it wants to shine in th' golden sun.

A prose work, the *Dorotea* has often been condemned as tedious in its long-drawn-out discussions, five extended acts of them, with the action rather accidental.[24] But much of the precious talk—smart in the current American sense—was presented by way of humorous exaggeration. The deeper meaning was a confessional, an accusation of the aging poet against the artificialities and superficialities and amoralities of his youth. Lope's conscience, none too strong in life, poetically represented the all-engulfing *vanitas vanitatum* in *Dorotea.* The thought of the fleeting, transitory, the elusive and perhaps meaningless quality of life permeated all.

One of the most penetrating students of this period, reminding us of the spirit of Don Quixote, has pointed out that *Dorotea* unfolds the drama of

[23] Vossler, *op. cit.,* 220.
[24] Pfandl, *op. cit.,* calls it "a trial of patience." But is not this also true of the *Divina Comedia* and *Paradise Lost?*

ın indulgent literary and artistic world which revels in gallantry, senti-
mentality, amorousness and melancholy. In sharp contrast to modern
ealistic tendencies, the reader was invited to join this world of playful
nake-believe; no problems were allowed to torment the reader.[25]

The man who gave perhaps the most extreme expression to the formal
ınd artificial in baroque letters was Luis de Góngora y Argote. The
:ontrast usually drawn between Lope, the naturalist, and Góngora, the
:ultist, is an oversimplification. There was much that was artificial and
.llusionist in Lope, as we have just seen, while Góngora at times displayed
ı very genuine, popular strain. But Góngora was somber, haunted, full of
ınxieties. His favorite themes were death, pain, and the fickleness of
fortune and human attachment:

> The lass most beautiful in the entire land
> Left who only yesterday him had on her hand
> Who today is gone to the wars with a band
> To her mother she laments how he's inconstant:
> "Oh, let me weep on the wide oceanstrand." [26]

These lines are clear enough, but in the most brilliant pieces of Góngora,
the metaphors, allusions and complex subtleties are so numerous that they
are well-nigh untranslatable. "Here we find the most extreme form of a
poetical convention concerning a language of metaphorical allusions which
put an unreal wall between the meaning and the object it refers to." [27]
Perhaps Lope's comment was as sensible as any put forward since his
day; he had a real regard for Góngora, in spite of the latter's often dis-
agreeable attitude. Lope's delightful spirit, gay and yet passionate, but at
all events unwilling to take itself seriously, enabled this genius to maintain a more balanced view. In his *Discorse sobre la nueva Poesia* (*Discourse about the New Poetry*) (about 1617) Lope wrote:

Many have been carried away by the novelty of this kind of poetry, nor have
they been mistaken; for in the older style they would never in their lives have
been poets, and in the modern style they are such in one day; for with these
transpositions, four ideas and six Latin words or emphatic phrases, they find
themselves elevated to a degree that they do not know themselves . . . the
whole foundation of this edifice is the transposition of words. . . . For to

[25] Vossler, *op. cit.,* 175 ff.
[26] Translated from the German of E. Geibel.
[27] Dámaso Alonso, in the introduction to his edition of the *Soledades* (1927); Miguel
Artigas, *Don Luis de Góngora* (1925); and Elisha Kent Kane, *Góngorism and the Golden
Age* (1928).

make the whole composition into figures, is as vicious and unsuitable, as i
a woman who rouges herself, instead of putting the colour on her cheeks—
very proper place—should put it on her nose, brow and ears.[28]

Yet Lope did not lack considerable appreciation for Góngora's achieve
ments; he took the moderate view that the genius of the master shoul
be respected, but that his excesses should be avoided:

The genius of this gentleman whom I came to know 28 years ago, I valu
as one of the finest in Andalusia and am ready to put him beside Seneca an
Lucian. . . . We possess precious works in the purest language by him. . .
But not content with these achievements, he set himself the task of enrich
ing our language and enhancing it by newly invented, never before see
figures of speech and ornamentation.

Lope then alluded to the inspiration Góngora might have received from
Marini,[29] but of course the popular poet condemned this search for the
artificial and esoteric. Lope was the poet of the people, whereas Góngora
like Mérimée, Stefan George, and T. S. Eliot in our day, wished to with
draw from the multitude into an elect circle of refined spirits.

Pedro Calderón de la Barca, one might say, represents a merging of the
two divergent poetic strains. He has been called the poet of the palace, bu
his enormous popularity makes that appear a rather artificial judgment
To be sure, Calderón had a stately, somber quality which contraste
sharply with Lope. Yet to call his plays "affected and monotonous," a
does Rennert, seems unjust, even when coupled with the observation tha
Calderón is "superior to any dramatic poet of his age in grandeur o
theological conception and metaphysical subtlety," and hence "the poet o
Catholicism *par excellence."* [30] Calderón in truth represented a more fully
developed stage of baroque drama, more nearly like that of Corneille
Vondel and Gryphius. Religious devotion has become more completely
merged with the renaissance sense of natural passion to produce a
mystical, all-pervading feeling for the divine powers.

Besides Calderón's most famous *Life Is a Dream,* a symbolic drama
other striking plays were his tragedies, *The Mayor of Zalamea, The*

[28] H. A. Rennert, *The Life of Lope de Vega* (1904).

[29] This reference is obscure, because he refers to a Genoan without name, whereas Marin
was Neapolitan; this has given rise to controversies, for which see Rennert, Vossler, *et al.*
op. cit. Lope attributes Marini's obscurity to his not knowing pure Tuscan. Hence the argu
ment would apply, regardless of whether he was Genoan or Neapolitan, and considering
Lope's carelessness in all detail, I believe he means Marini.

[30] Rennert, *op. cit.,* 395.

Painter of His Dishonor, and *The Physician of His Honor.* The numerous "sword and mantle" and "corpse" comedies—two categories of traditional Spanish shows running into the thousands in the century of Lope's and Calderón's lifetime—while often admirable in their way, did not represent the genius of Calderón in its most characteristic form. But his religious dramas did, and among these *The Constant Prince* was probably the most celebrated, though the greatest was perhaps *The Excellent Magician.* In no other play did Calderón achieve quite the same balance and depth, combined with skilled execution. It has often been compared with Goethe's *Faust;* for Cypriano, the magician, searching for truth and finding it through the faith in God, resembles Doctor Faustus. And yet, what a difference between the philosophizing, experimenting, ever-restless Faust, and the passionate Cypriano, who is tempted forever by his sensuality.[31] *The Constant Prince* portrayed a saintly ruler, Ferdinand of Portugal, as he triumphed over all passions and humiliations. The play was a special favorite of the romantics, like Schlegel and Shelley.

It stands to reason that Calderón's religiosity should have led him to devote special attention to the *autos sacramentales,* the religious shows produced on the festival of Corpus Christi. Indeed, the story goes that as Calderón lay dying on Corpus Christi, 1681, one of his plays was being performed in virtually every city of Spain. He had achieved universal acclaim, just as the *autos* were about to be abandoned; for soon afterward they disappeared from Spanish life. These plays were allegories in which the mystery of the Eucharist was symbolically presented. Calderón, then, perfected the genre, and did so with the greatest variety of themes, stories from the Bible, from the lives of the saints, from ancient mythology and even from history. Among the more remarkable, representing different themes, mention should be made on *The Meal of Balthasar, The Sacred Parnassus, The Divine Orpheus*—the latter a strange combination of Greek and Old Testament mythology, linking the fall of man to Orpheus. Finally, *The Great Theater of the World,* one of Calderón's most resplendent *autos,* dramatized even in its title one of the key ideas of the baroque: the stagelike vanity of this world.[32] Very characteristic of the period was *To God for Reason of State,* in which Christianity triumphed over the other religions, including atheism. In these religious plays, Calderón was unsurpassed. His deep devotion and his subtle

---

[31] *The Excellent Magician, The Constant Prince,* and several others were translated into English by McCarthy, while Fitzgerald translated *The Mayor of Zalamea.*

[32] This and the preceding were translated by the German romantic, Eichendorf.

understanding of theological issues were combined with his superb lyrical language to produce pieces of unique beauty. The mystical strain in baroque letters has nowhere found more artistic expression.

The modern reader is somewhat handicapped in reaching a full appreciation of Calderón by his inability to recapture the rich settings and musical accompaniment of these shows. Indeed, the popular passion for the "show" went so far that the poetry was at times quite lost, much to the chagrin of the poet. Calderón, as we noted, took orders in 1651 and refused to write any more plays, so disgusted was he with such pagan tendencies; only after many years was he prevailed upon by the aging king to resume the writing of plays.[33]

Among the many other writers of distinction who competed for the acclaim of king and people one might mention Ruiz de Alarcón, who wrote only about thirty plays; but they have been gaining in repute. Guillem de Castro (1569–1631) was noteworthy because he authored the *Ciud,* which provided Corneille with materials for his most celebrated drama, *Le Cid* (1635).

(c) France

The traditional view is that Corneille, and indeed French culture generally, did not participate in the development of the baroque, but proceeded from renaissance through classicism to rococo. That this view is untenable should have been suggested by the recognition of rococo as one of the French styles par excellence. For what is rococo but a lighter and more gracious baroque? The French genius merely brought to the baroque world picture some specifically French sentiments which resulted in greater stress upon gravity and severity of form than in Spain. Corneille especially was a dramatist of true baroque quality in the abstract and type-formed character of his figures, the ornate quality of his language, and the climactic enhancement of formalized conflict situations. If this was true of Corneille, it was even more true of the other literature and poetry of the period. Knightly romances were the rage at the height of Richelieu's career, and in a sense it can be said that the very classicism is baroque in its stagy unreality.[34]

Corneille was so deeply baroque that only recently has he been "revived" by a generation with a new feeling for formal beauty. *Le Cid,*

---

[33] For the *dramma di musica* and opera see next chapter, pp. 86–7.

[34] See below, pp. 199–201 for Richelieu and Father Joseph, and below, pp. 67, 76–9 for painting and architecture, pp. 111–7 for philosophy.

which precipitated a violent controversy among literary men and led to an inquiry by the new Académie Française, founded in the very year of its appearance, seemed like a revelation to its contemporaries. Corneille, who remained obstinate in defending *Le Cid* against its detractors,[35] nevertheless was profoundly affected by the proceedings against him. Ever after he remained troubled by the rules of dramatic art which Aristotle was presumed to have laid down for all time. Some feel that this was a permanent loss for the French theater, but insofar as "limitation reveals the master" (Goethe) this was hardly true. Lope de Vega and his Spanish compatriots also worried about these rules; but instead of letting them thwart their exuberant spirits, they confessed themselves to be lowbrows and sinners against the higher verities, while continuing to write as they and their audiences felt. Lope simply blamed it on the audience, who wanted it so. But in the France of Richelieu a truly baroque majesty surrounded the all-knowing state, which set itself the task of enforcing uniformity to what was considered artificial truth. Hence there developed the preference for precision and refinement of style, the so-called "preciousness" which only later and as a result of its exaggerations became a derogatory term and provided the stuff for Molière's *Les Précieuses Ridicules* (1659). At this time, *les précieux* crowded the salons which set themselves the task of aiding the literary and poetic directions of the court.

Corneille founded the French tragedy upon a Spanish base, but significantly altered it and greatly developed it. *Horace* and more especially *Cinna* represented a striking revolution. It might be said that passing from *Le Cid* to *Horace* is like passing from a world of painting to one of sculpture. It is unfortunate that space limits forbid sufficient quotation to make this contrast vivid. *Le Cid* was the drama of honor par excellence, not only of Spanish, but of French and universal baroque honor; everyone was moved by the feeling that all other values must be subordinated to this supreme challenge. Against the appeal of the courtier that he should submit to the king's will, the Count asserted:

> *Et l'on peut me reduire à vivre sans bonheur*
> *Mais non pas me résoudre de vivre sans honneur.*

[35] In a letter to his friendly rival Boisrobert he wrote about 1639: "Le Cid *sera toujours beau, et gardera sa réputation d'être la plus belle pièce qui ait paru sur le théatre.*" Quoted in Jean Schlumberger, *Plaisir à Corneille* (1936), a delightful anthology with commentary which makes the best lines readily available to the modern reader who does not wish to read Corneille's plays entire—as he should.

Likewise, after the suitor of his daughter had killed him in a duel, the daughter's honor demanded of her that in spite of her love she seek the death of her father's slayer, as she saw it; in turn, the young man who had quarreled with the Count and felt himself insulted, countered with:

> *Il me prête la main, il a tué le Comte,*
> *Il m'a rendu l'honneur, il a lavé ma honte.*

The inextricable net of conflicting emotions was superbly portrayed in an encounter between the two lovers:

Chimène: *Malgré des feux si beaux, qui troublent ma colère,*
Je ferai mon possible à bien venger mon père;
Mais malgré la rigueur d'un si cruel devoir,
Mon unique souhait est de ne rien pouvoir.
Rodrigue: *O miracle d'amour.*
Chimène: *O comble de misère.*
Rodrigue: *Que de maux et de pleurs nous couteront nos pères.*
Chimène: *Rodrigue, qui l'eut crû?*
Rodrigue: *Chimène, qui l'eut dit?*
Chimène: *Que notre heure fut si proche et sitôt se perdit?*

The skill with which the rigid armor of the Alexandrine verse is hammered out to fit the pulsating passion of such an encounter displays a unique power of formalized representation of the emotions. Nothing like it had ever before been sounded upon the boards of the French stage. The spectators, including the king, listened spellbound. Richelieu, too, recognized the superb quality of Corneille's craftsmanship, though he condemned the dueling and suicide on the stage, as he did in life.

For his equally fecund, lone comedy, *Le Menteur,* Corneille likewise started from a Spanish model, Alarcón's *Verdad sospechosa,* itself a superb creation. Upon this foundation, Molière was to build the unique achievement of his thirty-odd great comedies; but they belong to the decade beyond 1660. In 1659 Corneille had emerged from a self-imposed retirement with his *Oedipe,* which was followed by about ten more plays until 1674, after which he wrote no more, although he did not die until ten years later. The great tragedies of the decade from 1640 to 1650 all show the superb craftsmanship of a man who, unlike his Spanish contemporaries, never tired of improving and amending his verses, thus making good Lope de Vega's whimsical: "The corrections show thought." People will presumably always dispute the rank of *Horace, Cinna, Polyeucte, Rodogune,* and the rest. In the skillful use of classical themes they resembled the great canvases of Poussin; in their somber and often fierce and rigid display of the passions they dramatized the philosophy of Descartes; in their highly ornamental language they offered a perfect vehicle for the baroque figures which walk upon his stage.

(d) Holland and Germany

Although the Alexandrine verse form of Corneille was peculiarly adapted to the metric rhythm of French, poets of other European countries, especially Germany, imitated the dramas of Corneille. They also derived inspiration from the greatest Dutch dramatist, Joost van den Vondel (1587–1679).[36] Born in Cologne, as the child of religious refugees from Antwerp, this thoroughly Dutch poet preserved all his life a deep veneration for the great free city on the lower Rhine, and often compared it with Amsterdam. Since his folks were tradesmen, he acquired his education in piecemeal fashion, but more especially in one of the "chambers of rhetorics" which then flourished in the Low Countries, animated by an ardent enthusiasm for humanism and the classics. Vondel's world was that of the local trade and craft guild, of painters and etchers who thronged the crowded streets of Amsterdam, Haarlem and Leiden.

Vondel was an ardent partisan of the party of Oldenbarneveld. To protest the latter's execution, he wrote one of his finest plays, *Palamedes,* or *Murdered Innocence* (1625). Perhaps his greatest drama, however, was *Lucifer* (1654), which, together with Hugo Grotius' *Adamus Exul,* is generally credited with having had a considerable influence upon Milton. In truth, all three and many more poets of the age were developing a baroque version of a dramatic theme that had been in the making for centuries. We say baroque, because all three combined Christian and classical (humanist) elements of thought and form and thus created a newer and more powerful dramatic effect. In any case, both Milton and Vondel received inspiration from a common source: *Le Sepmaine* of the French Huguenot, Du Bartas, available in England in the form given it by Joshua Sylvester in his *Divine Weeks.*[37] Vondel also shared the dislike Milton conceived for Calvinist orthodoxy, especially the doctrine of predestination. Hence in *Lucifer,* as in *Paradise Lost,* the idea of man's free decision is a central theme. No doubt, Vondel would have subscribed to Milton's

---

[36] J. A. Barnouw, *Vondel* (1925).
[37] See James H. Hanford, *John Milton, Englishman* (1949), 174–77.

> Son of heav'n and earth,
> Attend: that thou art happy, owe to God;
> That thou continu'st such, owe to thyself, . . .
> And good he made thee, but to persevere
> He left it in thy power; ordained thy will
> By nature free, not over-ruled by fate
> Inextricable, or strict necessity.[38]

It was straight Arminianism, but also in keeping with older Christian doctrine, except that there was lacking an adequate emphasis upon grace—as was generally true in Milton the humanist and aristocrat. Vondel had, by the time he wrote *Lucifer,* joined the Catholic Church (1641); a friend of Grotius and like the Vischers inspired by humanist letters and learning, he shared the dislike of strife over theological doctrines; in 1648 he celebrated the longed-for peace by an allegorical masque, *De Leeuwendalers.* J. Huizinga has written that "Vondel in the often clumsy, but always aspiring majesty of his elevated, solemn language is the perfect baroque poet." The depth of his sense of power is, as in Milton, most strikingly portrayed by his Lucifer, who at one point exclaims:

> If only I'm struck down with my gold'n crown
> Upon my head, the sceptre in my fist,
> Together with this honorary guard
> Of thousands of our party's followers;
> The fall brings fame and never-dying praise.
> Much rather in the lower realm the first
> Than in the blessed light be second.

Besides his great dramas, Vondel wrote many lyrics, as well as stately poetry for special occasions, especially for the departed. But if he showed in these moving pieces that typically baroque propinquity to death, Vondel could be very gay; his childlike heart had a wonderful capacity for enthusiasm.

In spite of his lack of psychological depth—Vondel's figures were even more rigidly "stuffed" than Corneille's—this greatest of Dutch poets had a majesty and purity, a wealth and felicity of expression, which made his words shine and sparkle, and gave to his stately Alexandrines a royal dignity. Unfortunately, his very lyricism prevented his becoming generally known outside Holland; even there a prosaic age has ceased to read him.

[38] *Paradise Lost,* V.

Vondel exercised a decisive influence upon the leading German baroque poets of the stage, especially upon Andreas Gryphius (1616–64). Martin Opitz, the most celebrated of this so-called Silesian school, set the tone by his *Book of German Poetry (Buch von der deutschen Poeterey)*, which appeared in 1624. He stressed purity of language, style and verse, along lines similar to the ideas of *les précieux* in France. But his poetry, while skillful and achieving truly baroque perfection, lacked a counterbalancing depth of feeling.[39] Much more genuine in this respect was the somber Gryphius, the "founder of German 'bombast.' "[40] A suffering, melancholic man, Gryphius was truly the poet of the Thirty Years' War. Deeply moving were some of the lines from his sonnet on the Thirty-first Psalm:

> With weeping and with groans, with labor, woe and fear
> I'm wasting hour and day, and February's grimness
> Ruins me, like the flight of the swift time the year,
> Let's hardly me lament my bitter woe, my mis'ry!

> (*Mit Thraenen und mit Ach, mit Arbeit, Weh und Zagen*
> *Verschleiss ich Stund und Tag, des Feber grimmes Leid*
> *Nimmt mit dem Jahr mich hin, die Flucht der schnellen Zeit*
> *Laesst mich mein herbes Weh, mein Elend kaum beklagen!*)

But Gryphius carried the baroque violence of expression to greater lengths than any of the other major poets of the age. In his sonnet on Hell the following verses are astounding in their exclamatory desperation:

> Ah! and Woe!
> Murder! Clamor! Groans! Terror! Cross! Torture! Worms! Plagues!
> Pitch! Torment! Hangman! Flame! Stench! Spirits! Cold! Fears!
> Ah Perish! .
> High and Low!
> Sea! Hills! Mountains! Rocks! Who can bear the pain?
> Swallow, abyss, oh swallow! them who forev'r shall clamor.

It may well be asked whether this was still poetry. Gundolf has suggested that it was straight virtuosity; yet, as he rightly added, only the mind can follow these violent counterpoints. The poem leaves one cold.

Very different in spirit and influence was the *Simplicius Simplicissimus* (1669) of H. J. C. von Grimmelshausen (1625–76), a striking novel of adventure, modeled upon the picaresque romances of Spain. The hero

---

[39] See Karl Vietor, "Das Zeitalter des Barock," in *Aufriss der deutschen Literaturgeschichte* (1930).

[40] Cf. Friedrich Gundolf, *Andreas Gryphius* (1927) for a penetrating, brief study.

was a quite ordinary fellow, a bit of a rascal who, having lost his parents in the early part of the war when marauding soldiers attacked his home, wandered about and grew up to manhood under the lawless and wild conditions of Germany. Stylistically, Grimmelshausen bore a relationship to Gryphius similar to that of Bunyan's *Pilgrim's Progress* to John Milton—or for that matter of Frans Hals to Velasquez. His was the naturalistic, realistic and sensuous side of the baroque, full of spirits mocking God and men.

V. ALLEGORY AND MYSTICISM

John Bunyan, born in 1628, was the poet of the epic of the English common folk in the mid-seventeenth century, as Grimmelshausen was the poet of the Germans. Of humble origin, Bunyan lived through Commonwealth and Protectorate as one of the ordinary men whose aspirations the revolutionaries represented. His book was an inward drama portraying the ardent religiosity of a people who rivaled the Spaniards in their devoutness of spirit.[41] While Bunyan's work, properly, belongs to a later period, *Grace Abounding* being published in 1666 and *Pilgrim's Progress* in 1678, the events which shaped it are so much part of the revolution that mention must be made of it here; after all, *Paradise Lost* did not appear till 1667 either.

John Bunyan's work was perhaps the outstanding allegory of the period; and allegory was one of the favorite devices of the baroque poet. We have already commented upon the extensive use of allegory in Spanish literature. It was part of the general inclination toward mysticism. Each country produced its mystics in this period of intense religiosity, and most of them were highly significant from a literary standpoint. Pascal and Böhme will occupy us in the course of the next chapter. Here a word might be added concerning Angelus Silesius (1624–77) who in 1653 became a convert to Catholicism. His most important work was *Der cherubinischer Wandersmann* (*Cherub-like Wanderer*), a collection of sayings which, while often extremely baroque, were permeated by an intense religious feeling and probed the depth of mystical insight. As in Spain, so in Germany, the lines run back from this flight into mystical absorption to the medieval tradition which had produced Master Eckhart and others.

If, in concluding, we sum up what these many different writers had

[41] See below, pp. 154–6, 296–7.

in common—the baroque language—we can say that it was rich in simile and metaphor, in ornamental adjectives and stately formalities. Nouns were piled up and ejaculation occupied a central place. Indeed, with the more radical baroque writers, literary language became an end in itself; thought was sacrificed to expression, meaning to sound. And yet, with all the brocade and declamation, there occurred the occcasional luminous vistas of utter simplicity:

> freely we serve,
> Because we freely love, as in our will
> To love or not; in this we stand or fall.

VI. CONCLUSION

The extraordinary poetical power of the visions of the mystics might well be the occasion for including more detailed discussion of their work here. But this will be taken up later, and it therefore remains only to sum up the literary work as an expression of the "spirit of the age." The sense of power in all its forms, spiritual and secular, scientific and political, psychological and technical is the only common denominator which enables us to conceive of them as varied expressions of a common view of man and the world. The startling achievements of man led to a sense of potential might which alternated with a crushing realization of human limitations in the face of an infinite world created by a remote and all-powerful being transcending all human comprehension. The inherent drama of such a view provided a magnificent setting for poets of true grandeur. It is the glory of the baroque age that everywhere men rose to this unique challenge. Milton and Vondel, Corneille and Calderón, Lope de Vega and Grimmelshausen—they all spoke the language of an age when man's dignity was his most prized possession in the face of the powers of this earth and those of the beyond.

Chapter Three

BAROQUE IN ART AND MUSIC

I. ARCHITECTURE AND SCULPTURE

The beginnings of baroque art are traditionally found in the field of architecture and traced to Rome,[1] often called the birthplace of baroque. Certain historians and art critics have urged that the late work of Michelangelo, who died in 1564, must be considered the beginning of the baroque. The problem resembles in some ways that of Shakespeare in literature. It is argued that Michelangelo's architectural plans, especially those for St. Peter's, are closely akin to early baroque plans and buildings. In any case, the earliest clearly baroque building is Il Gesù, built by the Jesuits in Rome between 1568 and 1584, a basilica centered in a cupola. Thus, it combines the longitudinal tradition of medieval churches with the centered buildings of the renaissance. Furthermore, the free-floating effect achieved in this cupola, supported by much statuary pointing upward to heaven, which is part and parcel of the structuring of its space, suggests a longing for the infinite and the all-high. Emotional agitation is presupposed. The new in Il Gesù may be called "a movement of physical nature toward spiritual goals, expressed in the progression of spatial elements, by the encounter and resolution of contraries."[2] Eternity is not unchangeable, but ever-changing.

It is in keeping with the general feeling for space as a fluid that baroque architecture and sculpture go hand in hand. The search for dynamic effects called for the fullest possible use of the decorative possibilities of sculptural detail. On the other hand, the setting of *mise en scène,* the space within which it was to live and breathe, became ever more vital for this dramatic plastic art.

The early baroque filled the latter part of the sixteenth century; soon after 1600 its full flowering in Italy, Spain and the Netherlands studded the European landscape with castles and churches, bridges and fountains,

---

[1] A. Riegl, *Die Entstehung der Barockkunst in Rom* (1908).
[2] Werner Hager, *Die Bauten des deutschen Barock* (1942), 48.

theaters and country houses in incredible profusion.[3] No major European city is imaginable without this rich harvest of baroque architecture and sculpture. More especially Rome and Vienna, Munich and Madrid, Warsaw and Prague are veritable museums of the creativity of this period. No style, neither Gothic nor Renaissance, has left so vast and dominant an imprint upon the European scene. Unfortunately little more than a few hints at the most celebrated monuments built between 1610 and 1660 can be attempted here. During these two generations much of the finest work of the high baroque (*Hochbarok*) was built, forming a startling contrast to the devastations of the fierce religious wars. Many of these buildings were paid for out of the destruction and booty which these very wars put into the coffers of men like Wallenstein and Richelieu, Urban VIII and Mazarin. They also rested upon the extravagance which others, like the kings of Spain, could ill afford; their enthusiasm for art was greater than their determination to be successful on the field of battle.

Confronted by such an embarrassment of riches, it is difficult to select particular artists or works for especial emphasis. It seems best to treat architecture and sculpture together, because they enter into so intimate a relationship that the one is inconceivable without the other, and most of the great architects were also sculptors and vice versa. Ever since the Renaissance this ideal of universality had animated the world of art. The incredible range of a Leonardo and a Michelangelo had become a fixed aspiration in this period, especially in the Latin countries. Not only the incomparable Bernini, but many others tried their hand at all the arts, as well as letters, with varying success.

Among the greatest, most marked figures in sculpture and architecture Lorenzo Bernini was outstanding. Son of a great father, Pietro Bernini, he was born in 1598, so the beginning of our period marks also the start of his amazing productivity. As far as Italian architecture and sculpture are concerned, Bernini has been called the Michelangelo of the seventeenth century. He was the daring genius who fully embodied the spirit of his age. Next to him, F. Boromino (1599–1667) and G. Guarini (1624–83) were pre-eminent among the Italians. Among the French, F. Mansart (1598–1666) maintained strongly classicist elements, and Claude Perrault (1613–88) was outstanding as the creator of the Louvre, for which his design won over Bernini's more extravagant baroque proposal.

[3] Cf. the inspired if one-sided chapter of Lewis Mumford, "Uprising of the Libido," in *The Condition of Man* (1944).

Another leading architect was Louis Leveau the younger (1612–70). Among Spaniards, none was equally distinguished, but even the great Velasquez participated in the completion of the Escorial. More important than the Spaniards were the artists of the Low Countries, especially Rubens (see below) and Jacques Franquart (1577–1651) in the Spanish Netherlands, Jacob van Campen (1595–1657) and Pieter Post (1609–69) in the United Provinces. The latter two developed the work of the two masters of the transition period, de Keyser (1621) and de Key (1627). From these centers, as from Italy, a host of minor architects went to the many courts of Germany. In England, always somewhat apart from the rest of Europe in her architectural development, the dominant personality was Inigo Jones (1572–1651) who, inspired by the work of the great Andrea Palladio (1518–80), created a number of masterpieces in the "classical" tradition, especially the castles of Greenwich and Wilton. Christopher Wren (1632–1723), who built more nearly in the spirit of the baroque, got his chance only after the great fire in London (1666) and therefore must be left to a later volume. The same is true of the great masters of German and Austrian baroque architecture, Fischer von Erlach, the brothers Asam, Neumann and the rest. Like their Slavic brethren, they were destined to carry the baroque to its ultimate perfection and reckless extravagance, but their work, which shaped Vienna, Dresden, Würzburg, Munich and many smaller cities, came to fulfillment only as the ravages of the Thirty Years' War were healed by the consolidation of society under "benevolent" absolutism. It is unavoidable that a style so rich and far-flung in its ramifications as the baroque will be somewhat artificially truncated by the selection of a fifty-year period, such as that between 1610 and 1660. There is little question that as far as architecture and sculpture are concerned, our discussion must be focused upon the Italians.

Even so, a great difficulty presents itself. Besides Il Gesù, which belongs to the sixteenth century, St. Peter's in Rome is perhaps the most imposing, certainly the most widely known, among the architectural creations of the early baroque. One is tempted to include a discussion of this remarkable creation, completed in 1612, especially as Bernini contributed the baldachino, a fanciful structure over the high altar (1627–33). But since the basic conception of this great cathedral was Michelangelo's, we would be carried far beyond the confines of our period. How far Michelangelo in fact transcended the architectural ideas of the renaissance in the direction of the baroque, a comparison of the ground plan he prepared with that of Bramante will easily show.[4] But in view of Palladio's classicist conception, which dominated the second half of the century, we have to recognize the anticipatory vision of the genius in Michelangelo's remarkable plans. The new ideas which the early baroque, following these visions, had developed by the time we are here primarily concerned with, were the following: a predominant position assigned to the main spatial unit; suppression of separate independent parts, such as chapels in churches; rhythmical relationship of all spaces within the total complex. This matter of rhythm deserves some further comment.

Rhythm, basically a musical category, is of central significance in appreciating baroque style. Indeed, the one-sided emphasis on simplicity so characteristic of much modern architecture tends to let one forget that the more complicated forms of building raise inevitably the problem of the relation of various rooms to each other. Brinckmann, who has particularly urged the importance of rhythm in baroque art, has said that "spatial rhythm develops when common relations of measurement (*Masstabbeziehungen*) connect one room with another, when there are found relations between the shapes of the several rooms."[5] As one looks at the blueprints of baroque buildings, this fluid quality of their rhythm becomes very clear, especially in the churches. Among the most striking features of baroque buildings are the sweeping staircases, the best of them veritable triumphs of rhythm in stone. Similarly balustrades and façades acquire something of the rhythmic quality of waves; they are music become stone.

The most significant turn toward high baroque occurred around 1630. This turn was closely associated with the maturing of Bernini and Boromino. But the fulfillment of this development would carry us far beyond our period; for a full hundred years the ideas which animated the creators of the high baroque occupied architects and sculptors throughout Europe. The decorative element thereby became of decisive importance. Perspective, and shadow effects which heighten it, achieved central significance. Everywhere there was movement and dynamic challenge. Heavy, often somber, baroque building, whether secular or ecclesiastical, was full of life and challenge.

A great difficulty confronting anyone who tries to select outstanding buildings for special attention in this period is the vast number of churches and palaces, villas (country houses) and theaters which still

---

[4] A. E. Brinckmann, *Die Baukunst des 17. und 18. Jahrhunderts* (1915), 2.
[5] A. E. Brinckmann, *op. cit.*, 53.

dazzle us with their beauty. Furthermore, their builders paid no attention to our concern with 1610–1660, but rather started building before or
ended them after this set of dates. It is perhaps one of the striking features
of architecture in this period that oftentimes more than two generations
elapsed between the beginning and the end of such an enterprise. We
have already spoken of St. Peter's in Rome. The Palazzo Barberini in
Rome was begun at the time Urban VIII became pope, in 1624, and
according to Maderno's plans. The building was continued after 1629 by
Bernini, who changed some basic features and added a great central stair-
way. Afterward Boromino added other details, and the palace may not
have been finished until after 1700.[6]

Among churches of similar significance, we might mention Boromino's
S. Carlo alla Quattro Fontane, built 1638–40, and S. Ivo (1642–60), both in
Rome, and S. Lorenzo (1634–87) in Turin, in which Guarini participated
after 1666. In all these churches, the blueprint reveals an extraordinarily
complex interlocking of curving lines. From Guarini's *Architettura civile*
we know that mathematics was the recognized basis of these architectural
masterpieces, *more geometrico.* "Architecture depends upon mathematics,"
Guarini wrote.[7] The several spatial units in these extraordinary buildings
were so arranged that they seem to intertwine and to penetrate each other.
At the beginning of the high baroque the effort was made to enrich the
spatial groupings, but without altering the subordination of all spatial
units under a main room. The curves became more agitated. The relation
between the several spatial units became more intimate, and the various
spatial units interpenetrated. This process was further enhanced by the
introduction of plastic elements, which were projected into one or more
of the spatial units. Thereby all clear demarcation of spatial units was
telescoped; straight walls were transformed into flowing lines, and the
several spatial units melted into one all-embracing conception. Light and
shade were skillfully employed to aid in this process of welding the
several units into one all-engulfing whole. It may be of interest to compare the treatment of window-casings by successive masters of the baroque, showing the increasing richness and complexity by which the
original wall was extended and molded into curves.[8]

In France, by contrast, and in consequence of the French classicist

[6] *Ibid.,* 90.

[7] This statement follows Brinckmann, but with some alterations and qualifications. See
Brinckmann, *Die Baukunst,* 89.

[8] *Ibid.,* 106.

preference for moderation and restraint, baroque tendencies were held in check. Baroque buildings like Saint Roch and Saint Sulpice in Paris were begun in 1653 and 1655 respectively and were finished only in the eighteenth century. The effects here were more nearly linked to earlier Gothic traditions, with great clarity in the over-all structure. Anyhow, a considerable number of France's finest castles and town houses (*hôtels*) were built in this period. Richelieu's palace, now the Palais Royal, has been changed so much over the years that the original plans of Lemercier and Mansart are hard to recognize, but the Hôtel Lambert, built around 1650 by Leveau, presents a beautifully proportioned structure in the spirit of French classicist baroque, in which especially the staircase is of superb and novel design. The skillful blending of variously shaped rooms and the linking of building and garden represent a unique achievement for the period. We find the same tendencies in some of the most famous country castles, such as the Château de Blois which Gaston d'Orléans had rebuilt by F. Mansart between 1635 and 1660. Here again the staircase was of grand design. Very important also is the Château de Veaux-le-Vicomte, built by Leveau for Fouquet, Mazarin's minister of finance, between 1657 and 1660, with the co-operation of Lebrun and others. Especially striking is the French quality in the Château de Maisons, also built by F. Mansart, between 1642 and 1650. Claude Perrault was so enthusiastic that he called this one of the most beautiful things in France.[9] But the most important of all was of course the Louvre. Here again, Leveau took over toward the end of our period, followed by Perrault, who won out, as we have mentioned, against Bernini. But the Louvre was not finished even during the eighteenth century, thereby once again illustrating the difficulty of discussing architecture within this short compass.

Among the sculptors of the period, Lorenzo Bernini was so uniquely powerful that we may consider him representative of the entire effort in this field. Among his many striking works, none has received greater praise, nor has been more roundly condemned, than his Theresa altar figure in S. M. della Vittoria in Rome.[10] In the middle of the altar, Theresa is seen swooning upon billowing clouds, with golden rays falling upon them from above. The saint is completely overcome by her beatific vision. An angel is facing her; of uncertain sex, the angel smiles "sweetly, knowingly and a bit cruelly." The obvious erotic analogies have

---

[9] An excellent recent study is Anthony Blunt, *François Mansart and the Origins of French Classical Architecture* (1941).

[10] See illustration.

scandalized successive beholders, but according to the best authorities, "there can be no question of lascivity." Such questions are hard to settle; the two-faced quality of baroque feeling, oscillating between the extremes of mystic devotion and sparkling sensuality, is strikingly merged in this celebrated altarpiece. The use of light and shadow, including colored windows to spread a golden light, heighten the over-all effect which is that of a great painting in its fluid, animated liveliness.[11]

Equally striking was the sepulcher for Urban VIII, Bernini's great protector. Using differently colored marbles for pictorial effects, Bernini ordered all the figures in such a way that attention is centered upon the Pope, who dwells above a variety of allegorical figures, untouched, immortal. This celebrated monument became the model for numerous later baroque sepulchers. We omit comment on Bernini's last phase, which falls beyond our period and seems weak in comparison to his earlier period.

Not of equal weight, but also great was the work of Alessandro Algardi (1602–64), who created the magnificent sepulcher of Leo XI as well as many remarkably realistic portrait busts. He was anti-Berninian in his general outlook, and a great favorite of Pope Innocent X, whose sepulcher he likewise fashioned. These works showed a classicist tendency, though the relief in marble called Expulsion of Attila revealed the curvature of the baroque, albeit in a more harmonious and balanced design. The third outstanding sculptor of Roman baroque in this period, was François Duquesnoy (1596–1646), really of Flemish origin. Let mention be made only of his S. Susanna in S. M. di Loreto in Rome. It is one of the most characteristic statues of the high baroque. To sum up, we might say with Brinckmann, probably the best interpreter of baroque sculpture:

The spread of high baroque in sculpture took place between the poles of Bernini and Algardi, regulated and made warmer by the influence of Duquesnoy. But it did not oscillate indecisively; rather the line culminated in the direction of Bernini and only after a last and highest jubilation, after the glittering burning out of the baroque fireworks, the line settles toward the quiet plains of classicism.[12]

It is a curious fact that no other country has anything of comparable intensity to place beside the work of Bernini, Algardi and Duquesnoy, except possibly the work of some Flemish artists, like Artus Quellinus

[11] See S. Franschetti, *Bernini* (1900) and the valuable discussion of other sculptural works in *Die Barockskulptur* (1919).
[12] Brinckmann, *Die Barockskulptur*, 260.

(1609-68) and Luc Fayherbe (1617-97). These men, like Duquesnoy himself, were deeply influenced by P. P. Rubens and thereby illustrate strikingly the palpable fact that baroque sculpture sought to paint in plastic materials. The role of the "picturesque" in baroque art has often been remarked upon, as has its musical quality of expressiveness. It is natural, therefore, that painting and music should have achieved a unique flowering in this period.

II. PAINTING

The same general tendencies which molded architecture and sculpture in the baroque period were at work in painting, of course. But the baroque developed certain formal elements peculiar to painting. Among the outstanding traits of the new and vital style were chiaroscuro (contrast of light and shade); the extensive use of tonal gradation rather than clear colors, combined with the gradual elimination of distinct outlines and the merging of objects into the surrounding background; and finally the employment of large quantities of pigment and the consequent visibility of brush strokes. Continuing the trends of the renaissance, the baroque painter decorated the interior of palaces and chapels, created great altarpieces, but also developed further the landscape and the portrait as movable decorations for the rooms of princes and wealthy burghers alike. A truly adequate appreciation of the art of baroque painting would necessitate, just as in the other arts, a discussion of the early baroque and of the so-called mannerism of the late sixteenth century. The towering genius of Michelangelo would once again have to be considered together with such masters as Carracci and Caravaggio. Titian, Tintoretto and Veronese would likewise have to be analyzed.

Assuming these antecedents of early baroque, we may say that all the great nations of Europe, except England and Germany, produced magnificent painters in the period of the high baroque. At the opening, around 1600, we find the Italians in the lead with Guido Reni (1575-1642) whose mature period began with his famous Aurora, and more specifically with Pietro da Cortona (1596-1669) whose frescoes in the Palazzo Barberini were among the most jubilant creations of the high baroque. At the other end of Europe, the first phase of high baroque was unquestionably dominated by the brilliant work and outstanding personality of P. P. Rubens (1577-1640). Ill-reputed among moderns on account of his lusty and sensuous female nudes, Rubens actually painted with a verve and a sense for the glittering beauty of colored surface that makes him unique in the history of painting. Trained in Antwerp and Italy (1600–1608) he was profoundly stirred by the magic color effects of Titian and his school, especially Tintoretto, as well as by the two incomparables: Raphael and Michelangelo. With the inception of our period, Rubens began to dissolve the fixed and isolated figure of renaissance painting. Figures were placed into more animated relations with each other, and an increasingly unified movement pulsed through his great canvases. At the same time, the colors gained in richness, variety and interrelationship. Pathos and sensuality combined to fill Rubens' canvases with a life that shows cosmic unity in all its parts; after 1620, some magnificent landscapes showed the same profound change. His success became overwhelming, and he developed a large workshop at Antwerp in which many assistants executed the great dynamic designs which he sketched. But after his great diplomatic mission to Spain and England, 1628–30, during which he tried to re-establish peace, Rubens withdrew and a late, more spiritual style appeared which was less vital but more subtle. Among his greatest, most celebrated works were the altarpieces now in the cathedral of Antwerp, Venus Facing a Mirror (1618), The Fall of the Damned (1620) and the Drunken Silenus (1618) at Munich, the Medici cycle painted for Marie de' Medici's Luxembourg Palace (1621–25)[13] and now in the Louvre, the Altar of St. Ildefonso and The Festival of Venus (1630–32) at Vienna; and from his final period The Garden of Love (1635) and the great landscapes showing his country estate at Steen. From Rubens influences radiated into Italy, France and Spain; but perhaps his greatest follower was Anthony van Dyck (1599–1641).

Van Dyck was a member of Rubens's workshop from 1616 to 1620, then went, via England, to Italy, returning to Antwerp in 1627. In 1632 he became the court painter of Charles I and remained in that position until his early death. Van Dyck was most renowned for his portraits.[14] In his later period he imposed a marked restraint upon baroque forms. In this respect his artistic development resembled trends in France. Van Dyck was more reserved and subtle than Rubens, and displayed a delicate taste in his use of color. No one has ever portrayed the noble grandeur of British aristocracy more convincingly than he, and his influence is clearly recognizable in the work of Gainsborough and Reynolds.

[13] See below, pp. 215–7.
[14] See illustration.

Among the most celebrated of van Dyck's canvases I should mention The Betrayal of Christ (1620) at Madrid, Susanna and the Elder (before 1622) now at Munich, Madonna with Ste Rosalia (1629) at Vienna, Lamentation (1630) at Berlin, Maria Louise de Tassis (about 1628) in the Liechtenstein Gallery, Queen Henrietta (1634), Charles I on Horseback (about 1635) at London, and The Children of Charles I (1637) at Windsor. No greater contrast can be imagined than that between van Dyck's affinity for all that is noble and reserved, and J. Jordaens's (1593-1678) and Adriaen Brouwer's (1605/6-38) earthy, lowbrow scenes of peasant life. Yet these scenes, apart from their subject matter, were extraordinary in their masterly handling of complex design and highly dynamic motion.

The true kinship of Van Dyck was with Diego de Silva y Velasquez (1599-1660), who served Philip IV and Olivárez throughout his life.[15] Velasquez was a student of F. Pacheco (1564-1654), whose daughter he married. Pacheco in turn was the center of a remarkable group of artists and writers in Sevilla which included Cervantes, Góngora, Quevedo. Like Zurbarán (1598-1664) he deserves an independent evaluation, but Velasquez towers above them both as one of the very greatest painters Europe has produced. In some ways, the baroque had no more striking representative than Velasquez. His portraits like those of King Philip IV are unrivaled as embodiments of the divine right of kings to rule and to be honored as representatives of God on earth. His Góngora (1622) now at Boston, caught the haughty and self-centered personality of this quintessentially baroque poet. Velasquez evolved from a relatively rigid style of painting which clearly separated figures and shapes toward a much looser and dashing treatment which exerted a profound influence upon the French Impressionists. In his most brilliant period he painted such extraordinary canvases as The Surrender of Breda (1635) now at Madrid, and the numerous portraits of Philip IV and of Olivárez, especially the famous ones on horseback. His portrait of Pope Innocent X (1650) now at Rome is among the most striking psychological studies of the period; only Rembrandt probed as deeply into the personality of the human beings he painted. His numerous studies of court dwarfs,

---

[15] See the remarkable monograph by Carl Justi, *Velasquez und sein Jahrhundert,* which is classic, in spite of its Burckhardtian preference for Renaissance and Italian standards which we reject as inadequate for interpreting baroque art. Jacob Burckhardt's own *Erinnerungen an Rubens* (1897) suggest the turn toward the new view: an English translation with 140 reproductions has just been published by Phaidon Press (1950).

like those of Sebastiano de Morra (1643) revealed the same penetration. Among his late paintings, The Tapestry Weavers (1657) and the Venus (1657–58) now at London were especially impressive in their subdued vitality. Velasquez was twice in Italy, in 1629–31 and in 1649–51, and the result of these visits was a loosening of his style. Deeply affected by the art of Tintoretto and Titian, Velasquez always retained an unbaroque quality of clear and distinct coloring; sharp contrasts were not lacking, and a certain static element, while rooted in his temperament, gave his painting a "classic" aspect which links him to French tendencies. The art of the renaissance was similarly alive in B. E. Murillo (1618–82), called "the Raphael of Sevilla." Characteristically Spanish in his merging of naturalism and mysticism, Murillo was probably the most universally admired Spanish painter. Many of his most celebrated canvases belong to our period, like The Flight to Egypt (1648) and the somewhat saccharine scene of a small Jesus offering refreshment to a small St. John, as well as the great representations of the legend of St. Francis (1645–46). But Murillo was above all the painter of the Madonna, tenderly portrayed as the virginal mother of Christ. His compositions were devoid of tightness; he used the chiaroscuro with exceptional warmth, fitting soft pastel colors like cirrus clouds into the sunset of a summer evening. The contrast between Murillo's gentleness and Zurbarán's monumental and heroic figures conveys something of the rich range of Spanish life and art, comparable to the contrast between Lope, Calderón, and Góngora. (See Chapter Two.)

No clear lines ran from the great Spanish painters to France's outstanding men, Poussin, Claude Lorrain, Champaigne, the brothers Le Nain, Vouet, who all conveyed a specific French flavor, modified by Italian and Flemish influences. Indeed, these painters present a problem comparable to that of French literature, which is highlighted by the term *classicism*. This classicism has been treated as an absolute antithesis to the baroque; but, as we have pointed out earlier in the general discussion, it was a specifically French form of baroque, modified when compared with Italian, Flemish or Spanish baroque, but differing from it no more than the persistent folkways of these peoples.[16]

Simon Vouet (1590–1649) spent many years in Italy, and while he brought to France the baroque ideal of bodily beauty, he nonetheless modified Italian ideas sufficiently to become the teacher of an entire

---

[16] Cf., e.g., R. Kautzsch, "Kunstgeschichte als Geistesgeschichte," *Belvedere*, VII (1925), 6–15.

generation, more especially of Eustace Le Sueur (1616–55) and Charles Le Brun (1619–90). Le Sueur, who is spoken of as "the French Raphael," was deeply religious and infinitely refined. This very French artist achieved his greatest triumphs in twenty-two canvases which he painted for the Hôtel Lambert, between 1645 and 1648. Le Brun was, in a way, the first of a long line of French artists who, superb craftsmen, have nevertheless exerted an unfortunate influence by their tendency to be academic intellectuals who permitted their clear thoughts to dominate their cool hearts. Greatly admiring Poussin, whose formal perfection he urged as the ideal against Rubens's powerful colors, Le Brun was in no way comparable to Poussin's willful and stubborn genius. Indeed, the two greatest French painters, Nicolas Poussin (1593–1665) and Claude Gellée, called Lorrain (1600–1682), spent most of their lives in Italy, and more especially in Rome, where Poussin played a vital part in the passionate rivalries which divided the artists of the Eternal City.

In many ways Poussin was the counterpart of Corneille. His many striking landscapes, with classical themes, could easily be visualized as stage settings for Corneille's stately dramas. The constructed, stagy effect was as baroque as was Corneille's characterization, and the handling of colors and scenery similarly resembled the ornamented diction of the great dramatist. Following Carracci, Poussin painted wide, open, heroic landscapes which breathed order. Yet there always seemed to be an undercurrent of passion, of mysterious subdued tension—a strange expectancy enlivens these great scenes for the beholder, if he takes the time to contemplate them as idealized reality. Besides, Poussin painted some magnificent scenes of earthy and sensuous pleasure, of mighty clash of arms. Among his greatest (and they are difficult to reproduce in small compass) are the Bacchanal with the Lute Player (after 1630) at the Louvre, the Parnassus (1630) at the Prado, The Rape of the Sabine Women (1637–39) at the Metropolitan, the Triumph of Pan (one of four painted for Richelieu) at the Louvre. The great landscape canvases of his late period, especially the Winter of the Four Seasons cycle (1660 and later) also at the Louvre, was as baroque in conception and execution as any painting of the period; but Landscape with Diogenes (1648) at the Louvre and Apollo and Daphne (1665) at the Louvre were likewise baroque in conception and execution. Only the brief period 1640–47, the first two years of which he spent in Paris, showed an academic effort to paint like Raphael, but I must confess that a picture like The Discovery of Moses (about 1645) at the Louvre strikes me as intensely baroque in its very setting.[17]

If Nicolas Poussin may be called an epic painter who depicts the heroic in all its ramifications, Claude Lorrain was the lyric painter par excellence. Goethe, in his conversation with Eckermann, remarked that there was "not a trace of reality in his pictures, but the highest truth. Claude Lorrain knew the real world by heart down to its smallest detail, but he used it as a means for expressing the cosmos of his beautiful soul. This is true idealization; it knows how to use real means in such a way that the truth which appears produces the illusion of being real." It was one of the most curious features of Lorrain's remarkable achievement that he remained free from all dominant Italian influences though living in Italy most of his life. Claude Lorrain was the incomparable master of sunsets and their golden sheen upon the waters of quiet harbors, of the indirect light through mist that makes a pastoral landscape glow, of the balanced elaboration of a welter of palace fronts, ships with their masts and sails and the manifold appointments of a waterfront. It is almost impossible to gather from any black and white reproduction the limitless peace and the cosmic sense which emanates from these canvases. The baroque sense of unity was superbly expressed. A bachelor all his life, Lorrain lived in virtual retirement from the world, painting the quiet scenes which were much in demand for the great baroque palaces of Rome and elsewhere. Among the greatest were the following: Harbor in Mist (1646), Landscape with Flight to Egypt (1647), Adoration of the Golden Calf (1653), and the wonderful cycle of Morning, Noon, Evening and Night (1661–72). Lorrain kept a diary of his development, the *Liber veritatis,* containing many sketches which show the vivid animation underlying his great paintings.[18]

Compared to the genius of Poussin and Lorrain, the splendid craftsmen who remained in France seem academic and weak, with the single exception of the brothers Le Nain. Their extraordinary work, much of it concerned with life on farms and in inns, showed the baroque spirit of naturalism at work in true polarity to the stately, even pompous, paintings of Philippe de Champaigne (1602–74). The latter's Richelieu as well as his Louis XIII were singularly vivid examples of the courtly

[17] Poussin's own view was that he was "classic"; his was a reasoned eclecticism; see *Correspondance de Nicolas Poussin,* ed. January (1911).

[18] Walter Friedländer gives, in an appendix of his *Claude Lorrain* (1921), a discriminating evaluation of the *Liber Veritatis.*

side of baroque art. All the splendor, the theatrical gravity, found perfect form in these portraits of the two men who by their singular combination of talents did more than any others to consummate the task which the baroque sense of power and unity called for in the political field, and which the emergence of the modern, national, bureaucratic state institutionalized—to repeat once again our major theme. That Champaigne should at the same time have painted with depth of appreciation representative figures of Port Royal is testimony to his artistic sensitivity, which intuitively grasped the basic polarity of the age.

This basic polarity is perhaps nowhere as clearly seen as in the contrast between a great court painter, such as Champaigne or Le Brun, and the work of the greatest Dutch baroque, rooted in the life and feeling of the common folk, the burgher and peasant of the Dutch lowlands, especially as exemplified in Frans Hals (1584-1666) and Rembrandt Harmenez van Ryn (1606-69). Among the incredible welter of brilliant talent that strode upon the scene of western paintings, these two were perhaps the most striking baroque figures, although van Ostade, van Goyen, Hobbema, Ruysdael, Vermeer, Jan Steen and Wouwerman certainly have great claims upon our recognition and attention. Especially Vermeer has had a renaissance; his extraordinary capacity to elicit in the beholder the poetic qualities of a simple scene has found many admirers; his clearly demarcated treatment of color and line made him, however, a somewhat typical figure without the more striking characteristics of the baroque age.

Frans Hals was perhaps the most extreme representative of that lust for life and nature, of that abandon and physical impulse which the age offered. Who does not know his famous Malle Bobbe, his lute players and fisher lads, his startling self-portrait, so-called. But Frans Hals must have had a unique psychological insight into the recesses of "abstract" thought and what produces it: his portrait of René Descartes [19] is probably the most remarkable picture of a great philosophic genius. This aspect of Frans Hals's nature and art has only recently found adequate interpretation. It has now been shown that underlying his dash and naturalistic vivacity, there was a hard, geometric core of structure and design which gave his compositions a Cartesian quality of rationalist rigidity.[20]

Although Hals's portraits are most widely known and provided him

---

[19] See illustration.
[20] See Willi Drost, *Barockmalerei in den Germanischen Ländern* (1926), 131–46.

with the greatest immediate fame, his Banquets of Officers (five in all, dated 1616, 1624, 1627, 1633 and 1639, all at Haarlem) were the most striking products of his art. His manner of painting was revolutionary in its impressionistic liveliness and vivacity. The colors were brilliant, but fused; only in his later period did Hals employ black extensively. The individual figure in his group portraits lives a distinct life of its own, yet there is always a unity achieved through interrelated movement. Hals has been called the most sober, the most guarded of Dutch painters. This is true only in the sense that he possessed a veritable passion for reality. If one goes over the several great feast scenes, from the Officers in Georgedoelen (1616) to the same topic in 1639, one finds an increasing unity of design. But the most extraordinary symphonic accord was achieved in his late group of Regents of the Old Men's Hospital (1664), where he himself spent the last years of his life, evidently quite impoverished. Other key paintings: Jonkheer Ramp and his Sweetheart (1623) at New York; The Merry Drinker (about 1627) at Amsterdam; Malle Bobbe (about 1640) at Berlin; and The Gypsy Girl (about 1635) at Paris.

In the work of Rembrandt baroque painting rose to universal significance and appeal. Like Raphael, Leonardo and Michelangelo, Rembrandt is in his most personal works "for all times and nations." At the same time, we have to recognize that Rembrandt was clearly and strongly linked to the baroque in such masterpieces as The Night Watch (1641), which has been called the greatest baroque painting. In a very striking manner Rembrandt from the outset struck against the idealizing tendencies coming from Italy. With startling realism, he depicted the human body with all its shortcomings of age. Witness Rembrandt's Ganymede, where an idealized youth was transformed into a terrified child, wetting in its distress at being carried off. Like Jordaens and Brouwer, van Ostade and others, Rembrandt appears to have reveled in the ugly, the lowbrow, the coarse. Among paintings he owned, Adriaen Brouwer occupied a high place. It was a result of the determined search for man and nature as they appear to common folks in street and field. This insistence upon realistic representation had even a political significance: the protest of the Netherlander who had won his freedom from the mighty king of Spain, surrounded by his courtiers and elegant ladies as portrayed by Rubens and Velasquez. Similarly, Dutch painters preferred the simple charms of farm life to the heroic landscapes of a Poussin. But we must not forget

he corresponding scenes in the work of the brothers Le Nain, and the
ccasional canvases of Velasquez (see above).

Starting with the cult of a "realism," Rembrandt eventually achieved
a new spirituality by somehow investing all that is human with an un-
uspected inner life.[21] His expressive handling of light and dark and his
aroque efforts at unity and universality through the complete dissolv-
ng of outline were unique. His pictures were the quintessence of what
painting can accomplish when it sets itself the task of portraying the
"soul that lives in all things," of which Spinoza was to formulate the
definitive philosophic statement. Color and light, surface and space were
made to serve the purpose of rendering visible the inner life of all being
and more especially of man. The complete freedom and independence
upon which Rembrandt insisted all his life, even when it meant suffer-
ng and poverty, was an essential condition of his achievement.[22] "The
external tragedy of his life—economic ruin after great success and social
ostracism after brilliant rise which made him ever greater and more
sovereign—is closely connected with this willfulness of the genius who
abandons all social bonds."[23] In Rembrandt's work, nature became
animated and spiritualized.

Among his greatest paintings must be counted, besides The Night
Watch already mentioned, The Anatomy of Dr. Tulp (1632). Here we
have the first group picture which seems to live a life of its own in the
situation it portrays: the passionate interest in a problem of natural
science. Therefore light is concentrated on the arm of the corpse. Sam-
son's Wedding (1638) showed a marked development of Rembrandt's
style in the direction of atmospheric chiaroscuro. The bride, flooded by
light, was surrounded by a waving, flowing commotion of human
activity. The Night Watch (1641) carried this tendency further; each
individual was made an integral part of the drama of the whole. Working as if a spectator of the great scene, Rembrandt recreated a moment
of intense activity, when the parade was gathering, moving toward
order, but as yet free, in entirely unpremeditated activity.

Rembrandt's bold innovation in transforming a group portrait into a dramatically animated crowd stemmed from truly Baroque impulses. He created
a tremendous burst of movement of utmost complexity, brushing aside all

[21] Jacob Rosenberg's Rembrandt (2 vols., 1948), 177–78.
[22] This aspect has perhaps been most movingly described in H. van Loon's novel-like
biography, The Life and Times of Rembrandt van Ryn (1930).
[23] See Hamann, Kunstgeschichte (1933), 592.

remnants of the more static order which the Renaissance tradition had continued to impose upon his forerunners. The Baroque favored both complexity and unification of movement, and Rembrandt succeeded in expressing both subtly subordinating the diversity of action to a concentric trend within the whole.[24]

A similar extraordinary scenic effect was achieved in some of his great etchings, more especially the one where Christ is shown in the midst of a multitude (Hundred Guilder print) (before 1650). But Rembrandt had still a long way to go before he arrived at his greatest heights, the superb art with which he captured the quintessence of a human being. After about 1650 he became primarily occupied with this almost superhuman task; for who "would know what is in another's heart"? In this last period, the surrounding space and all decorative detail tended to disappear. For example the famous Portrait of an Old Lady (1654) now at Leningrad,[25] concentrated upon the face of the old woman, lost in meditation. Her eyes are turned inward, her hands quiet and absorbed. "Design and outline are those of a monument and the painting is great and significant, but the picture is not monumental in the usual sense of rigid immortalization. All forms are softened and instead of eternity, the elusive, fleeting quality is caught of a life which is here concentrated in one changeable moment."[26] In this, as in other paintings of this period such as The Man with Golden Helmet (after 1650), we find the peculiar treatment of light, luminous and illuminating, yet devoid of a clear source, often like a fluid emanating from a misty atmosphere of darkness. A new clarity, a combination of outer brilliance and inner life (excelling Velasquez and van Dyck), was reached by Rembrandt in such portraits as that of Jan Six (1654), and in this same spirit he painted the grandiose scene of The Syndics (1661–62). A final and perhaps ultimate combination of all of Rembrandt's originality was revealed in The Return of the Prodigal Son (1668–69). The intense religiosity of Rembrandt, which his sketches of the Life of Christ so beautifully embodied, was here given final form: the inner light of Protestant faith animates not only the painter, but the face of the father, forgiving and sorrowful, the abject figure of the son, and the reverent attitude of the onlookers wrapped in darkness. Here what is penultimate in the spirit of baroque feeling was achieved.

[24] Rosenberg, op. cit., I, 75–76.

[25] Actually this picture is now believed to be a portrait of his brother's wife. Rosenberg, op. cit., 59. Cf. also Table 94 in Vol. II.

[26] See Hamann, op. cit., 606.

III. INTEGRATED WHOLES: CITY, CASTLE, OPERA

Remarkable as were the individual works of art in architecture, sculpture and especially painting, in some ways even more extraordinary were the skillful blendings of these several forms of art into integrated wholes. The castle, within its setting of a great park, adorned with statuary and fountains; the city, laid out according to an over-all plan, a comprehensive conception which blended all works of art, architecture and nature in accordance with a rational design; and finally the opera as *dramma di musica* with its combination of song, dance, instrumental music, elaborate stage decorations, conceived in the spirit of baroque architecture, sculpture and painting—these represent the culmination of that spirit of extravagant vitality and complex mathematical design, of overweening sense of unity and power as the meaning and significance of creative effort. In creating thus, man truly worked in the image of God, the Almighty.

It is a striking feature of Europe that in contrast to the many beautiful cities which are evidently the result of slow growth over the centuries—cities like London, Florence, Antwerp, Stockholm, Copenhagen, Bern and the now destroyed cities of Germany—others are clearly the result of a rational plan and a determined decision to "make" a city where there was none before: Versailles, Karlsruhe, Darmstadt. Plans which have survived show that many more were conceived, though never executed. Still others, above all incomparable Rome and Paris, are a combination of the two, adding or indeed thrusting the constructivist spirit of baroque design into the ancient pattern. Thus, as everyone knows, the Paris of the Place Vendôme and of the Opéra is a different Paris from that of the Cité and of Notre Dame, although the former certainly today overshadows the latter.

Probably the greatest achievement of baroque city architecture in our period was the Piazza di S. Pietro in Rome, which Bernini [27] constructed between 1656 and 1667. Here gigantic spaces were handled with easy elegance and woven into a single, unified whole of interrelated parts. The two vast semicircles of colonnades, at once vital and willfully shaped, enclose a space which provides a magnificent setting for the mighty cathedral. Its center is pointed up by an obelisk, characteristic feature of many baroque squares (which typically are not square, but round!). From the portals of St. Peter a great vista across the mighty

[27] See above, p. 68.

piazza opened into wide streets, now greatly altered. The startling constructivist power of this creation was intensified by the way in which
was forced into the ancient surrounding city, a veritable triumph of
baroque willfulness. A similar piazza of lesser dimensions was built i
this period by Pietro da Cortona in front of S. M. della Pace.

The baroque rebuilding of Rome found an inspired, if capricious
sequel in Salzburg. Here the three great baroque bishops, Wolf Dietrich (1587–1612), Marcus Sitticus (1612–19) and Paris Lodron (1619–33)
undertook to reshape a medieval city in the new style. "Wolf Dietrich
fell upon the city, as if he wanted to destroy everything in blind fury."[28]
There is a tale, well-invented, if untrue, that the archbishop, when told
that the cathedral was in flames, remarked calmly: "Let it burn." His
successor, though not his equal, created the charm of Castle Hellbrunn
Paris Lodron carried out the passionate dreams of Wolf Dietrich, and
thereby completed an extraordinary feat: to recreate a whole city in the
image of the Counter Reformation and of its Italian center: Rome. The
result was something unique and uniquely beautiful. The great square
in front of the cathedral and the archiepiscopal palace, set off by the
dramatically baroque fountain, is an achievement of the highest order.

Fountains of unique dramatic power were often used to enhance the
unity of the spatial whole. In the early period such fountains tended to
avoid all figures; great columns or cascades of water were utilized to
point up the severity of early baroque structures, like the Maderno fountain on the piazza di S. Pietro in Rome. Later, baroque returned to the
use of figures, but in a new and agitated form. Works like the Fontana
di Tritone (1640) and the Fountain of the Four Rivers (1516), both by
Bernini, made the figures grow from the rock and brought them into
dynamic relationship with the water.

It has often been remarked that the castle or palace occupied the place
in baroque architecture that the cathedral possessed in the gothic period.
We have mentioned a number of the greatest of these buildings in discussing architecture. But besides these structures themselves, baroque
artists undertook to shape the entire setting by molding the surrounding
landscape into great gardens and parks constructed in accordance with
baroque ideas of spatial relationships. In contrast to the balanced and
static garden of the renaissance, the palaces of the baroque period projected their power outward, so to speak, and the designs of these palaces
were set into a park or garden in such a way as to show clearly the

[28] Herrmann Bahr, *Salzburg* (undated).

artists' idea: to conceive of the entire spatial unit as one single whole. In keeping with these notions, all disturbing detail, like flower gardens and the like, were pushed to the side or hidden away, and all was subordinated to one great central axis, indicated with fountains and long avenues of trees to which the castle or palace formed the cross axis, set in firm rectangle to it. Great staircases led from the building in sweeping curves onto this central axis, offering views of often overwhelming power and beauty. Statuary was set into this highly structured park to bind the various elements together, and often minor buildings, little intimate palaces, were erected at some distance from the main palace to provide variety and further animation. While the greatest of these creations, enriched by the unique genius of the French landscape architect, Lenôtre, namely the royal palace at Versailles, belongs to a later period, units of comparable beauty were built in Italy during the first half of the seventeenth century, as well as in France and elsewhere. Thus the Villa Doria Pamphili (1650 by Algardi) though only a partial realization of the artist's conception [29] was so closely tied in with the surrounding gardens as to form a complete unity. While still very angular, it represented clearly the new style, as did with perhaps even more striking effect the Villa Aldobrandini, built at the beginning of the century.

In England, by contrast, baroque building was held back by the influence of Palladio's classicism which dominated artists like Inigo Jones. While we find baroque elements here and there, the dominant type remained a static and balanced building, placed rigidly into an unrelated surrounding, e.g. Whitehall. In Germany, on the other hand, a striking beginning was made with the comprehensive conception of the castle and park as integrated wholes by the intensely baroque duke of Wallenstein, who built the Palais Waldstein in Prague (1621–28), and the even more striking castles at Gitschin (1626–34) and at Sagan (Silesia, begun 1627). In these castles, although their heavy, severe character seems to forbid it, a vital relationship to the surrounding parks and gardens was worked out in typical baroque fashion. But many of the most striking creations upon Austrian, Bohemian and German soil were the product of a later time; the ravages of the Thirty Years' War brought with them an exhaustion of both human beings and their resources which caused more than a generation's delay in this development.

If the city and the palace set within its gardens and parks are mag-

[29] See A. E. Brinckmann, *Die Baukunst*, 171–72.

nificent testimony to the baroque's determination to mold nature i
man's image and display the power of the human spirit, even more ex
traordinary, albeit fleeting, integrated wholes were put upon the stage i
the form of an entirely new art form, the *dramma di musica* or oper.
While its beginnings antedated the seventeenth century and were th
outgrowth of that passionate enthusiasm for the work of classical an
tiquity—a misunderstanding about the newly discovered Greek traged
played a significant role—Claudio Monteverdi (1567–1643) with his *Orfe*
(1609) entered upon that period of his artistic effort to which we ow
the most magnificent baroque operas: among them *The Rape of Prose*
pina (1630), *The Return of Ulysses* (1641), *The Marriage of Aenea*
(1641) and *The Coronation of Poppea* (1642). Unlike the rather sti
productions of his predecessors, these operas of Monteverdi were all con
ceived in the spirit of unity and power, of deep emotion and stately ritua
in which the baroque gloried. Here music and painting, sculpture an
architecture were all united to produce one all-embracing unity.

Looked at from the opera as developed by Mozart, Wagner or Verd
these productions seem strange, indeed. While the music was subord
nated to the words, at the same time a constant effort was made t
express restrained emotion in a strictly nonsentimental fashion. If Lop
de Vega and Calderón were bothered because their language was over
shadowed by the musical accompaniment of interwoven songs an
dances, of choral pieces and the like, these various elements were worke
into a comprehensive unity by the genius of Monteverdi. In short, w
may say that the *dramma di musica* was transformed into an opera unde
his influence. Unfortunately, we do not know what these production
really looked and felt like. Even rather detailed contemporary descrip
tions and pictorial records do not succeed in reproducing the magi
which their real performance must have breathed. Linked to great fes
tivals, often performed in the open, and suited as they were to fill th
very spaces which we have been describing, these new operas may b
considered the crowning fulfillment of that life of baroque man, at onc
stately and playful, enchanted by illusion and yet full of life, reachin
out for the infinite in an ecstatic sense of man's power and at the sam
time full of a sense of cosmic unity and of the passing of time, of th
death that seals all life's ambitions and glories.

One of the most famous and grandiose was the performance of an
Italian opera, *Chi soffre speri,* by Rospigliosi (text) and Mazzochi-Maraz
zuoli (music), given at the Barberini palace on February 27, 1639, befor

3,500 spectators, including Cardinal Mazarin. Bernini provided the stage designs, which were so marvelous that Bernini's biographer thought their fame would endure forever. Between the acts, *The Fair of Farfa* was enacted by a great multitude of players, spilling over into the audience and garden. Every kind of scene from real life at a Roman carnival was made part of the gorgeous entertainment, while the Cardinal Barberini entertained his guests. Among these was none other than John Milton.

IV. MUSIC

It is often claimed that music develops last those modes of expression characteristic of a particular style.[30] Thus baroque music is seen to have achieved its fullest flowering in Bach and Handel after 1700. But so did Poehlmann build the marvelous baroque *Zwinger* in Dresden during the same period, while on the other hand Monteverdi and his contemporaries created the opera after 1600, and Heinrich Schütz wrote the most expressive religious music of the Protestant baroque in the midst of the Thirty Years' War. In short, the long sweep of the baroque, extending from the end of the sixteenth to the beginning of the eighteenth century, was closely paralleled by the unfolding of a new style of musical composition in which naturalism and formalism, emotionalism and rationalism found a dynamic outlet comparable to the creations of architecture and painting, and indeed surpassing them. For music is as much akin to baroque as it is to romanticism. This most abstract of all art forms is at the same time the most intimate and emotional. Mathematics and music are the children of the most intense introversion.

Besides the opera we have already discussed, oratorios, instrumental concerto music, cantatas, and chorales constituted the most characteristic musical forms of this period.[31] Italy provided the leadership in all but the chorale, which owed its flowering to the Protestant service, especially in Germany. It may in fact be said that along with architecture, music was the peculiar passion of Italian man during the early baroque period. Rome and Venice celebrated the greatest triumphs, Gabrieli, Monteverdi and Frescobaldi being acclaimed throughout Europe and attracting eager pupils from all countries. The ardor of religious controversy was forgotten over the universal excitement for the new expressive style. Thus,

[30] See H. Leichtentritt, *Music, History and Ideas* (1938), 136 ff.
[31] A splendid general account of baroque music in English is at last available: Manfred F. Bukofzer, *Music in the Baroque Era* (1947), to which general acknowledgment is made here.

when the ardently Calvinist, Duke Maurice of Hesse, was struck with the intense musicality of a poor young law student at the University of Marburg in 1610, he gave him a scholarship to go to Venice. The consequences were far-reaching for the future of music, for the young man was none other than Heinrich Schütz, the greatest baroque composer of Germany (1585–1672). Four years he remained at Venice, first working with Gabrieli, and after the latter's death with his greater successor Monteverdi.

Claudio Monteverdi (1567–1643) was the Beethoven of the Baroque. Besides the operas we have discussed, Monteverdi developed the madrigal in a series of striking compositions from the earlier forms. His style known as the monodic, moved from the original form through successive stages marked by his eight books of madrigals (1590, 1592, 1603, 1605, 1614, 1619, 1638). His *Lettera Amorosa* (*Love Letter*) of 1614 and his *Partenza Amorosa* (*Love Parting*) of 1619 were particularly impressive examples of this monodic style: baroque expansiveness combined with moderation in harmonics and complete indifference to the base.[32]

Another important development was the oratorio, in some respects the spiritual branch of the monodic style. Among the masters of this form G. Carissimi (1605–74) was probably the greatest and most influential. His works were characterized by a beautiful melodic quality, a brilliance of picturesque expressiveness related to the words of the text, and an elegance and fluidity of form which was universally admired. Another great master of the oratorio was S. Landi (1590–1655); *La terra e cielo* (1626) is especially noteworthy.

Generally speaking, the oratorio, as well as the *dramma di musica,* developed out of the *cantada,* which they transformed in a typical baroque fashion. The three "styles" which G. Doni (1594–1647) had distinguished in his *Trattato della musica scenica* were the monodic or recitative style, the representative, and the expressive style. The first comprised every kind of melody, provided the words of the text were clearly enunciated. The notes were few, and the key problem was how to portray the commotion of the "soul." The representative style was proper only for the stage, and was intended to represent the nature of a given action or situation. The expressive style, finally, was specifically intended for lyric poetry; it was to express its *Stimmung.* The arias of composers like Peri and Caccini were illustrative of this style, which Monteverdi then

[32] Robert Haas, *Die Musik des Barock* (1934), 50.

carried to greater heights. This "new music," programmatically announced by Caccini in 1602 in his *Nuove Musiche,* steadily progressed in wealth of expression and dramatic power. From Grandi (1620) to Carissimi and Rossi, the *cantada* was typically an aria in several strophes, giving variations supported by a *basso continuo.* Its richness provided the musical substance for operas and oratorios; its possibilities in an instrumental direction were first explored by Monteverdi.

Besides these artists, one other master deserves brief, all too brief, mention, and that is G. Frescobaldi (1583–1643). A member of the artistic world which Urban VIII created to adorn his court, as organist for St. Peter's, Frescobaldi was more celebrated as a performer than perhaps any other musician of this period. But his many *canzoni, capprissi, toccate* and *partite* show a man of extraordinary inventiveness, of sparkling vitality, and of truly baroque temper. From 1614, when his first collection of toccatas and partitas appeared, until his death he stated and restated the great musical ideas of the Roman school in instrumental, and more especially in organ, works. A hundred years later, Johann Sebastian Bach still found inspiration in this music, so startlingly reminiscent of the bubbling fountains with which his great contemporary Bernini embellished the piazzas of eternal Rome.

Alongside this glittering display of Italian music, the production of the countries north of the Alps seems rather thin. Especially in France and England we find mostly echoes of this Italian productivity. But there is one country in which the first signs of later glories were beginning to appear, and that is Germany. Yet in contrast to Italy, where music was more and more separated from the church and shaped the whole nation's culture,[33] the central task of music in Germany, and the basis for its development, was the Protestant church service. In fact, music took an ever-greater part, until protests arose to curb such extravagance. The most important core of this growth was the Protestant chorale, so auspiciously initiated by Martin Luther himself. But around it various kinds of music injected themselves, mostly in the form of organ preludes and cantatas of varied length.[34]

Among the musicians who carried forward this development, Paul

[33] Leonardo Olschki, *The Genius of Italy* (1949), Ch. XVI, "The Triumph of Music." "Music became the only free and autonomous manifestation of the Italian artistic spirit in a period when thought, science, literature, and the figurative arts were all under strict tutelage and authoritarian control." (P. 410.) Cf. also remarks concerning Monteverdi, p. 421.

[34] See Albert Schweitzer, *J. S. Bach* (1934), Vol. I, Chs. II–VI.

Gerhard (1607–76) was probably the greatest chorale composer, but as a
all-round musician Heinrich Schütz (1585–1672) deserves the palm. Nex
to him, J. H. Schein (1586–1630) and S. Scheidt (1587–1654) were th
most important leaders; indeed the latter two went beyond Schütz i
the development of instrumental music.

These composers abandoned the traditional choral melody and sough
new and often startling expressive monodies, such as Schütz's spiritua
concert, *"Wenn meine Augen schlafen ein,"* which is one of the piece
in his *Kleine Geistliche Konzerte* (1639). But the most important fiel
for monodic self-expression was found in the prose of Holy Script. Whil
as in the past the Psalms were made the subject of great choral work
the oratorical style, as Schütz called it, was developed as a melodic adorn
ment of various Bible texts. Thus Schein composed a symphonic inter
pretation of *Marias Verkündigung* (in his *Opella Nova*, 1626), an
another of Jesus' entry into Jerusalem. His music for the Lord's Praye
was of unique power. Scheidt composed a *Dialogue of Christ with th
Blessed and the Damned* (1634). But the greatest achievements wer
those of Schütz. Following his Venetian masters, he created a new styl
which he called recitative for the Psalms, for several choirs which h
made recite the text without repetition, occasionally injecting an ex
pressive solo voice. In the years 1629, 1647, and 1650 Schütz publishe
three volumes of *Sacred Symphonies*. Stimulated by a second visit t
Italy, he went ahead with very bold harmonic combinations, involvin
daring dissonances, similar to those which Monteverdi employed in hi
later work. Arias, duos, cantatas—they were all now developed accord
ing to the new monodic style, favoring such scenes, laden with emotion
as *David's Lament for Absalom,* in which a choir in four voices o
trombones was employed for accompaniment. The *Kleine Geistlich
Konzerte* (I, 1636, and II, 1639) realized the potentialities of monodi
treatment for spiritual music. When one considers that these musica
creations were composed at a time when German towns and village
were sinking into ruins as the Thirty Years' War continued on it
disastrous course, one is struck by the capacity of man to transcend dis
aster, perhaps even to put it to positive account. For human voices
especially deep bass voices, play a central role in all these compositions—
their somber quality had a great appeal in this period. Unique amon
the cantatas, full of passion and anxiety, is the celebrated "Saul, Why D
You Persecute Me" (in his *Sacred Symphonies,* 1629). It is, in view o

these masterworks, a lamentable loss which has robbed posterity of Schütz's *Dafne,* produced in 1627 upon a text by Martin Opitz.[35]

Besides these works, Heinrich Schütz's two histories of the resurrection and three Passions belong to the immortal creations of this time. Dated 1623 and 1664-66,[36] these works possess extraordinary dramatic power, partly as a result of the unusual economy of the means employed. While based upon traditional passions in chorale form, they contain recitations which without any supporting music achieve remarkable heights of expressiveness, while great choirs heighten the dramatic impact of these simple recitals of Holy Script. Devotion is combined with great power of expression.

Instrumental music as such was not Schütz's, but Scheidt's and Schein's concern. Scheidt, a pupil of the Dutch master J. P. Sweelinck (1562-1621) (the last of a great tradition) wrote *Seventy Symphonies in the Manner of Concerts* (1644); Schein greatly advanced the art of the suite in his *Banchetto Musicale* (1617). But on the whole, Germans in these fields were following Italy's leadership, or carrying on the Dutch and English tradition. As this music is still largely unknown, we must here remain content with a mere mention.[37]

V. CONCLUSION

As one beholds the vast array of wonderful creations in literature, the arts and music that constitute the high baroque, one is tempted to proclaim it the high-water mark of European creative effort. Surely it was one of the most productive periods in all these fields. The sense of limitless power, checked by an overwhelming sense of cosmic relationships, produced a style which startles by its contrasts, yet exhibits a singular and unique unity. Its creators thought of themselves as continuing and developing the art of the renaissance, the letters of humanism, yet recapturing something of the spirituality of gothic Christianity. Many of the artists and writers could surely have been greatly surprised to be called "baroque" as they strove for classic design and perfect beauty. Like its great predecessor, the gothic, the baroque received its name from critics who could not sympathize with its profound intensity, its sweep-

---

[35] See above, p. 63.

[36] The *Lukas Passions* has been assigned to an earlier date; see F. Spitta, *Die Passionen von Heinrich Schütz* (1886) and *Heinrich Schütz, ein Meister der Musica Sacra* (1925).

[37] Cf. the discriminating discussion by Robert Haas, *op. cit.,* for this topic, as well as the general analysis of baroque music.

ing vitality, its heaven-scaling grandeur. The rationalist theoreticians of a calmer age might fasten upon the baroque extravaganzas of its cruder moments, without realizing the thinness of their academic disquisitions. Just as the mystic fervor of a Böhme was inaccessible to the dispensers of the rational religion of deism, so the artistic and literary creations of a Poussin, a Corneille or a Rembrandt were alien to the theorists of a rational art like that of Pope. Some of the most marvelous fulfillments of baroque art were yet to come, especially in music and architecture in Germany and Austria. But their style was firmly and definitely set by 1660.

Chapter Four

RELIGION, PHILOSOPHY AND THE SCIENCES

"BUT you have ordered everything according to measure, number and weight." This line from the Wisdom of Solomon (11:21) was a favorite Bible quotation in the early seventeenth century. It may be called the "motto" of all scientific effort since that time. The quantitative analysis of all phenomena, while begun in the renaissance, became the dominant method in the seventeenth century. But it was as characteristic for the period that such an outlook should express itself by a quotation from the Bible. Religion and the sciences were closely related to each other, and the effort to achieve scientific insight was believed to be undertaken "for the greater glory of God." Kepler's mystical belief in aliveness and related-ness of all things in the universe, which permitted him to engage in astrology, served him as a foundation for his great astronomical achievements. Significantly, when his aged mother was tried for witchcraft, he could avert her certain condemnation not by rational scientific argument but only by the weight of his great authority. Yet, during the course of the decisive fifty years after 1600, the place of religion and science changed radically and science was well launched on the triumphal career which was to culminate in our time. The mathematical and cosmological speculations of Galilei, Kepler, and Descartes laid the foundation for the new world view which Newton and Leibniz came to expound in the period following. Characteristically, all three still acknowledged the superior authority of religion, if not of theology; few writers saw fit to deny the existence of a personal God, until Spinoza came to identify God and nature.

I. CATHOLICISM AND PROTESTANTISM

In 1610, roughly two generations after the Council of Trent, the forces of the Counter Reformation were everywhere on the advance. Protestantism seemed to have lost its great revolutionary fervor. The rival factions of Lutherans and Calvinists appeared in many countries to be more concerned with combating each other than with resisting the ever-broadening advance of the Counter Reformation. The particular version of reform which owed its inception to Zwingli in Switzerland, and the Thomistically rational Protestantism of the Elizabethan settlement, as summed up by the "judicious Hooker" at the end of the century, provided further divisions and resulted in corresponding weaknesses in the Protestant camp. The aspirations of a James I to be a Protestant pope and an ecclesiastical oracle upon a secular throne were only an extreme instance of the absurd implications of the cynical principle, *"Cujus regio, ejus religio,"* which the Reichstag of Augsburg had enunciated in the midst of the Council of Trent's efforts to reunite Christendom (1555).

If one asks what really divided Christendom in 1610, what in other words were the residual basic disagreements between Catholics and Protestants, between Lutherans and Calvinists, the answer is not easy. Questions of church government certainly played a very important role; doctrinal issues, such as those of the immaculate conception, of predestination and of the communion, were hotly debated by intellectuals and simple folk alike, while the ethical implications often provided the more tangible source of immediate conflict in family, town and court. We really ought to know much more about the human stories by which conversion from one of these faiths into another came about, to enable us to speak with any degree of assurance of the strictly religious aspect of the matter.

Yet by 1610 thoughtful men throughout Europe were beginning to weary of the endless arguments. When the great Grotius published his *De Veritate Religionis Christianae* (1627) he achieved an instantaneous European success. Why? Because Grotius suggested that the views of all Christianity might be reconciled, if a common basis of piety were stressed, and doctrinal differences minimized; on the basis of scriptural evidence, he set forth a series of propositions common to all Christianity. In the center he put the idea that:

I was used to consider it incumbent upon me to control for the truth; to contend, indeed, for such a truth, as I myself could inwardly and cordially approve . . . I selected therefore, as well from ancient as from modern authors, whatever appeared to me the best and most authentic. . . . For my design was, to compose something that might be serviceable indeed to my fellow citizens in general, but especially to the sea-faring part of the community. . . . I urged them to employ that art . . . not only for the service of their private ends . . . but also for the propagation of the *true,* in other words, the Christian religion.[1]

This was two years before the Edict of Restitution (1629), high-water mark of the policy of conversion by force,[2] sought to destroy the secular power of Protestantism in northern Europe. In it the aggressive efforts of the Society of Jesus overreached themselves and brought on the dramatic reversal associated with the campaigns of Gustavus Adolphus.

II. THE JESUITS

Ever since the establishment of the Society of Jesus in 1540, this new order had been growing in influence. Forcefully led and devotedly concerned with the renewal of the Church of Rome as the universal order of Christianity, the Jesuits by 1610 had achieved a position of extraordinary leadership within the rising tide of Counter Reformation effort. Originally inclined to take the side of the papacy against the Hapsburgs, they had by this time become so firmly entrenched in the government councils at Vienna and Madrid that they tended to take the Hapsburg side. As a result, Urban VIII (1623-44, born 1568) was hostile to the order, and in alliance with the crown of France, struggled to reduce the influence of both Hapsburgs and Jesuits. In this work, a rival order, ably represented by Père Joseph, Richelieu's "Gray Eminence," played a decisive role. The Capuchins were the close rivals of the Jesuits, anyhow, in the work of diplomacy and statecraft. Like the Jesuits, they sought to direct princes through becoming their confessors.[3]

But the Jesuits were far the more interesting from a religious standpoint, because their strictly political work was incidental to their great efforts in the field of education, and in the arts, especially architecture and the drama. These efforts were doctrinally rooted in their central tenets, contained in two writings of Ignatius of Loyola, the founder. The *General Examen,* together with the celebrated *Spiritual Exercises,* constituted the foundation of the order. Its opening statement proclaimed

---

[1] Quoted from *An English Translation of the Six Books of Hugo Grotius on the Truth of Christianity* (1814) by Spencer Madan, pp. 2–3 (italics in the original). In this translation there is included a series of prefaces by John Leclerc, in one of which he succinctly remarks that "the main object of this work is to place in a clear light the truth of the Gospel, totally unconnected with the bias of any party or sect whatsoever; and that solely with a view to general virtue, evangelical virtue, in the minds of men." (P. IX.) Grotius, in short, sought out the ethical common ground of Christian teachings.

[2] See below, pp. 173-7.

[3] See Chapter Seven, pp. 199–200.

the aim of the society as "not only to seek with the aid of the Divine Grace the salvation of one's own soul, but with the aid of the same earnestly to labor for the salvation and perfection of one's neighbor." Here was the keynote to the aggressive proselytizing of the new order. When taken together with its devotion to the ideal of a universal church, and its insistence upon the personal leadership of Christ, which the *Exercises* sought to rivet upon every Jesuit, this concern with each human being gave the order its popular slant and its determination to use every available means to reach the heart and mind of even the lowliest man. Thus one might say that the Jesuits expounded a doctrine which within the church corresponded to the concept of divine kingship over national communities in the secular realm: they exalted the position of the ruler (pope) in the interest of the mass of followers, while curbing the intermediate powers. As a result, the Jesuits were keenly interested in all the intellectual and artistic currents of sixteenth- and seventeenth-century Europe. Humanism and classicism, music and the theater, painting, sculpture and architecture all became means for their mission of working for "the greater glory of God." Instead of the antithesis between the religious and the secular, between Christian and pagan forms of thought, which had been the characteristic feature of the renaissance,[4] these opposites were resolved into a new unity. The churches the Jesuits built, like Il Gesù in Rome, were striking expressions of this new spirit. Thus the baroque style was born; a marriage of Christian and pagan forms.

At first predominantly Spanish, the Jesuits had, since the last quarter of the sixteenth century, experienced great internal controversies. Torn between an Italian and a Spanish faction (since the generalate of Aquaviva[5]), the learned fathers of the society had become politically committed to the house of Hapsburg as the best prospect for a revival of the medieval unity which in 1610 was still cherished by many as the ultimate goal of the Counter Reformation. By 1660 all such hopes had vanished and the waning power of Spain, as well as the consolidation of national kingdoms, especially in France and England, suggested a basic reorientation. Yet the tendency of the order to enhance the position of the papacy continued; it troubled the work in a country like France where tendencies toward an independent national church—for that is the essence

[4] Note the famous sentence in Machiavelli's *Prince*, Ch. XV, where this typical Renaissance intellectual pointedly contrasts his approach with that of the medieval mirror of princes.

[5] See Ranke, *Geschichte der Päpste*, II, 278 ff.

of Gallicanism—had deep roots. Not only politically, but doctrinally, the toughest opposition to the Jesuits arose in France. The movement known as Jansenism, and most brilliantly represented by Pascal, was violently anti-Jesuit.

After the generalate of Aquaviva, the Jesuits became increasingly worldly in their outlook and viewpoint, under the long, but weak, leadership of Mutio Vitelleschi (1614-45). In this period control of the order passed to the senior members who were allowed to own property and who, in contrast to earlier times, occupied the positions of administrative leadership in the order.[6] The order also engaged in industry and commerce. This affected their general policy. After 1651, when Oliva became general vicar of the order, its policy tended to favor the French crown against the papacy. Instead of permeating the world with religious enthusiasm, the Jesuits themselves surrendered to the world. They strove mainly to become indispensable to other men and shaped the confessional to this purpose. This is not said in a spirit of hostility or distortion. The Jesuits themselves wrote numerous works defending their viewpoint. Some of these books were even put on the Index. In the center of their teaching in this respect they placed the conception of sin as a voluntary deviation from a divine rule. This notion was violently attacked by Pascal. What angered the more pious in such an approach was the notion that man apparently was the more likely to sin the more aware he became of divine rules, while the ignorant or passionate might be considered free of blame. It is impossible to consider the subtleties of the resultant controversies and distortions. Perhaps with undue asperity, Ranke remarked that "all life would have had to be gone from the Catholic Church, if no opposition had arisen against such pernicious doctrines." Such opposition arose among many Catholics, individuals and organizations; but it took its most radical form in the movement known as Jansenism.

III. THE JANSENISTS AND PASCAL

Jansenism, as contrasted with Jesuitism, belonged fully to the period after 1600. Its originator, Cornelius Jansen (1585-1638), was a scholar of Dutch origin who was associated during most of his creative life with the University of Louvain. There he joined the anti-Jesuit group which

[6] See H. Boehmer, *The Jesuits* (1928) as translated from the German; see also Paul von Hoensbroech, *Der Jesuitenorden, eine Enzyklopädie* (1926-27). The change in the internal situation of the Society of Jesus is described, on the basis of an unprinted document, by Ranke, *op. cit.*, III, 122 ff.

expounded Augustinian principles while the Jesuits continued the scholastic tradition. An ardent Catholic, stressing the inner life, Jansen sought to rival the Protestants in interpreting the Bible in a "mystical and pietistic" manner. From 1630 to 1638 he devoted himself to scriptural interpretation at Louvain, while completing his magnum opus, *Augustinus*. This work appeared posthumously in 1640. It contained a careful digest of St. Augustine's teachings with emphasis upon the problems confronting the seventeenth century. Antischolastic in outlook, Jansen urged that religious experience, as contrasted with theological dogma, was the heart of religion. Consequently, the "love of God" and faith in Him was more important than any ritual. Since divine love was a gift, "conversion" was the core of religious life. Yet such conversion itself sprang from God's inscrutable will—a doctrine which brought the Jansenist view close to that of Calvinist predestination. In spite of such similarities, Jansen and his school remained ardent Catholics. They would not hear of justification by faith, any more than of salvation outside the Holy Church. Jansen set this forth clearly in his *Augustinus:*

The liberation of the will is not the remission of sin, but a delectable relaxation of the bond of concupiscence which the dependent soul serves until it is brought to love the highest by grace, as a celestial sweetness is infused [into it].[7] . . . The rules for living and the light, immutable and ever-lasting, of the virtues is nothing but the eternal law.[8]

Therefore, the man who is among the elect, loves God, truth and justice and by his devotion and love frees himself from sin.

While Jansen was a scholar, his followers, led at first by his friend Duvergnier, then by Antoine Arnauld, established themselves as a religious movement, with its center at Port Royal, a Cistercian abbey a few miles southwest of Paris. The reforming ardor of the abbess, Angélique Arnauld, had brought her into contact with Jean Duvergnier of Saint Cyran, the friend and sympathizer of Jansen. Thus, when the plague had driven the nuns away in 1626, a group of religious men, mostly relatives of the abbess, established themselves at the abbey to practice what Jansen had preached. But Père Joseph, as adviser of Richelieu, did not approve of this group, and persuaded his master to incarcerate Saint Cyran. After the death of Richelieu, Arnauld in 1643 published *Frequent*

[7] Cornelius Jansenius, *Augustinus*, Vol. III, Bk. I, Ch. II. Cf. also Pascal, *Letters*, No. XVIII.
[8] *Op. cit.*, Bk. V, Ch. III.

Communion, which caused great agitation throughout France. All the ardor of noninstitutional religiosity, which had fed so much of the Protestant ferment, rose once again and greatly disturbed the established powers, reinforced by Jesuits who had already fought violently over the issues involved. The government, in the spirit of Richelieu, strongly supported the forces of order and conformity. Upon an appeal to Rome, Pope Innocent X declared five central propositions of Jansen's work heretical, namely, that: (1) the commandments of God are impracticable to men; (2) grace is irresistible; (3) we have no free will to do either good or evil; (4) Jesus Christ did not die for all men, but (5) died only for the elect.[9] The Jansenists refused to admit that these propositions were actually contained in Jansenius' *Augustinus.* Thereupon Blaise Pascal (1623–62), who at twenty-four had discovered God as he was revealed by the Jansenists, entered the fray, though anonymously. As F. Mauriac has written:

The power which Jansenism exercised over certain minds stemmed from its clear, simple attitude toward corrupt nature. . . . Being tainted from birth we go inexorably toward evil. . . . Believing in predestination, Pascal nevertheless did not despair. One hope remained: perhaps we are loved by God. Some of us are. . . . But since the sin of Adam, that grace was accorded only to those few who were chosen from all eternity. . . . We would not believe that such heresy could have attracted a young man if we did not know that the more terrible the doctrine, the greater the efforts of the believer to find reassurance.[10]

What Mauriac, along with so many traditionalists, did not see was the appeal of radically irrational views to the most penetrating minds, *because* they are irrational. The very intellectual despair of such superintellectuals gives birth to mysticism.

Pascal's sudden conversion, as contrasted with Pascal's intellectual otherworldliness, was perhaps the most moving testimonial to the mystical ardor of the period. "The Mystery of Jesus," contained in Paragraph 552 of *Pensées,* and published only after Pascal's death, belongs among the immortal documents of that variety of religious experience.[11]

In his *Provincial Letters* (1656–57) Pascal undertook most skillfully to

[9] This is the brief formulation given them by Blaise Pascal in his *Provincial Letter XVII,* dated January 23, 1657. For Jansenism in general, cf. C. A. Saint-Beuve, *Port-Royal* (new edition, 1926–28), J. La Porte, *La Doctrine de Port-Royal* (1923).
[10] See his Preface to *The Living Thoughts of Pascal* (1940), 2.
[11] See for the text *Pascal's Pensées and The Provincial Letters* (ed. by Saxe Commins, 1941), 175 ff. See also below, pp. 114–5.

controvert the position of the Jesuits by a series of presumed discussions between them and the Jansenists on such subjects as "proximate power," "sufficient and actual grace," "attrition," and the various vices. The radically ascetic attitude of the Jansenist moral perfectionism shone forth as truly Christian when contrasted with the worldly rationalism of the Jesuits. The latter's defense of such actions as assassination of tyrants, usury (the taking of interest) and the like, was made the butt of a most telling incrimination. The *Letters* caused an immediate sensation; they were distributed by the thousands thoughout France. But they did not save Arnauld, and the suspected author himself had to go into hiding. In 1660 the convinced authoritarian Louis XIV, as one of his first independent acts, had the Jansenists condemned. The following year all suspects were forced to sign a solemn renunciation. Yet the Jesuits in France never fully recovered from the shattering logic of Pascal's attack; four generations later their order was actually suppressed.

The Jansenist controversy, raging as it did during the very years that the sectarians of the inner light battled for the freedom of religious conscience in Protestant England, may be summed up in Pascal's proposition that the church persuades by reason, and that "the popes may be surprised." But this deep mysticism in matters of inner experience was coupled with a radical assertion of scientific rationalism regarding outer, sensory experience. On points of fact, the testimony of the senses must be yielded to, and reason—natural reason—must be regarded the proper instrument for determining unrevealed truth, while only with respect to supernatural truth were scripture and the church decisive. Quoting St. Augustine and St. Thomas, Pascal proclaimed that any other position "would render our religion contemptible." Entering therewith upon the decisive issues of science and religion in his age, Pascal told the Jesuits that "it was to equally little purpose that you obtained against Galileo a decree from Rome, condemning his opinion respecting the motion of the earth. It will never be proved by such arguments as this that the earth remains stationary; and if it cannot be demonstrated by sure observation that it is the earth and not the sun that revolves, the efforts and arguments of all mankind put together will not hinder our planet from revolving, nor hinder themselves from revolving along with her." Thus at the end of this subtle argument about freedom and determinism, about predestination and grace, the victory of science over authority was triumphantly adduced as conclusive.

IV. THE INNER LIGHT: J. J. BÖHME

There has been a tendency among Protestant and secular writers to deal with the doctrine of the inner light as if it were an exclusive discovery of the Reformation. Antagonists of the new religious movement have often spoken in a similar vein, and have even made it in recent years the basis of propagandistic interpretations à la "from Luther to Hitler." Actually, the inner light has played a significant role throughout the history of Christianity and is closely related to the doctrine of revelation. The distinctive outlook of the more radical reformed sects in the sixteenth and seventeenth centuries consisted in this: they placed the doctrine of the inner light at the very center of their faith. Their mysticism was not the peculiar possession of a select few, but the common heritage of all. If we take the word mysticism in its broad meaning, as "a conviction of certainty that the person's own soul has found its goal of reality in God," [12] then we might say that the sectarians of the inner light, as indeed the Jansenists and Pascal, believed that there was something mystical and awe-inspiring in every man. This sense of mystery gave them the exalted quality of a Bunyan which so troubled and exasperated their more rational contemporaries.

In the chapter on the Commonwealth and Protectorate it will be shown how this spirit manifested itself in the realm of government. The extraordinary, near-mystical language of a Cromwell was a striking testimonial to the vigor of this sentiment; yet it was only a pale reflection of what men like Winstanley wrote and said. Much of it echoed the thought which had animated the Anabaptists who rose in the wake of the Lutheran challenge.

Both Luther and Calvin had been scared by the anarchic consequences of such radical doctrines. Yet they found it difficult to escape such implications of their doctrine of faith without sliding back into the institutional and authoritarian pattern of the Catholic Church. Whether it was Luther's reliance upon the prince, with its caesaropapist potential, or Calvin's readiness to adopt a theocratic pattern, the compromise was to prove less stable than the authoritarianism which it replaced. In opposing all such authoritarianism, the mystic depended upon and lived by his direct communion with the Lord Almighty. No matter in what poetical

---

[12] See Rufus M. Jones, *Mysticism and Democracy in the English Commonwealth* (1932), 13, a book to which the author is greatly indebted for the whole subject of the "inner light."

form he clothed his experience, he would live in the fellowship which this experience created for him. It is one of the most characteristic features of the baroque age that the worldly sense of power, manifest in figures like Richelieu and Wallenstein, found its counterpart in a spiritual sense of power which animated Spanish Catholics as much as English seekers, Jacob Böhme as intensely as Pascal or Kepler.

A striking figure, representing the deep faith in learning and science, was the Czech, J. A. Comenius (1592–1670). A Moravian, Comenius conceived of scientific research and of making universally known the knowledge resulting from such research as the best means for resolving the religious and international conflicts of his time. Himself several times the victim of the ravages of the Thirty Years' War, he finally found an abode in Holland and, like Rubens and Grotius, became preoccupied with the problem of how to maintain peace. But whereas Grotius thought of law, Comenius pinned his hope on learning and more effective education. Although his great scheme for universal learning perished when the town he had lived in was burned down, he outlined his "pansophism" in a sketch, *Conatuum Comenianorum Praeludia,* which was to be presented to the English parliament for consideration; but then the civil war intervened. Toward the end of his life, Comenius composed a moving plan for peace entitled *Angelus Pacis* or the *Angel of Peace,* addressed to the English and Dutch ambassadorial conferees at Breda. While not containing a general program for universal peace such as one might have expected from the author of pansophism,[13] it is a stirring general plea anticipating the more detailed programs for universal peace of the next century.

The note of mysticism involved in Comenius' work was much more marked in that of Jacob Böhme, a small shopkeeper of Silesia, who published a first account of his mystical visions in 1612 under the title *Aurora.*[14] Claiming direct divine light as his source, he drew upon the ground of grounds (*Urgrund*) to interpret and resolve all conflict. God, he taught, is all and nothing—he is the world-generating being which

---

[13] Comenius in fact suggested that wars of religion were more excusable than those over commercial rivalry (as the English-Dutch war had been), on the ground that they "seem zealous for the glory of God and the salvation of the soul." See paragraph 20 of *Angel of Peace.* But such wars cannot really be justified. "Should Christians wish to be wiser than Christ?" he asks, and then points to the Waldenses, to England, the Netherlands, and Bohemia as showing how little is accomplished by violence.

[14] See for this *Jacob Böhme: Studies in His Life and Teachings* by Hans L. Martensen, revised edition, Stephen Hobhouse (1949).

projects from the bottomless abyss (*Urgrund*) a variety of essential phenomena, such as love and visible variety. The world which results has different ends in three successive periods, but the last brings the victory of good over evil. Man, compounded of spirit, soul and body, must have a rebirth before he can achieve the true knowledge of God. These views, related as they were to those of Paracelsus, seemed as heretical to the Lutheran pastorate as Jansen's did to the Jesuits and the Holy Father, but nevertheless they spread. They represented the most extreme statement of the doctrine of the inner light that the age produced. Characteristically, Böhme's followers in England eventually merged with the Quakers.

V. ANGLICANISM AND CALVINISM

Such mystic ardor was a far cry from the sane and moderate rationalism of Richard Hooker. His *Law of Ecclesiastical Polity* may well be called the most balanced statement of the Anglican religious position. Its judiciousness appealed even to so avowed a deist as John Locke. But in the three generations which elapsed between Hooker's treatise and Locke's consummately skillful summary of English constitutional traditions, Anglicanism was violently torn between a caesaropapist Lutheranism and a strongly Puritanical Calvinism. The word *Puritan,* due to its later signification in the English revolution and the pioneering of the Pilgrim Fathers, has been the subject of much confusion and abuse. It has no distinctive theological meaning but indicates rather a general attitude toward life which was found among Anglicans, Calvinists and Sectarians alike. Between Anglicanism and Calvinism the line was more perceptible. The most heated controversies concerned problems of church government, but underneath these disagreements lay the explosive issues involved in predestination and free will. Calvinists generally, and the Scotch Calvinists in particular, tended to push the predestinarian position to its radical extreme. There was no hope for anyone except those whom God had elected to be saved; all men could do was to labor at their calling with all possible diligence in the hope of snatching a glimpse of the divine will by their success in contributing to God's greater glory. The Calvinists "disparaged" reason, as Hooker had put it, and while they believed in an elite of the elect in heaven, they were no respecters of earthly pomp and circumstance. It was a fierce and somber doctrine. The Anglicans, including Archbishop Laud, inclined to side with the

Thomist tradition which, in the Reformed movement, had been most eloquently represented by Melanchthon and Jacobus Arminius, founder of the Remonstrant school of Reformed religion.[15] This tradition was significantly elaborated in our period by Simon Episcopius (1583–1643), whose views were condemned at the Synod of Dordrecht (1618). At the heart of the Remonstrants' struggle lay the insistence upon freedom of the will and the consequent significance of manifesting one's Christianity through practical ethics. It was clearly humanist in its implications, just as was the corresponding doctrine of Erasmus and of Molina, the Jesuit. Indeed, this humanism strongly reinforced its appeal to the upper classes in England and the Netherlands. Refined and civilized urbanity, such as animated the court circles of Charles I, was more readily compatible with such a doctrine than with the fierce challenge of predestination, which suited such tempers as Maurice of Orange, Cromwell and Milton.[16]

The Calvinists, forever haunted by their bitter concern with predestination, were the spearhead of the Protestant forces opposing the advancing phalanx of the Counter Reformation. They put the amiable Frederick of the Palatinate upon the throne of Bohemia; they worked upon the kings of Denmark and Sweden to enter the war which raged in the Holy Empire; they challenged the growing absolutism of Richelieu and Charles I; they brought Buckingham and Laud to the scaffold; they double-crossed Wallenstein, the invincible, and they conducted the policy of the rising Hohenzollerns. As has rightly been said:

The Calvinist system and plan of life . . . was an imperial structure of thought that could compete in dignity, in grandeur and in august authority with the Roman Catholic system itself.[17]

There was also a distinct relationship between some aspects of Calvinism and the rising spirit of science. It is well known that modern natural science is based upon the belief that there is a rational pattern inherent in nature, and that it is the task of man to discover this rationality, to discover the laws or regularities which govern nature.[18] Stemming

---

[15] For the violent political upheaval resulting from these issues in Holland, see below, Chapter Five.

[16] But Milton turned against predestination. For his dislike of the doctrinal aspect, see the quotation above, Chapter One, p. 32.

[17] Jones, *op. cit.,* 18.

[18] The implications of this problem are discussed by A. N. Whitehead in his *Science and the Modern World* (1925). Cf. also my discussion in the Introduction to *Johannes Althusius' Politica* (1932), pp. lxxv ff.

from Hellenic as well as Judaeo-Christian cosmologies, this approach was even more clearly in accord with the Calvinist conception of God. Decidedly one and only one—though the doctrine of the trinity was retained—Calvin's God was predominantly a God of power, of majesty and of will. This God, who created the universe according to inexorable and universal laws, had set before man the task of seeking to discover his laws and thereby glorify his power. It was man's task to discover God's rational plan and to act in accordance with it, as far as possible. It was a matter of unshakable faith that there must be an order according to laws. But while man's rational faculties afford him a chance of discovering these laws, they are not themselves "rational." These laws can be discovered only by a diligent observation of the facts, combined with a determination to abstract from the details of observation in order to perceive the regularities and to formulate such regularities as generalizations. "Generalizations based upon observed matters of fact"—this key to the methodology of seventeenth-century science—were well in accord with Calvinist determinism and predestination. To be sure, two generations earlier Calvin himself had been ready to assent to the burning of Servetus, an early scientist. For Calvin and his more literal followers, the "word" of Holy Script took complete precedence over all generalizations based upon observed matter of fact. That this was indubitably the orthodox view has obscured the link between Calvinism and science. Yet the piety in the face of nature's majesty which is so characteristic a trait of many great scientists [19] served as an emotional underpinning for the scientists' scrupulous regard for factual evidence, as partaking of that majesty.

VI. SCIENCE AGAINST SUPERSTITION: ASTRONOMY VERSUS ASTROLOGY

In spite of, or maybe because of, the growing scientific spirit among the intellectual elite of the seventeenth century, the belief in sorcery and witches continued to prevail, and some of the worst witch-hunts belonged to this period. In England and Scotland, as well as in Germany, Spain and elsewhere on the continent, witches were burned by the hundreds. These superstitions, based upon the mistaken attribution of troublesome effects, such as sickness, madness and death, to human agents, were rooted quite generally in an overestimation of man's power. Is it too

---

[19] Even in the nineteenth century, men like Helmholtz urged acceptance of St. Thomas' famous dictum: *"Ignoramus, ignorabimus."*

fanciful to suggest that in the age of the baroque, with its fantastic feeling of power as well as of insecurity, the very mystery which surrounded the startling discoveries of the men of science contributed to such outrages? King James I, who is generally credited with having brought on an intensification of witch-hunting,[20] actually had quite an interest in the new scientific developments, and Charles I even called upon the great Harvey to supervise an examination of a group of women accused of witchcraft by scientifically minded medical men who rejected the claims of the accusers. Contrariwise, some of the Puritans, notably Matthew Hopkins, the "Witch-Finder General," in the forties engaged in a veritable orgy of witch-burning. One James Howell spoke of it as follows:

We have likewise multitudes of Witches among us, for in Essex and Suffolk there were about two hundred indicted within these two years, and above the one half of them executed: More, I may well say, than ever this Island bred since the Creation, I speak it with horror, God guard us from the Devil, for I think he was never so busy upon any part of the Earth . . . nor do I wonder at it, for there's never a Cross left to fright him away.[21]

Such views were common throughout the seventeenth century, even among scientific men; the great Boyle, for example, seems to have given credence to witchcraft as late as 1670. Earlier in the century, Bacon, with all his vaunted scientific method, accepted witchcraft—it incidentally illustrates strikingly the weakness of his conception of scientific as the inductive method of mere observation. Only by the slow spread of the scientific spirit, as well as by general enlightenment, combined with broadening toleration, did this scourge of superstition in sorcery and witchcraft gradually subside. There were many more doubting Thomases in 1660 than in 1610. It is one of the glories of Thomas Hobbes that he never succumbed to the lure of this superstition. His general skepticism regarding supernatural causes served him in good stead and helped him not to "philosophize like a Lord Chancellor."

But there were other superstitions of a hallowed kind, more especially the notion that the earth was the center of the universe, which yielded to the onslaught of scientific advance in this period. In 1609, Galileo

[20] This charge is derived from the king's *Daemonology* (1596); George L. Kittredge has shown how unjust and exaggerated the prevailing view is in *Witchcraft in Old and New England* (1928), especially Ch. XVII.

[21] Quoted by Kittredge, *op. cit.*, 331–32. Kittredge shows that there was nothing specifically Puritan about this outbreak; on both sides of the religious fence there were believers in witchcraft, as well as opponents of it.

Galilei (1564–1642) heard that two Dutchmen had built a new instrument for magnifying man's vision, the telescope. He immediately set to work to build a similar but more powerful one. No sooner had he succeeded than all his doubts about the Copernican system were dispelled by the new vistas. Jupiter he discovered to be a great sphere circled by moons, Venus to show phases like the moon, the sun to have spots which show its rotation. Galileo was so enthusiastic about his discoveries that he became a strong public advocate of the ideas of Copernicus. It was the enthusiasm of the experimenter who is primarily concerned with observed matter of fact. For years he had struggled with the problems of gravitation, formulating the law of acceleration. Experiment and calculation, factual observation, coupled with daring hypotheses concerning their rational interpretation—these together constituted the new outlook. But the hypotheses were of a very special kind: for the factual observation was primarily quantitative. Measuring, counting and weighing were the crucial methods. The refinement of the instruments employed for these tasks became a central concern of the scientist. Anyone who failed to appreciate the importance of this method was a devotee of superstition.

Until the invention of the telescope by Jansen and Lippershey (1608) and its perfection by Galileo (1610 and later), the Copernican system had remained in doubt. In fact, the great Tycho Brahe had, with infinite patience, compiled observational detail to reconstitute the Ptolemaic system. In 1600 he had called Johann Kepler (1571–1630) to his assistance, but the younger man was in fact a Copernican. After Tycho's death the next year, Kepler commenced to explore the vast observational material assembled by Tycho in order to further support and develop the system of Copernicus. To him the mathematical rationality of the universe was an article of deep and abiding faith. Ever-renewed calculations were undertaken to find a further simplification for the complex data which the observation of the heavenly bodies provided.

Under the impact of these efforts, superstition acquired a new meaning, the modern one, used to this day. Superstition came to mean the human tendency to believe explanations which are demonstrably contrary to established matter of fact, or for which no observational basis can be adduced. The fight for science and against superstition, begun in the sixteenth century, eventually was symbolized in Galileo's famous, if apocryphal, remark, "And yet it moves." It was supposedly made as he left the chamber where the Holy Inquisition had queried him concerning his Copernican teachings and had made him recant and admit that the earth did not move around the sun. "And yet it moves" became the battle cry of the antitraditionalist observer of the realities of nature who was ready to challenge pope, emperor, great council and philosopher in the interest of scientific truth. This famous anecdote combines into one brief incident what was historically a matter of sixteen years. For in 1616, after Galileo had frankly raised the Copernican issue in his *Letters on the Solar Spots* (1613), Pope Paul V admonished him and ordered him not to teach or defend the proposition that the earth moved around the sun, after the theologians of the Holy Office had declared the doctrine heretical. Sixteen years later, in open and flagrant violation of this papal injunction, Galileo published his *Dialogues Concerning the Two Largest Systems of the World* (finished in 1630), a book which was widely acclaimed but soon put upon the Index, whereupon the Inquisition made the author appear for examination under threat of torture. Galileo recanted and was condemned to protective custody. But he was allowed considerable freedom and was soon permitted to return to his villa near Florence where he spent the remaining years of his life in scholarly seclusion. During this time he produced the ripest fruit of his research, the *Dialogues Concerning the New Science* (1638). In this work, Galileo set forth the principles of the "new science" of experimentation and of the mathematical formulation of the regularities observed. It was the testament of the greatest genius of the new scientific spirit; indeed a much more effective "And yet it moves" than a defiant casual remark thrown in the teeth of the defenders of superstition.

But not only theologians defended the views of the past. Many of the more ardent "liberals" of the new humanistic learning were as attached to authority as the representatives of organized religion. To them the ancients were the gospel. The clash which thus occurred between learning and science was well illustrated in the refusal of Galileo's colleague, Cremonini, to look through the telescope. He was a free spirit but an ardent Aristotelian, and he reportedly feared that what he might see would be contrary to what he had read in Aristotle. Here was superstition at the highest level of learning; it was this superstition which science—the new organon—was going to rout and destroy.

While Galileo formulated the principles of the new scientific spirit in close connection with the actual experiments and calculations he had carried on, Francis Bacon (1561-1626) undertook to expound what he believed to be the philosophical implications of the new world view. "The school of experience," as Spinoza later called it, was the only school which Francis Bacon would admit, and by experience he meant actual observation by the senses. But this was only one side of the new science of men like Galileo; the other was mathematical calculation, as we have seen, and of this vital aspect Bacon showed scant appreciation. He likewise lacked real understanding of the significance of quantitative data for the study of social and economic problems; his was a trumpet call to arms, rather than the battle. Yet in his personal life he demonstrated, as a warning symbol understood by all too few, the dangers inherent in a strictly pragmatic approach to man and human society.[22]

Did these enthusiasts, generally speaking, realize the dangers inherent in such a view—dangers which have gradually become more visible as the scientific approach has engulfed man in all his social relations? There were those who did, and those who did not, but the excitement of the new discoveries swept all before it. Perhaps nowhere was the spirit of the baroque, of the new sense of power, more violently at work than in these scientists. Indeed, one is tempted to see here the core, the central dynamic element, upon which the sense of power fed.

VII. GALILEO AND KEPLER

Among the many workers in the field of the "new science," as it was called by the man who was perhaps its greatest exponent,[23] there grew up after 1600 a sense of a great mission. In no other field was the feeling of European unity more pronounced than among these crusaders for a new world view.[24] Yet they were also sharply divided amongst themselves, not only on specific scientific issues, but also on the broad philosophic basis of their work. Of none was this more true than of Galileo and Kepler. Kepler confused his brilliant achievements by the retention of mystic notions which aroused the ire of Galileo. This in turn misled Galileo into neglecting the discoveries of Kepler in celestial mechanics, thereby weakening his own work in astronomy. Galileo's genius was dedicated to experiment and calculation, Kepler's to mathematical speculation. Their antagonism was symptomatic of the age's preoccupation:

---

[22] For a summary of *The New Organum* (1620) see below, last paragraph. For a clear case of statistical, in the sense of quantitative, data see the work of Giovanni Botero, especially his *Relazioni Universali* (1590–96) and his *Delle Cause della grandezza delle città* (1588). Significant it is that Botero was the inventor of the term *ratio status* (see above, Chapter Two).

[23] Namely, Galileo Galilei in his *Dialoghi della nuova scienza* (1638), already cited.

[24] Among the most fascinating documents of this spirit were the letters exchanged by these men, such as the *Correspondance* of Descartes, cited below.

should one try to bracket cosmological issues, "stay away from theology" as the Holy Father had demanded of Galileo, or should one try to develop a new cosmology which would at once be compatible with the new discoveries and with the essence of Christian theology? John Donne, who throughout his life was greatly troubled by the "new philosophy" which "calls all in doubt," suggested the characteristically Protestant inclination toward the second alternative in a letter to Goodyear: "Methinks the new astronomy is thus applicable well, that we which are a little earth should rather move towards God, than that He which is fulfilling, and can come no wither, should move toward us." This striking attempt to adapt the Christian religion to the Copernican universe would have been acclaimed by Kepler, no doubt, who himself entertained similar notions.[25]

Galileo, as we have said, was very averse to mystic ideas of this kind. He strongly objected to Kepler's attempts to invest the sun with a sentient soul which listened to and animated the "celestial harmonics" of the solar system—an idea first hinted at in Kepler's *Mysterium Geographicum* (1596), but fully developed in *De Harmonice Mundi* (1619). Disgust with such mystical nonsense misled Galileo into overlooking the fact that Kepler's treatise also contained the third law of celestial mechanics, a law which established a connection between planetary periods and distances. The first two laws had been set forth by Kepler in 1609 (1610?) in his *Astronomia Nova,* which is considered, from an astronomical standpoint, the most noteworthy of Kepler's many works,[26] because of these laws. The first of them stated that the planets in the solar system moved in elliptical orbits, the second that the areas described were equal.[27] Finally, after years of devoted labor, Kepler was able to publish his *Rudolphine Tables* (1627), containing, besides predictive calculations of the motion of the planets, tables of logarithms and of refractions; a list of 1,005 stars was included. These tables were considered authoritative for over a

[25] For the letter see Edmund Gosse, *Life and Letters of Dr. John Donne* (1899), I, 219–20. I owe this reference to my friend Ed. Kemler, who is at present writing a biography of Francis Bacon.

[26] See Ch. Frisch's biography in the last volume of his authoritative *Joannis Kepleri Opera Omnia* (1858–71). On Kepler's cosmology see also H. A. Strauss, *Die Astrologie des Johann Kepler* (1926).

[27] More precisely stated, Kepler's first law says that the planets move in elliptical orbits, one focal point of them being the sun; the second law that the areas described, in equal times, by a line drawn from the sun to the planet were strictly equal; the third that the squares of the periods of circulation around the sun of the several planets are in the same ratio as the cube of their mean distances.

hundred years, although they contained some errors, and have in principle never been superseded. Kepler had a distinct anticipatory sense of some such force as gravitation, but since he was not cognizant of the law of inertia he still pursued the will-o'-the-wisp of a prime mover, which he located in the sun. Kepler thus ignored the most significant of Galileo's discoveries, especially his law of acceleration. Thus two new basic lines of inquiry were kept apart by the philosophic antagonism of their pre-eminent exponents, and it remained for Sir Isaac Newton to draw the two together when he formulated the law of gravitation as the key to the new cosmos he constructed out of the elements Kepler and Galileo had provided two generations earlier. Newton, by making full use of the mechanical laws first enunciated by Galileo, provided a more satisfactory hypothesis than the notion of vortices, first adumbrated by Kepler, but more fully developed by René Descartes in his *Principia Philosophiae* (1644).[28]

VIII. MATHEMATICS OF THE INFINITE

In his study of Pascal, Leon Brunschwicg, after observing that the beginning of the seventeenth century was the turning point at which the essential character of modern civilization crystallized, remarks: "Through the arrival of positive science, man acquired as a new sense: the sense of truth which brusquely revealed to him the infinite." But it was not only positive science, the observations of a Galileo, which revealed the infinite, but even more so the new mathematics. Fermat's and Descartes's discovery of analytic geometry (between 1630 and 1640) together with Pascal's work on probability were the most decisive developments, prior to Newton's and Leibniz's work on the differential and integral calculus in the succeeding period.[29] Descartes's approach to geometry (and mathematics in general) may be called dynamic, in contrast to the static approach of classical Greek mathematics. He observed, so to speak, geometrical figures in the process of becoming, rather than contemplating them as fixed verities. More specifically he concerned himself, therefore, with the properties of curves, which he undertook to describe by placing them within a system of co-ordinates, and then stating the relation of successive points on the curve to these co-ordinates in the form of equations.

[28] See below, pp. 113–14.

[29] Compare the nice summary in Clark, *op. cit.*, Ch. XIV, which includes developments after 1660 and hence is more complete than our account here.

Here is the most elementary illustration, showing a parabola which results when the general proposition, $y=f(x)$ $(xy)=0$, is given the specific form: $y=x^2$.

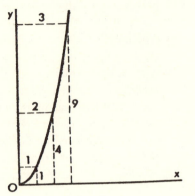

This leads to the general proposition: if x and y are the rectangular co-ordinates of a point in a plane, then $y=f(x)$ or $(x,y)=0$ may be represented by a curve in this plane.

Analytical geometry converts geometrical, spatial figures into numerical or algebraic equations; these are seen as two different forms of the same underlying set of relations; they may be considered two different "languages." While the conversion of the traditional figures of Euclidean geometry was perhaps the more immediately significant achievement, the reverse process, by which equations are made visible in figures and curves, became eventually of equal significance, especially in those fields where statistical data are the primary given of experience. The function, as it was called, could thereby be projected. For example, if the years are indicated on one of the co-ordinates, and the increments of population on the other, the points at which the parallels to these co-ordinates, drawn through these points on the co-ordinates, meet will constitute a curve showing the rate of population growth.

Of comparable significance, and intended to cope with the difficulties of comparing an arithmetic with a geometric progression [30] is the system of logarithms, invented by John Napier and Henry Briggs (around 1615), which was at once introduced by Kepler into his astronomical calcula-

[30] An arithmetic progression is a sequence of numbers in which each successive number results from adding the same increment to the preceding one, while a geometric progression results from multiplying each successive number by such a constant factor.

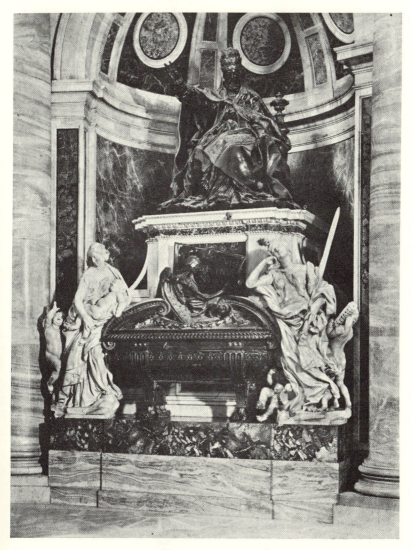

1. Tomb of Urban VIII: Bernini
St. Peter's, Rome

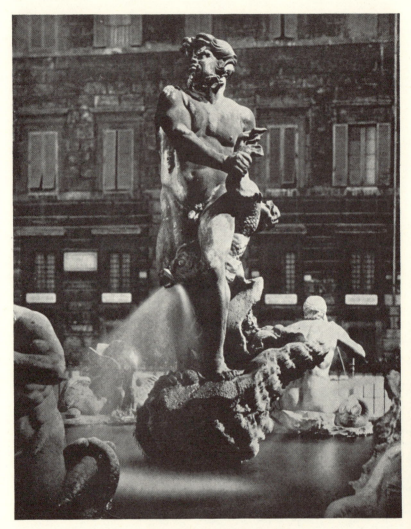

2. Fountain of the Moor: Bernini
Borghese Gallery, Rome

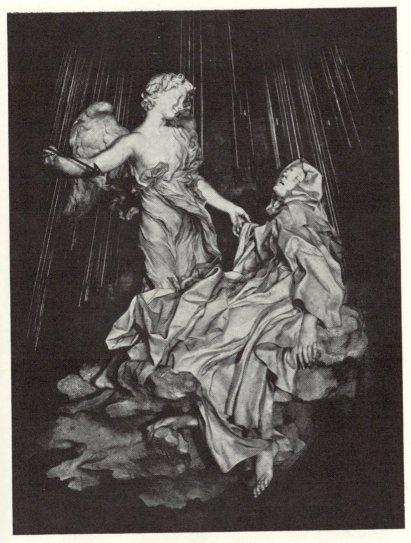

3. St. Teresa in Ecstasy: Bernini
s. Maria della Vittoria, Rome

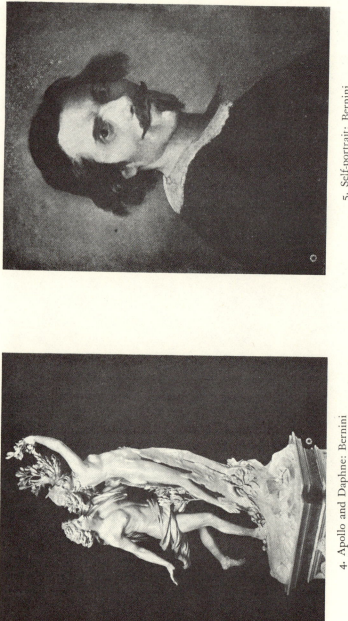

5. Self-portrait: Bernini
Borghese Gallery, Rome

4. Apollo and Daphne: Bernini
Villa Borghese, Rome

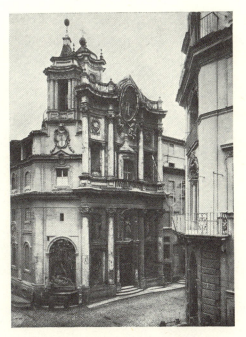

6. Church of San Carlino of the
Four Fountains: Borromini
Rome

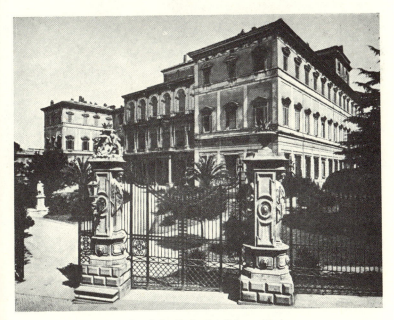

7. Façade of the Barberini Palace: Maderno
Rome

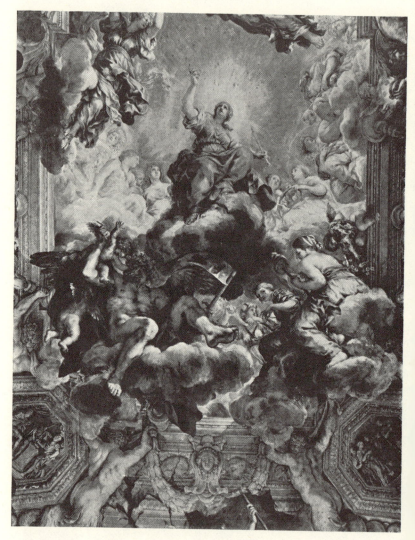

8. The Triumph of Glory: Pietro da Cortona
Ceiling Decoration, Barberini Palace, Rome

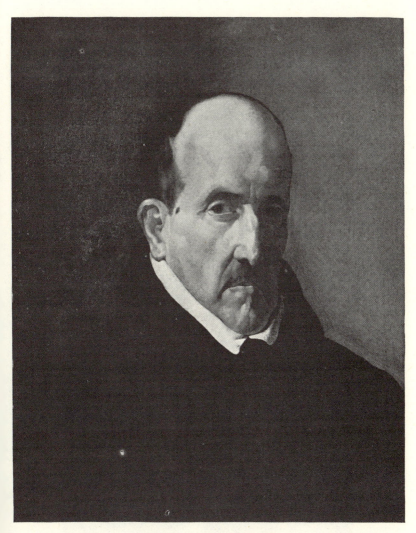

9. The Poet Gongora: Velasquez
Courtesy of the Museum of Fine Arts, Boston

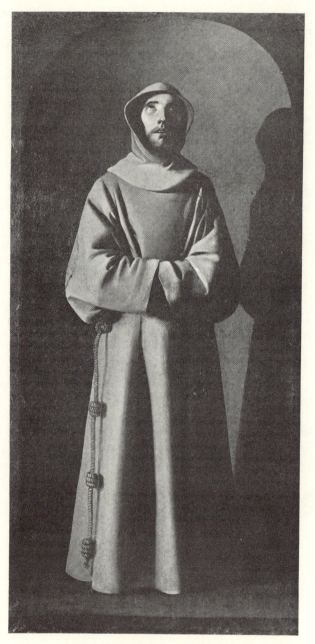

10. Saint Francis: Francisco Zurbaran
Courtesy of the Museum of Fine Arts, Boston

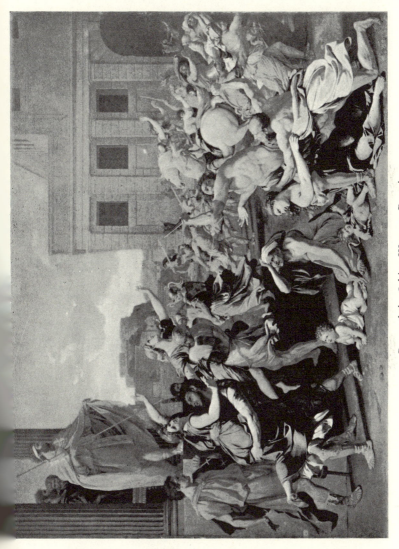

11. Rape of the Sabine Women: Poussin
Courtesy of the Metropolitan Museum of Art, New York

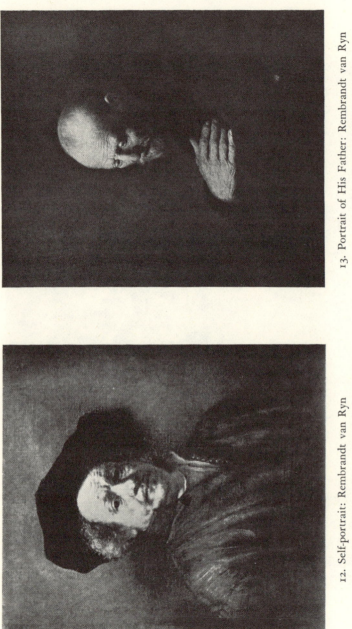

13. Portrait of His Father: Rembrandt van Ryn
Courtesy of the Museum of Fine Arts, Boston

12. Self-portrait: Rembrandt van Ryn
Courtesy of the Metropolitan Museum of Art, New York

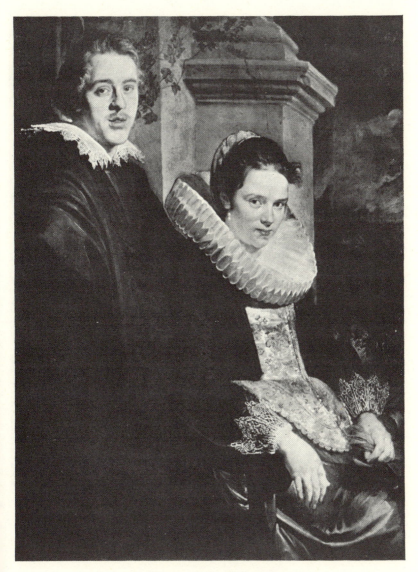

14. The Master and His Wife: Rubens
Courtesy of the Museum of Fine Arts, Boston

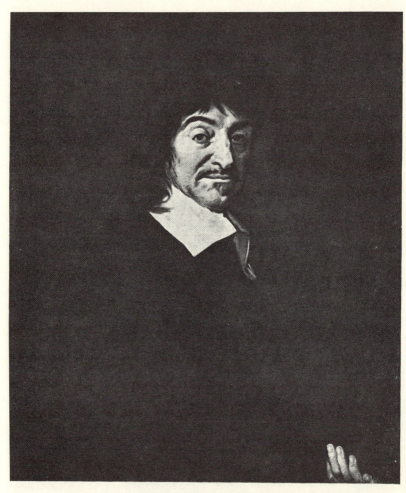

15. Descartes: Frans Hals
Louvre, Paris

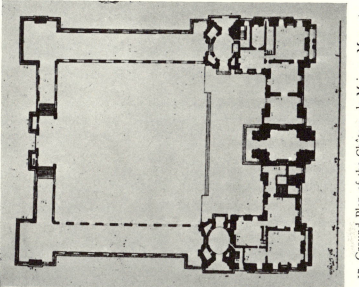

17. Ground Plan of the Château de Maison: Mansart

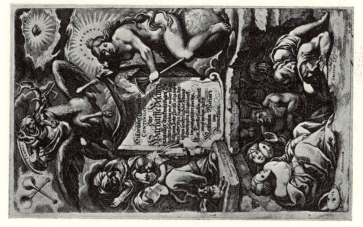

16. Title Page of Matthäus Merian's
Theatrum Europaeum, 1629-1635, vol. II

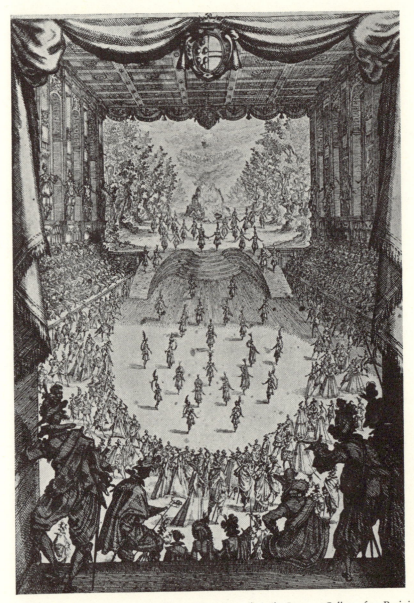

18. First Interlude of the *Vaglia della Liberatione* (1616): Jacques Callot, after Parigi
Theatre Collection, Houghton Library, Harvard College

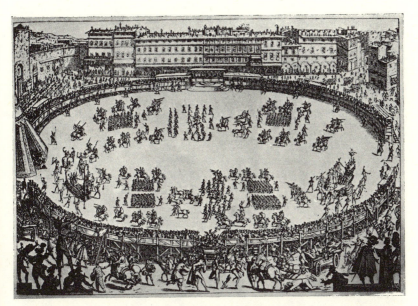

19. La Guerra d'Amore: Jacques Callot
A Tournament Opera, Presented upon the Piazza di San Croce (1615) from Haas,
Musik des Barocks

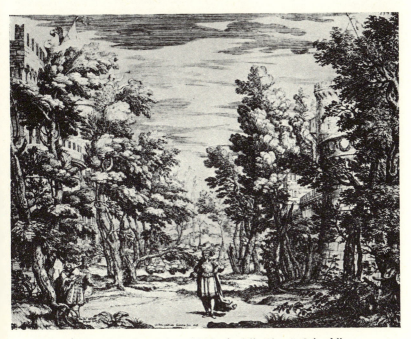

20. Landscape Scene for "Il Trionfo della Pieta." Grimaldi
Theatre Collection, Houghton Library, Harvard College

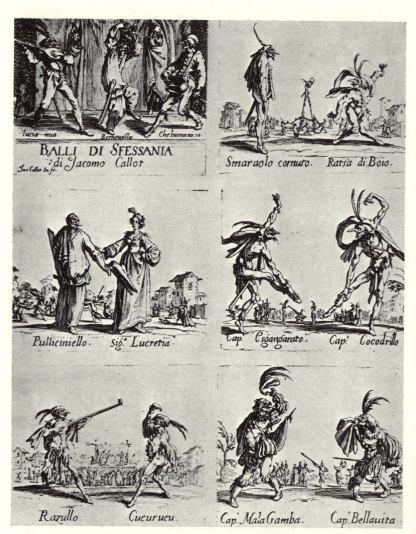

21. Balli de Sfessania: Jacques Callot
Theatre Collection, Houghton Library, Harvard College

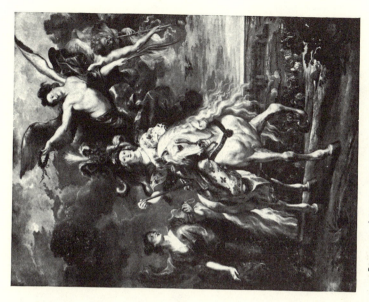

23. Journey of Marie de' Medici to Pont de Cé: Rubens
Louvre, Paris

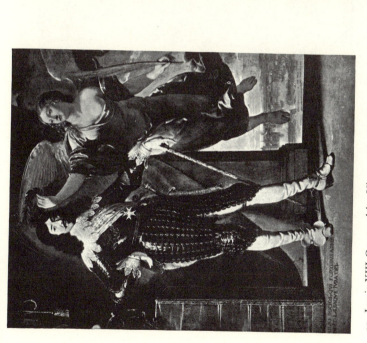

22. Louis XIII Crowned by Victory: P. de Champaigne
Louvre, Paris

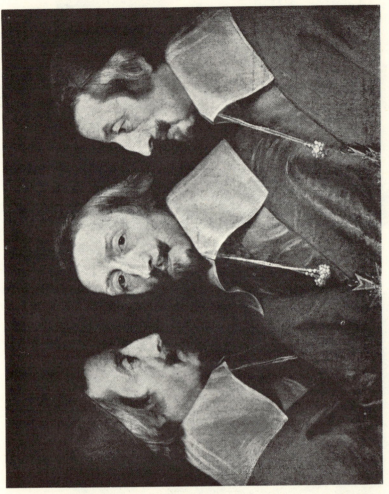

24. Richelieu: P. de Champaigne
National Gallery, London

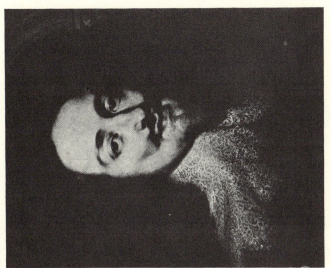

26. Charles I of England: Van Dyck
Pitti Gallery, Florence

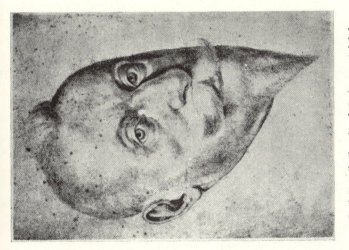

25. Red Pencil Sketch of Gustavus Adolphus
(1632): L. Strauch
from *Generalstaben Sveriges Krig*, 1611-1632,
vol. VI

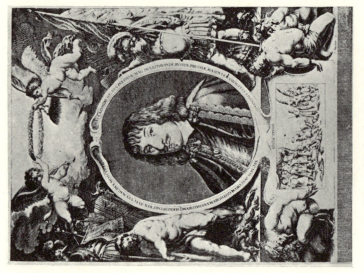

28. A Dragoon
from an engraving in Francis Gross'
Military Antiquities

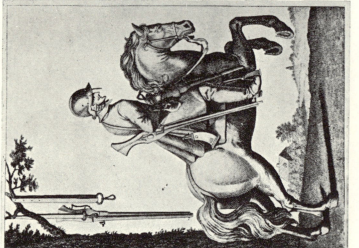

27. King of Poland: John Casimir
from *Polska jej Dzieje i Kultura*, vol. II

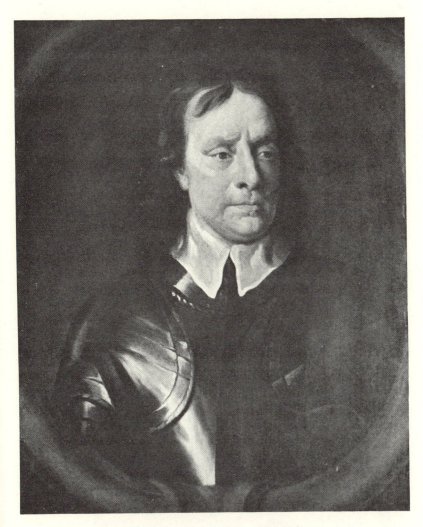

29. Oliver Cromwell, Aged 58: Artist Unknown
Photographed by George M. Cushing Jr.
Courtesy of Prof. Charles C. Abbott, present owner

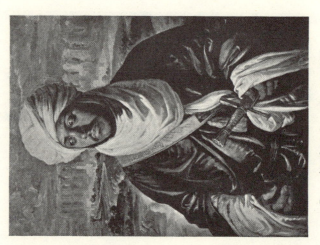

31. Portrait of Mulay Ahmed: Rubens
Courtesy of the Museum of Fine Arts, Boston

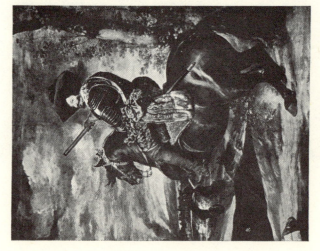

30. Equestrian Portrait of the Duke of Olivares:
Velasquez
Prado, Madrid

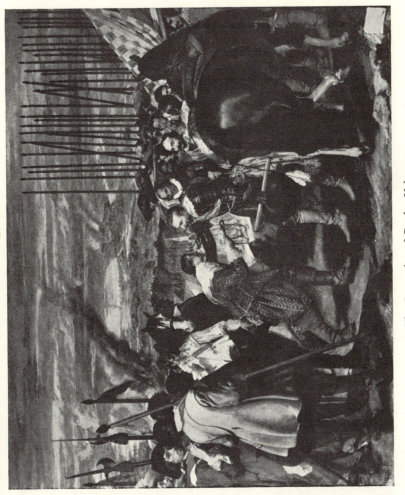

32. The Surrender of Breda: Velasquez
Prado, Madrid

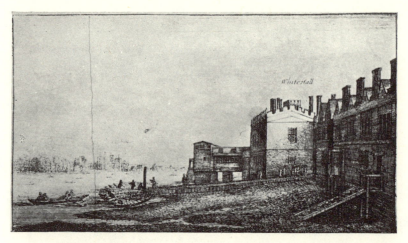

33. Whitehall from the River, with Lambeth in the Distance

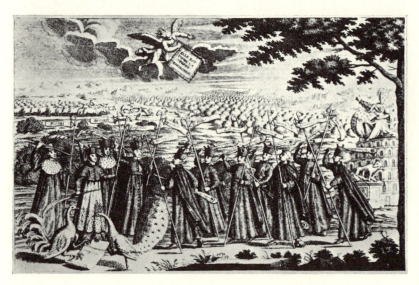

34. Jesuits and Jansenists, Contemporary Caricature
"While the shepherds fight, the wolves devour the herd."

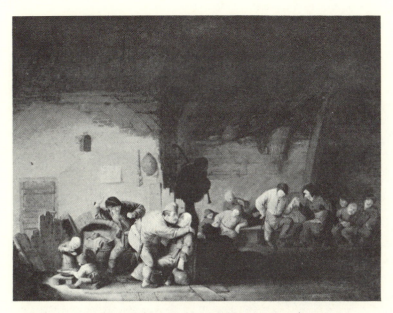

35. Peasants Merrymaking: Adrian van Ostade
Courtesy of the Museum of Fine Arts, Boston

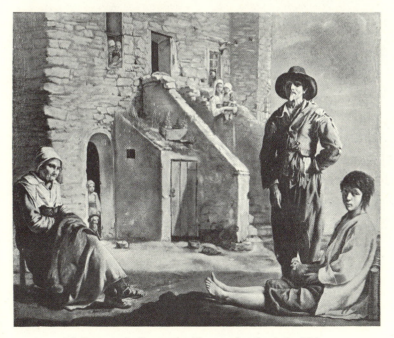

36. Peasants in Front of a House: after Louis Le Nain
Courtesy of the Museum of Fine Arts, Boston

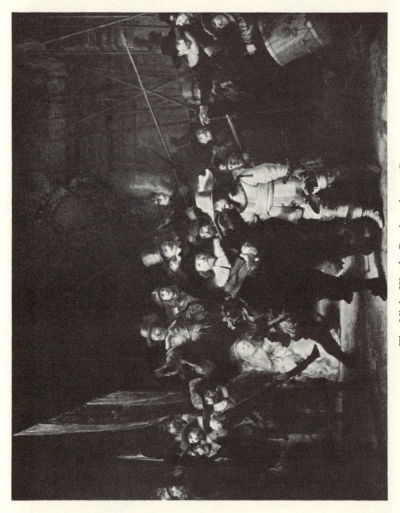

37. The Night Watch: Rembrandt van Ryn
Rijksmuseum, Amsterdam

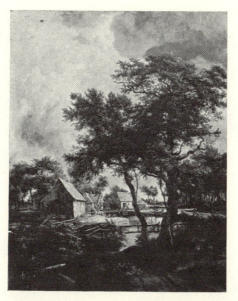

38. Landscape with Mill: Hobbema

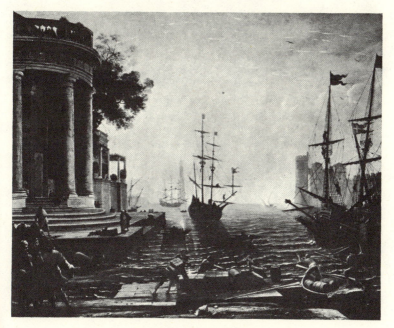

39. Seaport: Claude Lorrain
Courtesy of the Museum of Fine Arts, Boston

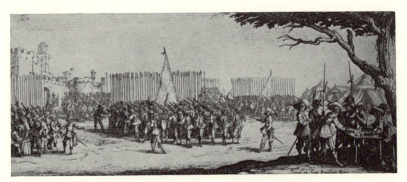

40. The Enrollment of the Troops: Jacques Callot
from *Les Grandes Misères de la Guerre*

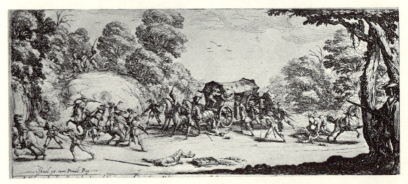

41. Attack on the Coach: Jacques Callot
from *Les Grandes Misères de la Guerre*

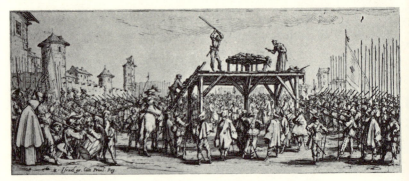

42. The Wheel: Jacques Callot
from *Les Grandes Misères de la Guerre*

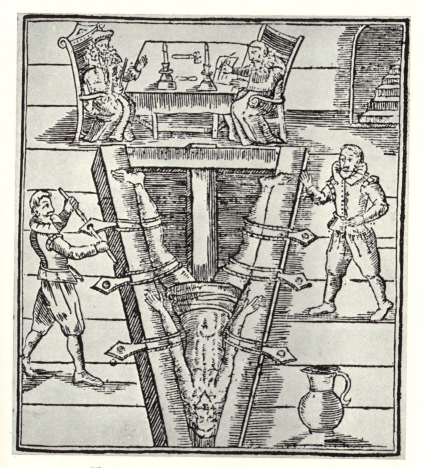

43. The Author in the Rack at Malaga: William Lithgow
Rare Adventures, 1632

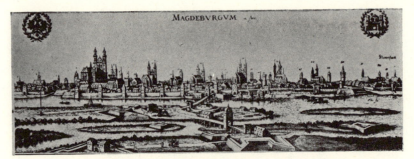

44. View of Magdeburg (before the destruction)
from Matthäus Merian's *Topographia Germaniae,* 1642

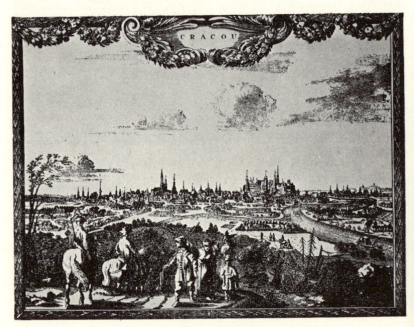

45. View of Cracow
from *Polska jej Dzieje je Kultura,* 1927, vol. II

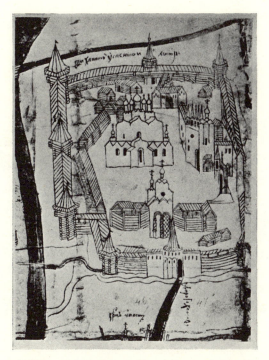

46. Tishvenski Monastery, Drawing of 17th Century
from Hans von Eckhardt, *Russisches Christentum,*
1947

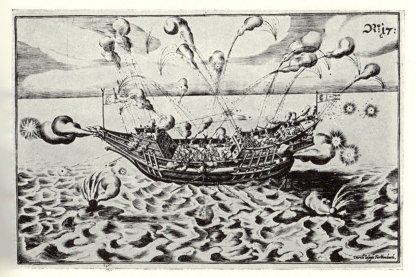

47. A Turkish Terror in Action
from J. Furtenbach, *Architectura Navalis,* 1629

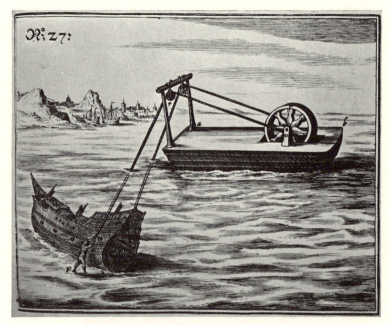

48. Engine Lifting Sunken Ships
from J. Furtenbach, *Itinerarium Italiae,* 1627

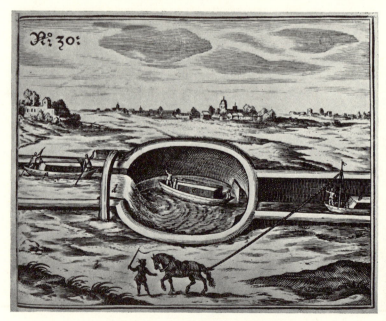

49. Lock between Bologna and Ferrara
from J. Furtenbach, *Itinerarium Italiae,* 1627

tions. Logarithms are a calculating device for infinitesimal fractions; one does not need to understand their principle in order to use them; indeed the slide rule was soon invented to enable people to read off the results of logarithmic calculation mechanically. This proved invaluable for all kinds of complicated calculations involved in the new quantitative approach to science.

The name "analysis" was given to this new dynamic approach to mathematical problems, for it analyzed these problems instead of depending upon guesswork for the formulation of hypotheses. As a consequence problems which had baffled mathematicians for centuries became manageable and were either solved or proved impossible of solution. Thus the celebrated "squaring of the circle" (and of other curves) was approached in terms of the infinitely small segments of space through the addition of which the content of the circle may be approximately measured.[31] Thus standard symbols such as π in the case of the circle were developed to designate these new data.

Similarly the calculation of probabilities, as exemplified in chance games, was coming within reach; both Pascal and Pierre Fermat (1601–65) made highly significant discoveries in this field, but its full development, including its significant application to statistical materials, occurred only later in the century.

IX. DESCARTES AND PASCAL

The limits of Descartes's overemphasis on mathematics as part of a comprehensive and systematic theory of all of nature—Descartes's philosophy in this respect resembled Kepler's notions—were highlighted by his critical comment upon Galileo's work. After praising him, Descartes continued: "He does not stop to examine all that is relevant to each point; which shows that he has not examined them in order, and that he has merely sought reasons for certain particular effects, without having considered the first causes of nature; and thus he has built without a foundation."[32] Descartes's effort to deal scientifically with the first causes of nature, to apply mathematics to the universe, aroused the fierce antagonism of Blaise Pascal (1623–62), whose religious spirit revolted against

[31] For the mathematical detail, the reader may consult any text on differential calculus; cf., e.g., W. F. Osgood, *Differential and Integral Calculus* (1919), 111 ff.
[32] In his letter to Father Mersenne (March, 1638), see his *Correspondance* (ed. by C. Adam and G. Milhaud), III (1941), 76. Descartes formed a low opinion of Galileo in a personal encounter in 1638. Cf. his letter to Mersenne (March 31), *op. cit.*, II (1939), 223.

the proud rationalism of Descartes's assertion, "There is no phenomenon in nature which has not been dealt with in this treatise."[33] And even though Descartes at the end of his treatise declared that all his opinions were "submitted to the authority of the church," Pascal protested against Descartes's whole outlook. "I cannot pardon Descartes," he wrote in *Pensées* and denounced Descartes's mathematical principles as "useless and uncertain."

Pascal, in thus objecting to Descartes, at the same time struck at the work of Hobbes and Spinoza, respectively the authors of a politics and of an ethics *more geometrico*. To the conceit of a self-contained system of definitions Pascal opposed the ever-repeated, central proposition that experiences (the French *expériences* also at this time covered experiments) have much more power to persuade in physics than reasoning; he went even so far as to state that experiences are the only principles, the true masters of physics.[34] One "stubborn fact," as William James was to call it, has, according to Pascal, the power to destroy any hypothesis, no matter how securely grounded it had previously been. This viewpoint is usually associated with Francis Bacon, who wrote in *The Advancement of Learning*: "All true and fruitful natural philosophy has a double scale or ladder, ascendant and descendant; ascending from experiments to the invention of causes, and descending from causes to the invention of new experiments."[35] But neither Bacon nor yet Hobbes nor Spinoza was a mathematician; indeed they might even be considered mathematical illiterates, when contrasted with Descartes and Pascal. But whereas Descartes overestimated the potentialities of mathematics, and of ratiocination generally, Pascal in a scientific spirit more generally adopted in recent years appreciated that all generalizations upon established matter of fact are hypothetical, and hence his outcry: "To write against those who made too profound a study of science: Descartes."[36] Descartes's exaggerated sense of the power of the mind was in its very emphasis typically and dramatically baroque. Perhaps no passage is more revealing in this respect than his own summary of the crucial argument in his *Meditations:*

. . . and finally all the reasons from which we may deduce the existence of material things are set forth. Not that I judge them to be very useful in establishing that which they prove, to wit, that there is in truth a world, that men

[33] The treatise in question is his *Principia philosophiae*, of which a convenient extract is available in Ralph M. Eaton's *Selections* (1927). The statement cited is on p. 309, and constitutes Principle 199.

[34] Pascal, *Oeuvres* (ed. by Strowski), I, 95, 133, 402.

[35] Bacon, *Works* (ed. by Montagu) (American edition, 1842), I, 195.

[36] Pascal, *Pensées*, No. 76.

possess bodies, and other such things which never have been doubted by anyone of sense; but because in considering these closely we come to see that they
are neither so strong nor so evident as those arguments which lead us to the
knowledge of our mind and of God; so that these last must be the most certain and evident facts which can fall within the cognizance of the human
mind. And this is the whole matter that I have tried to prove in these Meditations.[37]

Against such a view, Pascal made two trenchant observations: (1) "The
perceptions of our sense are always true,"[38] and (2) "Mathematicians
wish to treat matters of intuition mathematically, and make themselves
ridiculous, wishing to begin with definitions and then with axioms, which
is not the way to proceed in this kind of reasoning."[39]

Pascal was enabled thus to perceive the limits of the scientific spirit
more clearly than perhaps any other scientist or mathematician of his
age, because he had himself experienced God in the most intense and
dramatic way. As Sainte-Beuve was to show,[40] Pascal possessed to the
highest degree of intensity the feeling of the human person. One might
add that Pascal also to the highest degree of intensity possessed, or at
any rate acquired, the feeling of the Divine Person. His anger over
Descartes's rationalist God, as when he wrote that Descartes "in all his
philosophy would have been quite willing to dispense with God," was
rooted in this powerful personal experience and conception. It may well
be true that in his view of man Pascal was guided by Montaigne; but in
his view of the Deity he was worlds apart from the skeptic of the Renaissance, and a true child of the new religiosity; his ardor matched that of
any of the mystics who crowded the religious life of the seventeenth
century, in Spain and in Germany, in France and in England.[41] His
famous memorial of the night of November 23, 1654, cried out: "Certitude, certitude, feeling, joy, peace, God of Jesus Christ . . . grandeur of
the human soul . . . joy, joy, joy, tears of joy."[42]

[37] Descartes, *Selections* (ed. by Eaton), 88.

[38] *Pensées*, No. 9.

[39] *Pensées*, No. 1, which Leo Roth has rightly called Pascal's own "discourse on method."
Compare Roth's skillful summary of Pascal's criticism of the *Esprit géométrique* in his
Descartes' Discourse on Method (1937), 132–34. Basing his argument on Pascal's own
fragment, *De l'Esprit Géométrique*, Roth concludes that "logic cannot follow the geometrical
model, and that the geometrical intelligence is incompetent in the fields of morals and
religion, according to Pascal"—a position which was to be elaborated by Kant.

[40] In his *Port-Royal*, Vols. III and IV, entitled "Pascal."

[41] See above, Chapter Two and pp. 64–5.

[42] For the text and a partial reproduction of the memorial in Pascal's own hand, which
he carried sewn into his coat, see Leon Brunschvicg, *Pascal* (1932).

To a man who had had that kind of *Erlebnis,* there was no need for "proving" the existence of God, as Descartes had tried to do. As noted before, Pascal called one of the most extraordinary passages in the *Pensées* "The Mystery of Christ." Here the compassionate essence of divine love was presented in the form of an encounter between Christ and Pascal himself, culminating in Pascal's "Lord, I give thee all," and Jesus' answer: "I love thee more ardently than thou hast loved thine abominations." Quintessentially, the mystery of Jesus is that "Jesus suffers in His passions the torments which men inflict upon Him; but in His agony He suffers the torments which He inflicts on Himself." This was the background of feeling upon which Pascal's central criticism or, if you please, emendation of Descartes's philosophy was based: "The infinite distance between body and mind is a symbol of the infinitely more infinite distance between mind and charity: for charity is supernatural."[43] The piling up of infinities, paradoxical as it is and as it was intended to be, symbolized the intensity of Pascal's intuition of the Divine Being. This may be considered the clue to the difference between Bacon and Pascal in relation to experience: whereas Bacon underrated mathematics because he did not understand its role in scientific generalization, Pascal pointed out the limits of mathematics, because it could not cope with charity, with what men hold dear, with value, purpose and the loved end. Other mystics, more especially Jacob Böhme and John Donne, urged the point without clearly understanding its philosophical implications.

In contrast to so intensely human and even spiritual a conception of the feelings which stir man's heart, Descartes expounded the cold and presumably scientific proposition that "the action and the passions are always one and the same thing," but may be looked at either from the standpoint of the man to whom "it" occurs, or from that of the man who causes them to happen. Making a sharp distinction between soul and body, Descartes held that "the heat and movement of the members proceed from the body, the thoughts from the soul." This emphasis on thoughts as the essence of the soul's being was flatly advanced; "It is easy to recognize," Descartes remarked, after having perused "the functions which pertain to the body," "that there is nothing in us which we ought to attribute to our soul excepting our thoughts." These thoughts Descartes believed to be of two sorts: actions of the soul and passions of the soul, the first our "desires," the second our perceptions "or forms of knowledge found in us." Having thus radically divided soul and body—a

---

[43] *Pensées,* No. 792.

division which was in keeping with Descartes's dualism of mind and matter—Descartes was hard put to join them together again. In order to accomplish this feat, he decided to locate the soul in the pineal gland on the ground that "the soul is really joined to the whole body," and is "one and in some manner indivisible." So, since the "animal spirits" had been identified as "a very subtle air or wind" which passes through the nerves which "resemble little tubes," the movements which take place in this "interior part of the brain," "may alter very greatly the course of these spirits." And "how may we know that this gland is the main seat of the soul?" asks Descartes in Article XXXII of *The Passions of the Soul*. The reason which persuaded him was that all other parts of the brain are double, thus resembling the eyes, etc. This type of speculative reasoning on matters of fact, especially physiology and the like, was precisely what the experimentalists among the devotees of the "new science" most strongly objected to. Curiously enough, Descartes had just quoted (in Article VII) the opinion of Harvey as giving clear proof against the authority of the ancients. Yet what Descartes then set forth was so completely in the tradition of Galen (especially the notions of "animal spirits" and of "wind" in the arteries) that it is impossible to believe that Descartes had taken the trouble even to read Harvey's short treatise, let alone watch some of the crucial experiments. Descartes always remained the mathematician and the metaphysician; deduction was his strong point. Men of the stripe of Harvey were thoroughly opposed to this kind of argument. One may well wonder what Harvey might have said about Descartes, since he had observed that "Lord Bacon reasons about natural philosophy like a lord chancellor"—meaning that his conception of evidence was juristic, rather than scientific.

X. ANATOMY AND PHYSIOLOGY: HARVEY

William Harvey (1578–1657) was one of the greatest pioneers in experimental science. His discovery of the circulation of the blood, as set forth in his *Exercitatio anatomica de motu cordis et sanguinis* (1628), was an outstanding example of how to record accurate observations, implement them by skillful experimentation, and thus develop sound hypotheses based upon observed matter of fact. Harvey's work, like Galileo's, was neither mere induction nor mere deduction, but a sound combination and blend of both. Building upon the work of the great anatomists of the preceding century, especially Vesalius and Servetus, as well as his own teacher Fabricius at Padua, Harvey revolutionized medicine by proving a series of interrelated points, notably that the heart, a great muscle, propels the blood at regular intervals (pulse), that the blood in arteries and veins is the same, that only blood, and no "air" is propelled by the heart, and that this is done in a constant stream, from the heart, and not from the liver, as the ancients had taught.

Harvey's method was strictly scientific, although not leading to mathematical formulations, as did Galileo's work in mechanics. After learning all that had been previously written, he acquired through many dissections as complete a knowledge of the heart's anatomy as could be had without a microscope. He then proceeded to experiments with living animals to see how their hearts worked. He also utilized such information as proved useful from disease, and experimented with artificial blocking of the blood stream. Although his whole treatise was no longer than fifty-two pages, it constituted a close-knit demonstration that was never effectively challenged, but on the contrary became the starting point for further work in the field of anatomy and physiology. With the discovery of the microscope, M. Malpighi, Harvey's greatest immediate successor, was enabled to show the functioning of the capillaries which complete the circle. What a contrast between this kind of experimental demonstration and the speculations built by Descartes upon the faulty anatomy and physiology of Galen!

Harvey's other great labor was directed toward clarifying the problem of generation, but while the *Exercitationes de generatione* (1651) were based upon the same sound scientific methods, the results were much less lasting, because the smallness of the events involved presupposed the discovery of the microscope. Within twenty-five years his work was all but obliterated by that of Malpighi.

It is interesting that Harvey should have been the physician of Bacon, and yet have failed to communicate to Bacon the true essence of his scientific method. James I and Charles I both took a great interest in his work, and as physician in ordinary of the king, Harvey was with Charles I at Oxford during most of the civil war, becoming eventually warden of Merton College. After the king's defeat, Harvey went into retirement. An election to the presidency of the Royal College of Physicians he declined; he seems generally to have been a rather mediocre practitioner Aubrey says that he "never heard of any that admired his therapeutic way." Harvey himself did not believe that science should be guided by considerations of utility; yet even he made interesting practical applications of some of his basic findings to science.

XI. MECHANISTIC POLITICS AND PSYCHOLOGY

The contrast between the methods of Harvey and Bacon's panegyrics over the inductive method had its parallel in the social sciences. For if Thomas Hobbes carried through to politics the mechanistic notions which Descartes had sketched for the "passions of the soul," statistics was beginning even in the preceding generation to provide quantitative materials of a nonspeculative kind regarding the wealth and power of nations and states. Books like Giovanni Botero's *Delle Cause della grandezza delle città* (1588—English edition, 1606 and 1635) and Thomas Mun's *A Discourse of Trade* (1621)[44] were built on crude statistical material, but even so their methodology was genuine scientific empiricism.

Hobbes did not consider himself a follower of Descartes. Sharply hostile to Descartes's metaphysics—he wrote a highly critical comment on the *Meditations*—and unappreciative of Descartes's mathematics, which he presumably did not understand,[45] Hobbes proceeded to make a radical effort to interpret man and the state as mechanisms. It is curious that a man of his acumen should have considered himself working in the tradition of Galileo and Kepler when he wrote *De Cive* (1642), *De Homine* (1650), and *Leviathan* (1651), followed by *De Corpore* in 1655. Throughout these works, he assumed that matter and motion are the principles by which *all* events may be explained. "For seeing life is but a motion of limbs, the beginning whereof is in some principal part within; why may we not say that all Automata (Engines that move themselves by springs and wheels as does a watch) have an artificial life?" This sentence from the Introduction to the *Leviathan* was echoed again and again. In conjunction with expounding some very dubious analogies, such as that sovereignty is an artificial soul, or that the heart is "but a spring," he announced that the Leviathan, called a commonwealth or state, is but an artificial man created by the art of man. All this Hobbes believed to flow from an empirical basis:

---

[44] Even more important was his *English Treasure by Forraign Trade* written about 1628, but only published in 1664 after his death. Mun lived from 1571 to 1651.

[45] In his later years, Hobbes engaged in a protracted controversy over the squaring of the circle, which he believed himself to have solved. His comments on the problems of geometry, notably in *Principia et problemata aliquot geometrica* (1674), show that he did not appreciate the significance of analytical geometry. See also John Wallis' attack, *Geometriae Hobbianae Elenchus* (1656).

In the first place I set down for a principle by experience known to all men, and denied by none, to wit, that the dispositions of men are naturally such, that except they be restrained through fear of some coercive power, every man will distrust and dread each other, and as by natural right he may, so by necessity he will be forced to make use of the strength he hath, toward the preservation of himself.[46]

If Hobbes, on the basis of his conviction that the only ultimate facts are matter and motion, projected a comprehensive theory or philosophy of the universe in materialist terms as outlined in his "Preface to the Reader" in *De Cive* in 1642, it is only fair to remark that his political principles were not necessarily dependent upon this schema. They were published first, and were based upon Hobbes' observations and upon his thorough study of Thucydides and Aristotle. Nevertheless, Hobbes worked a harsh materialist dogmatism into his politics and psychology as a result of his preoccupation with mechanics *more geometerico*. He obviously went far beyond Descartes. If Descartes had spoken of the body as a "machine" (*Passions,* Article XXXIV), Hobbes completely rejected Descartes's sharp distinction between body and soul, and insisted that psychology must be studied as a branch of physics (mechanics) and grounded upon mechanical principles. Hobbes consequently was a radical determinist, and believed that all man's employment of the will, so-called, is the result of his perceptions, which in turn result from the impact of external causes.[47]

The first principles from which all is derived are the principles of mechanics. Hobbes was aware of the limits of the deductive method, but he also distrusted mere observation and induction in the manner of Bacon. Thought, he believed, must be combined with observed matter of fact to produce scientific insight. Since the laws of motion constitute the general laws of nature, as all change consists in motion, "all happens in nature mechanically." By this metaphysical proposition he subverted the very essence of the scientific work of men like Galileo and Harvey. But having made this extraordinary assumption, he proceeded to work out a deductive "proof" of the mechanistic premise, as well as of the axiom of inertia (law of continuity). One might sum up the rather

[46] *De Cive,* "Preface to the Reader." Cf. also what is said above, Chapter One, pp. 27–30, regarding Hobbes' views on the law of nature and on the state. The most searching analysis of this aspect of Hobbes's position has been made by Frithjof Brandt, *Den mechaniske Naturopfattelse hos Thomas Hobbes* (1921).

[47] Cf. for his point the discriminating discussion in Ferdinand Tönnies, *Thomas Hobbes, Leben und Lehre* (third edition, 1925), Chs. V, VI.

complex train of Hobbes' reasoning as follows: Space and time cannot be causing external events, because they are merely subjective. In a vacuum a body at rest cannot be thought of as getting into motion except by an external cause. Nor is it thinkable that a body moving in a vacuum could change its velocity or come to rest. Cause, according to Hobbes, is what makes it unthinkable that a certain change should not occur. Thus it is unthinkable that a body at rest remains at its location when another body takes its place; but that is the only condition on which it is unthinkable. It follows that only another moving body can be the cause of the motion. . . . In line with this, resistance is motion. This pattern of abstraction was admittedly derived from Galileo; there was nothing original in Hobbes' argument. Only when Hobbes went beyond the limited framework of Galileo's mechanics and asserted that these principles are applicable to all change in the universe, did he say something new. But was it sound?

Arguing from his mechanistic premise, Hobbes held that all thought was calculation. Furthermore, he interpreted calculation as adding and subtracting, and maintained that all things when transformed into thought could be so added and subtracted. In putting forward such a proposition, Hobbes made himself the highly representative, albeit exaggerated, expression of his age. But like Bacon and Spinoza, he was prevented by his mathematical ineptitude from appreciating the philosophical limits of any mathematics of the infinite. Unlike Kepler, Descartes and Pascal, whose mathematical genius made them realize the strictly formal nature of the mathematical insight, which in turn made them recognize the residual substantive problems of existence, Hobbes overestimated the cognitional value of mathematical insights. He rather clumsily attempted to cope with the problems resulting from such a view by suggesting a very small unit of motion as that which is occurring in the smallest conceivable space during the smallest conceivable time.[48]

Hobbes then defined this unit as $=0$,—an impossible proceeding, since he further suggested that by adding these units one arrives at larger entities; for what Hobbes was saying here is that $0+0+0 \ldots =n$, where "n" is a real number. Hobbes, in short, did not fathom the solutions offered by differential calculus and analytical geometry. Nor did he really understand the cognitional value of experimentation. His

[48] It is not permissible, in my opinion, to introduce the concept of quantum here, to characterize Hobbes' position, as Tönnies has done, *op. cit.*, 142; nor should Hobbes' mathematical failure be obscured by suggesting, as Tönnies does, *ibid.*, that the "smallest conceivable" is identical with "the infinitely small."

psychology, and the politics derived from it, were based upon introspec-
tion, implemented by an unproven major premise that all men are like
Thomas Hobbes. What resulted from such an approach we have discussed in a previous chapter.[49] The most extreme pantheistic position was
developed later in the century by Spinoza, who went beyond Hobbes.

XII. PANTHEISM AND NATURALISM

Both Hobbes and Spinoza were hotly attacked by their contemporaries
as atheists. When plague and fire swept through London in 1664 and 1665,
superstition raised its ugly head. Like the witch-hunters on a lower level,
divines and parliamentarians combined to silence the impious voice. The
previous year, 1663, Descartes's writings had been put on the Index.

That organized, rational religion should fight the deviations into mysticism and naturalism was nothing new; not only in the Middle Ages,
but throughout the sixteenth and earlier seventeenth century the struggle
had gone on. Nor need any particular church be singled out for special
censure. If the Anglican divines were after Hobbes, the Lutheran pastors
persecuted Kepler and Böhme, the Calvinist orthodoxy exiled Grotius,
the Jews ousted Spinoza from their congregation (1656), while the Holy
See pursued Galileo and the Jesuits Port Royal, Pascal, and Descartes.
And yet, later ages looking back at these proceedings have often been
puzzled. Not only did Spinoza seem to Goethe to have been the man
"drunk with God," but surely Kepler, Pascal, Böhme and Descartes were,
each in a different key, strongly religious men animated by a deep sense
of awe for what Kant was to describe as the two most profound sources
of wonder, "the starred heavens above and the moral law within."

The passionate concern of the age with nature and its secrets, the
persistent doubting of all human authority, was fed by what seems to
us now a faith of extraordinary depth and intensity—a faith in the power
of God to order the universe, and a corresponding faith in the power of
man to understand this order, and in the light of it to achieve the mastery
of nature and to order anew man's life on earth. Mysticism, pantheism
and naturalism were all logical forward projections of elements in the
older Christian orthodoxy, both Catholic and Reformed. When Bacon
wrote in his *Advancement of Learning* that he would separate metaphysics from the "first philosophy" and treat it as part of natural science,
he added that he would subdivide the inquiry into causes "according to
the received and sound division of causes; the one part which is physic

[49] See above, Chapter One.

inquires and handles the material and efficient causes; and the other which is metaphysic and handles the formal and final causes." Descartes thought along similar lines, though he was troubled lest one meddle with matters beyond one's understanding. "Finally we shall not seek for the reason of natural things from the end which God or nature has set before Him in their creation; for we should not take so much upon ourselves as to believe that God could take us into his counsels." For in Descartes's view, the entire world and all the permanent laws governing it which reason may discover rest upon God's will. As one commentator has said: "The supreme truth, the basic axiom, is that God exists." [50] Hence Descartes's view, customarily spoken of as dualistic, should really be considered trialistic. For existence, basic existence, is for Descartes compounded of God, mind and matter. These three are the three "substances"—two created, and one uncreated. To Pascal, animated by an intensely personal experience of God, this Cartesian God was little more than a fillip; certainly this God, though a first mover, was already dangerously close to a pantheistic deity which becomes submerged in nature. It was toward the end of our period that Baruch (Benedict) Spinoza formulated such an all-engulfing pantheism. In his *Short Treatise on God, Man, and His Well-Being,* probably composed in 1559–60,[51] Spinoza started from the propositions that: (a) God exists; (b) God is a being of whom all or infinite attributes are predicated, of which attributes everyone is infinitely perfect in its kind; (c) God is the cause of all things, to which may be added his providence and predestination. A completely deterministic universe resulted in which "the big fish devour the little fish by natural right." It was Spinoza's glory that he pursued to the bitter end the implications of the Cartesian philosophy and its mathematical and physical antecedents. It was only in our time that the practical implications of such a conception came fully into view. The God whose quintessence is power, who causes all events in a nature which is itself a congeries of power relations, is a curious expression of the dual trend toward mysticism and skepticism which pervaded religion, philosophy and science during the two generations whose poets included Donne as well as the late Shakespeare, Calderón and Milton. It was the age in which the world-view of the modern man took definite shape and organized itself for the conquest of mankind. Whether it was a glorious achievement or a disastrous betrayal of human destiny seems more controversial today than it was in the intervening three hundred years.

[50] Eaton, *op. cit.,* p. xxxi.
[51] See A. Wolf, *Spinoza's Short Treatise on God, Man, and His Well-Being* (1910).

Chapter Five

THE SULTRY YEARS OF PRECARIOUS BALANCE: THE DUTCH ASCENDANCY

I. INTRODUCTION

The world of 1610 was a complex one. Throughout the chancellories of Europe there was great uneasiness and a sense of impending doom. In the Hradschin at Prague sat the weakling, Rudolf II, trembling amidst his art treasures lest his more vigorous brothers take away his authority and his throne. The Pope, Paul V, though a vigorous and able master, had suffered greatly through his efforts to combat the Republic of Venice when it persisted in violating the ecclesiastical jurisdiction. Spain, though externally presenting its traditional splendor and grandeur, was rapidly deteriorating under the weak and pleasure-seeking Philip III. The duke of Lerma, who ruled the country in Philip's behalf, sought vainly to accomplish by cruelty what his ability failed to achieve. The truce which Spain had concluded in 1609 with the United Netherlands had at long last recognized the success of the Dutch struggle for independence. Here a master of politics, John of Oldenbarneveld, brought all the resources of his small country into play to give it a commanding position in the international sphere.

Unquestionably, if one were to divide Europe at that moment into a Catholic and a Protestant camp, Oldenbarneveld was the unrivaled leader of the newer creed. James I, who might have procured this position of leadership among the Protestants, allowed himself to be absorbed by the professional pursuits of controversial theology. His timidity in action was compensated by the most extreme claims of royal authority, the divine right of kings to do what they considered right. In defense of James it must be said that to divide Europe into Catholics and Protestants is a somewhat misleading simplification, though more nearly true within Germany. Outside the Empire, it is only necessary to look at Henry IV of France. This able ruler, with the aid of the duke of Sully, had built up a position almost matching the established predominance of the Hapsburgs by a skillful policy of balancing powers, which manifested

124

itself most strikingly in his simultaneous collaboration with the Pope and the Dutch Republic. In 1610 it was Henry who caused everyone the greatest worry. For Henry, so all insiders knew, was about to go to war with Rudolf of Hapsburg and his cousin in Spain. Indeed, the beginning of the campaign was set for the spring of that year. The Protestant princes of Germany were in league with the king of France, and expected to join him, or, to look at it from their angle, Henry was to join them in a vigorous effort to establish Protestant supremacy within the Empire. For within the fluid boundaries of what was in part to become Germany 250 years later, the division between Catholics and Protestants was the central issue. To be sure, the territorial princes' ambition to be rid of the imperial overlordship readily fed upon the religious controversy, but Catholic princes, like the powerful Maximilian, duke of Bavaria (1573-1651), were as determined to assert their "sovereignty" as any Protestant. In fact, the Holy Roman Empire of the German Nation, as the unwieldy remnant of the medieval empire was termed, was a complicated feudal federalism, with its nobles, cities and estates. Within the representative machinery of this federal colossus the division between Catholics and Protestants had brought about a state of tension. Each side watched with alert suspicion any sign of a change in the existing distribution of power.

II. THE ISSUE OF THE JÜLICH-CLEVES SUCCESSION

Unhappily, in 1609 the death of John William, duke of Jülich, Cleves, Berg, Mark and Ravensberg, had created a problem which involved upsetting the balance within the Empire which had been so tenuously maintained. These rich duchies were looked upon by Protestants and Catholics alike as their rightful possession, particularly since the population was almost evenly divided between the two faiths. These territories covered the fertile regions of the lower Rhine and Ruhr valley; they stretched from Aachen in the west to Soest in the east. It is not necessary here to disentangle the various claims to succession. For in those days of monarchical government it was universally admitted that the right to rule depended upon legitimate blood descent. The elector of Brandenburg and the Count Palatine of Neuburg both presented claims which were recognized by the Protestant party in Germany as well as by Oldenbarneveld and Henry IV as legitimate. The emperor on the other hand asserted his right to the duchies on the basis of ancient privileges as the feudal overlord of all German princes, since John William had died without leaving a male heir. Naturally, the imperial rights were favored by the Catholics. Both parties had attempted to prejudice the settlement in their favor. The Brandenburger, John Sigismund, and the Count Palatine, Philip Lewis, had been established with the aid of Dutch arms at Düsseldorf, the capital of the duchies. They were to hold and administer the duchies together, until the claims of the emperor could be warded off. This had occurred in May, 1609. Soon afterward, in July, Bishop-Archduke Leopold of Hapsburg had, as the representative of Rudolf, seized the fortress of Jülich. It was this impasse which Henry IV was presumably planning to break by marching into the duchies and cutting the Gordian knot by force of arms. In order to do so he had to march through the Spanish Netherlands, and he therefore blandly proceeded to demand the right of passage from Archduke Albert, who ruled in Brussels under the nominal overlordship of Spain. Albert, though brother of the emperor, proceeded to grant Henry his request. He did not wish to become embroiled in this war although the Hapsburgs in Austria and Spain were openly committed to fight against Henry.

III. THE GRAND DESIGN

Why should the French king, presumably not motivated by any religious partisanship, allow himself to be drawn into this conflict? Why, more particularly, should he plunge his country, which was just beginning to recover from the devastations of the religious wars, into this risky and formidable encounter with the greatest military powers on the continent? Such questions of deeper purpose are bound to be among the most mooted problems of history. Various interpretations have been advanced. According to some, Henry considered the moment opportune for destroying the overweening power of the Hapsburgs. Others have maintained that the French king had designs of his own upon these rich duchies, which would have extended the boundaries of France to the Rhine and beyond. Still others insist that the whole project was conceived as a great demonstration on behalf of Henry's Protestant allies, the Dutch and German confederates. But the most extraordinary, indeed unbelievable, conception has been attributed to the French king by his close collaborator and minister of finance, Maximilien de Béthune, duke of Sully (1560–1641). In his *Mémoires* Sully, after some general historical and moral

reflections in which he sought to anticipate the objection that the grand
design was a chimera, relates:

I remember the first time the King spoke to me of a political system, by
which all Europe might be regulated and governed as one great family. I
scarce paid any attention to what he said, imagining that he meant no more
by it than merely to divert himself, or perhaps to show that his thoughts on
political subjects were greater, and penetrated deeper, than most others: my
reply was a mixture of pleasantry and compliment. Henry said no more at
that time. . . . I was astonished when, some time after, he renewed our conversation on this head, and continued, from year to year, to entertain me with
new regulations and new improvements in his scheme. . . . I had never
thought seriously about this scheme. . . . Strongly prejudiced . . . I used my
utmost efforts to undeceive Henry . . . (but) . . . having viewed all the
parts of the scheme in their proper light, and weighted them thoroughly . . .
I found myself confirmed in the opinion, that the design of Henry the Great
was, upon the whole, just in its intention, possible, and even practicable in all
its parts, and infinitely glorious in all its effects, so that upon all occasions I
was the first to recall the King to his engagements, and sometimes to convince
him by those very arguments which he himself had taught me.

It has been argued learnedly that this is all pure fiction. Perhaps so,
though there seems to be nothing inherently improbable about the imaginative Henry trying to persuade a mentor of such stern morals and
parsimonious principles as Sully by appealing to the latent idealism of
his highly constructivist mind. Be that as it may, the fact remains that
a design for the federal unification and pacification of all Europe was
invented by Henry or Sully at this early date to take the place of the
medieval unity which had now definitely vanished.

The Grand Design started from the premise that three religions, the
Roman Catholic, the Calvinist and the Lutheran, had become so definitely
established "that there is not the least appearance that any of them can
be destroyed." Hence "all that remains to be done is to strengthen the
nations who have made choice of one of these religions . . . and those
nations whose inhabitants profess several religions should be careful to
observe those rules which they find necessary to remedy the ordinary
inconveniences of a toleration." These enlightened notions were, unfortunately, not shared by the vast majority of people at that time. In
writing that "the Protestants are very far from wishing to force their
religion upon any of its neighbours . . . and the Catholics, doubtless,
are of the same sentiments," Sully is here engaged in some pretty fanci-

ful, wishful thinking: the most formidable religious war was yet to come. Upon this premise of mutual toleration of the three religions, the design constituted a general council in which all the princes and other governments would be represented. In order to eliminate the problem which the vast possessions of the Hapsburgs would have created in such a federation, the design proposed to divest this house of all its possessions except Spain and to recompense it by giving it all dominions overseas. In this respect the plan was typical of Sully's anticolonial views. Without going into the details of how he proposed to distribute the Hapsburgs' dominions, it may be said that the plan included liberal portions for everyone whose support was needed for the execution of the project.

Germany was to be federally united under an electoral emperor, and Italy similarly under the Pope, who was besides to become a secular prince of an enlarged papal state. "Among all these different dismemberings, we may observe that France received nothing for itself, but the glory of distributing them with equity." No grander application of the ancient adage, *"Divide et impera,"* has surely ever been designed. "The purport of the design . . . was to divide Europe equally among a certain number of powers, in such a manner that none of them might have cause either of envy or fear." In short, a perfect federation was to be constructed. Six great hereditary monarchies, five elective monarchies, and four sovereign republics: France, Spain, England or Britain, Denmark, Sweden and Lombardy (Savoy) constituting the first; the Empire, the papacy, Poland, Hungary, and Bohemia the second; and Venice, Italy, Switzerland, and the Netherlands the third group. Permanent ministers were to constitute a senate "to deliberate on any affairs which might occur; to discuss the different interests, pacify the quarrels, clear up and determine all the civil, political and religious affairs of Europe, whether within itself or with its neighbors." The ten larger states were to have four permanent delegates, the others only two. There might also be regional councils in different parts of Europe. All powers were to contribute according to their strength to a common army and a common treasury. Non-Christian states were to be excluded. Such was the grand design by which the duke of Sully, with the powerful imagination of a visionary, glorified the motivation of his admired master, Henry the Great.[1]

---

[1] *Mémoires de Sully, Nouvelle Édition* (1814), V, 27 ff.

Nineteenth-century historians with their materialistic cult for *Realpolitik* have scoffed at this flight of the human genius. The present generation which made two active, though half-hearted efforts to accomplish something like the grand design has reason to admire this extraordinary scheme. It was indeed chimerical. But it shows that at the very moment when the modern national state, centralized within and dividing Europe into mutually hostile camps, emerged from the ruins of medieval unity, the ablest minds realized that eventually a new unity would have to be built out of these distinct entities, a United States of Europe, and of the World.

IV. THE DEATH OF HENRY IV

Whether Henry was the author of this magnanimous project or not, it is clear that his preparations for a war in the spring of 1610 were directed against the house of Hapsburg. Since the enemies of Hapsburg were rather numerous, Henry stood really at the head of a far-flung coalition which included the United Netherlands, Venice, Savoy and the German Calvinist princes. James of England had also half-committed himself. Of these confederates, the Netherlands were doubtlessly the most reliable and resourceful. Indeed, Oldenbarneveldt had played as great a role in the preparation of the war as Henry, and it was through him that the Protestant princes and England were held in line, while Henry handled the Pope, Savoy, and even to a certain extent Bavaria and the Catholic League in Germany.

Many of his contemporaries speculated upon Henry's chances of success, and the balance of opinion inclined in his favor. For neither Rudolf nor Philip could provide effective leadership, and although the physical resources of Hapsburg were great, Henry's plan was to attack not only in the duchies, but in Italy as well, thus necessitating a dispersion of Hapsburg resources. Yet, until the very last, even his closest associates, such as the foreign minister, Villeroi, remained doubtful of the execution of the program. A curious and dramatic episode had intertwined itself with the great affairs of state. As Richelieu says in his *Mémoires:* "Love was not the last cause of this famous journey; for it is true that he [the king] wanted to use this occasion to force the archduke [Albert] to return the Princess to him." This princess was the charming, gay, and irresponsible Henrietta-Charlotte de Montmorency with whom Henry, in keeping with his habits, had fallen violently in love the previous year.

Since she was the daughter of a peer, he had proceeded to marry her to his creature, the Prince de Condé. This unattractive favorite became violently jealous of his master, however, and forced his wife to flee with him to Brussels, where Archduke Albert took Henrietta-Charlotte into custody and refused to surrender her without permission from her husband, in spite of urgent requests by herself, her parents, and the king, her lover. Meanwhile, her husband went the round of the Hapsburgs, seeking active support against Henry. Indeed, Condé's intrigues extended to endeavors to have Henry's children by Marie de' Medici declared illegitimate so that he might claim the throne of France as cousin of the king. It is, of course, absurd to imagine that Henry was making war solely for the purpose of capturing this damsel. Still, following Richelieu, it seems impossible "not to consider how dangerous this passion is to princes, because it makes them excessively blind to the consequences of actions dangerous to their persons as well as their estates." Indeed, the legend shows how far absolutism had progressed in the minds of men that they could imagine this sort of romance as the genuine origin and purpose of a major war.

Love and war came to an abrupt end when the king was murdered in the streets of Paris by Ravaillac on May 14, 1610. Many accusations were at once rumored concerning the authorship of this crime. The Pope, Spain, the Jesuits, the nobles were all involved in a variety of dark tales. But all we know for certain is that the official record claimed that Ravaillac refused to give any information about his accomplices, indeed denied that he had any. He admitted having been stirred by some radical sermons in which the king had been accused of plotting the destruction of the Catholic Church, but for the rest, his deed was that of a fanatic. However, the results were so favorable to Spain and to certain groups of French nobles, that a suspicion has lingered of their having been implicated in the affair.

Queen Marie de' Medici's immediate concern was, of course, to secure the succession for her son, Louis XIII. It was only natural that upon the sudden death of the king, whose internal policy had been to tame the great nobles, the feudal lords should raise their heads once more and demand a share in the government of the country. Marie, helpless in the face of men like the Duke d'Epernon, who could count upon the support of a large part of the army, took refuge in a system of bribes. Huge sums were handed out on all sides, as well as provincial governorships and other revenue-yielding positions of all sorts. If to the victor belong the spoils, then certainly the nobility was victorious over the monarchy after the death of Henry IV.

In foreign affairs a much more cautious course was adopted by Villeroi, thus giving rise to accusations that this minister of Henry IV had been in the pay of Spain. The piety of the queen accounts for her turning to the papal nuncio, Ubaldini, for advice and counsel. This forceful ecclesiastic, though by no means pro-Spanish, any more than his master, Paul V, counseled peace and moderation. Two favorites of Marie, the Florentine adventurer Concini and his wife, who had belonged to the queen's immediate household, acted as go-betweens in these transactions. But it does not appear that Concini, who was basically a timid man and without political ideas, attempted to do more than to get along as best he could with his limited abilities. The main concern of the Concinis was undoubtedly to enrich themselves while the sun of royal favor shone upon them. Anyone who seemed ready to help them in these efforts was favored, while opponents like Sully were pushed aside. In sum, the death of Henry IV resurrected all the forces of incipient feudal disorder and showed on what slender foundations royal authority rested. France in the next few years slipped back into feudal anarchy and chaos.

V. THE ENGLAND OF JAMES I: THE PARLIAMENT

James I, who had ascended the throne of the Tudors after the death of "Good Queen Bess" in 1603, had by 1610 succeeded in muddying the waters of English constitutionalism. Puritan divines, about three hundred of them, had been driven from their benefices because they would not acknowledge the Prayer Book as the word of God; parliamentary privilege had been infringed; and the traditions of constitutional legalism had been flouted. The lingering fear of Spain had been aroused by a policy of *rapprochement,* following the inherently sensible peace of 1604. Finally, and contradictorily, the Catholics had been placed into the position of outlaws, following the Gunpowder Plot (1605), by a new Oath of Supremacy and a tightening of the penal laws and fines. The king, a man of whom it has been said that one could love or despise but not hate him,[2] had good qualities such as learning, tolerance, and a measure of good will bordering on weakness, which helped him little to govern well, while he also had bad ones which made his ideas on government or king craft, as he put it, ineffectual pedantries: his vanity, his stubbornness, above all his lack of judgment of men and measures. Of able men who might have assisted

---

[2] George M. Trevelyan, *England Under the Stuarts* (1906), 75.

him there were many; but he either drove them into opposition, like Coke and Eliot, or allowed them to be discredited, like Bacon and Raleigh. James was no fool, but he inclined to overcleverness, and the contrast between what he conceived to be a king's right and position and what he was willing to do to live up to such pretensions bordered in its irresponsibility upon levity. As a result James, who liked to speak of himself as the "establisher of perpetual peace in Church and Commonwealth," precipitated the great controversies which wrecked the Stuart monarchy: when he dissolved parliament in February, 1611, the constitutional conflict was already beginning to take shape.

Unquestionably, the most distinctive feature of England was coming to be her parliament. Rooted in the medieval tradition of government-with-estates,[3] the English parliament was rapidly overcoming the division into such hostile estates which a prince might use to rule over them. In a memorable passage, George M. Trevelyan has summed up the background of the parliament which James faced at the time of his accession:

The forms and functions of the English Parliament derived from medieval origins. The baron, able, when he chose, to let war loose over the land from his cattle-yard, consented to spare his country so long as he was compensated with an hereditary share in the counsels of state. The gentleman, the burgess and the yeoman, in days when the central power could do little to strengthen the hands of the tax-collector against the passive resistance of a scattered population, consented to fill the royal treasury, so long as they were consulted as to the amount and reassured as to the necessity of the royal demands. Such was the original meaning of House of Lords and House of Commons.

The Tudors retained the forms but altered the significance of our Parliamentary institutions. By destroying the Barons and their armies, the King removed the only political power that could presume to name his Ministers or dictate his policy . . . the English Parliament preserved its privileges and increased its functions by becoming part of the theory and practice of English absolutism.[4]

However, parliament had not been so completely merged into nor become so integral a part of Tudor absolutism as to be unable to extricate itself when the policies of James provoked its animosity. In contrast to medieval precedent, the house of commons now developed as the center of opposition and eventual resistance. Representing the middle classes, it combined uniquely the lower gentry in town and country with the mer-

[3] See above, pp. 14–25 and below.
[4] *Op. cit.*, 100.

chants and yeomen, and this sharing of the representative system gave to the Commons a national unity lacking in the estates' assemblies of many continental countries (though English historians incline to overstress the difference, and to neglect the close parallels existing in some other countries). Genuine elections, though based on a restricted suffrage, were common throughout England, and since yeomen and burgesses inclined to send gentlemen to parliament to represent them—the overwhelming preponderance in the membership was drawn from the gentry—the commons achieved a measure of genuine national integration.

Being as yet uncorrupted by court life or long "seasons" in London, the English parliaments were unique in their genuine patriotic sentiment. Trevelyan feels that "as an opposition, no assembly of men at once so shrewd and so stalwart ever met to resist the abuse of power." They were largely rough and simple country squires, "now at last informed by Elizabethan culture; and now at last spiritualized by a Puritan religion." But as they began to shape themselves into an opposition to arbitrary royal government in their sessions of 1610, they aroused the king to such anger that he for ten years tried to get along without them. The clash of 1610 by which James took himself "out" of parliament, contrary to the ancient tradition of the "king in parliament" as the highest authority in England,[5] was rather unnecessarily provoked by the king, who had been engaged in theoretical disputes with the Jesuits, especially Cardinal Bellarmine, concerning the "divine right" of kings. This issue had boiled up in 1604 when parliament had humbly begged James not to allow himself to be misinformed regarding the commons' rights and privileges: they do not enjoy them by the grace of the king, but that "our privileges and liberties are our right and due inheritance, no less than our very lands and goods." [6] Now the king, pedantically insistent upon his divine grace theory, on March 21, 1610, asserted:

The state of monarchy is the supremest thing upon earth: for kings are not only God's lieutenants upon earth and sit upon God's throne, but even by God himself they are called gods. . . . I conclude with this axiom of divinity, that as to dispute what God may do is blasphemy . . . so is it sedition in subjects to dispute what a king may do in the height of his power. . . . I will not be

---

[5] See Sir Thomas Smith *De Republica Anglorum*, Bk. II, Ch. II ff., and the comments in Charles H. McIlwain, *The High Court of Parliament and its Supremacy* (1910), 124 ff. But McIlwain overstresses the judicial aspect.

[6] G. W. Prothero, *Select Statutes and Other Constitutional Documents* (1913), 288.

content that my power be disputed upon; but I shall . . . rule my actions according to my laws.

James then outlined three matters he would not have the Commons discuss: his policies, which he called his "craft," his ancient rights and possessions, presumably the prerogative rights, and finally any established or settled law. By this last injunction James did not suggest that he was the sole fount of law; far from it. He said: "Now if any law or statute be not convenient, let it be amended by Parliament, but in the meantime term it not a grievance." To these propositions the commons on May 23, 1610, replied by reasserting their broad right to debate and criticize:

We hold it an ancient, general and undoubted right of Parliament to debate freely all matters which do properly concern the subject and his right or state; which freedom of debate being once foreclosed, the essence of Parliament is withal dissolved.[7]

They returned more specifically to the issue of the rule of law in a further petition of July 7 of the same year when they stressed the require-ment of assent of the parliament, and insisted that the king's subjects had enjoyed "a certain rule of law which giveth both to the head and members that which of right belongeth to them, and not by any uncertain or arbitrary form of government." They therefore claimed to be entitled to protection of lives, bodies or goods except for penalties provided by authority of laws and statutes agreed to by common consent. In short, the commons reasserted the principles of constitutional government against the king's extension of royal prerogative. But James would not hear of it; he dissolved parliament in February, 1611, and, except for the ineffectual "Addled Parliament" which sat for two months in 1614, did not call it again until 1621.

During these fateful years James ruled with the aid of personal favorites, first Robert Carr, duke of Somerset, and then George Villiers, duke of Buckingham; for in 1612 Robert Cecil, earl of Salisbury, and Prince Henry, the king's eldest son, passed away, and therewith disappeared the two men most able and ready to restrain the king, since they occupied independent positions. In spite of, or perhaps more truly because of, his anti-Spanish policy, Cecil had received a secret pension from the king of Spain, as did most of his fellow councilors—an amazingly baroque habit considering the fact that these very men persecuted poor parsons of tender

---

[7] Prothero, *op. cit.*, 297. For preceding quotations see *ibid.*, 293 ff.

conscience for "treasonable" activities.[8] Is it surprising that once this stalwart leader of the Elizabethan policy of the middle way was gone, tendencies toward compromise with Catholicism and Spain should make their appearance, since the king favored them? James, though fancying himself the leader of Protestantism, also entertained the vain conceit that he might "compose" the difficulties and heal the rift which divided Christianity: he curiously resembled the Elector John of Saxony in this policy, got enmeshed in similar duplicities, and like him has been bitterly condemned. Yet these men and others like them stood for a deep longing and widespread impulse of their time.[9]

Three fateful events followed the death of Prince Henry. Almost immediately, in February, 1613, James gave his daughter Elizabeth in marriage to Frederick, Count Palatine, and thereby permitted the mistaken presumption to be made that Britain would back the acknowledged leader of Protestantism in Germany and assist the aggressive policy of his government to succeed; James' later efforts to dissuade his son-in-law were unavailing.[10]

Thereafter, in 1614, James called a parliament containing the emerging opposition leaders, John Pym, Thomas Wentworth and John Eliot, which came to nothing, because the commons insisted on raising again the question of impositions on trade which had given trouble since the beginning of James' reign. Governmental expenditures rose from a little over 400,000 pounds at the end of Elizabeth's reign to between 500,000 and 600,000, thus leaving a deficit of around 100,000 pounds. The commons feared that trade impositions might destroy the ancient "power of the purse" as commerce grew, and so had been trying, without success, to have them based on law rather than prerogative.

Finally James, after a brief interlude signalized by Raleigh's hapless expedition against Guiana in 1617–18 which sent this leader of the war party to the block, compounded his ecclesiastical, dynastic and pacific policies into a long-drawn-out endeavor to marry his son and heir Charles to the Spanish Infanta, Anne of Austria. This was the ill-fated "Spanish Match" which prevented effective leadership by the British in the Protestant struggle against the Counter Reformation during the decisive years 1619–23. This policy was spoken of as a "revolution" in the established

---

[8] See below, pp. 281–2.
[9] See Hugo Grotius, *De Veritate Religionis Christianae* (1627), and above, pp. 24–5, and below pp. 147–9.
[10] See below, pp. 165–6.

system of church and state, since it might reverse British foreign policy, unloose Catholic propaganda, and ripen Britain for an overthrow of Protestantism by the forces of the Counter Reformation. In view of what happened to Henrietta, such suggestions seem a bit farfetched, retrospectively. It is, however, undeniable that the policy raised precisely such fears among the people, and thus undermined the monarchy's position. "For a hundred years the foreign policy of the Stuarts drove the forces of nationalism to aid the cause of Protestant enthusiasm and civic freedom."[11]

The Spanish Match ended in an episode as baroque as any of the age. In February, 1623, Buckingham and Prince Charles set out in secret to win the hand of the princess by wooing her in Spain. The lordly Escurial treated the royal suitor politely, but distantly. Having never intended the match as anything but a skillfully designed ruse for the purpose of inactivating James while the renowned Spanish infantry seized the Palatinate, Olivárez and his ambassador in London, Gondomar, were sore perplexed to discover a way of ridding themselves of these Don Quixotes without getting into war. Stately festivities and stiff ceremonial were interposed, until finally the two gallants returned home (October, 1623).

VI. THE UNION AND THE LEAGUE

While these reactionary developments were occurring in England and France, decisive changes were under way in Germany. After long-drawn-out negotiations, alliance systems had been constructed in 1608 and 1609 by both the Protestant estates and the Catholic estates. These alliances, called the Protestant Union and the Catholic League respectively, were of such importance later that their composition must be briefly sketched. Though formally concluded only in 1609, the Catholic League had been long advocated by its foremost protagonist, the Duke Maximilian of Bavaria, as the only method for stemming the tide of Protestant progress throughout Germany. His appeals were primarily directed toward the princes of the church whose position was patently threatened by the continuous extension of Protestantism. More especially the archbishops of Cologne, Trèves and Mainz, as well as the powerful bishops of Würzburg, Augsburg, Constance, Regensburg, and Passau, were to be united in such a group. But the foremost prince amongst them, the Archbishop of Mainz, was a very cautious man who feared the military power of his Protestant neighbors in the Palatinate. Hence the leadership fell to Maximilian,

[11] Trevelyan, *op. cit.*, 117.

perhaps the most remarkable ruler Bavaria ever had. Steadfast and courageous, but opposed to all adventures, of a high order of intelligence tempered by profound piety and loyalty toward the Catholic Church, he was not only a statesman of real distinction, but a military leader as well. The problem which he had to solve was how to buttress and defend the Catholic position in Germany without sacrificing his sovereignty to imperial pretensions. The League was his instrument for effecting this purpose. It provided him with the broad foundation for Catholic leadership, and created a counterpoise to the power of Hapsburg. It was characteristic for this situation that Sully in his Great Design proposed to enlarge Bavaria by considerable Hapsburg possessions and to have the duke become a candidate for the imperial office, a plan which had actually been pushed by the Protestants themselves (1611). It is typical also that Maximilian rejected such projects as too far-flung and risky. He was satisfied to build slowly and steadily so as to be prepared for any eventual conflict. As director of the League and commander of its forces, Maximilian occupied the foremost place among the Catholic princes in Germany apart from the Hapsburgs.

No such clear-cut leadership and direction proved possible among the Protestants. Indeed, their religious convictions as well as their practical interests were diversified to the point of serious conflict. Hence the establishment of the Union was more difficult and its eventual employment for effective action remained more doubtful. Lutherans and Calvinists fought each other with much venom. The doctrinal controversies over the communion and predestination were reflected in practical politics: the Calvinists were active and progressive, the Lutherans passive and conservative. The latter's conservatism more particularly attached itself to the constitution of the Empire: "Be obedient to the authorities which are set over you." This injunction of Luther's was ever before their minds. Convinced that Protestantism was winning in Germany, the Lutheran princes were satisfied to progress by small gains, here and there.

It is true that at the beginning of the seventeenth century Germany was predominantly Protestant. But it was hardly Calvinist. More ascetic and radical reformers, the Calvinists were deeply aroused over the sloth and intemperance of many Lutheran courts. They felt that the Reformation had only just begun. The leading prince of this group was at first the Elector Palatine, and later the elector of Brandenburg. Closely associated with them was the landgrave of Hesse-Cassel and the count of Nassau. Such leadership as would naturally have come from the Palatinate was actually in the hands of Christian of Anhalt, a man of great ability and restless ambition, but not too steady and persistent in the pursuit of his objectives. He was officially the governor of the Upper Palatinate and as such the leading councilor of and spokesman for the Elector Palatine.

The main pressure in favor of the Union came naturally from these south German Calvinists. In the actual negotiation of the agreement certain south German Lutheran princes played, however, a leading part. They had been deeply stirred by the vigorous proceedings, in 1607, of Maximilian of Bavaria against a small south German town, Donauwörth, after the emperor had outlawed it for disturbing the peace of Augsburg. Duke Philip Ludwig of Neuburg, whose territory bordered immediately on that of Bavaria, Duke Frederick of Württemberg and the margrave of Baden, both of whom were neighbors of the Hapsburg lands in the west of Germany, as well as certain great free cities, like Ulm, had come to feel that Protestant interests in Germany would hereafter have to be defended by force of arms. They proceeded to found a defensive alliance with the south German Calvinists. Later a number of German princes and free cities, such as Nürnberg and Strassburg, were added, until at the beginning of our period the Protestants faced the Catholics as one armed camp the other. For the Protestants too had decided to establish a common treasury, and to set up an armed force.

The Union was hampered from the beginning by the animosities between Lutherans and Calvinists. But under the stress of common danger, they accepted the Elector Palatine as their leader. Unhappily for them he was by no means so commanding a personality, nor were his physical resources so great as those of Maximilian of Bavaria. A further complication arose from the continued disinclination of the elector of Saxony to join the Union. With his lands bordering upon Bohemia, the elector found it to his advantage to adopt a policy of deference to imperial authority. Descendant of the calculating Maurice, through whose treachery Charles V had been enabled to triumph over the League of Schmalkalden (1547), the elector of Saxony and his council remembered that they owed the electoral dignity to playing the game of the emperor without regard to religion. Deeply attached to Lutheran views, to hunting and drinking, the Elector Christian II held aloof. As leader of the Protestants among the estates, he insisted that he must maintain the constitution. However unreal, however inadequate to cope with the existing difficulties, the constitution must nevertheless be upheld. Thus history repeats itself!

Once these hostile camps had been organized, so that the estates of the

Empire were getting ready for war, each allied with foreign powers, the League with Spain and the Union with France and England, the stage was set for a European conflagration. But it took ten more years until the spark was set to this tinderbox. Nor did the conflict originally break out between members of the two camps; both were drawn into a conflict between crown and estates, between Catholicism and Protestantism in Bohemia. It is necessary to look into these internal dissensions under Hapsburg rule.

VII. EMPEROR MATHIAS

In 1610, Rudolf II still ruled in Bohemia, as in the Empire. But his government was a shadowy specter of the emerging modern state. Indeed, the weakness of Rudolf had enabled the estates of Bohemia to secure concessions which seemed to belie the universal trend toward monarchical absolutism. These concessions set the stage for the bloody Bohemian civil war which in 1618 initiated the Thirty Years' War, once a more resolute ruler had ascended the throne. But before these things came to pass, extended efforts were made to redress the balance by peaceful means. These efforts filled the reign of Emperor Mathias, king of Bohemia since May, 1611. This younger brother had been pushing Rudolf successively out of his several positions, supported by the other archdukes who had, in 1606, entered into a formal agreement among themselves to co-operate in saving the house of Hapsburg from destruction. The leading spirit in these negotiations as well as later had been Bishop Melchior Klesl, the son of a Bavarian baker. At first animated by a strong ambition to further the Counter Reformation in Austria—he was bishop of Vienna—he eventually became the leading advocate of the policy of reconciliation. By the sheer logic of events which his calculating mind could not but accept, he was pushed along the path of shifting maneuvers on behalf of his master, Mathias. Klesl, though much criticized at the time, has on the whole been vindicated in his persistent efforts to avoid a clash. The more determined Catholics, however, to whom his policy of "composition" was hateful, caused his downfall and imprisonment shortly before the death of Mathias (1618). After the Pope rescued him in 1625, he lived in exile till shortly before his death (1637). But there can be little doubt that whatever Mathias achieved was largely to the credit of this commoner. The six years of his reign were the lull before the storm.

The internal politics of the several Hapsburg realms can only be sketched here. Amidst all the complex detail, two forces stood out in bold relief: the conservative Catholic policy of the house of Hapsburg and the progressive Protestant efforts of the several estates. There were of course quite a few Catholic members in the several estates' assemblies, but the Protestants dominated and continued to gain adherents, except where checked by the determined efforts of their prince. The system which the house of Hapsburg had developed in these parts was to farm out, so to speak, the several subdivisions of its far-flung possessions to younger sons, called archdukes. In some of these constituent parts, the power and privileges of the estates, usually composed of lords, knights, and burgesses, had become much more considerable than in others. Hungary and Bohemia certainly led the way. In the latter, the estates had secured the *Majestätsbrief,* or Letter of Majesty (Sovereignty) (July 9, 1609).[12] It was an agreement limiting sovereignty, and eliminating the rule, *"cujus regio, ejus religio,"* from Bohemia. For according to this agreement complete religious equality and freedom were to prevail; nobody, not even a simple peasant, was to be alienated from his church by either the civil authority or the clergy. Though the provisions were broadly drawn, they left plenty of openings for further controversy, as we shall see. Here as elsewhere it is difficult to say whether the religious conflict brought about the demand for political rights on behalf of the estates, or whether the surge toward popular participation enhanced the appeal of the new religion. Undoubtedly a close connection existed; yet the constitutional division of power between princes and estates had existed for a long time. Only when the new religion had appeared, did the problem of supremacy present itself.[13] Since the monarchical exponents of Catholicism were united in the house of Hapsburg, it was natural that the estates of their several realms should seek to combine to further their claims. Hence the estates of Bohemia, Silesia, Moravia, Hungary, Upper and Lower Austria formed a series of leagues which in turn sought to collaborate with the Protestant estates of the Empire, more particularly the Protestant Union. These negotiations, never quite conclusive, had a threatening portent. Through such an alliance, a civil war in Bohemia might spread to the whole decaying structure of the Empire.

The Empire's composite feudal constitution was clearly moribund. In

---

[12] It is traditional to speak of this Letter as "Letter of Majesty," but it is important to remember that *majestas* means "sovereignty."

[13] See above, Chapter One, for the theoretical issues.

1608 a group of Protestant estates, led by the representatives of the Elector Palatine, had broken up the imperial diet at Regensburg. In doing so, they gave vent to the profound disgust of the Protestants over the execution against the little free city of Donauwörth undertaken the previous year by Maximilian of Bavaria at the behest of the imperial chancellery. Under the imperial constitution, the country was divided into circles, each with its own representative assembly and executive officer (*Oberst*). In case one of the component units of the Empire, like the free city of Donauwörth in the Bavarian circle, refused to comply with the decisions of the imperial authorities, the executive officer might be called upon to "reduce" the recalcitrant member to obedience. But one of the great complaints of the Protestant party was that the imperial court council had, like the Star Chamber in England, taken unto itself the jurisdiction of the regular courts, more particularly the imperial court (*Reichskammergericht*). No agreement having been possible, the Elector Palatine and his allies had left the diet, and none had been held thereafter. Instead, as we have seen, Protestants and Catholics had organized themselves; the Union and the League faced each other like hostile camps.

But there were important estates outside the two groups. On the Protestant side, the elector of Saxony, leader of the Protestant estates in the diet and ardent orthodox Lutheran, continued to pursue his policy of loyalty to the Emperor, remembering also that the Hapsburgs were his close neighbors to the south. Moreover, the Hapsburgs themselves were entirely outside the League. Maximilian feared their dominance as well as their commitments abroad. This situation seemed to provide the entering wedge for a policy of reconciliation. Both League and Union contained members who would have liked to see a revival of the constitutional methods: the great free cities on the Protestant side and among the Catholics certain prelates, like the archbishop of Mainz. Consequently Mathias, at the instigation of Klesl, decided to call a diet once more, which met in Regensburg in 1613. Although the Imperial Proposals laid before the diet placed judicial reform ahead of everything, even aid against the Turk, nothing was achieved. No compromise proved possible between the warring factions.

As a result of the failure to reunite the estates of the Empire, Mathias was obliged to compromise in the east. Confronted by the concerted opposition of the estates in his own territories, he had to ascquiesce in the ascendancy of Bethlen Gabor who, after the murder of Prince Bathory, had made himself master of Transylvania, under Turkish protection.

Fierce, unscrupulous and astute, this adventurer showed little interest in the sultan's protection, as soon as he could secure recognition from Mathias (1615). But his equivocal position remained a liability for the future. Emboldened by success, he was bound to look abroad for conquests, and soon began to intrigue with the opposition in Hungary and Bohemia. Mathias' endeavors to limit the expansion of the estates' power by a strict interpretation of the existing agreements aroused the ire of the more radical Protestant elements and stimulated ever more far-reaching pretensions. Repeated diets in the several principalities, as well as a general diet at Prague (1615), served merely to make more evident the state of armed peace which prevailed in these territories.

The war clouds on the eastern frontier of the rickety Reich had a counterpart in dangerous developments in the western territories. In the Jülich-Cleves duchies things had taken a turn for the worse. The possessory princes, Brandenburg and Neuburg, had, after a half-hearted attempt at reconciliation, moved in opposite directions, both politically and religiously. Wolfgang Wilhelm of Neuburg, after returning to the Catholic faith, had married the sister of Duke Maximilian of Bavaria (1613). Thereafter he was supported in his claims not only by his brother-in-law and the League, but also by Spain and Archduke Albert in the Catholic Netherlands. Johann Sigismund of Brandenburg, on the other hand, had finally become a Calvinist, and hence was more vigorously aided by the United Netherlands and the Calvinist action party under Palatinian leadership in the Reich. As a consequence, a rather curious campaign took place in the summer of 1614. At first the Dutch and Brandenburgers seized the fortress of Jülich. Thereupon the Spaniards under Spinola proceeded against Aix-la-Chapelle and re-established the Catholic magistrates in that predominantly Protestant city. Spinola then turned and captured Wesel, important fortress on the Rhine, in the duchy of Cleves and very near the Dutch frontier. This was a severe blow to the Protestants and the Dutch, for Wesel had been a stronghold of Protestantism. Hence Maurice of Nassau marched into the duchies, occupying a number of fortified places, but not attacking Spinola, who, passing by Maurice, installed himself in Soest. The reason for this curious maneuvering was that a truce existed between Spain and the United Netherlands. Each could come to the aid of its allies in the duchies but could not fight with the allies of its allies! Stately proceedings without an issue, symbolizing the helpless impotence of the Holy Empire, these events intensified the stress.

Meanwhile decisive influence was exercised by the Dutch upon internecine strife elsewhere in northern Germany. In the county of Eastern Frisia, the count and the estates, more particularly the wealthy city of Emden, were engaged in the typical seventeenth-century struggle over control, embittered by religious conflict between the Lutheran count and the Calvinist city, which was often spoken of as the "Geneva of the North." When the situation became critical, the Dutch put a garrison into Emden and arbitrated the controversy contrary to the findings of the imperial authorities to whom the count had appealed. In this typical environment, Johannes Althusius elaborated his doctrines, first composed when he was councilor of the count of Nassau, a member of the radical Calvinist party among the imperial estates. But Emden was not the only city which the Dutch supported. The Hanse, though long past its zenith, still lingered on as a league of north German commercial towns. It had lately been engaged in an extended controversy on behalf of one of its members, the city of Brunswick, with the dukes of Brunswick-Wolfenbüttel. Again, the estates-general intervened by sending an army and when the duke backed down, the Dutch negotiated an agreement (December 31, 1615). This was followed by an alliance between the United Netherlands and the Hanse (1616). Formally, of course, the Dutch were still part of the Reich, but in fact they must be reckoned a foreign power. Their settlement of these disputes, where the imperial authority had failed, was striking evidence of the decomposition of political authority in the center of Europe.

Mathias, dawdling away his time with his sweet and pretty wife, enjoying the art treasures which his brother Rudolf had collected, and occasionally strutting forth in the glittering display of his imperial emblems of power, failed to make a lasting impression upon the world around him. Naturally indolent, impulsive but without persistence, he had neither the inclination nor the resources to transform the Empire or even his own territories into modern states. He lived between two worlds, neither of which he fully comprehended. The last two years of his reign were filled with the struggle over his succession, a story which must be told in connection with the outbreak of the civil war in Bohemia. But Mathias was a passive victim of forces over which he had no control. His cousin Ferdinand, profoundly opposed to any policy of compromise and conciliation, had chosen to side with the Catholic party long before he ascended the throne of Bohemia and was elected emperor. The middle course of Bishop Klesl died with his master, Mathias (1618).

VIII. DUTCH POLITICS

The truce which the Dutch had concluded with Spain in 1609 had provided them with an opportunity to consolidate the position they had won in the course of their struggle for independence. What were they going to do with their newly won freedom? That they played a decisive role in the various conflicts dividing the Empire we have already seen; under the skillful guidance of John of Oldenbarneveld [14] they had made themselves arbiters in the north. But while the new-born Republic thus gave an impression of imposing strength, internal dissensions presaged a stormy future. The government of the Dutch Netherlands was based upon a genuine federation of independent and sovereign provinces, each with its own estates and executive officer. Under the Union of Utrecht (1579), the constitutional charter of the Republic, deputies were sent from each of the component provincial estates to a national assembly. Among these Holland, by far the wealthiest and most populous, was dominant. Oldenbarneveld, as Advocate of Holland, headed the delegation from that province and, by the mere weight of Holland's position, came to direct the policy of the country. As Motley tells us, he took the lead in the deliberations both of the estates of Holland and the estates-general, moved resolutions, advocated important measures, saw to their execution, summed up the proceedings of the meetings, corresponded with and instructed ambassadors, and negotiated with foreign ministers, besides directing home policy and the rapidly growing colonial system of the Republic.

All this Oldenbarneveld had been doing for many years. There was, however, one very serious complication. Maurice of Nassau, who had succeeded his father, William the Silent, as governor (stadholder) of the several provinces, was looked upon abroad as the princely sovereign of the Republic. Indeed, so strong was the inclination of the age to seek a personal sovereign that the United Provinces had finally planned to confer the sovereignty upon William the Silent. He, like Washington, hesitated, and was murdered before the project materialized. As the father had been in doubt, the son hesitated to aspire to the monarchical distinction. Oldenbarneveld was even more dubious. He had persuaded Maurice's mother that for Maurice to seek the sovereignty might possibly spell ruin. The Dutch, having escaped from the royal absolutism of Spain, would be loath to commit themselves to a personal sovereign. All subsequent events

---

[14] J. H. Motley, in his magistral biography calls him John of Barneveld in the title but later in the text often uses the more familiar name.

suggest that Maurice resented this frankness. Being one of the leading military figures of the age, scion of a proud princely house, he evidently felt that Oldenbarneveld's opposition was inspired by personal rather than objective considerations. Maurice was realistic enough to appreciate that he could not pursue the plan without the Advocate's support, as long as the latter was in power.

Later, the advocate was apparently willing to put the proposal before the states-general as an amendment to the constitution, the Union of Utrecht (1573), but so doubtful was he of success that he requested Maurice to agree beforehand to Oldenbarneveld's resigning and leaving the country if the proposal failed.[15] That Maurice should not have taken him up on so lukewarm a proposal, cannot be wondered at.

In any case, Maurice was too noble a man to proceed on purely personal grounds. He had to convince himself that the advocate's policy was detrimental to the country. He opposed the conclusion of the truce which in several respects he did not approve. Spurred by personal animosities, other far-reaching disagreements soon developed between the two men concerning Dutch internal and external policy.

The death of Henry IV of France greatly weakened the foreign policy of Oldenbarneveld. Built as it was upon close collaboration with France, it became involved in the civil conflicts of that country. Francis Aerssens, the Dutch ambassador and a creature of Oldenbarneveld, had given brilliant service while Henry lived, because the king liked him. After Henry's death Aerssens, being suspicious of Villeroi and the queen on account of their Spanish and papal connections, commenced to intrigue with the Huguenot opposition, and thus eventually incurred the violent anger of the French court. He believed he had reasons for blaming Oldenbarneveld for this, some of his reports having come to the attention of the French through official Dutch channels. When his recall became unavoidable, he turned against the advocate. For some time he had acted as an intermediary between the French Protestant nobles and Maurice. Such contacts made the Huguenots look upon Maurice as their natural ally, if not their leader. It seemed, indeed, arguable whether collaboration with these rebellious aristocrats was not better policy at the time. In retrospect, there can be little doubt that the advocate's policy of collaborating with the official government in France as best he might was

---

15 *Verhooren van Oldenbarneveld* (1850), 169. This report, together with Hugo Grotius' *Verantwoording,* serves not only as the basic source for Oldenbarneveld's trial, but also for the history of the period.

the correct one in the long run. But we must not forget that at that time it was not yet decided whether France was to be an aristocracy, like England, or an absolute monarchy. Richelieu had not yet arisen.

France having become so uncertain an ally, Oldenbarneveld had to tread cautiously in his relations with Spain and the Spanish Netherlands. These were complicated by the conversion of one of the possessory princes in Jülich-Cleves, Wolfgang Wilhelm of Neuburg, to Catholicism (1613). As we have seen, Neuburg's claims were supported by Spain and the League against those of Brandenburg, with whom the Dutch were allied. Oldenbarneveld hesitated to act decisively when a Spanish army invaded the duchies and seized Wesel (1614). Since this important Rhenish fortress had been a stronghold of Protestantism right close to the Dutch border, its loss became a symbol of Oldenbarneveld's failure in foreign affairs, deeply resented by the Dutch masses.

But why did Oldenbarneveld not reorient his foreign policy toward England? He found it impossible to do so. One difficulty arose from James's interest in a Spanish marriage for his son. Incomprehensible as such an ambition appears in the light of later developments, for James it possessed an undeniable attraction. It seems that it would have meant to him a symbolic act, by which England's position as a great power would be attested. There were also personal vanities involved, especially the desire of James to be considered the equal of Elizabeth and Henry IV. Since the latter's children were being married to Spain, why not James'? This courting of Spain stood in the way of any frank and straightforward co-operation with the Dutch Republic and the Protestants. As such it was very unpopular with a majority of Englishmen.

Were the theological quarrels in which James engaged with Oldenbarneveld merely a cloak? The spirit of the age of which James is so picturesque a representative would make one doubt it. It seems incredible today, but James's ambassadors used to address long discourses on predestination to the estates-general of the United Netherlands. The occasion was extraordinary. Oldenbarneveld and many other wealthy merchants in Holland were inclined toward views which softened the pristine harshness of Calvin's doctrine. Following Jacobus Arminius (1550–1609), a professor at Leiden, they pleaded for a certain measure of free will. It was natural that Oldenbarneveld and his friends should, on the death of Arminius, want to call a man of his views to Leiden. Their choice of Conrad Vorstius (1569–1622) aroused the ire not only of orthodox Calvinists in Holland, led by Professor F. Gomarus of Leiden, but of James as well. The king of England, looking upon himself as the protector of the United Provinces, addressed the fiercest protests to the Dutch. His ambassador, Sir Ralph Winwood, had to hand the estates a long catalogue of the blasphemies and heresies of Vorstius. Winwood demanded that Vorstius' works "should be publicly burned in the open places of all the cities" for "the friendship of the King and heresy of Vorstius are quite incompatible." Vorstius had written on the nature of God, but without taking much heed of James' work on the same subject.

Some of the irritation of a vain academician animated James's diplomacy at the Hague. When he found that Oldenbarneveld was slow to do his bidding, he conceived a strong dislike for him. Such effect as it had was detrimental to Oldenbarneveld's diplomacy. Although Vorstius did not lecture at Leiden, he remained at the university, and the orthodox Calvinists accused Oldenbarneveld of shielding him. The conflict followed a typical pattern: The clergy denounced the government for not doing its duty in suppressing heresy; the government criticized the clergy for trying to use the government in the settlement of religious controversies and for seeking to erect a theocracy. On this score, Oldenbarneveld hoped that he might enlist James' sympathy; he frequently called the orthodox Gomarist party "Puritans." In 1613 Oldenbarneveld even succeeded in persuading King James to write a letter on five contested points concerning predestination, counseling moderation and toleration. But the king soon shifted his position. As Motley remarks, he might object to Puritans in England, but would favor them in Holland. In any case, he believed in the divine right of kings, and the Republic was a thorn in the side of monarchical absolutism. James had to admit his strong opposition to clerical pretensions to control the government; still he hesitated to accept the idea of outright government supremacy in ecclesiastical matters, later known as "Erastianism." Nor had James any need to do so, since he looked upon himself as the head of the church. Oldenbarneveld, less favorably placed, leaned in the direction of governmental supremacy.

IX. OLDENBARNEVELD AND MAURICE OF NASSAU

These conflicts assumed an ever-wider importance. The orthodox party demanded a national synod to settle the points at issue. Oldenbarneveld and his group opposed such a synod, insisting that each province had the right to settle such matters by its own sovereign estates, as unquestionably they had under Article 13 of the Union of Utrecht. The mass of the common people, particularly in the poorer agricultural provinces, were little concerned over constitutional niceties but followed the lead of their preachers in supporting a national synod. Even in Holland the powerful city of Amsterdam was on that side. Here anger over the advocate's opposition to the West India Company played an aggravating role. Insurrections occurred in a number of cities. Finding that the regular army under Maurice was unwilling to support the government of Holland on this issue, that province and Utrecht on the advice of Oldenbarneveld organized a mercenary troup, the *Waartgelders,* to insure order. By this time, Maurice had become the recognized leader of the Orthodox party seeking a national synod. Modern sympathy tends to be with Oldenbarneveld and his friends, who evidently stood for toleration and sanity. They also had the constitution on their side. But from a democratic standpoint, one's sympathies might well turn the other way. There can be little doubt that the majority of the provincial estates favored a synod, in fact, eventually voted for it. The formal provisions of the Union of Utrecht, especially Article 13, made the taking of such a vote very questionable; each province had been guaranteed religious autonomy. But when has a constitution ever withstood widespread popular discontent? Attempts to uphold it in the face of strong feelings have a way of dissolving into violence; the young Dutch Republic was no exception to the rule. Maurice, as stadholder, could claim emergency needs. Behind all the theological indignation hard economic rivalries also played a role.

As we have noted, the Amsterdam merchants resented the wealth and power of the East India Company; they were angry at Oldenbarneveld's refusal to permit them to organize a West India Company instead. The advocate was the key official of the East India Company; his friends, like Grotius, were closely associated with it. Foreign complications had resulted from the conduct of the company, for the Dutch East India Company was a competitor of the British East India Company, as well as of the Levant Company. Henry IV's desire to share in the rich returns from this trade by organizing a French East India Company had strained his relations with Oldenbarneveld considerably.

All this helped to feed the indignation of Amsterdam. Throughout Holland there were many men who felt cheated by the exclusive, monopolistic conduct of this company, but particularly in Amsterdam there were many merchants who wished to organize another company to compete with the East India Company. All these efforts Oldenbarneveld adamantly opposed. Maurice, who with all his military prowess was very

fond of money, sympathized with others who wished to see the East
India Company's hold on the country's government and diplomacy
broken. But so skillful was the hand of old John Oldenbarneveld, so
steady and experienced was his course, that only when the religious issue
and the national synod stirred the people to the point of wanting to see
him dislodged, did he fail. In such a body the rigid orthodoxy of the
clergy triumphed over all suggestions of toleration and decreed religious
uniformity.

It was in response to such general clamor, reinforced by his convictions,
that Maurice decided to act to "save the state." First he assured himself of
adequate popular support, then he disarmed and disbanded the *Waartgelders,* arbitrarily changed the magistrates in Utrecht and other key
cities, and finally arrested Oldenbarneveld, Grotius and two other leaders
(August, 1618). He could claim to have done this on orders of the states-
general but since, under the Union of Utrecht, these states-general were
not "sovereign," his and the states-general's actions must be viewed as a
"cold revolution"—in any case, a skillfully manipulated *coup d'État* by
which the constitution of the United Provinces was in fact changed from
a loose into a close union.[16]

The proceedings against Oldenbarneveld were carried out in the greatest
secrecy, and from a study of the record no modern student can escape the
feeling that the trial was little more than a pretentious façade for the
elimination of a political rival. Oldenbarneveld had unquestionably over-
played his hand. The charges against him, though very numerous and in
part contradictory, may be summed up under three heads: political,
religious and economic. He was charged with having opposed Maurice's
assumption of "sovereignty" and of having under the influence of bribes
pursued a policy friendly to Spain; with having fostered Arminianism
and opposed the calling of a national synod; and with having prevented
the establishment of the West India Company while favoring the East
India Company, to the detriment of the country and its international
relations. There was something to all these charges. As a moderate and a
promoter of the truce of 1609, Oldenbarneveld had tried to avoid open
conflict with Spain; the East India Company's plans, for example, of
doing business by plundering Spanish merchantmen, could not appeal to

---

[16] Motley's one-sided presentation was skillfully corrected and revised by two Dutch
scholars, Fruin and Groen van Prinsterer, who based their conclusions upon the then newly
published *Correspondance* of the house of Orange. See the illuminating, though very disorganized volume by Van Prinsterer, *Maurice et Barneveld* (1875).

him. It would lead us too far afield to sort out all the charges and replies. If his answers had been given in the form in which a parliamentary leader today replies to his critics, he probably would have been defeated, and that would have been the end.

It was inexperience with constitutional democratic government that led to these quasi-judicial proceedings—in fact a mockery—and that ended in the condemnation and beheading of the all-powerful advocate (May, 1619). In vain did the French ambassador, Du Maurier, plead before the assembly that the prisoners ought to be discharged, unless they could be convicted of treason. There had been no indictment, no testimony had been taken, no defense had been permitted; even paper was denied the aged statesman to write out his views. Motley was right in concluding "that there had been no trial whatever" [17] and the whole proceeding was as much a judicial murder as the "trial" of Charles I thirty years later. Little did the vain talker on the English throne suspect that the kind of proceedings he had encouraged by fanning theological fanaticism would bring his son to the block. But what both events demonstrated was the depth of religious passions in this, as in preceding generations, sweeping all before them. Not until they were spent had men who favored toleration an opportunity to prevail.

X. THE NETHERLANDS AND SPAIN

After the death of Oldenbarneveld, the Dutch drifted back into war with Spain. When the truce ran out in 1621, hostilities were resumed, but without clear-cut results. Whether the advocate could have kept the peace, it is difficult to say. That the desire to prevent him from doing it was part of the efforts to destroy him, seems clear enough. When, in 1625, Maurice passed away, the Dutch had become thoroughly embroiled in the great war that was being fought with increasing bitterness, as we shall show in the next chapter. As far as Spain was concerned, one thing is certain and that is that the truce, concluded in 1609, had been a hard thing for the pride of His Catholic Majesty to bear. But it was in a sense a statesman-like act of the corrupt and inefficient duke of Lerma, Philip III's favorite till near the death of this weak, well-meaning, bigoted king. Looking upon his position as one to exploit for personal enrichment and pleasure, Lerma seems yet to have had an appreciation of Spain's inherent weak-

---

[17] J. L. Motley, *The Life and Death of John of Barneveld* (1874), in 2 vols. II, 355. Motley's interesting and detailed account of the trial is marred by his partiality toward Barneveld.

ness. As long as the pro-Spanish policy of Marie de' Medici [18] was carried on, Spain was relatively secure in the far-flung possessions she had amassed during the great days of her conquistadors, admirals and generals. Such fighting as Spain carried on during this period was intermittent and primarily done underhandedly in Italy. There one of her most overbearing and ruthless viceroys, the duke of Osuna, had engaged in warlike actions against Venice, while ruling first Sicily and then Naples. It seems that the king and his minister pretended not to know about these undertakings, which eventually culminated in an extraordinary event the nature of which has remained controversial to this day. According to Venice, the Spaniards sought to overthrow the sovereignty and subject the Republic to Spanish rule. The suspicion of some historians that this Venetian claim was a cover-up for an actual move for concerted action by Venice and the duke of Osuna to enable the latter to make himself independent seems doubtful. But it is highly characteristic of the corruption of Spanish rule that such accusations were sufficiently plausible to be made the basis for a trial of the duke after Lerma had fallen (1621).

The real disaster of Spain was the inability of her government to master the economic problems she faced and to utilize her vast overseas possessions for the buttressing of her domestic productive resources. A rather poor country at best, vast fiscal levies of all sorts strangled her foreign trade and ruined her peasantry.

XI. THE PURITANS

On May 26, 1612, the city of Emden concluded a contract or agreement with the "English Society which call themselves Puritans." Concluded on the morrow of Cecil's death, it provided for aid to these orthodox Calvinists, hard-pressed by James' hostile policy and preparing themselves for all-out opposition. The fact is worth mentioning because it highlights the religious preoccupation of the Puritans, who were as ready as any to go beyond national boundaries when their faith required it, although this is sometimes forgotten in the light of the strong patriotic flavor of many of their arguments against the Stuarts as stressed by the historians of a later, national-minded age.

James had from the outset been hostile to the Puritan position. Like Elizabeth, he was troubled by their inclination to put ecclesiastical above

---

[18] See below, pp. 286-8.

secular authority. While he shared their abomination for the heresies of
Vorstius, whom he had tried to prevent from joining the faculty at Leiden
by vigorous diplomatic protests, still the potential Erastianism of the
Arminians was objectionable to James for a different reason: his belief
in the episcopal majesty of kings and the divine right and grace with
which he considered them endowed.[19] The king, so he held, was God's
representative on earth, with heavy responsibilities, for which, however,
he was responsible to God alone. His powers included the complete
disposal over goods, persons and their doctrinal views; neither ecclesiastical
nor temporal boundaries limited it.[20] Against this the Puritans and Presbyterians had set the view that "Christ Jesus is the King of the Church
whose subject King James is, and of whose kingdom he is not a king,
nor a lord, nor a head, but a member." [21]

We have seen already how James challenged the parliamentary tradition by his divine right doctrine; it was of tremendous historic significance
that this parliamentary tradition, intrinsically no more weighty than
similar traditions elsewhere, gradually merged after 1610 with the political
outlook of the Puritans' religious faith. As if this dual ideological mixture were not explosive enough, James reinforced it with economic self-
interest by creating the grievance of the ship money; out of such a con-
vergence of religious, legal and economic frustrations the revolutionary
cramp arose.[22] But in this particular age, the age of power through faith
and of faith through power, the religious ingredient was probably the
most important; certainly those who were strong in the Puritan faith
took the lead in resistance to the royal pretensions.

Throughout Europe the Calvinists were the activists in the Protestant
camp, as we have seen. But the broader Calvinist fraternity looked upon
the Puritans as a regional "society," a special grouping with a distinctive
outlook. Perry Miller has perhaps probed most deeply into the Puritan
mind; he has given a sketch of its predominant features. Basically religious, it was moral and esthetic into the bargain. A revulsion of refined
sentiment against the grossness and license of "merry old England" was

---

[19] Charles H. McIlwain, *The Political Works of James I* (1918), Introduction, pp. xvi ff.
McIlwain rightly puts in the forefront James' remark that "Jesuits are nothing but Puritan-
Papists." Reversely, one might call the Puritans "Jesuits without a pope." See also John N.
Figgis, *The Divine Right of Kings, passim* and above, pp. 103–4.

[20] *Ibid.*, p. xxxiv.

[21] Figgis, *op. cit.*, second edition, 286.

[22] We owe some striking insights into the prerevolutionary tensions and strains of a disturbed society to George S. Pettee, *The Process of Revolution* (1938).

a powerful motif which the harsh bigotry of the Puritans in power has tended to obscure. The great cultural gains it secured have been all but obliterated by the easygoing civilized liberalism of the nineteenth century.

During the reign of James, the differentiation of viewpoints which developed in the course of the civil war did not as yet divide the many different varieties of Calvinists who all desired to purify Christian life and achieve that sanctification in this world which inspired young men like Milton, then a student at Cambridge. To be sure, the more radical Congregationalist groups encountered sharp hostility even on the part of the suppressed Presbyterian Puritans. There was inherent in the very approach of the Puritan a tendency toward increasing radicalization; purity is a matter of degree and its achievement a perfectionist ideal. Since Luther's doctrine of faith and grace had stressed the importance of direct communication between each soul and its Lord and Creator, an anarchic mysticism lay embedded in its teachings. Luther and Calvin both and each in his characteristic way had sought to keep these radical forces under control. Luther had stressed the need for submission to secular authorities in all outward actions; Calvin had developed the insistence upon rigid discipline in all personal conduct as enforced by the religious community through its elders. The Puritans, in line with the latter approach while the government of James favored the former, felt strongly that the work of faith could only work its miracles if ecclesiastical organization were reduced to a minimum, rituals and ceremonials were eliminated, and "the Word" of Holy Script were substituted for all traditional interpretations. But a deep conflict rent the Puritan's feelings. "A Song of the Puritan" at the beginning of our period mockingly said:

> Pure in show, an upright holy man,
> Corrupt within—and called a Puritan.

The dangers inherent in all self-righteousness are familiar enough in the moral field. How they project themselves into politics was aptly put by Macaulay in his essay on Milton (1825):

The Puritan was made up of two different men, the one all self-abasement, penitence, gratitude, passion, the other proud, calm, inflexible, sagacious. He prostrated himself in the dust before his Maker; but he set his foot on the neck of the king.

The trouble was that he really set his foot on anyone who disagreed, as men like Lilburne were to discover.

The gradual merging of Puritan and parliamentary sentiment led to a number of parliamentary moves in favor of Puritanism, more especially for restricting the presumed jurisdiction of the High Commission,[23] which had been authorizd under Elizabeth. That the bishops or "prelates," as the Puritans liked to call them, should thereupon incline to support the royal prerogative did not contribute to their popularity nor make it easier to maintain their ecclesiastical authority. As Milton remarked of the prelates in his *Of Reformation in England* (1641): "Though they had renounced the popism, they hugged the popedom, and shared the authority amongst themselves." This was in Henry VIII's reign. Yet, after surveying the role of episcopacy through the succeeding reigns, he concluded:

That in England episcopacy is not only not agreeable but tends toward the destruction of the monarchy, that the mortallest diseases and convulsions of the government ever did proceed from the craft of prelates. . . . Let us not be so overcredulous, unless God hath blinded us, as to trust our dear souls into the hands of men that beg so devoutly for the pride and gluttony of their own backs and bellies, that sue and solicit so eagerly, not for the saving of souls . . . but for their bishoprics, deaneries, prebends and canonries: how can these men not be corrupt?

By such passionate sentiments was the Puritanical spirit animated. It was a sentiment, and "purification" was its inner core. While there were many different strains, some dogmatic, some truly tolerant, some desiring restraint on bishops, others their abolition in favor of presbyteries, still others straight congregationalist, they all shared a strong dislike for Catholicism.

XII. THE PILGRIM FATHERS

In the history of overseas European colonies, the relatively small and unpromising settlements of North America have come to occupy a unique place, due to the astounding later development of the United States. In the short space of three hundred years these seemingly insignificant groups of Puritan settlers have grown into the mightiest nation on earth. It is natural that so startling a series of events should have led to poetical embellishment of the early beginnings. Thus the Pilgrim Fathers who

---

[23] Petition of the House of Commons, July 7, 1610; see Prothero, *op. cit.*, 302 ff.

set out on the *Mayflower* in 1620 to found a genuinely saintly common-wealth of true believers have come to be looked upon as the little acorn from which grew the mighty oak which today overshadows the globe. The small community of faithful had followed their godly pastor, John Robinson, to Holland to escape the persecution to which Puritans were exposed in England if they refused to submit to the established church and to participate in its ritual. They found themselves troubled by the alien setting. Perhaps the vehemence of the theological controversies also disturbed them. At any rate, they decided to depart for a more secluded spot in which to build their community. They first tried to go to a Dutch colony, but failing to get the necessary support, they accepted help proffered them by a group of Englishmen. It seems that their original destination was the Chesapeake Bay, but storms and the advanced season made them land at Plymouth, where fourteen years earlier a chartered company had tried to start a settlement, similar to the one which had been established in Virginia. It is a touching picture, these pious and poor people, setting forth on the tiny vessel, landing in the wilderness and struggling to survive—a picture painted with charm and poetry by their leader, William Bradford.[24]

Being thus passed the vast ocean . . . they had now no friends to wellcome them, nor inns to entertaine or refresh their weatherbeaten bodys, nor houses or much less townes to repaire too, to seeke for succoure. . . . And for the season it was winter. . . . For summer being done, all things stand upon them with a weatherbeaten face; and the whole countrie, full of woods and thickets, represented a wild and savage view. If they looked behind them, there was the mighty ocean which they had passed, and was now as a maine barr and goulfe to separate them from all the civill parts of the world. . . . What could now sustaine them but the spirite of God and his grace? [25]

What could sustain them but the spirit of God and his grace, indeed? And what held true of the little colony of ardent spirits whom Bradford governed until 1650, applied with equal though less generally recognized force to the many other settlers up and down the Atlantic Coast. Plymouth Colony was soon to be merged with Massachusetts Bay, where

---

[24] See Kenneth B. Murdock, *Literature and Theology in Colonial New England* (1949), 78–84.

[25] William Bradford, *History of Plymouth Plantation*, ed. by W. C. Ford (1912), as cited by Murdock, Ch. I, 83.

the statesman-like John Winthrop was governor most of his life during the early years of the Massachusetts Bay Colony. New Hampshire and Maine, Connecticut and Rhode Island were each to come into their own, Rhode Island owing its distinctive origin to the determination of Anne Hutchinson, reinforced by the saintly perseverance of Roger Williams, who would not submit to the bigotry of the clergy in Puritan Massachusetts. All these settlements had their first great expansion between 1630 and 1640, but encountered substantial difficulties during the civil war and Protectorate. Though their natural sympathy lay with the Commonwealthmen, the sharp conflict in the homeland could not help but throw its shadow over the new and unstable communities in the wilderness.[26] When, in 1660, the king returned, new charters were sought and obtained by Rhode Island and Connecticut.

The pride of these godly Puritans in their work has tended to obscure the rapid strides which were made in the same period, by the Dutch and Swedish colonies on the Hudson and Delaware, in the Chesapeake Bay region, in Virginia and Maryland. Indeed, Virginia had been developing ever since 1606, but upon a slightly different pattern, more nearly akin to the usual colonial enterprises of the period. A royal chartered company, the London Company, had been developing the land, making grants of varying size on the basis of contributions and performance. The very different climate and resulting agriculture soon brought the cultivation of tobacco into prosperity, and as a consequence the plantation of a thousand acres (and often many more) soon became predominant. Indentured servants and tenant farmers were brought over to work the ever-larger estates, and the government of the "Old Dominion" thereupon took an aristocratic turn.

In all these company-promoted colonies the royal charter provided, as it had in such charters since time immemorial, for the effective participation of those who held property under them. Whether the governor was appointed by the company or the king, he was bound to work with and through a council, as well as listen to some kind of assembly representing those who held shares. In Massachusetts, the actual management removed to America, so the charter could readily be transformed into a constitution of a sort. Elsewhere, analogous developments took place. While it would be a great mistake to assume that the leaders of these colonial settlements were democrats by conviction, the nature of frontier life soon brought about a co-operative pattern of government. This was especially true in the townships of New England, where the ancient English parish organization was re-created for broader purposes of local administration. It has often been claimed that the very fact of a charter limiting the exercise of authority started Americans on the road to an appreciation of limited constitutional government. No doubt the charters helped to solidify such thoughts. But they were in fact a common heritage of Europe in this period, as we have shown elsewhere. The competitive struggle for predominance which brought absolutism into being on the continent, as it threatened to do for a period in England, did not concern the colonists, although at times it touched them, as in the conflicts with Canada. So the older tradition could be preserved and brought to a new fruition. As popular government had had a first flowering in the free cities of the later Middle Ages, so it now struck a new root in North America. Unnoticed by the powerful of the baroque age, remote from the inspiration of that age and its style, the Puritan settlers and their fellow pioneers, whether Lutheran or Catholic, laid the foundation for a civilization which was eventually to challenge the modern national state with its sovereignty and its bureaucratic and military imperialism.

XIII. COLONIAL RIVALRY

The first half of the seventeenth century was the great age of colonizing activity. During the second half of the sixteenth, English, Dutch, and French sailors had commenced to defy the original Spanish and Portuguese supremacy. Now as Spain declined—and this decline was itself related to the colonial rivalry—the new powers themselves engaged in colonizing on a large scale. The West Indies, West Africa, North America, India and the Malay were the areas of keenest competition. These colonies provided challenging opportunities for the overflowing vitality of the European nations, and a ready escape for some of the more unruly elements. Cromwell's comment,[27] that he would have gone to America if the parliament had not sustained a motion he favored, is characteristic for this aspect of the matter. We have shown in an earlier chapter how the development of colonial resources aided the development of the modern state;[28] it remains to indicate here briefly the story

27 See below, p. 294.
28 See above, Chapter One, pp. 7–9.

of the colonial exploits of the three key nations, England, France and the Netherlands (Holland).

Until about 1650, the Dutch were by far the most aggressive of the colonial competitors of Spain. Since they were at war until 1648, except for the brief period during the truce of 1609, they could act with great vigor and they took full advantage of their opportunity. They seized islands in the West Indies, such as Curaçao (1634); they occupied a large part of Brazil (1624–54) and Guiana; they settled the Hudson Valley and founded New Amsterdam (New York) in 1614. This area as far south as Philadelphia had, by 1624, become New Netherland. In the eastern direction, the Dutch established themselves on the Cape of Good Hope (1651), occupied the larger part of Ceylon, and set up a number of establishments on the mainland of India (1616 and later). By 1619 they had taken firm hold of Batavia and thus secured one of their lasting colonial possessions. Their interest in the Malay Archipelago was in fact the focal point of Dutch colonizing efforts. After expelling the Portuguese, they became virtual masters of the entire area of the Spice Islands, securing from them an enormously profitable trade. From the Malays the Dutch extended their trade to China and Japan; in 1642 they came into possession of Formosa. Ranging the seas, the Dutch discovered New Zealand and Australia, but their resources were insufficient to settle these large dominions. But in Japan they virtually monopolized trade, after the suppression of the Christians and the expulsion of all foreigners, even though under humiliating conditions (1641). Clearly, the primary interest of the Dutch in establishing colonies was trade, rather than the settlement of Dutch people.

The English, on the contrary, settled overseas in large numbers. This emigration was due, as we have noted, to the oppressive religious policy of the Stuarts; once commenced, it continued until the crowding of the limited island resources provided persistent economic incentives instead of religious and political ones. We have sketched the Puritan settlement of New England. South of the New Netherlands another important area was developed, starting from Maryland and Virginia (1587, 1607, 1634). The English also established themselves firmly in the Caribbean, in the Barbados (1624), in the Leeward Islands (1625), in Surinam (1640), and in Honduras (1638) they built plantations of lasting success. In Africa they seized parts of the Gold Coast (1618) and Gambia. In Asia the English, after the massacre of Amboina (1623), focused their attention upon the mainland of India. The Mogul emperor allowed them a settlement at Surat (1616), and in 1622 they wrested Ormuz from the Portuguese. Fort St. George on the east coast was established in 1639, after protracted fighting with the Dutch.

The French became active only after the rise of Richelieu had consolidated their kingdom. In 1636 they acquired Martinique and Guadeloupe; earlier they had made their possession of part of Guiana secure. The colonial settlements in Canada, which Samuel de Champlain had started in 1605 (Port Royal) and 1609 (Quebec), were made more permanent by the Company of the Hundred Associates, founded by Richelieu to colonize New France after 1634. Montreal was founded in 1642. As compared with these undertakings, the efforts of Danes and Swedes (Delaware, 1639), Austria and Brandenburg were of little consequence and no lasting effect. Preoccupied with the great wars raging in central and eastern Europe throughout this period, there was little excess energy left for colonial rivalry with the great maritime nations.

Looking back upon this period of colonial expansion, it is not difficult to perceive that the spreading of the Gospel, the lure of gold and silver, strategic considerations, the need for outlets for surplus population, the search for sources of raw materials and markets, the effort to increase governmental revenue and naval training, together with the psychology of adventure and escape, all played their roles, in fact and in propaganda.[29] The lust for power, the basic motif of the baroque age, was involved in all of them. But not only the lust *for,* but even more perhaps the reveling *in* the gorgeous feeling *of,* power were most wonderfully at work in this field. If one confronts the slave trader and the Puritan, the "get-rich-quick" speculator and the Quaker mystic and pacifist as they sailed the seven seas and expanded Europe until it circled the globe, one beholds once more the basic polarities of the baroque. Both the search for inward and outward power propelled the colonial expansion of Europe between the beginning of the century and 1660 more definitely than ever before or since.

It seems a fitting conclusion to this story of England's heroic age to quote its poet, John Milton, in one of his moving passages written at the time the great revolution of spirits was at its height:

[29] See the penetrating study by Klaus E. Knorr, *British Colonial Theories—1570–1850,* Introduction and Ch. I. Though concentrating upon Britain, Knorr's findings apply, *ceteris paribus,* to the other nations as well, before 1650, because England was then much more like them than since that time.

Methinks I see in my mind a noble and puissant nation rousing herself like a strong man after sleep, and shaking her invincible locks: methinks I see her as an eagle mewing her mighty youth, and kindling her undazzled eyes at the full midday beam.

Chapter Six

THE THIRTY YEARS' WAR AND THE LIQUIDATION OF THE MEDIEVAL EMPIRE

I. INTRODUCTION: WAR OF RELIGION

IT HAS been the fashion to minimize the religious aspect of the great wars which raged in the heart of Europe, over the territory of the Holy Roman Empire of the German Nation. Not only the calculating statecraft of Richelieu and Mazarin, but even Pope Urban VIII's own insistence lent support to such a view in a later age which had come to look upon religion and politics as fairly well separated fields of thought and action. Liberal historians found it difficult to perceive that for baroque man religion and politics were cut from the same cloth, indeed that the most intensely political issues were precisely the religious ones. Gone was the neopaganism of the renaissance, with its preoccupation with self-fulfillment here and now. Once again, and for the last time, life was seen as meaningful in religious, even theological, terms, and the greater insight into power which the renaissance had brought served merely to deepen the political passion brought to the struggle over religious faiths.

Without a full appreciation of the impossibility of separating secular and religious issues, it becomes impossible to comprehend the Thirty Years' War. Frederick, the unlucky Palatine, as well as Ferdinand, Tilly and Gustavus Adolphus, Maximilian of Bavaria and John George of Saxony, they all must be considered fools unless their religious motivation is understood as the quintessential core of their politics. Time and again, they appear to have done the "wrong thing," if their actions are viewed in a strictly secular perspective. To be sure, men became increasingly sophisticated as the war dragged on; but even after peace was finally concluded in 1648, the religious controversies continued. Ever since the Diet of Augsburg (1555) had proclaimed the startling doctrine that a man must confess the religion of those who had authority over the territory he lived in, *"cujus regio, ejus religio,"* the intimate tie of religion and government had been the basis of the Holy Empire's tenuous peace. Born of the spirit of its time—Lutheran otherworldliness combining with Humanist indifferentism—this doctrine was no more than an unstable compromise between Catholics and Lutherans, the Calvinists being entirely outside its protective sphere. But in the seventeenth century not only the Calvinists, who by 1618 had become the fighting protagonists of Protestantism, but likewise the more ardent Catholics, inspired by the Council of Trent, by the Jesuits and Capuchins, backed by the power of Spain and filled with the ardor of the Counter Reformation, had come to look upon this doctrine as wicked and contrary to their deepest convictions.

When Ferdinand, after claiming the crown of Bohemia by heredity, proceeded to push the work of counter reformation, his strongest motivation was religious; so was the resistance offered by the Bohemian people, as well as Frederick's acceptance of the crown of Bohemia on the basis of an election. Dynastic and national sentiments played their part, surely, but they reinforced the basic religious urge. The same concurrence of religious with dynastic, political, even economic motives persisted throughout the protracted struggle, but the religious did not cease to be the all-pervasive feeling; baroque man, far from being bothered by the contradictions, experienced these polarities as inescapable.

If religion played a vital role in persuading Ferdinand II to dismiss his victorious general, it was even more decisive in inspiring Gustavus Adolphus to enter the war against both the emperor and the League. The nineteenth century, incapable of feeling the religious passions which stirred baroque humanity and much impressed with the solidified national states which the seventeenth century bequeathed to posterity, was prone to magnify the dynastic and often Machiavellian policies adopted by rulers who professed to be deeply religious, and the twentieth century has largely followed suit in denying the religious character of these wars. But it is precisely this capacity to regard the statesman as the champion of religion, to live and act the drama of man's dual dependence upon faith and power that constituted the quintessence of the baroque. The Jesuits, sponsors of the baroque style in architecture all over central and southern Europe, advised Catholic rulers, but more especially Ferdinand II, concerning their dual duties. The somber and passionate driving force behind so much unscrupulousness was religious pathos in all its depth. What the Catholics did, elicited a corresponding pattern of thought and action in the Protestant world: Maurice of Nassau and James I, Gustavus Adolphus and Cromwell, as well as many minor figures of the European theater, conceived of themselves as guardians of the "secrets of rule," the *arcana imperii,* to be employed for the greater glory of God and the Christian religion.

II. ESTATES VERSUS KING: THE BOHEMIAN WAR

Ever since the Golden Bull of 1356 had been issued by Charles IV, King of Bohemia and Holy Roman Emperor, Bohemia had remained a vital part of the Empire, together with the adjoining territories of Silesia, Lusatia, and Moravia. In a sense, Bohemia had been during the two and one half centuries which had elapsed by 1617 the richest of the Hapsburg possessions north of the Alps and Pyrenees. The Letter of Majesty of 1609 has already been mentioned as testimony to the relative freedom of the Bohemian people, both Czech- and German-speaking elements, especially in matters of religion. Yet, in spite of the predominantly Protestant sentiment, the Hapsburg rulers, Rudolf and Mathias, who both preferred Prague to any other capital, had favored Catholics for the chief offices of state, and the more ardent elements in the Catholic group were anxious to press for further advance against the Protestant position. Incidents had occurred where, as at Braunau, a Catholic prelate had on a questionable pretext seized a Protestant church and attempted to compel Protestants to attend Catholic services.

Under these circumstances it was not surprising that the Protestant leaders should cast about for a candidate of their own religious persuasion to be elected to the Bohemian throne. To be sure, the Hapsburgs held that their right to the Bohemian crown had become hereditary, but the estates held this view to be incorrect. Unfortunately for them, the Protestants were divided among themselves, the usual antagonism between Lutheran and Calvinist being further complicated by the native tradition of Hussite sentiment and of the more militant Bohemian Brethren. In any case, while the Lutheran group was inclined toward the elector of Saxony, whose lands bordered on Bohemia to the north, the Calvinists and Hussite factions definitely preferred the Elector Palatine, whose Upper Palatinate bordered Bohemia in the west, while the Hapsburg dominions lay, of course, to the south.

The situation was aggravated by the fact that the Hapsburgs had settled upon Ferdinand of Styria as the most appropriate successor to Mathias. Ferdinand, chosen because he had children, had a record of rather ardent Catholic sympathies. A pupil of the Jesuits, he had made every effort to restore Catholicism in Styria, while at the same time reducing the position of the estates to the minimum. Such a man was likely to be more unwelcome in Bohemia than either Rudolf or Mathias. But when Emperor Mathias precipitated the issue, on June 17, 1617, the large majority of Protestants, under weak and divided leadership, timidly voted for Ferdinand. They then insisted upon Ferdinand's guaranteeing the Letter of Majesty, which he did, not because he intended to keep it, but for "reasons of state." Thus the stage was set for a violent clash between estates and king. There was, however, a threefold division of outlook among those of the estates who were not Catholics and followers of the Hapsburgs: some were preoccupied with the constitutional position of the estates, for whom they desired an equal share in the government; others would subordinate all to the securing of religious liberty and freedom of conscience; a third group were Hussite nationalists seeking to free themselves of foreign domination. If the more ardent Catholics had not precipitated a conflict by a number of incidents, Ferdinand's election would probably have remained unchallenged.

Ferdinand in the meanwhile, after having secured the Bohemian kingdom and having arrested the compromising Klesl, successfully contended for the imperial election. Ever since the promulgation of the Golden Bull, elections had been restricted to the seven electoral princes: the archbishops of Cologne, Trier and Mainz, the king of Bohemia, the Elector Palatine, the duke of Saxony, and the margrave of Brandenburg. These seven were divided four to three as between Catholics and Protestants, but the latter were again divided between Calvinists and Lutherans. the latter being represented only by Saxony, after the Brandenburger had become Calvinist in 1614. For a while the Protestants had favored Maximilian of Bavaria, but in spite of his rivalry with Hapsburg, he did not covet the imperial office. It was typical of the oblique complexity of the situation that the Protestants could not agree on a candidate, but even if they had, they could not have elected him, once Ferdinand was king of Bohemia. So the inevitable happened, and in spite of everything that had been said and done in the long-drawn-out negotiations, Ferdinand was unanimously elected Holy Roman Emperor on August 28, 1619. Several days before, on August 19, the confederated estates of Bohemia, Silesia, Moravia and Lusatia had deposed Ferdinand and declared him no longer their king.

The events which led up to this dramatic culmination were essentially three. There were the religious incidents already alluded to, which provided the background; there were arbitrary acts of the government infringing the Letter of Majesty by unilateral action, such as the arrest of Protestants resisting the bishop's attempt to seize their church at Braunau; and there were finally the several moves by which the estates countered the royal actions, more especially the celebrated defenestration or *Fenstersturz*. Throwing imperial councilors out of a window, even though they lived to tell the tale, constituted open defiance and revolution, and it was so interpreted by all, by the immediate participants, by the Bohemian people and by Europe at large. In this age of rising monarchical power and authority, such a challenge to royal authority made even those hesitate who did not subscribe to the divine right of kings. To rulers like James I the whole proceedings were repulsive. His ill-considered marriage projects with the Spanish Hapsburgs reinforced his negative attitude.

The Bohemian revolutionaries, despite general lack of encouragement, proceeded to set up a provisional government, or directorate. Count Henry Mathew of Thurn, the spirited but conceited leader of the radical elements, became the commander-in-chief of the Bohemian forces. Ernest Mansfeld, captain of mercenary troops, illegitimate scion of a princely house, and self-made count, had been transferred to the service of the Bohemians by Charles Emmanuel of Savoy on the promptings of Christian of Anhalt. The latter may, in many ways, be considered the directing genius of the revolutionary movement. An ardent Calvinist and a somewhat unprincipled practitioner of "reason of state," Anhalt was the key councilor of the young Elector Palatine, Frederick. This prince, a charming, decent, but weak and unmilitary man, had won the hand of James I's daughter Elizabeth in 1613, and upon this fact alone many unsound hopes were built. In any case, the youth and inexperience of the Elector Palatine would have handicapped him in dealing with so dynamic a personality as Anhalt. Unfortunately, Anhalt was more persuasive than sound, and much inclined to build elaborate projects on speculative assumptions rather than on known facts. The European scope of his negotiations shows a man of exceptional political imagination and bold daring; projects like the exclusion of the Hapsburgs from the imperial office and the acquisition of the Bohemian crown for his prince excite the imagination. But Anhalt underestimated the inertia, envy and mutual jealousy of most men, and overestimated their attachment to ideal causes, more especially the cause of Protestantism. Hence the Palatine party, despite the devotion of their immediate adherents, failed recurrently at the decisive moment: the battles which are the pay-off for realistic preparation, they lost both in the political arena and in war.

Anhalt's earlier project of having Frederick elected king of Bohemia, instead of Mathias, while constitutional, had proved abortive. To a more penetrating statesman this defeat would have served as a warning and a revelation of the inner weakness of the Bohemian nobility. But Anhalt chose to revive his project when the revolutionary estates were casting about for a new king. Of the four princes whose realms abutted on Bohemia, they would have liked the elector of Saxony, John George, best; but he was too cautious a legitimist and constitutionalist to enter upon such a career. So Frederick was elected, and after some hesitation accepted. There is little doubt that a sense of religious obligation played an important part in the decision, as did a sense of pride in the face of his handsome and truly regal wife, who had some years earlier been given to understand that she was marrying a future king.

If Frederick had been tough, if he had taken the gamble for what it was worth and had demanded that the electing estates make sure of the kingdom which they were offering, while he himself secured the defenses of the Palatinate through adequate support from the Netherlands, England and the Scandinavians, he might possibly have succeeded in staking out a claim of lasting value. Instead he went to Prague as if the kingdom were secure, only to find himself unsupported by the estates in the vital matter of ways and means for the maintenance of an army able to defend the kingdom against the combined forces of the Hapsburgs and the League. For the League of Catholic princes, ably led by Maximilian I of Bavaria, had the dual interest of monarchical legitimacy and the extension of Catholic Christianity to unite them against the Bohemian revolutionaries. In Maximilian's case, this interest was reinforced by the desire to capture the electoral dignity, promised by Ferdinand, as well as large parts of the Palatinate, especially the Upper Palatinate, between Nürnberg and Ratisbon.

In a sense the debacle at the election of Ferdinand II as emperor in 1619 foreshadowed the catastrophe of the Bohemian war. This catastrophe was decisive in the sense that it alarmed all Europe and thus set the stage for the long sanguinary struggle which was to follow, yet the Bohemian campaign itself was quite short. After some indecisive operations in 1618 and 1619, the actual declaration of war—the imperial demand to Frederick to leave Bohemia by June 1, 1620—was followed by one Protestant setback after another. King Frederick was even unable to settle the issue of the command as between Count Thurn and Prince Anhalt. His troops were disorderly, ill-equipped, ill-paid and lacking in morale as a result. Unlike the League, the Union of Protestant princes remained inactive, paralyzed by constitutional scruples and by the animosity between Lutherans and Calvinists. The latter was obvious, but the modern student tends to forget that the ancient constitution of the Empire was a factor of real concern to many of the German princes. Maximilian had been constitutionally invested with the imperial authority to quell a rebellion; what was asked of princes like the elector of Saxony was to come to the aid of revolutionaries. They either did not act at all, or moved so slowly and assisted so weakly that it was truly "too little and too late."

Consequently, the battle of the White Mountain (November 8, 1620) lasted for only about an hour and ended in a complete rout of the Bohemian forces. It was not an interesting battle in a military sense for it was a battle of surprise. It is interesting, however, that the victorious leaders were sharply disagreed on whether to risk it; it was Maximilian, the civilian, who correctly assessed the opponents' inner weakness and who insisted that a battle be attempted. The impending winter with its inevitable losses from epidemic disease, and the approaching reinforcements of the Transylvanian, Bethlen Gabor, also were factors in the shrewd prince's calculations. Bethlen Gabor had right along played a rather erratic role in supporting the Bohemian Calvinists. Himself an ardent Calvinist, Bethlen Gabor was yet primarily an adventurer, both political and military. Wedged in between the Hapsburgs and the Turks, he had to play a wily diplomatic and military game, shifting sides as the situation commanded. Faced with the Bohemian collapse, he withdrew after the battle of the White Mountain had been lost.

Frederick, when apprised of the rout of his forces, decided to abandon Prague and retreat. His attempts to rally Lusatia or Silesia having failed, he was destined to play the sorry role of the luckless pretender so familiar in our own days. Certainly his precipitate flight, in which military and civilian leaders joined him, made all further resistance hopeless. Bohemian patriots in modern times, lamenting the failure of Frederick to fight for his crown, have been inclined to forget that the inner weakness of the revolutionaries was itself the basic cause of the collapse. Perhaps, had they known what fate was in store for them, Frederick and his Bohemian subjects would have rallied. But the ruthless determination of the restorers of the faith, who had gone into battle with the cry, "For the Virgin Mary!" was only to become manifest in the sequel to the Bohemian surrender.

In the wake of their victories, the Catholics, with full imperial backing and authority, instituted a thorough liquidation of their enemies. In Bohemia three successive commissions, that of execution (1621), of confiscation (1622–23) and a follow-up *commissio transactionis* (1629–30) first meted out to the revolutionaries severe penalties of death, prison and expropriation, then continued the confiscations of their property on a vast scale. It is believed that perhaps half of all landed possessions in Bohemia changed hands, so that certain skillful manipulators, with free funds and inside information, made great fortunes. Albrecht von Wallenstein, the future duke of Friedland, was one of the most successful of these "carpetbaggers." Not only in Bohemia, but in the Palatinate and elsewhere, the Jesuit Order moved in, taking over schools and universities, proscribing Protestant clergy and teachers, and forcing the people to attend Catholic services. Large numbers became refugees, leaving their possessions behind and swelling the ranks of mercenary soldiery. Lusatia fared somewhat better, since it was administered by the elector of Saxony, who had acquired it as a pledge for what the Emperor owed him, and Silesia also succeeded in maintaining greater religious liberty.

The "Winter King," as Frederick was now mockingly called, instead of returning to the Palatinate to rally it in its own defense, started on a tour of other courts in the vain hope of persuading them to support his Bohemian cause. In the process of maintaining his claim upon the Bohemian crown, he lost in the end even his German principality. Attempts to forestall this outcome on the part of Palatinate forces, assisted by Dutch and British contingents and by the mercenaries of Mansfeld, failed in the face of the superior forces of Spain and the League. The able Spanish general, Marquis Ambrogio de Spinola, having trained a first-class professional army in the Netherlands for the impending war with the Dutch Republic—the armistice had lapsed in 1620—was easily able to seize the Palatine's lands west of the Rhine, while Count John Tilly, the equally able general of Maximilian, and victor of the battle of the White Mountain, conquered most of the territory east of the Rhine, including the fortess capital of Heidelberg. Thus Spain secured its communication by land with the Low Countries, provided it could pass through the Valtelline. (See next chapter.)

After these striking Catholic successes, a settlement was made in 1623. It was not truly a peace, any more than the later treaties of Lübeck (1629) and Prague (1635). Maximilian of Bavaria received the Upper Palatinate and the Lower Palatinate, east of the Rhine; the elector of Saxony obtained control over Lusatia for his aid in subduing Bohemia. By these acts, the two most important princes of the realm suggested that theirs was a policy of personal aggrandizement, even as they headed their respective coalitions of Catholic and Protestant princes. Of these, the Bavarian move was to prove the more obviously disastrous, since it blocked the road to peace, and kept the determined adherents of the Elector Palatine at work seeking support for a restoration of Frederick; but in a negative sense, John George of Saxony bore as heavy a responsibility, for he might, had he insisted upon a more equitable compromise, have kept the Bavarian claims within bounds.

III. THE DANISH PHASE

While Hapsburg and its allies settled down to the task of reconverting to Catholicism the lands they had conquered, the Protestants inside Germany, and more especially the supporters of the Elector Palatine Frederick, cast about for some new source of support with which to challenge the outcome of the Bohemian and Palatinate wars. James I having failed the Protestant cause, and the Dutch being heavily committed against Spain after the lapse of the armistice, anti-Hapsburg diplomacy turned to the Scandinavian kingdoms of Denmark and Sweden. There two able and ambitious rulers, both descendants of native houses but by their German mothers and wives related to Germany, had come to the throne in recent years: Christian IV in Denmark, Gustavus II Adolphus in Sweden. They both entered the great war, but not together. Their marked rivalry, which had already flared up in a war between them (1611–13), stood in the way of a joint enterprise, but perhaps even more importantly Gustavus Adolphus was occupied in a protracted conflict with the kingdom of Poland under John Sigismund, whose crown Gustavus Adolphus claimed as rightfully his.

Christian of Denmark was a prince of the German Empire through his possessions in Holstein, which was part of the Lower Saxon District (*Kreis*). As the sentiment of resistance to Catholic pressure increased, Christian was elected head (*Direktor*) of the district, which put him in charge of the local military forces. Throughout his campaign, Christian maintained that he was engaged in the conflict as a result of the emperor's unconstitutional actions toward the Elector Palatine. Passing over the intricate local issues, involving numerous petty dynastic squabbles and pretensions over secularized episcopal sees, one may say that the religious issue was being superseded by the struggle for political power as Christian of Denmark entered the field, although for the people at large religion remained vital, as it did for Ferdinand.

It had been Christian's original hope and expectation that he would be strongly supported by the various powers having anti-Hapsburg interests and commitments. But although some assistance came from all these sources, it was quite inadequate for the purpose of reconquering the lands the Hapsburgs and the League had seized. As a consequence the war remained largely confined to the territories of the Lower Saxon District and immediately adjoining territories, including Denmark itself. Like Bohemia and the Palatinate, the district was devastated from one end to the other by the depredations of the armies. The desperate spirit of self-defense of the people, deprived of their livelihood, with their women raped and their children murdered, has been brilliantly portrayed by Hermann Löns in his *Werwolf*. These scenes in all their brutality had earlier found classical expression in Grimmelshausen's *Simplicissimus,* the great epos of the Thirty Years' War discussed earlier.

In this period just before the establishment of modern fiscal methods and a fully developed bureaucracy, armies were quartered on the land and lived off it to an extent only recently revived by the totalitarian governments. As a result, an army settled like a swarm of locusts upon a prosperous district and sucked it dry, after which it moved on. The excesses which such a system begot caused a formidable toll in human suffering throughout Europe. At the same time, this system greatly affected strategy. Anyone looking at the map of the campaigns of the Thirty Years' War is puzzled at first that armies were to be found anywhere except in the country for which they were presumably fighting. Most princes were anxious to keep armies away from their dominions at all costs. Recurrently, the generals would be forbidden to move into the home country. Since the regulars were largely hired mercenaries, they would be as little concerned with the suffering of one country as another. It was a main task of skillful generalship to secure winter quarters in a territory that had not yet been mulcted. This system of army maintenance, when combined with the unsanitary conditions and resulting loss of manpower through epidemics, provided a perfect setting for the strategy of exhausting the enemy which seeks to avoid battles while maintaining a superior force.

Christian of Denmark was not sufficiently aware of the superior resources of an enemy with vast defense in depth. The delays imposed
upon him by the flaccid attitude of his allies made him lose the two
summers of 1624 and 1625 with relatively insignificant, albeit frequently
adverse, encounters. But as the Catholic prospects brightened, in the
course of 1625, the emperor received vast new support from an unexpected quarter: Albrecht von Wallenstein (Waldstein), soon to be made
duke of Friedland, undertook to put an army of 24,000 into the field,
arm and equip them and come to the support of Tilly, the League's
general. Wallenstein, along with Gustavus Adolphus, Richelieu, and
Cromwell, was one of the "heroes" of the first half of the seventeenth
century. He sought to do for the emperor what we shall later describe
as Richelieu's actual accomplishment: create central authority adequate
to establish peace and order throughout the Empire. In a decisive negotiation with the emperor, he undertook to accomplish this vast design on
the battlefield, only to be defeated by the enemies he had made at
court. Richelieu, by contrast, was the statesman and diplomatist first and
never relinquished his hold upon Louis XIII.

One of the strangest things about this strange man, Wallenstein, was
the prognostication of his future on the basis of an astrological horoscope
prepared by the great Kepler. "Kepler," Ranke wrote, in paraphrasing
the horoscope,

emphasized the conjunction of Jupiter and Saturn which occurred in the first
house, the house of life. Saturn suggests melancholic, continually fermenting
thoughts, neglect of human rules and even of religion, lack of fraternal and
married love. For this star makes a man pitiless, impetuous, combative and
undaunted. But since Jupiter joins Saturnus, it may be hoped that most of
these faults will be reduced by maturity and age.

Kepler opined regarding the young Wallenstein that he had a restless
mind and more thoughts than he revealed, and that he would seek innovations by untried means. Kepler concluded, from Saturnalian and
Jovian influences, that Wallenstein's exceptional personality qualified him
for high achievements. He attributed to him a thirst for power and glory,
stubborn pride and bold courage, so that he might some day be the leader
of malcontents; he would have many and great enemies, but would
triumph over most.[1]

---

[1] Translated by the author from Leopold von Ranke, *Geschichte Wallensteins* (third
edition, 1872), 1–2.

Wallenstein's appearance upon the scene altered Christian of Denmark's position materially, and caused him in the spring of 1626 to dispatch part of his forces under Mansfeld to Silesia, in the hope of diverting Wallenstein to the defense of the Hapsburg dominions proper. Mansfeld, though an able *condottiere,* met with crushing defeat at the bridgehead over the Elbe River at Dessau, which Wallenstein had been fortifying through the winter. Wallenstein might have pursued and annihilated him, and it has often been argued that he should have done so. From a strictly military viewpoint such a course would have been defensible, but Wallenstein was ever aware of the political implications of his moves, and such an attempt would have forced him to violate the neutrality of the elector of Brandenburg's territory, into which Mansfeld had fled. This would probably have brought both George William, the Brandenburger, and his brother-in-law, Gustavus Adolphus, into the war, and maybe John George of Saxony as well, since the latter was jealously guarding his neutral rights. But eventually Wallenstein moved through Silesia and Moravia in pursuit of Mansfeld, who had joined forces with the ever restless Bethlen Gabor. But Wallenstein did not do this without leaving behind, under his circumspect subcommander, Count Aldringen, some eight to nine thousand of his best troops. These superior contingents enabled Tilly to take the offensive against Christian of Denmark, whose demoralized Danes and other troops suffered a complete rout in the battle of Lutter am Barenberge (August, 1626). After this disaster Christian vacated all of Brunswick and retired to his duchy of Holstein. Lutter am Barenberge demonstrated Tilly's remarkable ability to strike and strike hard at the right moment. Not really an exponent of the strategy of attrition, Tilly won a considerable number of important battles by his ability to select the right moment for attack. But he left the strategic and political exploitation of his victories to others, more especially to his princely master, Maximilian, who ever asserted his own authority over Tilly.

While Tilly thus destroyed the fighting strength of Christian, Wallenstein outmaneuvered Mansfeld and Bethlen Gabor, and successfully protected the Hapsburg dominions and Vienna. He did so under most adverse conditions, which lost him a considerable part of his army. He had to defy the court at Vienna in order to secure adequate winter quarters for what troops he could hold together, but the following spring he reached a broad settlement regarding strategy with Vienna, raised an even larger army, said to have numbered seventy thousand men, and set forth once again to annihilate Christian and secure control of the Baltic for the Empire, if possible. It was at this time that Wallenstein showed his divinatory strategic genius by remarking that the Swedes would prove worse than the Turk, as he dispatched one thousand horses to the aid of the king of Poland.

The campaign in the north proved eminently successful, and was, after Tilly's being wounded, conducted by Wallenstein alone. Wallenstein occupied all of Denmark, except the islands, as well as Mecklenburg, Holstein and parts of Pomerania. However, his sweep was brought to a standstill before the free city of Stralsund. Stralsund had refused to pay the large sum Wallenstein's general, Arnim, had demanded, for not having imperial troops quartered upon its territory. Wallenstein thereupon laid siege to the city, and might have subdued it, but for the support given from the sea by Christian and Gustavus Adolphus, when the common citizenry, rejecting a compromise negotiated by their city council, decided to fight it out (July, 1627). Wallenstein could not effectively deploy his vast forces against this water fortress, and in August lifted the siege.

This successful act of resistance provided enough of a counterpoise to permit a settlement with Christian. Due to Wallenstein's counsels of moderation, a peace was concluded at Lübeck on May 22, 1629, after several months of negotiation. While Christian gave up all claims to German sees as well as the directorship of the Lower Saxon District, he received back Jutland, Schleswig and his part of Holstein, did not have to pay an indemnity, and altogether "escaped with a blue eye," as the Germans say. Wallenstein persuaded the emperor to accept these terms, because of new and greater dangers, more especially those threatening from Sweden, which in the meantime had come to terms with Poland.

IV. THE EDICT OF RESTITUTION: REACTION TRIUMPHANT

Even before peace was concluded with Denmark, Ferdinand II had taken a step much at variance with Wallenstein's conception of imperial absolutism, but dear to the heart of the emperor and expressive of his religious convictions. On March 8, 1629, he issued the Edict of Restitution.

The Edict, without sanction or discussion by the diet or Reichstag, as required under the constitution in all matters of major legislation, proclaimed all alienation of church lands since 1552 (Convention of Passau) null and void, called for their restitution to the rightful proprietors, authorized the latter after such restitution to expel all who would not confess according to the preference of the ruler of the territory, and outlawed all Protestant confessions except the Lutheran of the Augsburg Confession (1530), and more especially the Calvinists. There was here involved the principle of the ecclesiastical reservation, which had been intended to prevent the alienation of church lands by individual church dignitaries becoming Protestants, formally reasonable enough, if the church is viewed as a body corporate and the bishops, abbots and the like as its officials and employees. But this bureaucratic view of church office had not in fact prevailed after 1555, and many sees had become alienated, fairly enough in the light of the prevailing Protestant sentiment of the inhabitants of such sees as Magdeburg, Halberstadt, Minden and Bremen. The inherent contradictions involved in church officials acting as territorial princes were all implicit in these bitter controversies over the ecclesiastical reservation, especially when coupled with the bland principle of the religious peace of Augsburg (1555) that a man was to confess the religion of the lord of the territory he inhabited. Now the Edict of Restitution proposed to compound the inherent immorality by restoring these lands to Catholics and then enforcing the iniquitous principle.

For the enforcement of the Edict, imperial commissioners were authorized. Against their decisions there was no appeal. In concrete terms, this meant the re-establishment of two archbishoprics and twelve bishoprics in territories now largely Protestant, such as Augsburg and Magdeburg, and of approximately five hundred monasteries, foundations and the like. In the sequel it meant the expulsion of tens of thousands of industrious and peaceful citizens, e.g., from Augsburg, where only a few hundred Catholics had remained in a population of about thirty thousand. The situation in Bremen, Magdeburg, Minden, Halberstadt and other sees which had long been secularized was very similar, as was indeed that of many knights and simple peasants throughout these domains.

As events were to show, Ferdinand by this arbitrary and nonconstitutional act was "reaching for the stars." His attempt to undo the development of three generations was the high-water mark of imperial power and Catholic reaction; soon the balance was to be redressed. For the Edict convinced even the most pacifically inclined Protestant princes that the house of Hapsburg meant to destroy the ancient constitution of the

Empire and the "liberties" of the German people, institutionalized as they were in the rights and privileges of princes, knights and burghers, of electors and free cities, in short, of all the estates of the Empire save his own. They realized that even foreign intervention must be countenanced in order to cope with so formidable a threat. Sweden and France, Gustavus Adolphus and Richelieu, stood ready to take advantage of the situation. So helpful did the Edict prove to the anti-Hapsburg policy of Richelieu that the rumor could spring up that it had been proposed by Richelieu. If anyone, Pope Urban VIII would be more nearly entitled to claim such Machiavellian design; for he unquestionably urged the restitution, while seeking the destruction of the house of Hapsburg.

In the meantime, a sharp clash had arisen over the succession in the Italian duchy of Mantua, and as usual in these dynastic and hereditary contests, there were arguments on both sides. A campaign largely won by the imperial forces, who had taken Mantua, placed the emperor in a position where he might hope to bargain with France and to secure concessions in return for a compromise on Mantua. In fact, such hopes proved illusory and provided a trap into which imperial diplomacy was led by France's wily negotiators. However, the Mantuan war marked the resumption by France of Henry IV's policy of combating Hapsburg power by every available means. In this policy, France was continually encouraged by Urban VIII, whose over-all conception of ecclesiastical strategy called for the extension of Catholic influence without relying upon the house of Hapsburg for the purpose. Indeed, the Pope desired to check the ascendancy of Hapsburg, and in this effort went so far as to suggest to Maximilian of Bavaria that it might be well for him to ascend the imperial throne upon the death of Ferdinand II. It was entirely in keeping with such a policy that a French subject, and a man ardently supporting Catholic Counter Reformation, the Duc de Nevers-Gonzaga, should become duke of Mantua. The intrachurch struggle between the two most aggressive orders of the Jesuits and the Capuchins played its role behind the scenes, the Jesuits favoring Hapsburg and the Capuchins Bavaria and France.

The Edict of Restitution and the Mantuan war set the stage for the electoral gathering (*Kurfürstentag*) at Regensburg as it assembled in early July, 1630. While Ferdinand II hoped to obtain the election of his son to the imperial throne, Bavaria, reinforced by a secret agreement with France, planned to secure the dismissal of Wallenstein as imperial general, whereas the Protestant electors, now reduced to two, intended to have the Edict of Restitution either revoked or modified. The gathering provided an ideal opportunity for the skillful diplomacy of France, now becoming aggressive after Richelieu's hands had been freed by the reduction of the Huguenots and the seizure of Savoy, and this opportunity was, according to all accounts, used with consummate craftsmanship by one of the many remarkable figures of the period, the almost legendary Capuchin, Père Joseph—the "Gray Eminence" who trotted about Europe in brown hood on bare feet as an "observer" and "adviser" for the court of France and its foreign minister.[2] Père Joseph on his way to Regensburg had stopped briefly with Wallenstein, and, according to his own report, had succeeded in goading the general into one of his more fateful indiscretions. Some doubts about this report remain, for while it is evident why the calculating Capuchin might misrepresent the general to Richelieu, it is not at all clear why Wallenstein should ever have made such statements to him. In any case, Père Joseph's diplomacy fits into the French policy of sowing discord between the emperor and his electors, especially the Catholic ones, in anticipation of a Swedish attack upon the Empire. This attack was possibly intended, and certainly worked out in the end, to be a prelude to French military intervention. In any case, the results of the electoral gathering were highly favorable to French policy: Wallenstein was dismissed, Ferdinand's son not elected, and a further breach caused over the Edict of Restitution, with Brandenburg and Saxony refusing to adhere to it, but securing agreement only on a further meeting to discuss it.

That Ferdinand should have assented to the dismissal of Wallenstein, and that a majority of his council should have favored such a step shows them to have been basically unaware of the trend of the times. In the case of Ferdinand himself, it was partly weakness, partly perhaps a desire to reassert his imperial authority, and partly a persistent dissatisfaction with Wallenstein's indifference toward the religious cause. Not only had he opposed the Edict of Restitution, but he had enforced it only where it fitted into his broader political strategy. In a historical hour, Ferdinand opted for religion and medieval conceptions of government, while Louis XIII at the very same time resisted all pressures along similar lines and retained his cardinal—who like Wallenstein was prepared to subordinate all, including religious considerations, to the require-

---

[2] For further background, see next chapter.

ments of royal absolutism. The state and its *raison d'État* fought medieval constitutionalism, taking full advantage of its inner divisions, as the cardinal and his monkish emissary faced the emperor and his electors. Such a statement may sound rhetorical, but it was decisive for this period that Ferdinand faltered when confronted with the full implications of establishing the centralized power of a modern state over the scattered dominions which he nominally ruled. Could he have succeeded, if he had backed his imperial general to the hilt? Did the military and economic resources he controlled suffice to accomplish so vast a revolution? And could he have avoided an even more complete dependence upon his major domus than the French king had to accept? It may well be doubted that the answer to any of these questions could be in the affirmative. Nineteenth-century historians, looking back nostalgically at the successful consolidation of the national state in France and the dynastic division of Germany into a number of kingdoms, have conjured up sympathies for Wallenstein's dreams of imperial integration and national unity. But the solid territorial footing of the princes of Germany, as well as the rapid progress of the modern state in adjoining realms suggests that any decisive move in this direction would have brought together against imperial Hapsburg a grand alliance infinitely more determined to prevent imperial absolutism than the one that actually emerged after the gathering at Regensburg. Hence the intrinsic reasonableness of the dismissal of Wallenstein has been obscured by the startling successes on the battlefield of a new and brilliant commander: King Gustavus Adolphus of Sweden.

V. FOREIGN INTERVENTION: THE SWEDISH CHALLENGE

Gustavus Adolphus, when he landed in Germany on July 4, 1630, was only thirty-five years of age but had already been king of Sweden for nineteen years, and had spent most of that period in protracted wars with his neighbors, Denmark, Russia and Poland, all of which had been defeated by this "happy warrior." Descendant of the native line of Vasa kings, Gustavus represented in modern garb the hoary idea of the Germanic warrior king, ruling and leading his people in battle by right of the intrinsic authority derived from an overweening capacity for leadership. Yet Gustavus Adolphus was a genuine pathfinder of the modern nation state.[3] Hostile to the aristocracy, who quite recently had hoped to

---

[3] For further detail see below, Chapter Eight, pp. 258–9.

convert Sweden into a "republic" ruled by the nobles like Poland, Gustavus Adolphus had carried forward the work of establishing a centralized administrative state and a productive industrial society; even overseas colonization was not neglected, as the Swedish settlements in North America testify. The king had worked out arrangements for something approximating a general draft, and had succeeded in professionalizing his army to an extent astonishing for the period. This professional national core of his army was to prove of decisive significance in his battles, and is entitled more particularly to the credit for the crucial victory at Breitenfeld. By bringing his army into the German war, Gustavus Adolphus provided a genuine counterpoise to the Spanish professionals on the Catholic side.

A good part of Gustavus' achievement was due to his extraordinary personality. Though the son of a German mother, he was the idol of the Swedish people. A great nineteenth-century historian has drawn the following character sketch of Gustavus Adolphus:

He was very reserved, sincere, unapproachable, an enigma even to his most intimate entourage, who were accustomed to execute his commands without asking for reasons. He recognized with sureness the means which would most rapidly lead to the set goal, but often genius carried him beyond [such goals], the *impetus ingenii,* as Oxenstierna called it. Thus Gustavus rushed from plans to plans so that his faithful Oxenstierna had difficulty in restraining him. He was hardened and without indulgence to himself. He shooed away attacks of fever by having a sword duel. . . . Contemporary historians tell of Gustavus that he did not sleep in rooms when in war but on his ship and in tents. From time to time northern coarseness and the wildness of his tribe broke through the majesty of his spirit. . . . This hard, brusk and reserved lord, this *leo arcticus,* was taller than the tallest of his men, broad shouldered with light blond hair, white colored face and slow movements . . . he loved soft music. . . . He seems like northern lights, so great, so marvelous, so luminous and yet so cool.[4]

There was a deep-felt relationship between Gustavus Adolphus and his people. It found striking expression in the words he addressed to the estates in 1630, before departing for his extraordinary adventure. After speaking of his having to die some day, "as it generally happens that the pitcher is carried to the water till it breaks," and commending them all

---

[4] Droysen, *Gustaf Adolf* (1869), 60 ff., translated by the author from the German original.

to the care of God, the All-highest, he turned to the peasants at last: "My wish for the common man and peasantry is that their meadows may be green, and their fields give a hundredfold, so that their barns may be filled, and that they may all grow and increase in prosperity and so that they may cheerfully and without murmur perform their duties and exercise their rights." The next day the king went on board ship, and with favorable winds set sail to rescue the cause of Protestantism, and render his people secure against the offensive of the Catholic Counter Reformation. That this struggle was coming, he of all people had been most certain. Three years earlier he had warned: "As one wave follows another in the sea, so the papal deluge is approaching our shores." What he perhaps did not know was that the Pope was suspected in Vienna of rejoicing at the king's decision, and an open attack was made upon Urban by some of the cardinals in Rome. But what he did know was that a cardinal of the church, Richelieu, not only rejoiced, but was prepared to finance his undertaking on a substantial scale, if not to support it by arms. "Reason of state" triumphed over religious loyalties in the giving and taking of that support. The most dramatic "religious" intervention was to prove the turning point from a religious war into a struggle for political power.

The progress of Gustavus Adolphus against the disorganized and dispirited imperial forces was rapid. The dismissal of Wallenstein had removed from the scene the one strategic genius who would have been a match to Gustavus Adolphus. One fortified place after another capitulated, so that by the end of the year the Swedish king was in control of most of Pomerania and was threatening Brandenburg. Considering the elector's vacillating policy toward his brother-in-law during the period when Gustavus fought in Poland, the Swedish king could hardly be expected to pay much heed to diplomatic niceties in forcing Brandenburg to co-operate. The German princes were nonetheless slow in entering into engagements with Gustavus. More especially the elector of Saxony, John George, was greatly disturbed at the appearance of the Swede as protector of Protestantism. Not only did he consider himself the constitutional leader of German Protestantism, but he was forever hoping to re-establish peace on the basis of the old constitutional order, and an agreement with the Swedish king would have been contrary to this settled policy. From the standpoint of this Protestant constitutionalist, it would have been much the best thing if Gustavus Adolphus had remained in Pomerania—a distant threat rather than a conqueror and

eventual destroyer of the German states. But the king was no compromiser; indeed he was a bold, even reckless, champion of the Protestant
cause, believing himself divinely appointed to smash the power of Hapsburg and the antichrist forever. This being so, Gustavus Adolphus had
no hesitation in concluding at Baerwalde, January 13, 1631, a five-year
treaty with Richelieu's skillful ambassador, Hercule de Charnacé, providing for the advance of an army of 36,000 Swedes into Germany to
rescue the German estates and their "liberties." These German liberties
had been a French concern for almost a hundred years, in keeping with
the old adage: *"Divide et impera."* The French were to provide a subsidy of 400,000 thalers in support of the cause. Freedom of the seas, more
especially of the Baltic, and freedom of commerce were also agreed upon.

This strong French backing enabled Gustavus Adolphus to compel the
co-operation of the reluctant German princes, including the king's
brother-in-law George William, Elector of Brandenburg. But this did not
prove easy. Brandenburg was secured by a series of moves which gave
the king control of the fortresses of Spandau and Frankfort an der Oder.
In mid-May Gustavus concluded an agreement with the elector of Brandenburg. Unfortunately, if understandably, John George of Saxony still
hesitated.

Meanwhile a crisis had been developing at Magdeburg, key city of
central Germany and a pivotal point of controversy as a result of the
secularization of its archbishopric. Christian William, the brother of the
Brandenburg elector, had returned the previous summer to resume his
post as "administrator" of the achiepiscopal lands, on the strength of a
promise of Gustavus Adolphus to support him. The city council was
fearful, but a military force of over three thousand men provided by the
administrator and which the friendly dukes of Weimar promised to increase, helped to allay their fears. In the spring of 1631, however, the
imperial army under Tilly was continuing the siege of the city, begun
by the daredevil Pappenheim. Gustavus Adolphus might have moved to
relieve the city immediately after taking Frankfort an der Oder, but
he hesitated in the hope of securing the backing of Brandenburg and
Saxony. While their failure was offered afterward as his main excuse,
Gustavus Adolphus must have had poor intelligence about the defensive
strength of the city. Having placed Dietrich von Falkenberg, a reliable
if somewhat intemperate soldier, in charge, the king depended upon the
latter's promise to hold the city through May and June. Tilly and Pappenheim knew that time worked against them. They needed the city's

resources, and learned that the king was near. So they attacked, on May 17. After two days of assault upon the outworks, the city council wanted to surrender, and was about to do so, when the imperial army stormed and took the city on May 20, 1631. Fire broke out while the soldiers were plundering, and within forty-eight hours one of Germany's finest cities lay in complete ruins. Who caused this disaster? Certainly not Tilly, whose position was gravely imperiled by the loss of the city's resources. Probably not the fanatical defenders either. The great Gothic cathedral was almost the only building standing on May 22, but with true baroque feeling for the great stage of history, General Tilly had a *Te Deum* sung and the cathedral rededicated to the Virgin Mary, declaring that the city's name should henceforth be Marienburg.

The destruction of Magdeburg came as a profound shock to Protestant Germany and Europe. The elector of Saxony could hesitate no longer and concluded an agreement with Gustavus Adolphus, as did many another prince. At the same time, the Swedish king was eager to wash away the ignominy of the serious disaster which Catholic sympathizers were not slow to blame upon him. Ever a believer in the decisive battle, though forced by the conditions and the temper of the age into a skillful strategy of exhaustion, he sought and found the enemy in the broad plain north of Leipzig and decisively defeated him in the battle of Breitenfeld (September 7, 1631).

This victory was a remarkable feat, for while the two opposing forces were fairly evenly matched at the start, the entire Saxon contingent under John George himself was decisively routed and lost, exposing the king's flank. But Gustavus Adolphus had developed new tactical devices: smaller squares of cavalry interspersed with infantry as against the large solid squares of infantry. He also had light artillery in greater numbers. These innovations (developments of ideas of Maurice of Nassau), together with the superior morale of the Swedish troops, enabled the king to rout Tilly who never recovered. The Swedish king was now free to act. Friedrich Schiller, in his wonderfully poetic story of the Thirty Years' War, says of Gustavus Adolphus after the battle of Breitenfeld that he "readily confused his cause with the cause of heaven, and therefore saw in Tilly's defeat a decisive judgment of God against his enemies; himself he saw as a tool of divine wrath."

However, Gustavus Adolphus, who was averse to the strategy of annihilation, did not march upon Vienna, as many expected him to do, but asked the Saxon elector to take charge of the Bohemian conquest,

while he himself turned west and conquered a chain of Catholic territories: Bamberg, the Upper Palatinate, Würzburg, Mainz. This decision
has been the subject of extended controversy ever since. It certainly complicated the king's relations with Richelieu, for not only the attack upon
the territories of the Catholic League, which Richelieu in a secret treaty
with Maximilian of Bavaria had guaranteed neutrality, but the appearance of Sweden on the frontier of France gave the cardinal thought.
Yet Gustavus Adolphus' decision made sense in political, religious and military terms. For his march through the "priests' alley" or *Pfaffengasse*
greatly encouraged the numerous German princelings and territorial lords,
as well as the great free cities, to make common cause with him, liberated
the oppressed Protestant elements, more especially those in the two
Palatinates, gave the Swedish king the yet unspoiled resources of this
rich region, and cut the lines of land communication between the Spanish
Netherlands and the Hapsburgs of Vienna and Madrid. On November
27 the king arrived in Frankfort am Main, key center of the Holy
Empire's constitutional structure. The total armed strength of Gustavus
Adolphus at this time was estimated at eighty thousand, and he proposed to raise another hundred thousand or more. Is it to be wondered
at that, when talking to friends like the duke of Mecklenburg, he is reported to have mused: "When I am emperor. . . ." For there was no
formal constitutional reason why he might not be elected; only some
four generations earlier Henry VIII of England and Francis I of France
had vied with Charles V for the ancient crown.

Fascinating as were the multifarious activities, military, political, and
administrative, which filled Gustavus Adolphus' year of triumph between
the battles of Breitenfeld and Lützen, three only were of major importance: his proposal for a Protestant confederation (*corpus Evangeli-
corum*) under Swedish leadership; his failure to break Wallenstein's
armed camp and general strategy of attrition; and his consequent proposal
for a general peace.

In the middle of the summer of 1632, the king advanced his broad
project for the settlement of the German war: the Protestant princes
should unite in a general union with Sweden after dissolving their bonds
with the Empire. This proposal, joined with Swedish acquisition of
Pomerania, was submitted to and approved by the Swedish estates
(*Riksråd*), and was put forward about the same time at Nürnberg. The
Saxon elector took a dim view of the plan: it was unrealistic not only
in terms of German national sentiment and dynastic interest, but also

because of Richelieu's natural dislike for such a block of united Protestant strength.

The French having failed to bring about a compromise between the king and the Catholic League, because of Bavarian objections, Gustavus Adolphus resolved to carry the war into Maximilian's carefully preserved lands. He systematically devastated Bavaria and, upon Tilly's death after the battle on the Lechfeld, took Munich. However, when Wallenstein at long last moved into Franconia, threatening Nürnberg by constructing a vast encampment near Fürth, Gustavus Adolphus marched thither and took up a position in and around the famous town. His attempts to interfere with the construction of Wallenstein's camp failed; thereupon Gustavus Adolphus resolved to take the camp by storm, but in vain; on September 5, he drew back. Wallenstein had succeeded, by a brilliant feat of strategy, in halting the Swedish king's advance.

Gustavus Adolphus, in keeping with his usual moderation, now put forward his proposals for a general peace settlement. Whether he expected them to be considered will always remain in doubt. Some historians have then and now considered them fair and moderate, others have felt that they were no more than a ruse. For himself the king claimed Pomerania and therewith the position of a prince of the Empire (*Reichsfürst*); Saxony was to receive Magdeburg; the dukes of Mecklenburg were to be restored, as were the electors Palatine and of Mainz; Brandenburg, Wallenstein and Bavaria were to be compensated respectively by Halberstadt, a Franconian duchy and Upper Austria; the Edict of Restitution was to be revoked.

It cannot be denied that these proposals represented roughly the balance of power at that moment. They also resembled closely the compromise reached in the eventual peace; but they ran counter to many deep-seated feelings, which were still held with much determination. In any case, Wallenstein declined to negotiate and merely agreed to forward the terms to Vienna, where they were treated with indifference. Gustavus Adolphus realized that Wallenstein meant to continue the war. Since he was outnumbered by the great organizer, he at first tried to divert him. But Wallenstein invaded Saxony, in the hope of forcing John George to abandon Gustavus Adolphus. Thereupon the king, honoring his agreement with the Saxon, turned and pursued Wallenstein. The latter evidently did not expect the king to attack, and therefore split his forces for better wintering. An egregious error, as it turned out: Gustavus Adolphus seized his chance, threw himself upon Wallenstein southwest of Leipzig, near Lützen, on November 6, 1632, and, after a fierce struggle, utterly routed the imperial forces. But the king himself lost his life upon the battlefield. The magnificent campaign, resembling in more ways than one the meteoric conquests of Alexander the Great, thus came to a dramatic close.

Had Gustavus Adolphus been a lone wolf, like his rival Christian of Denmark, the Swedish armies would have dissolved on the battlefield on which the king fell. But, as a matter of fact, Gustavus had not only very able military lieutenants, like Horn and Banér, but also the sagacious chancellor, Axel Oxenstierna, working with and under him. Indeed, Oxenstierna had often moderated the king's flights of temper and fancy, and was intimately acquainted with every detail of Swedish policy.

Oxenstierna has perplexed modern historians who fail to take religious motivation into full account. Kind, thoughtful, generous and of great ability, the Swedish chancellor's obvious course would have seemed to be to conclude a peace on the best possible terms and then to withdraw from the German scene. But to a man of Oxenstierna's loyalty such a course would have meant not only a betrayal of the dead king and of the valiant Swedes left dead upon the battlefields, but also lack of faith in the true religion which the arms of Sweden were to rescue from the wily intrigues of the Jesuits and the power-loving bigotry of the Haps-burg dynasty. Only in these perspectives is the chancellor's persistence understandable, especially after the military setbacks which he suffered.

In this connection, it is vital to bear in mind that Wallenstein con-tinued negotiations looking toward a general settlement and, what is more, avoided taking any decisive action to follow up the king's death either immediately after the battle of Lützen or later, in 1633. The ever-active Bohemian exiles and their Calvinist friends among the supporters of the Elector Palatine continually exerted themselves to encourage such hopes and expectations by reports which at times were pure fancy. Men like Count Thurn out of natural optimism, others like Count Kinsky and Rasin from a love of intrigue and a desire for revenge, but all of them motivated also by genuine religious and national sentiments, traveled about between Prague, Friedland, Dresden, Kassel, as well as between Paris, the Hague, Copenhagen and Stockholm, not to mention the smaller courts of the Holy Empire, keeping alive the idea that peace, while a good, could not be concluded by good Christians unless they attained also the greater good of making the Protestant cause secure.

Humanitarian sympathy for the common people, for the farmers and craftsmen who suffered ever more unspeakable horrors through the ensuing years, together with the religious indifferentism of a liberal age, have obscured the true tragedy of the years after Gustavus Adolphus' death. There can be little question that the contending forces might well have settled for some such terms as those agreed upon at the peace of Westphalia fifteen years later. But the truth of the matter is that Ferdinand II was not willing to make broad concessions to the Protestants, while the Protestant war party, including Sweden, was not yet ready to admit its inability to support its brethren throughout southern Germany, and Richelieu was not prepared to relinquish the opportunity of weakening Hapsburg power afforded by the war in Germany. In this situation, the elector of Saxony, John George, cannot be blamed for seeking to reestablish peace on a compromise basis, but he need not be praised for his ineffectual methods either. Personally a gluttonous phlegmatic, John George might well have been of decisive help either to the peace party, if he had followed the advice of his marshal, von Arnim, or to the Protestant cause, if he had yielded to the urgings of his wife and her friends, who wanted to make effective common cause with the Swedes. By doing neither, he bore as much responsibility for the continuance of the war by his inaction as Oxenstierna, Ferdinand and Richelieu by their belligerency. The same charge applies to Wallenstein. He, too, failed to produce either peace by compromise or by victory as a result of his shilly-shallying and elusive intrigue.

The sharp controversies occasioned by Wallenstein's last years and the disaster in which they ended will probably never be composed. To some he has been the traitor to the Catholic cause, to others the thwarted protagonist of a German national state, to still others the ruthless, self-seeking mercenary caught in the meshes of his own nets. A sympathetic perusal of the available evidence leads to the conclusion that Wallenstein was all of these things and more. "Uncertain, his portrait fluctuates in history," Friedrich Schiller was to say of him in his historical drama *Wallenstein's Tod*. A cold, calculating man, the duke of Friedland was surrounded by astrologers; pitiless in collecting contributions for his army and in venting his wrath upon those who crossed him, he was an extraordinarily industrious and successful administrator of his vast estates, keenly concerned with the welfare of his subjects even to the point of minutiae. The eighteenth and the nineteenth centuries, increasingly rational, prosaic, decent and informal, have puzzled over this quintessentially baroque figure. In keeping with the style of his age, Wallenstein's very contradictions, contrasts and tensions reflected his true nature. Somber and highly dynamic, he elicited universally those intense emotions of admiration and hostility which only the truly representative figure of an age is capable of arousing. Indeed, how else could Wallenstein have departed this earth than by some such means as a great state murder? Condemned in secret conclave for a treason which he could not, within his own premises, commit, he was murdered because he could neither convert the tottering Empire into a modern state nor substitute a modern state for the tottering Empire. The latter would have called for his becoming "Caesar" himself—an idea which cropped up in casual remarks and was bandied about by his enemies. Such an idea, eventually embraced when the Corsican crowned himself, was at once too rational and too romantic for a baroque leader to pursue in earnest. Combining medieval faith and superstition with a renaissance sense of power and artistic performance, baroque man was forever walking upon a stage: European history was a theater and the beauty of a performance was enhanced by a dramatic exit for the tragic hero. Results were incidental.

Wallenstein's death at Eger, February 24, 1634, once more raised hopes of a general peace. But instead, Protestants and Swedes suffered an overwhelming defeat in the battle of Nördlingen, in September, 1634. Confronted by the combined forces of the Austrian and Spanish Hapsburgs —the cardinal infant of Spain had been able to bring up more than eight thousand Spanish professionals through the crucial Valtelline Pass that summer—Gustavus Adolphus' two generals, Marshal Horn, the son-in-law of Oxenstierna, and Duke Bernard of Saxe-Weimar engaged in ill-considered rivalry over the command. Acting either too late, by allowing the cardinal infant to join with the king of Hungary, or too early, by not awaiting the reinforcements, which were on the way, these two able generals brought the Swedish phase of the war to a hapless close almost exactly three years after Gustavus Adolphus' victory at Breitenfeld had seemed to open the prospect for a victory of Protestantism. Thereafter the son of the emperor, the future Ferdinand III, was able to recapture most of southern Germany for Catholicism. Indeed, the prospects of the Hapsburgs became so bright after this victory that the French were induced to cross the Rubicon and enter the war openly as the protectors of German "liberties," that is to say the medieval constitution and its Catholic and Protestant beneficiaries, the lesser German princes. It thus came to pass that the most skillful promoter of the modern state in France, Cardinal Richelieu, who systematically destroyed the French "liberties" of feudal times, fought to keep them intact in Germany as a check upon the house of Hapsburg.

VI. MODERN STATE VERSUS MEDIEVAL EMPIRE: A COMPROMISE PEACE?

The five battles of the White Mountain, Lutter am Barenberge, Breitenfeld, Lützen and Nördlingen, were the decisive ones of the great war; after Nördlingen many a bloody engagement was fought, but none turned the scale as these battles had done. It is a startling testimony to the inner weakness of the cause of the Counter Reformation that in spite of losing only one of these great encounters, it could not win the war in the end. The deeper reason was that the forces of the modern state were predominantly on the other side.

In any case, the battle of Nördlingen had sufficiently reduced the power of Sweden and with it the prospects of a sweeping Protestant predominance, to strengthen negotiations begun earlier in 1634 for an all-round compromise. In contrast to the French cardinal, who protested a desire for a general peace while fanning the flames of war, the German emperor and his estates proceeded to treat of peace among themselves and eventually arrived at a settlement which acknowledged the existing state of affairs. The peace of Prague (1635), the third of the peace treaties by which the great war was punctuated, might have brought the conflict to an end thirteen years earlier than the peace of Westphalia, had it not been for Swedish and French determination to reduce the Hapsburg power further and to secure extensive compensations for their sanguinary and financial efforts up to that time. The peace of Prague expressly challenged such pretensions by providing that any lands lost to either the emperor or one of the states, like Lorraine and Mecklenburg, should be restored to them, if necessary by force of arms. An army for the entire Empire was provided, and the liberation of German territories from foreign armies was made the express purpose of this army. As for the problem of religious peace, the doctrine of *"cujus regio, ejus religio"* was by implication reaffirmed, and the Edict of Restitution by similar implication set aside. Instead, it was provided that the ecclesiastical domains, foundations, monasteries and the like should be divided on the basis of actual possession at the time of the peace of Passau [5] and, for

---

[5] See above, p. 174.

those acquired after Passau, the date of November 12, 1627 should serve, but for a forty-year period only. There were a certain number of exceptions, and since Ferdinand was unwilling to grant religious toleration in his crownlands, especially Bohemia, in spite of strong Saxon representations, it was agreed that this matter might be further negotiated.

As a whole, the peace of Prague constituted an attempt to rally all German estates behind the ancient constitution and unite them against the foreign invaders, especially Sweden and France. Its operation depended upon its acceptance by a majority of these estates, and the unusual procedure of an agreement between the emperor and the Saxon elector was explained by the exceptional circumstance of foreign invasion. In this connection, it is significant that specific provision was made for the resumption of superior judicial authority by the *Reichskammergericht*, and that the emperor relinquished the pretended right to transfer cases to the *Reichshofrat*. The latter court was within the emperor's control, and while he conceded the admissibility of Protestant judges, he refused to have equality of representation such as was provided for the *Reichskammergericht*. Excluded from the pacification were the descendants of the former Elector Palatine, the duke of Württemberg and the margrave of Baden-Durlach, but these could be pardoned, and the emperor, at the insistence of Saxony, agreed to provide for the Palatine's family. Obviously this settlement was bound to look to France and Sweden more like a defensive alliance than like a peace treaty. Estates threatened by either French or Swedish forces could not but look upon the document in a similar light, since adherence to its terms entailed joining forces with the emperor and hence might bring about conquest by his enemies. As a result, its conclusion did not bring peace, but an intensification of the war.[6]

The historian may well be pardoned for not reviewing the sorry tale of this long-drawn-out disaster. Largely it was the story of a Swedish-French-Spanish struggle.[7] In 1637, Emperor Ferdinand passed away, unsuccessful and a victim of his bigotry and his delusions. Recurrently responsible for the continuation of the great war which he had himself allowed to get under way, he could look upon his crown lands, as well as upon the larger Empire, for which he was in his own conception of

---

[6] The text of the treaty is found in *Aller des Heiligen Römischen Reichs gehaltenen Reichstäge, Abschiede und Satzungen . . . und Friedens-Schluss* (Frankfurt am Mayn, 1720), 1018–32.

[7] See below, p. 220–9.

rulership the God-appointed shepherd, as not only devastated and exhausted, but also as no more Christian in the Catholic way than when he ascended his throne.

VII. FRENCH INTERVENTION AND THE PEACE OF WESTPHALIA

In 1635 Richelieu had finally *declared* war upon the Austrian Hapsburgs—France would never admit it meant the Empire—after having *participated* in it certainly since the entrance of Gustavus Adolphus. This step was in a sense the result of the battle of Nördlingen, in which the Spanish Hapsburgs had combined with their Austrian kinsmen to defeat the Protestants and Swedes. French intervention was also intended to counteract the peace of Prague. Since this peace had all but reunited the Empire, Richelieu was determined to split it again. He believed that the time had come to launch the final assault upon Hapsburg power, and if not utterly to destroy it, in any case to reduce it to the point where it could no longer threaten the imperial ambitions of France. If in the course of this, France secured Alsace and reached the Rhine, so much the better; but such was not a primary or initial goal of French policy. More important by far was the prospect of wresting control of Franche-Comté and the Spanish Netherlands from the Hapsburgs, since these territories constituted the eastern prong of the vise in which the Hapsburgs had held France for generations. If it meant the continuation of the war in Germany for another thirteen years, this was a regrettable incident to the more important goal of securing France against Hapsburg power.

The French aggression, though seemingly well supported by Sweden, the Netherlands, and the German Protestants, did not at first work out well. The Spanish, invading from the Netherlands, all but captured Paris; elsewhere, too, the French met defeat, due to incompetent commanders and lack of logistic support for badly organized armies. But in the face of these reverses, Richelieu showed his accustomed fortitude and perseverance, as told in another chapter. In due course, the internal weakness of Spain, highlighted by the successful revolt of Portugal in 1640,[8] was revealed in the crushing defeat at Rocroy (1643), which ended the legend of the invincibility of the Spanish infantry. The emperor thereupon authorized peace negotiations. Spain lost almost fifteen thousand men and never recovered from the disaster. This brilliant French victory was achieved under Enghien (Louis, Prince de Condé) (1621–86),

[8] See below, pp. 225–9.

one of two younger military leaders whom Mazarin, less eager for military glory than Richelieu, had gladly put into key positions. The other was Henry, Comte de Turenne (1611–75), whose brilliant strategy detached Maximilian of Bavaria for a time from the imperial cause and brought about the collapse of the Hapsburgs' western defenses.

After Rocroy, the Bavarian army had once again become the mainstay of the imperial position. It had successfully defended Württemberg against Turenne and Condé. But its dominance was due in part to General Piccolomini's being needed in the Netherlands, while General Gallas, through incompetence, wrecked the imperial forces in a vain attempt to check a Swedish attack upon Denmark (1644). Fortunately Queen Christina, now eighteen, mounted the throne of Gustavus Adolphus in that year. Determined to help secure peace, she insisted that the Swedish plenipotentiaries actively promote the negotiations. Furthermore, the Dutch, after Rocroy, had finally decided that France had become a greater danger than Spain, and were therefore quite willing to help further the peace which they more than others had ever been prepared to welcome. Finally, Pope Urban VIII, often the champion of the French cause, while at the same time keenly concerned over his own power, had died. In his place, the weaker and unaggressive Innocent X had mounted St. Peter's throne; by merely failing to support Mazarin and the French position with the energy of his predecessor, Innocent enhanced the chances of peace.

Actually, beginning about 1641, the preliminaries of a peace had for a number of years been under negotiation. They took definite shape after Rocroy when the emperor decided to go ahead. Crosscurrents of policy had previously caused the negotiations to be divided into halves. At Münster the treaty between the Austrian Hapsburgs, their allies and France was being negotiated, while at Osnabrück, some miles away, the Swedes negotiated with the Empire and its estates. There were endless wrangles over etiquette and protocol, but these disputes were often baroque designs, hiding deeper policy conflicts. Thus the refusal of the French ambassador to meet the Spaniard presumably served Mazarin's desire to avoid a peace settlement with Spain; seemingly senseless insistence upon forms for the furtherance of concrete policy was frequent.

The real difficulties arose from the complexity of the situation. France and Sweden both insisted that they were at war with the Hapsburgs, rather than the Empire, since part of the estates were on their side. The estates on their part insisted upon participation, not only to protect their territorial rights, but also to settle the constitutional and other internal issues from which the war had originated; for under the constitution of the Empire these were issues of immediate concern to them. Indeed, in 1640-41, the first representative assembly of the estates since 1603 had met at Regensburg, and had, after thirteen months of deliberation, concluded with an *Abschied,* as it was supposed to do.[9] But all attempts to keep them together failed, and on August 29, 1645, the emperor invited all those who were entitled to vote in the diet to participate. This meant a great complication in the negotiations, for each member of the estates could decide for himself whether to join the negotiations at Münster or at Osnabrück, and in each city there were established separate *collegia* of electors, princes, and cities. As a result, each decision called for agreement between the two separate respective *collegia* in Münster and Osnabrück, and then between all three of the *collegia* in turn, after which it had to be accepted by the emperor.

Unfortunately, two other factors besides the resulting clumsy procedure contributed to the extreme slowness of the negotiations. One was the fact that a number of other powers were brought into the negotiations. Richelieu's aspiration to make France the arbiter of Christianity favored this extension, but so did a variety of other ambitions, including the Holy See's similar desire. Thus Spain and the United Provinces, Portugal and Venice, Denmark, Poland and a number of others appeared on the scene. And while no peace was agreed upon between France and Spain, such a peace was worked out between Spain and the United Provinces.

The other, and perhaps the more serious difficulty, resulted from the failure to arrange for a cessation of hostilities, while the congress met. For not only was the course of negotiations continually being affected by the shifting fortunes of the battlefield, but some of the negotiating powers, notably Sweden and France, were thereby induced to intensify their war activities, in order to force a decision or effect an alliance. A striking illustration was the frightful devastation of Bavaria by French troops, undertaken in order to force the elector to abandon his connection with the emperor, May to October, 1648. At that point, fortunately, the peace was concluded, and the outrages came to an end. There can be little doubt that this would have happened much sooner if there had been a cease-fire agreement at the start, but the parties were too far

---

[9] This meeting was significant in showing that the "unity" of the Reich had, in a measure, been achieved by the peace of Prague, until French diplomacy and warfare disrupted it again.

apart at the outset to make this kind of agreement possible. So for five years they wrangled, maneuvered and shifted at Münster and Osnabrück, living in plenty while the surrounding countryside starved, and while terrible destruction was wrought upon the helpless mass of the people, not only in Germany, but in Italy, western France and elsewhere.

The main political and territorial provisions of the treaty, now generally known as the Treaty of Westphalia of 1648, were as follows: (1) Each German principality was declared a sovereign member of the body known as the Empire, and hence could declare war and make peace at its own discretion. (2) Alsace, with the exception of the free imperial city of Strassburg, was ceded to France, and the forcible acquisition of the bishoprics of Metz, Toul and Verdun by France was confirmed. (3) Sweden acquired the western parts of Pomerania (including Stettin) and the bishoprics of Bremen and Verden, thereby securing control of the mouths of three great German rivers: the Weser, the Elbe and the Oder. (4) Brandenburg, starting on its career of expansion, added most of eastern Pomerania to its possessions, along with the contested lands of the former bishoprics of Magdeburg, Halberstadt and Minden. (5) Saxony was confirmed in the possession of Lusatia. (6) Both France and Sweden, through their territorial acquisitions, were placed in a position to interfere in the affairs of the Empire at any time; since the treaties reaffirmed the constitution (Articles 8 of Osnabrück, 62–66 of Münster), any breach of the constitution was made a concern of France and Sweden; besides, Sweden was given the status of an estate of the Empire for Bremen, etc. (Article 10 of Osnabrück). France's full sovereignty over Alsace [10] precluded this status. (7) The vexatious question of the electorate and Palatinate, which had been so largely involved in the continuation of the war after 1622, was resolved by creating a new electoral office, so that both the duke of Bavaria and the son of Frederick could become electors; at the same time the Lower Palatinate along the Rhine was given back to the Elector Palatine, while the Upper Palatinate remained with Bavaria. (8) Status of full sovereignty was formally accorded to the United Provinces and Switzerland, which had hitherto been bound to the Empire by a shadowy dependence. (9) Calvinists, at the insistence of Brandenburg, were given equal status with Lutherans, and the year 1624 was chosen for determining ecclesiastical

---

[10] This is how it worked out; the actual provisions of the treaty were complicated and unclear.

control, while the terms of the religious peace of Augsburg were relaxed and greater toleration enjoined upon rulers. (10) On the imperial courts, the number of Catholic and Protestant judges was to be equal thereafter. The terms of treaty precluded objections by the church; consequently, Pope Innocent X forthwith condemned the treaty as unacceptable. While this ban was never lifted, the treaty remained as a symbol of the emergence of the modern state and of the system of many such states, facing each other as strictly secular sovereigns. The Counter Reformation's long-drawn-out struggle to recapture the unity of Christendom by force of arms had ended in failure.

The negotiations for the Treaty of Westphalia initiated what became a standing operating procedure of the new diplomacy; congresses of ambassadors at the end of a war to try to negotiate a peace settlement on the basis of the sovereign equality of victor and vanquished. This method with all its faults seems in retrospect superior to the more recent practice of dictating peace terms: its often elaborate compromises resulted in a greater degree of genuine pacification. But not always. The vague and in important respects contradictory provisions of the Treaty of Westphalia concerning Alsace served as a welcome pretext for Louis XIV when he decided to challenge them in the next generation. It is interesting that French opposition opinion—rather paradoxically, considering the substantial French gains under the settlement—attacked the treaty savagely and delayed its signing by France until 1651. Indignation was leveled at Mazarin because he had failed to establish peace with Spain at the same time. The anger of the public over this was an important ingredient of the commotion which led to the Fronde.[11]

But throughout Germany the announcement of the conclusion of peace was greeted with such joy as the utterly exhausted populace could still muster. There were celebrations upon celebrations, and all the baroque poets burst into heavily ornate song to welcome the dove of peace. Among the most solemn was the following "Song of Thanks for the Declaration of Peace":

> Praise God! Now has been heard
> The noble word of peace and joy
> That now shall come to rest
> The lance and swords' murder.
> Cheer and bring out again
> Your music, Germany,

[11] See below, pp. 235–42.

And sing again thine songs
In high and full-voiced Choir.
Lift now thine mind
To thine GOD and say:
Lord, Thy grace and kindness
Remains indeed eternal! . . .
We have deserved nothing
But heavy penalty and great wrath,
Because there still flourishes
Among us the fresh and mean tree of sin.[12]

Thus the greatest of them, Paul Gerhardt, greeted the coming of peace, concluding this solemn, chorale-like poem with a reminder that the peace of Christ is the truly eternal one.

In spite of the tendency of historical scholarship to tone down the doleful tales which are traditionally associated with the Thirty Years' War, there can be little doubt that its effects were not only disastrous in terms of the immediate future, but that the aftereffects of this war thwarted German life for a hundred years. It was only in the period of Goethe and Schiller that the German people seemed to shake off the pallor that had hung over the nation's cultural life. To be sure, there were noble exceptions, such as Leibniz and Bach, but on the whole the loss in human creative talent as well as the material devastation in town

[12] Gottlob! nun ist erschollen
Das edle Fried—und Freudeswort,
Dass nunmehr ruhen sollen
Die Spiess und Schwerter und ihr Mord.
Wohlauf und nimm nun-wieder
Dein Saitenspiel hervor,
Oh Deutschland, und sing wieder
Im hohen vollen Chor.
Erhebe Dein Gemüte
Zu Deinem Gott und sprich
Herr, Deine Gnad und Güte
Bleibt dennoch eniglich! . . .

Wir haben nichts verdienet
Als schwere Straf und grossen Zorn,
Weil stets noch bei uns grünet
Der freche schnöde Sündendorn.
See for this poem Karl Goedeke, *Gedichte von Paul Gerhardt*, in *Deutsche Dichter des siebzehnten Jahrhunderts* (ed. by Karl Goedeke and Julius Tittmann), Vol. XII. The Introduction summarizes the scant knowledge we have of Gerhardt's life (1607 or 1608 to 1676). The poem has a number of verses.

and country could not be overcome until after a long convalescence. Even worse, in the long run, was the institutional confusion which the war brought about. The perpetuation of a vast array of principalities large and small could only serve to prevent the growth of a healthy national spirit related to a suitable government and constitution. For a system of social order and government which had served well enough within the context of the medieval unity of church and empire could in the age of the sovereign state and nation lead only to endless frustrations and eventual violence in the search for a solution. It may be a bit far-fetched to trace an explanation of the violence of Fascist nationalism in Germany back to the Thirty Years' War.[13] But that the "monstrosity" which the young Pufendorf saw in the German constitution had something to do with the rise of Prussia few will deny. In any case, the Thirty Years' War marked the effective end of the medieval dream of universal empire, until the revolutionary first Napoleon revived it on a novel basis.

As to the actual physical destruction, even after all allowance has been made for the critical reduction of earlier figures, enough remains to stagger the imagination. There were very great regional variations, to be sure. But some reasonably well-established facts may serve to indicate the pattern. The worst-devastated lands were Bohemia and Württemberg, Saxony, and Thuringia. In Württemberg the number of men capable of bearing arms had, from 1623 to 1652, dropped from 65,400 to 14,800 (at best). The Countship of Henneberg in Thuringia lost half its families. In Württemberg more than half of all buildings were destroyed, 318 castles, 36,100 houses in the cities. The killing of cattle and horses laid large areas of farmland waste for many years; in a county of Brandenburg 822 of 1,878 hides of land, in another only 630 of 1,900 peasants were left. Comparable to the figures in agriculture were those in handicraft. Thus in Munich the number of master clothiers dropped from 32 to 10, that of weavers from 161 to 82.[14]

All in all, the toll in human suffering resulting from this greatest of the religious wars was staggering, the results in terms of the religious objectives practically nil. The high hopes of Ferdinand II and his Counter

---

13 This aspect is suggested in Peter Viereck's imaginative, if somewhat exaggerated *Metapolitics: From the Romantics to Hitler* (1941).

14 These figures are from Moritz Ritter, *op. cit.*, III, 614–15. The figures offered by E. C. Wedgwood, *op. cit.*, are admittedly fanciful; some of the remarks, e.g. about the improved situation of peasant farmers, are doubtful.

Reformation associates were finished, as were the Calvinists' projects for a predominantly Protestant Empire. The activities on both sides had merely succeeded in demonstrating that rather than surrendering their religious convictions, Germans would divide permanently into many principalities, each governed according to the formula of the religious peace of Augsburg: *"Cujus regio, ejus religio."* A vicious doctrine on the face of it, it nonetheless provided a tolerable compromise for the Germans as a people; a man could remove from one "sovereignty" to another, if compelled by religious scruples. Thus religion triumphed, in a negative sense, over the political requirements of building a modern national state. The outcome of the Thirty Years' War in this sense permanently shaped the course of German history, in contrast with England and France, where the religious wars led, eventually, to a consolidation of religious views, favoring Protestant predominance in one, Catholic in the other. To modify the "forcing of conscience" inherent in such unity, religious toleration—the willingness to let the individual decide for himself—served as the pathmaker for a later more pronounced individualism. In Germany, each "state" patriarchially protected the individual's conscience, while the nation remained a cultural community without firm political framework. Protestant Prussia and Saxony, Catholic Austria and Bavaria, not to mention the dozens of lesser princes, nobles and "free" cities, could proceed to develop a political absolutism, untempered by cultural aspirations. The fatal split in German thought and action between the realm of the spirit and the realm of material power had been started. The modern state emerged from the Treaty of Westphalia in all the kingdoms, duchies and principalities, but it was a crippled, barebones "state," a mere apparatus—a bureaucracy serving princely aspirations for power and aggrandizement. The nation remained outside.

Chapter Seven

THE MODERN STATE ABSOLUTE: FRANCE UNDER RICHELIEU AND MAZARIN

I. INTRODUCTION: ANTECEDENTS

THE same generation which witnessed the failure of Wallenstein to convert the Holy Roman Empire of the German Nation into a modern state saw the consolidation of such a state in France under Richelieu. Indeed, Richelieu resumed the task of internal and external aggrandizement which the first great Bourbon, Henry IV, had felicitously initiated. As we have seen, when Henry IV was felled by Ravaillac's knife in 1610 he was about to launch his assault upon the Hapsburgs in Spain and Austria, having consolidated his power in France. Though a convert himself, he headed a great Protestant coalition. When Richelieu resumed, Protestant prospects had faded in France and abroad, and to revive them abroad was one of his most persistent and difficult tasks.

In the meantime, France had gone through a turbulent period of internal strife. For a number of years after the death of the king (1610–17) the queen mother, Marie de' Medici, had ruled weakly and corruptly with the aid of her favorites. The great nobles of France had made the most of their opportunity, had milked the royal treasury of millions, and had made substantial progress in converting France into an aristocracy, wherein the most powerful nobles, controlling large areas of the country in virtual autonomy, would deal with each other almost like sovereign princes. Reinforced by religious interests and convictions, these centrifugal tendencies had all but triumphed when the young king, with the aid of his favorite, the (later) Duke de Luynes, seized control, killed his mother's helpers and banished her to Blois. Richelieu, who at the time had been put in charge of foreign affairs, was swept out of office with the rest, and only slowly made his way back to power as the adviser of the queen mother, whose reconciliation with the king he eventually effected at the latter's instance.

The period of De Luynes' predominance was one of confusion, intrigue and an unsteady foreign policy. With Urban VIII pope since 1623, a not unreasonable hope was entertained that Hapsburg and Spanish power would be checked. Fortunately, De Luynes died before his weakness could do much damage.

II. RICHELIEU'S ARRIVAL TO POWER

In 1622, Armand-Jean du Plessis, Duc de Richelieu, had become cardinal. He was still very much in the graces of the queen mother, and so he was made first minister after a weak successor to De Luynes had been eliminated. It was hoped and expected that he would carry on. Originally destined for a secular career, he was induced to take the vows in order to be able at the age of twenty to take over from his brother the bishopric of Luçon. Born in 1585, Richelieu was forty when he achieved the position of supreme power which he held till his death in 1640. A man of superb intellectual ability and overweening ambition, he was cold, calculating, ruthless and of tremendous energy and tenacity, though of weak physical constitution. Richelieu was a man of deep passions, which he knew how to control; he possessed superb political imagination, and a penetrating knowledge of men; generally he despised humankind. In his celebrated *Mémoires,* of many volumes, he described his conception of policy as compounded of three interrelated parts: destroying the Huguenot opposition, humbling the great nobles and reducing them to subjects, and raising the royal prestige and power abroad to its deserved place in the sun.[1]

These were really different aspects of one central objective: aggrandizement of the royal power at home and abroad to the point where true sovereignty, i.e. independence, would be achieved. Louis XIII, while a man of limited ability, had the judgment to support Richelieu as the mainstay of his own power and prestige. Richelieu, by making the achievement of "absolute" power by the king his one dominant goal, enhanced his own position accordingly. The political objective or plan of Richelieu was thus a very simple one, such as only a superb strategist of political power would adopt and maintain. Through him, a prince of the church, the claims of absolute secular authority were made to prevail, and the

---

[1] See Richelieu's striking statement of this position in his political testament: *"Je lui promis d'employer toute mon industrie et toute l'autorité qu'il lui plaisoit me donner pour ruiner le parti huguenot, rabaisser l'orguol des Grands, réduire tous ses sujets en leur devoir et relever son nom dans les nations étrangères au point où il devoit être."* Richelieu, *Testament Politique,* ed. with notes by Louis André, 1947, 95.

body corporate of the modern state came into being. Out of numerous beginnings and origins reaching far back into the Middle Ages, the state emerged from the hands of this builder, thereafter to be admired and feared, but to be copied by all. The state which Machiavelli had visualized as the most admirable work of art man can make thus emerged in true baroque style: not clearly against the church, but partly by its connivance. This extraordinary drama revolved around two remarkable personalities: Pope Urban VIII (Barberini) and Père Joseph, both of whom we have encountered before.

As conscious of *raison d'État* as Richelieu, Pope Urban VIII (1623-44), a markedly independent personality, was determined to avoid domination by Spain and Hapsburg, and to become once again *arbiter mundi* through firm territorial control of a growing papal state. Though at times clashing sharply with Richelieu, he was nonetheless fully aware of the fact that his policy could succeed only if France and other states were built up to balance the overweening power of the Hapsburgs. Actually, the papal policy failed, because the papacy was in the very nature of things ill-fitted to compete with secular princes in the building of a modern state. But while it lasted, it provided Père Joseph and Richelieu with a very important and sometimes crucial ally.

Père Joseph, a Capuchin, knew that no universal empire would restore the holy church, as the more ardent counterreformers of the Society of Jesus dreamed. Père Joseph had instead a dream of his own: a new crusade by which to eject the Turk from Europe and through which to unite Christian princes in a common cause. But this dream became entirely submerged in the struggle for the ascendancy of France. It was not an accident that a Capuchin should have been the one to do this. A scion of the minor French nobility and officialdom, François Le Clerk du Tremblay had been a soldier before he entered the Capuchin order in 1599. The Capuchins had been organized in the early sixteenth century by Matteo di Bassi (1520) as an offshoot of the Franciscans, who were devoted, in keeping with the original teachings of St. Francis, to extreme austerity, simplicity and poverty. After nearly one hundred years of growth, they were constituted an independent order in 1619. Together with the Jesuits, they were the chief protagonists of the Counter Reformation, and while their primary efforts were directed toward working with the poor, they also produced a number of skillful diplomatists. Among these latter, Père Joseph was unquestionably the greatest; indeed, the

Gray Eminence occupies a unique position in the annals of European statecraft. Père Joseph was probably as intensely stage-conscious as ever was a man of the baroque age. Incessantly traversing the length and breadth of Europe, in his gray hood and bare feet, shunning all comforts, yet readily admitted into the confidence of the most exalted, he mingled in his thinking to a superb degree the *raison d'État* with the *raison d'Église*. This enabled him to become a mystery man of the *Theatrum Europaeum* upon which he played his dramatic role. The rivalry of his order, Italian and French, anti-Hapsburg and anti-Spanish, with the Society of Jesus, which sought to promote the Counter Reformation at the hands of Spain and Hapsburg, no doubt provided an obscure backdrop to his extraordinary activity.

Père Joseph early recognized Richelieu's genius and promoted his fortunes. The extraordinary regard which Richelieu on his part had for the Capuchin was expressed in a letter written, presumably, immediately upon his return to power.[2] "You are the principal agent whom God has employed to lead me to all the honors which I have reached. . . . I beg you speed your voyage and come soon to partake of the management of affairs. There are pressing ones which I do not wish to confide to anyone nor to resolve without your advice." It was the letter of one friend to another, perhaps the only friend whom Richelieu had; it was a friendship born of a shared passion for power and politics as the essential vehicles for achieving a new order of things, a comradeship rooted in "understanding each other perfectly." They were both master craftsmen in the devious skills of diplomatic intrigue and of the secrets of empire—the *arcana imperii* which baroque man loved to picture as the motivating force behind the stage. As God governed the universe, superbly but perplexingly to mortal man, so the "earthly gods," the rulers of states, governed their realms "according to necessity." To know how, was the quintessence of "reason of state," as it was the quintessence of ecclesiastical statecraft. Richelieu knew, as did Père Joseph, that the Holy Father understood this problem. In a memorandum justifying the resumption of subsidies for the Dutch, which the Catholic party opposed (1624), Richelieu declared that in Rome matters were judged no less according

---

[2] G. d'Avenel in his *Lettres du Cardinal de Richelieu*, II, 3, dates this letter the end of April, but G. Hanotaux, in his *Histoire du Cardinal de Richelieu*, III, 2, suggests that it must belong to the second half of August, 1624, since Richelieu speaks of his becoming *premier ministre*. This, of course, happened in mid-August.

to the necessities of power politics than according to the interests of the church.

When Richelieu achieved the dominant position in the councils of the king, he had been for years close to the queen mother, Marie de' Medici, and hence was generally believed to be a probable protagonist of a Catholic and pro-Spanish orientation of French policy. While the middle of the road party of the politically minded *politiques* had had some intimation that the cardinal might move in their direction, they were generally apprehensive, though ready for the gamble. The Huguenots naturally expected the worst. Ever since the religious issue had arisen, the broad tendency of French politics had been to divide into a Protestant (Calvinist), feudally aristocratic and anti-Spanish camp, and into a Catholic, royalist-bureaucratic and pro-Spanish camp. There had been politicians who tried to straddle this division, and there had been startling exceptions like Henry IV and his great minister, the Duc de Sully. It was the strategic genius of Richelieu and Père Joseph to transcend this traditional partisanship, and by reviving the conception of the *politiques* to weld together the royalist-bureaucratic and the anti-Protestant and anti-Spanish positions and to make of the combination one solid foundation for the unity of France, her power and preponderance under an absolute monarchy.

Richelieu adopted the platform of the third estate which he had so eloquently opposed in the *États Généraux* of 1614: "That, as the king is the recognized sovereign in his state, not holding his crown but from God alone, there exists no power on earth whatever it might be, whether spiritual or temporal, which has any right over his kingdom. . . . The state of France depends immediately only upon God." This article embodied doctrine which has long since become accepted throughout the western world; at the time it challenged the newly defined pretensions of the Roman Church, rejected the decisions of the Council of Trent, proposed to settle the century-old conflict between Gallicanism and Ultramontanism, and in all these respects was not only deeply disturbing to the clerical estate, but obnoxious to the queen mother and her ultramontane circle, dominated by the great preacher, Cardinal Peter de Bérulle (1575–1629), the founder of the Oratory (1611). The conflict became insurmountable, and was finally compromised by a formula: it was said that it was no longer necessary to adopt the proposed article, since the crown considered it as "presented and received." Richelieu had been in the midst of this struggle, and his final address had been a masterpiece of double talk. Whatever his views at the time, by 1624 he had become profoundly impressed with the value of the national mysticism (*mystique nationale*) that expressed itself in the divine right of kings and their states as against the political pretensions of the Holy Church. Throughout the remainder of his life, he was to insist upon the prestige of the king and of his servants as embodiments of *l'État:* the royal prime minister took precedence over even the most exalted nobles and the princes of the blood.

As soon as Richelieu arrived in the councils of the king, a new note of hardheaded power politics appeared in French policy. Even before he was made prime minister, he had persuaded the council to renew the subsidies to the Dutch; similarly the king of Denmark, Christian IV, was promised an annual aid in support of his proposed war against the Hapsburgs in Germany. Yet, in spite of the fact that Christian's main antagonist would be Tilly, commanding the troops of the Catholic League, Richelieu also set to work to split the League, and especially Maximilian of Bavaria, from the Hapsburgs by promises of neutrality, protection for his Palatinate acquisitions, and other help. Finally, and perhaps most dramatically, a marriage was arranged between Henrietta Maria, the king's sister, and Charles, Prince of Wales (fall of 1624). Richelieu also renewed the treaties with Venice and Savoy (September 5, 1624). It all looked like a scheme for a great coalition against Spain, and Buckingham and his diplomats entered upon it with alacrity. Later, all these moves came to look more like an elaborate set of feints to scare Spain and the Holy See sufficiently to free the cardinal of their interference in domestic French concerns. Richelieu would be done with traitors.

But the first pay-off came in the form of a dramatic attack upon a key Spanish position: the Valtelline.

III. THE VALTELLINE

Ever so often, in the course of history, a small territory suddenly achieves a position of crucial significance. As a result, men of local stature suddenly find themselves involved in great power politics, and they often fail to measure up to the tasks thrust upon them. Such was the fate of the Valtelline and of its masters, the Swiss mountain communities of Graubünden (Gray League), *Gotteshaus* (League of God's House) and the *Zehngerichte* (League of the Ten Jurisdictions), together referred to as the Grisons or Rhaetian Leagues, attached to but not fully a part of the Swiss Confederation. The *Val Tellina,* Catholic and Italian, like the city of Chiavenna at its western end, stretches from the northern end of Lake Como eastward toward the headwaters of the Adda River, near the Ofen and the Stelvio passes in the Münsterthal, roughly paralleling the Engadin to the north. At its northeastern end, the town of Bormio balances Sondrio to the south. Its fighting strength, according to a Venetian report (and the Venetians had reasons to be well informed, since Venice recruited many mercenaries in this district), was about fifteen thousand in 1600, the total population of the Grisons and the Valtelline being about eighty thousand. The reason for its suddenly attaining the position of a key area was the valley's strategic position as a connecting link between the Spanish and the Austrian-German Hapsburg realms. For the passes out of the Valtelline linked the duchy of Milan, which Spain controlled, with the Tyrol, while both to the east and to the west the passes over the Alps were in the hands of hostile and/or Protestant powers: the Swiss Confederation, Savoy, France on the one side, the Republic of Venice on the other. Clearly, all those concerned with the power of the house of Hapsburg must try to control the Valtelline.

In the years between 1610 and 1640, a series of maneuvers were made by the two rival power camps to secure this control. The French and the Venetians sought to close the valley to Spanish troops by making treaties with the Grisons. Generous handouts to all the key leaders were combined with appeals to their religious sentiment and patriotism to achieve this result. Since the Grisons themselves were divided between Catholics, centered in the bishopric of Chur and the surrounding country districts, and the Protestants in the Gray Leagues and the God's House (Engadin), a protracted and at times extremely violent party struggle ensued. The human drama of these complex policies and passions has been celebrated by Conrad Ferdinand Meyer in his novel, *Jürg Jenatsch,* dealing with undoubtedly the most striking personality among the Protestant preacher-soldiers. But while the depth of conviction which motivated men like Jenatsch provides a noble chapter indeed in the struggle for freedom, their liberation from foreign domination owed more to the internal collapse of Spain than to their personal exertions or the efforts of their foreign supporters. It can fairly be said that these zealots risked their cause by the extremity of the violence committed in its defense.

After the conclusion of the treaty with France, the Spanish erected a fortress at the western entrance to the valley which challenged the

Grisons' control. Efforts on the part of the Grisons to secure its demolition, accompanied by tighter domination of the Valtelliners, precipitated a violent reaction. In 1621 a massacre of the few Protestants in the valley gave the signal for armed conflict. But the efforts of the Grisons to recapture the valley miscarried. French pressure, supported by the Pope, Urban VIII, got no further than a compromise: papal troops occupied the forts controlling the valley in 1623. But the negotiations for a settlement dragged on, and in the early summer of 1624 the French negotiator reluctantly assented to a treaty draft which gave the Spanish the right to pass through the valley, while leaving the forts under papal occupation. At this point, Richelieu entered the scene and radically reversed the French position. When Urban VIII refused to yield to the French, even when threatened with rupture, Richelieu instructed his ambassador in Switzerland, De Coeuvres, to gather an army and proceed to the reconquest of the Valtelline and the Grisons, since they had been put under French protection. This bold move, utterly unexpected, succeeded, and by the spring of 1625 France was in complete control. The indignation in the papal camp, and even more in Spain, knew no bounds, and there was talk of excommunication and other types of ecclesiastical coercion. Richelieu coldly drew the papal nuncio's attention to the fact that he had been given assurances by the Pope himself that if he took the premier's office, he would be free to act in accordance with necessities of the French state. Thus, what no negotiation could have accomplished, bold action brought to pass almost overnight. A key position was torn away from the Spanish system, a breach laid in their line of communications with the Low Countries and Austria. This action electrified all Europe. Like a flash of lightning, it revealed a decisive break between France and Spain, upon whose close understanding European relationships and the forward march of the Counter Reformation had hitherto depended. As Ranke comments, the French enterprise in the Grisons was like the announcement of a new epoch.

Yet the Cardinal's daring seizure of the Valtelline proved to have been overbold. When Richelieu became preoccupied with other internal and external issues, the Spanish and Austrian armies were able to reestablish effective occupation. As a result, Spanish troops and supplies could move from Milan to southern Germany in the crucial years of the Thirty Years' War. In 1635, the decisive victory at Nördlingen was probably made possible by the presence of twelve thousand Spanish professionals who had come up through the Valtelline and who helped administer the blow from which the Swedish forces did not for a long time recover.

The fascination of the intricate politics of the Valtelline in this period lies partly in the fact that the Grisons and their several leagues were democratic. The town meetings of the burghers and peasants in these mountain valleys and their gatherings in Chur have a peculiar appeal to the historical imagination. Here, by a primitive sort of popular referendum, issues of vast international import were settled according to local religious and patriotic views and emotions. It may, indeed, be said, that in the last analysis Richelieu lost out, in spite of the able and devoted efforts of De Coeuvres and later the Duc de Rohan, because the cardinal, skilled in the subtleties of cabinet intrigue, could not and did not grasp the simple fact that in the Grisons all depended upon the good will of the people. But the Grisons themselves likewise failed, and more crucially, because they did not realize that popular sentiment in the valley itself could not be coerced when religious convictions were involved. In this sense, the epic struggle in the Valtelline provides a curious parallel to that of the Pilgrim Fathers who in these very years set out to found a new commonwealth based upon a Christian covenant. The covenant proved mightier than the sword.

IV. INTERNAL TROUBLES: THE NOBILITY AND THE HUGUENOTS

A more pedestrian politician than Richelieu might have argued that internal enemies should be overpowered first, before any such touchy issues as the control of the Valtelline or the Dutch subsidies, let alone the marriage of the king's sister Henrietta with the Prince of Wales, should be raised. But it was part of Richelieu's genius to keep moving on all fronts while never losing sight of his central objective: the strengthening of the French state and its crown against all opponents at home and abroad. Actually, the Huguenots precipitated the issue in the autumn of 1624 by themselves rising against the royal authority. They had suffered a grievous setback in 1622, at the hands of the young king, and had lost all the strongholds guaranteed them by the Edict of Nantes, except La Rochelle, Montauban and Montpellier. It is difficult to understand why or how the Huguenots chose this particular moment for a decisive struggle, unless it was from a sense of impending doom. Richelieu had told the king that his position and crown could not be considered secure while part of his subjects constituted a state within the state, and that therefore La Rochelle must be conquered and destroyed.

The position of the Huguenots was indeed a curious one. Out of the protracted religious wars of the previous century (1562–98) they had, under the Edict of Nantes (1598), emerged as a recognized and protected minority. The higher nobility and the citizens of a number of cities and towns, including some fortified ones, were given the right to Protestant worship. They could hold public office, and participate in four of the *parlements* or provincial high courts. In the sequel, after Henry IV, the Huguenots had made common cause with the aristocratic factions. They had tried to create a political organization of the country similar to the Holy Empire's division into districts, with each district having a military force and captain of its own. They had held many assemblies. Since the more radical Calvinist preachers used these gatherings to stir people to action, Louis XIII had tried to suppress these assemblies, and after their defeat in 1622, the Huguenots had agreed not to meet without the king's leave. But they soon violated this promise. They asserted that it had been given conditionally and on the premise that the king would fulfill his part of the bargain. Especially important to them was the destruction of a fort threatening La Rochelle. This fort, far from being razed, was actually being built up, and the Protestants viewed this action with profound suspicion.

It must also be borne in mind that the Huguenots quite naturally looked upon the accession of Richelieu to power as a victory of the Catholic party, which the queen mother had long espoused. On the other hand, the marriage of Henrietta to the Prince of Wales (see below) and the payment of subsidies to the Dutch encouraged them to think that these Protestant powers would somehow aid them in their efforts. More especially, the duke of Soubise, who had a certain number of ships, thought he might achieve naval control. So he fell upon and captured the small number of ships the king had (January, 1625), seized the islands of Rhé and Oleron, commanding the access to La Rochelle, and roused the Huguenot corporation to make common cause. Richelieu, with unprecedented brazenness, thereupon secured Dutch and English ships, the latter without their crews, and inflicted a serious defeat upon Soubise. While the latter was thus engaged in the coastal areas of the northwest, his brother Henry, duke of Rohan, the ablest and most prominent Huguenot leader in the southwest, stirred up a comparable revolt in the country around Montauban. As in former days, the Spanish government gave help and encouragement to these movements, reinforcing them by persuading some great Catholic nobles to throw in their lot with the rebels. As we have seen, there was great indignation, anyhow, among the Catholics over the cardinal's deals with the Protestant powers, and some violent pamphlets were being distributed. It is a striking illustration of baroque politics that the Spanish ambassador could violently debate with Richelieu his Protestant connections, presumably at one point exclaiming that he was a cardinal of hell and not of the Holy Church, while at the same time his government was subsidizing the Huguenots.

In spite of Spanish aid, the Huguenots suffered setbacks on all sides and eventually sued for peace. The more devoted Catholics wanted, of course, to see them utterly crushed; but Richelieu refused to go further than a compromise. The peace of La Rochelle (February, 1626) was the result. Richelieu with puzzling shrewdness asked the English to negotiate this treaty and they succeeded in persuading the Huguenots. However, he thereby invited the intervention of the English a year later, when the Huguenots appealed to them as the power who had arranged the compromise. The English had carried through the negotiation in the hope and expectation of freeing France's hand for the great military effort of the Danish king to reverse the situation in Germany. They had hoped that the Danes would push back the Catholic forces, and possibly recapture the Palatinate for the elector and his wife, the sister of the new king, Charles I. The duke of Buckingham, England's prime minister, was filled with bitter hatred against Spain, because of his master's rejection as a suitor for the Spanish princess, Anne of Austria, now queen of France. Not only that; he was also vividly concerned with the English parliament's agitation over the government's failure to give effective aid to the Protestant cause. Unfortunately, Buckingham's plan was gravely imperiled by the sudden conclusion of a peace treaty between France and Spain. According to Richelieu, this treaty was negotiated behind his back, and he was confronted with it as a *fait accompli*. It is important to realize, then, that Richelieu was by no means in complete control of the situation. He had to win support for his policies in the king's council, and had to secure the king's own assent. It is fair to say, however, that Richelieu did not fight the treaty with great vigor.

Concluded at the instance of Father Bérulle, with the possible support of the queen mother, this Treaty of Barcelona (May 10, 1626) seemed to protect essential French interests: in the Valtelline the Spanish forts were to be razed and the state of affairs of 1617 to be re-established, with the Grisons reacquiring control over the valley. We have seen how unfortunate a concession this proved to be. But it was the general unrest throughout France, foreshadowing new revolts, which probably persuaded Richelieu to acquiesce, just as a few months earlier he had compromised with the Protestants and other opposition elements in order to be able to fight Spain. There is an element of vacillation here which does not fit the customary picture of Richelieu as the master politician; not until he had vanquished both Protestant and Catholic opposition groups did the cardinal succeed in securing full control and unified direction. In the meantime, the Catholic forces gained the ascendancy in Germany which culminated in the Edict of Restitution (1629).

In any case, the treaty with Spain, whether sought by Richelieu or not, freed his hands for the decisive blow against the Huguenots and the nobles. The situation had been complicated by a very baroque affair at court which revolved around the proposed marriage of the king's younger brother, Gaston of Orléans, with a rich heiress, Mademoiselle de Montpensier. Somehow the plotters seem to have thought that they could seize upon this issue for overthrowing, maybe even killing the cardinal. For a variety of motives, including the queen's increasing dislike for the cardinal, and her friend's the Duchesse de Chevreuse's love of intrigue, they seized upon this obscure issue. To make matters worse, Buckingham, allowing himself to be involved, mortally offended the king. It all ended in the complete victory of the cardinal, who made an example of a young and foolish nobleman, since he could not touch the king's brother. The latter proved a complete cad, betraying all his accomplices, yet being rewarded with the hand of the handsome heiress he had professed to dislike. The whole affair reads like a tragedy of Corneille, stagy and stately, the various personages playing their assigned roles without warm emotions, except the young and foolish lover who ended upon the scaffold. That his friends should have bought out the professional hangman, thereby forcing Richelieu to employ an amateur who succeeded in chopping off the plotter's fair head only after thirty-odd strokes, added that lurid touch so dear to the baroque.

If one were to object that such goings-on are not part of serious history, the answer must be that in the baroque age such an intrigue might well have led to the downfall of a less astute court politician than Richelieu. To clinch Richelieu's point, and to formalize his conception of the modern state, the king then called a gathering of notables (December, 1626), and had the government submit a set of propositions against rebellion: French subjects were not to communicate with foreign agents, not even the papal nuncio; the taking up of arms was to entail loss of all offices; in fact, no one was to collect arms, munitions or funds without the crown's authority; seditious libel was to be made punishable. To these propositions the gathering readily agreed; indeed it went beyond them and decided that the raising of arms against the government should be considered a crime, punishable by the loss of life and estates. The gathering's main counterdemand was the reduction of pensions by at least five million *louis d'or* and the razing of all fortresses not needed for the defense of the realm. Richelieu in turn suggested the establishment of a standing army of twenty thousand men, and the organization of an effective navy—not only for foreign war, but more especially for the maintenance of order and security at home. No objection was raised by the notables, since the assembly was composed to a considerable extent of the higher bourgeoisie, councilors of the *parlements,* and the like; both the high nobility and the clergy were sparsely represented. The prevailing sentiment was, as Ranke says, royalist and even governmental, which in this period meant "popular." The middle class was for the king and the state, as it was in England under the Tudors.

The peace of La Rochelle had proved to be only a truce of short duration. As in previous such agreements, neither party trusted the other, and both the crown and the Huguenots immediately started violating its terms, on the ground that the other party was planning to do so. Richelieu, one suspects, probably let the English negotiate this treaty partly because he had no intention of keeping it. After all, he had told the king in May, 1625, in a secret memorandum: "As long as the Huguenots in France remain a state within the state, the king cannot be master of his kingdom, nor can he do great deeds abroad." Therefore the Huguenot party must be crushed, as he allegedly had told the king upon his accession to power. As the violations of the treaty took more threatening form, as Fort Louis was not razed but strengthened, and various other agreements violated, the Huguenots began to present to the English government urgent requests for protection. To such entreaties Buckingham was the more ready to lend a willing ear as his situation in England was steadily deteriorating. He was burned in effigy in London and elsewhere and the opposition in parliament was growing (see next chapter). When it became known that the Treaty of Monzon (Barcelona) had been implemented by a treaty of alliance (April, 1627), Buckingham decided upon war. He was smarting under the humiliation which he believed he had suffered when the French king refused to have him come to Paris to negotiate. Back of that was Buckingham's behavior at the time of the marriage of Charles to Henrietta. Serious difficulties had since arisen. These difficulties all went back to secret clauses in the marriage contract, which sought to protect the queen's Catholic religion. At the time of the marriage (May, 1625) Buckingham had created a scandal by declaring himself in love with the queen of France, Anne of Austria. Remembering the knights-errant of old, he had staged a romanesque affair of tears and kneefalls, which thrilled the baroque courts of Europe, but outraged the timid and somber king of France. No wonder that Richelieu could inform the king, when Buckingham suggested the following year that he return to France, that "Buckingham's presence in Paris would be shameful for the king, noxious to the well-being of the state and inconvenient for the understanding of the two crowns." As events were to prove, the cardinal was quite wrong, if he meant to imply that the refusal to have Buckingham would be helpful to better understanding, for Buckingham, in accordance with the conventions of the baroque stage, drew the sword. On June 27, 1627, he sailed for France with a fleet and five thousand men, and a fortnight later appeared before La Rochelle. The hour of decision had struck for French Protestantism. "To be or not to be. . . ."

When Buckingham arrived at La Rochelle, he found the town hesitant to receive him. He, on his side, instead of establishing a wide belt of control on the coast surrounding the town, as Gustavus Adolphus was to do three years later when he invaded the Empire, landed upon the island of Rhé, which commands the approach to La Rochelle, and laid siege to Fort St. Martin, in the mistaken belief that he could quickly take it and thereby secure his line of retreat. Much baroque play-acting between himself and the gallant commander of the fort, Toiras, did not prevent the latter from holding out desperately, until finally relieved by a bold ruse, organized by Richelieu personally. On November 5, 1627, Buckingham decided to sail home, having accomplished nothing. By that time, Richelieu had strengthened the original force surrounding La Rochelle, and with the king was conducting the siege. The army was kept under strict discipline, men were paid on time, and by the fisc directly, and since the French crown's naval forces were still weak, Richelieu undertook to block La Rochelle's harbor and access to the sea by erecting a wall. This amazing enterprise succeeded in completely shutting La Rochelle off from outside supplies, and by the spring of 1628 hunger began to make itself felt; indeed the prospect of subjection through starvation loomed, unless outside help should manage to force the wall of concrete and sunken ships.

With the Dutch effectively neutralized through Richelieu's diplomacy—he had renewed the Compiègne treaty of mutual aid for another nine years, granting the Dutch subsidies on a grand scale—the only hope was the British. After Buckingham's ignominious return to England his position had become increasingly difficult. He made two attempts to relieve the situation, but both were unsuccessful, and the second was foiled by his murder in September, 1628. Lord Denbigh, commanding a small fleet, merely approached the blockaded city, but did not venture to attack the wall; Lord Lindsey, under specific instructions, tried to attack (October 3, 1628), but was frustrated by the refusal of his rebellious subordinates to fight and therefore withdrew. Thereupon the city, with its population reduced, so it is reported, from 25,000 to 5,000, surrendered unconditionally to the king. Richelieu, aided by Père Joseph, who had triumphed over all the intrigue hatched at the court against his master's determined effort to subdue the Protestant citadel, counseled moderation. In the session of the king's council where the very people who had tried to get the siege lifted now urged ruthless revenge, Richelieu declared:

Rarely has a prince had such an opportunity to distinguish himself before his contemporaries and posterity by his moderation; moderation and graciousness are the qualities by which kings are enabled to imitate the Lord God; for they can be his image upon earth only by doing good, and not by destroying and by exterminating. For the rest, the deeper the guilt of La Rochelle, the more purely will the generosity of the prince appear; by his victorious arms he has broken the resistance and has forced the rebels to submit nakedly to him and only to him. But his victory over himself will appear even greater, if now he forgives. The great name of this city will carry his fame to all the world, and will communicate it to coming generations.

This was indeed a noble sentiment, calculated to appeal to the romanesque chivalry of Louis XIII, who accepted the cardinal's advice. As a great historian has commented, if one wanted to talk of punishment, there had been punishment enough. There was something awesome about this uncompromising devotion to principle which had animated the proud burghers to bear the unbearable, to fight their fight till the very end of bodily self-sacrifice of man, woman, and child. As the conquerors rode into the city of the dead, the king, we are told, was overwhelmed by a sense of somber pride at the thought that Frenchmen could have endured such heroic sufferings in the service of an ideal. But while the pitiful remainder of the population was granted life, their possessions and the right to exercise their religion freely, the essential autonomy of the city, as of so many others throughout the breadth of Europe, and more especially of France, was destroyed. The proud autonomy of La Rochelle had rested upon its privileges, more especially upon its self-government under an elected council, its burgomaster, its local recruitment and taxation. All that was now gone; the modern state triumphed, with its officials and tax collectors; the walls and towers were razed never to rise again. Its last burgomaster, the fervent, marvelous, indomitable Jean Guiton, was deprived of his position and exiled from the city he had so undauntedly defended in its life-and-death struggle. With him and his city, the medieval period in French politics came to an end; the modern world had emerged. As if to mock man, a terrific storm blew in from the ocean in the week after the surrender, tore the cardinal's wall to shreds and opened once more the sea lanes for any who might have relieved the city on the rock. But could the forward march of history have been halted? Hardly. In retrospect, it appears a kindly fate which prevented the Huguenots at La Rochelle from continuing their resistance for another winter. Sooner or later their world of local autonomy was bound to crumble under the blows of the concentrated power of absolute monarchy. As Richelieu was wont to say, in justifying ruthless measures, severe measures are more kind, because they shorten the agony.

While Richelieu and Buckingham were thus committing their available resources to a war in which Protestantism was crushed in France, they left Christian of Denmark and the German Protestants without the promised help, so that Catholic Austria and the League could triumph over Protestantism in Germany. Things were going better for the master strategists of the Counter Reformation, including Père Joseph, than even they had planned, or indeed wished. For the Hapsburgs' sway in Germany seemed irresistible until Father Joseph succeeded in muddying the waters at Regensburg.

As a matter of fact, even after the conclusion of peace between France and Savoy (March) and between France and England (April, 1630), the Huguenots in southern France, the Languedoc, Provence and Gascogny, resumed the war of resistance against the crown under the brilliant military leadership of Henry de Rohan, but it was a losing fight. Within three months, filled with conquest, devastation and wholesale murder of surrendering Huguenot resisters, the king's armies conquered the key fortresses and Rohan sued for peace. The settlement was dictated: after the frightful revenge meted out during the campaign—against Richelieu's constant counsel of moderation and mildness—the Protestants were forced to consent to the complete destruction of all their fortified places, but for the rest the Edict of Nantes was reaffirmed, and toleration granted, much to the disgust of the more ardent partisans of a Catholic policy of Counter Reformation.

These recurrent efforts at reconciliation of the Huguenot faction, worked out by Richelieu or at his insistence, provided the Protestants would thereafter become loyal subjects of the French crown, helped to alienate further the queen mother, Marie de' Medici. Forever jealous of her son's advisers and favorites, bigoted and slow-witted, yet domineering and intriguing, Marie de' Medici had originally promoted the fortunes of Richelieu. A woman's intuition, reinforced by the skillful persuasion of Père Joseph, had made her sense the extraordinary ability of the cardinal; at the same time, she assumed that a prince of the church must needs promote the fortunes of the Counter Reformation. But as Richelieu became independent of her support, developed a direct relationship to the king, and forged a policy more and more closely resembling that of Henry IV, the situation became intolerable, as far as the queen mother was concerned. Her devotion to Father Bérulle, now a cardinal too, played its role in making this pretentious woman decide that the cardinal must be eliminated. But these after-effects of the campaign against the Huguenots and their destruction did not come into the open until after the Mantuan campaigns.

V. THE MANTUAN SUCCESSION

The fall of La Rochelle freed the cardinal's hands for urgent actions against France's external enemies. While the siege of La Rochelle was on, the ruler of the Italian duchy of Mantua and Montferrat had died, leaving his lands to Charles of Gonzaga, the duke of Nevers who, a distant descendant of the eastern Roman emperors, had dreamed with

Père Joseph of a new crusade to drive the Turks from Europe and re-capture the Holy Land. As a French subject, he was now seizing these two rich fiefs of the Holy Roman Empire, although the ruler of Savoy claimed Montferrat and Spain supported the rival claim of another descendant to the whole heritage. Between them, Charles Emmanuel of Savoy and the Spanish invaded Montferrat and laid siege to the key fortress of Casale. The Spanish party in France, of course, favored abandonment of the Mantuan claims and a settlement. But Richelieu, considering Italy "the heart of the world"—a natural sentiment for a prince of the church—urged immediate military action and secured the king's consent. With unbelievable swiftness an army was set in motion and in early January, 1629, Louis XIII was in the Alps at the head of his troops, and soon seized the key fortress city of Suza, com-manding a pass into Italy. In March, a settlement was concluded with the prince of Savoy. Charles Emmanuel, with the slyness of a mountain peasant, had once again changed his alignment; it must be remembered, however, that as ruler of his small and not very resourceful principality, he was wedged in between the two rival powers of France and Spain in such a way as to be confronted continuously with the danger of losing his independence.

The duke's restless spirit soon perceived new advantages to be gained by infringing the agreement just concluded and entering once more into relations with the Hapsburg power. New troubles had developed over the succession. This startling turn was due to the fact that Wallenstein had triumphed over Christian of Denmark and had induced him to conclude peace (May, 1629); imperial troops were able to seize the Val-telline and before long the sieges of Casale and Mantua were resumed, the Spanish under Spinola investing the former, the imperial forces under Collalto the latter fortress. Richelieu was occupied with internal intrigues too tedious to recount, but involving as usual the queen mother, Gaston of Orléans and some of the great nobles. It was natural that the Catholic party should, in light of the Edict of Restitution, have con-sidered the time ripe for concentrating on the task of Counter Reforma-tion, now that the Huguenots were crushed, and their best leader, Henry de Rohan, in exile at Venice. But Richelieu instead dispatched a bril-liant diplomat to free Gustavus Adolphus' hands for intervention against the Hapsburgs. He knew that the Swedish king was eager to assist the hard-pressed German Protestants, and hoped that he could counterbal-ance any ill effects of Swedish intervention by supporting Maximilian of Bavaria and the League. It is incorrect to say, as Hilaire Belloc and others have done, that he "hired" the Swedish king. Richelieu would have liked to, but Gustavus Adolphus would not agree, and concluded a treaty with the French for subsidies only after he himself could freely negotiate the terms (Treaty of Baerwalde, January, 1631). Nevertheless, by negotiating peace between Poland and Sweden, Richelieu accomplished the essential minimum and the Swedish king acted accordingly. This success proved decisive also in the Mantuan war.

Only by March, 1630, were the French ready to resume aggressive operations. The fortress of Pinerolo was seized soon after the cardinal reached the army, and in May Louis invaded and occupied all of Savoy. But just as the united French armies were ready to come to the relief of Mantua and Casale, Mantua was taken by the imperialists, and only the citadel at Casale held out. At the same time, both Charles Emmanuel of Savoy and Spinola died, thus weakening the Hapsburg position. At this point, Ferdinand II sought to settle the war at the electoral diet of Regensburg (Ratisbon). Père Joseph, Richelieu's plenipotentiary, skillfully played the electors against the emperor and both against Wallenstein, finally agreeing to a draft treaty on Mantua. It was a general settlement, such as the Hapsburgs desired and Richelieu did not. It was also ardently hoped for by the Spanish party in France and by the people, who were very tired of war. Père Joseph was motivated in negotiating such a settlement also by the news of Louis XIII's serious illness, which for several days in late September seemed to endanger the king's life. The shrewd Capuchin knew that Richelieu's position would be gravely imperiled by the king's death, but perhaps hoped that it might be saved by a peace. As it was, the queen mother had taken advantage of her son's illness to ingratiate herself with the king by her maternal solicitude, exploiting his weakness while at the same time undermining Richelieu's position. As a result, a serious crisis had developed between the king and his minister; yet, when the document arrived, Richelieu, flying into a passion of political indignation, tore up the paper, exclaiming: "The plenipotentiaries have exceeded their instructions." This bold, even reckless action was seized upon by the queen mother, now allied with the queen and one of Richelieu's chief aides, the Garde des Sceaux Michel de Marillac, to launch a full-scale attack upon the cardinal.

For a few days it looked as if everything was going perfectly for Marie de' Medici; the belief was general that Richelieu was finished. On November 10, 1630, the domineering Italian went to see her son for a decisive session, orders being given that no one was to be admitted. All doors were locked as the queen mother began to press Louis for a decision to dismiss the cardinal. She would probably have succeeded, had not Richelieu suddenly entered through a secret back door. Silently, he kneeled down before his sovereign, then murmured an abject apology. Thereupon, Marie pounced upon Richelieu with violent abuse, showering him with invective, accusing him of such absurdities as seeking the king's death, and giving the king no chance to say even a word. By her action, Marie unforgivably wounded the king's pride and sense of majesty. Such a scene in the presence of the king, God's anointed, was unbelievable in the baroque age; it was sacrilege. Finally the king interjected: "What are you doing, Madame? You are offending, you are insulting me." And when his mother, like a fishwife, thereupon resumed her tirade, the king ordered the cardinal to leave, then bowed to his mother without a word and departed.

Louis's mind was in a turmoil, but not for long. After brief reflection, he went to Versailles, commanding Richelieu to follow him. Marillac was told to go to a near-by village, where he was soon afterward arrested. At the decisive moment, when Richelieu once again had offered his resignation, Louis uttered these crucial words: "We are not concerned with the queen mother. I honor my mother, but I am more obligated to the state than to her." The king, seeing himself as the state's servant, in these words acknowledged the impersonal state's victory over the personal feelings and loyalties which ruled feudal society, as well as private men. Marie de' Medici, protesting, found herself confined, first at Compiègne, then at Moulins, whence she escaped to Brussels (Richelieu not at all interfering), never to return to France. The desperate move of the cardinal had succeeded and the day, November 10, 1630, became known as the "day of dupes." More than any other single day, it may be called the birthday of the modern state.

It did not take Richelieu long to recapture the initiative in foreign affairs, while the startling successes of Gustavus Adolphus helped persuade the Hapsburgs to accept a settlement of the Mantuan succession highly favorable to France. At Cherasco, in March, 1631, Charles of Gonzaga, Duke de Nevers, was confirmed as heir, but had to acknowledge allegiance to the emperor, whose fief Mantua was. Savoy, whose new duke inclined toward friendship with France, received a small part of Montferrat as compensation, while Pinerolo, decisive gateway between

France and Italy, remained in French hands. Richelieu could then turn his full attention to redressing the balance in Germany against Ferdinand. But before we trace this development, we must cast a glance at Richelieu's internal administration.

The striking successes of Richelieu's policy of strengthening the "state" internally and externally and the all but decisive victories which he had achieved by 1632 turned in the last analysis upon his unflagging detailed attention to certain key problems of administration. The army, the government service or bureaucracy, the navy, commerce and shipping, all underwent some sort of rationalization which twentieth-century engineers and efficiency experts like to call "streamlining." It was a passion of the age, oddly at variance, so it seems at first glance, with the baroque world of theatrical display, the grand gesture and the involved intrigue, but in fact born of the limitless dynamism and love of power. Technique now first detached itself from all higher purposes and became an end in itself. Richelieu has often been described as the most perfect practitioner of Machiavelli's statecraft. But this is not really true. Machiavelli conceived of the state as a work of art; he was a republican through and through and the civic spirit of a pagan past inspired his innermost being. He was a spokesman of the "city"—and in a very real sense the citizens of La Rochelle, making their proud efforts to defend their autonomy, were closer to Machiavelli than the cardinal who defeated them. In Richelieu's mind the state was not a work of art through which ancient virtue or manliness might express itself most nobly; it was an instrument for the achievement of many complex and interrelated purposes. It was the vehicle for making France great and prosperous, for thereby enabling her and her king to become the successful champions of the Counter Reformation, serving at the same time as a stage upon which to play the drama that was Armand-Jean du Plessis, Duc de Richelieu himself—severe, disciplined, the monk within this world, yet at the same time majestic, powerful, rich beyond the dreams of avarice.

That the armed forces, both on land and sea, were the backbone of power Richelieu recognized more fully than most; what is more, he realized that unless these forces were centrally controlled, i.e. were freed from feudal dispersion of responsibility, they were of little value. He was, of course, not alone in thinking so; it was the prevailing view. Indeed

Spain, the Netherlands and Sweden had each created a remarkable professional military establishment, and others followed. But here as in so many things Richelieu's greatness lay in carrying what was generally recognized to its penultimate and radical conclusion. We have already mentioned his plea for a standing army. Many of the methods which have since become commonplace had to be worked out in this period: regular pay for each soldier, discipline and a chain of command without hereditary officers to interfere, regularized provision of food, quarters, and clothing (though not yet the uniform, which was still limited to the ecclesiastical orders). Richelieu had no use for the traditional militia and the feudal ban of the nobility; in his *Testament* the Cardinal left a memorial of his settled low opinion of these formations. Instead, he built a sizable standing army around the royal guards, who served as an elite and a spearhead.

Perhaps even more striking than Richelieu's efforts in the army field was his determination and enterprise in creating a navy. Several of France's nearest neighbors and competitors in trade, Spain, England and the Netherlands, had pushed naval development. In his *Testament* Richelieu was to insist that "strength in arms requires the king to be strong not only on land, but also on the sea . . . the sea is [something] . . . over which the rights of sovereigns are the least clear. . . . The true title to this dominion is force, not reason. One must have power to claim it." When Richelieu arrived, the French navy was controlled by great nobles who inherited the title of admiral and who did no more than they chose. Soubise, as we have seen, made it an instrument of his rebellious actions and Richelieu had to borrow Dutch and English vessels to cope with the situation. Obviously the threat of invasion was everpresent under such conditions, as was indeed that of interference with fishing, commerce and communications. The cardinal therefore had himself made "grand-master, chief and superintendent general of navigation and commerce" (1626), abolished the admiralships (1627), and immediately set about having a royal navy of thirty vessels constructed and maintained at a cost of 1,500,000 *livres* per year, "so that his (the king's) neighbors will have the consideration they should have for a great state."

Armaments, however, require funds, and the state of France's fiscal affairs was lamentable in 1624, with a large floating debt and corruption rampant. Indeed, time and again great states have been brought to ruin by pursuing foreign and military policies exceeding their revenue resources. Sully, the great minister of Henry IV, had known this well, and under him revenue, amounting to some forty million *livres,* was well above the government's expenses. Richelieu held no such view, nor did he suffer a man to work under him who would have had the strength of character to insist upon it. His maxim was: "For no sum of money is the safety of the state too dearly bought." Hence his willingness to offer millions to men like Gustavus Adolphus at a time when his treasury was empty. The fact is that Richelieu, preoccupied with foreign affairs and with his own position at court, was a very poor administrator and financial manager. The figures tell an appalling story: according to accounts credited by Hanotaux, there were in

1626	18,243,045 *livres* received	44,657,161 spent
1636	23,471,254 " "	108,256,236 "
1640	43,454,166 " "	116,208,911 " [3]

These deficits meant, of course, a constantly swelling public debt; if interest on this had been about two million *livres* in 1624, it was ten times that at the time of Richelieu's death. Besides, the sale of public offices on a vast scale continued, report having it that half a billion was paid for such offices during the cardinal's rule, of which perhaps two-thirds reached the public treasury. The tremendous spread between what was collected from the unhappy taxpayer and what the state received was one of the clearest signs of the rottenness of financial administration under Richelieu, for customarily only about half of what was collected became available to the state. The other half was diverted to local use or pocketed by the collectors and financiers to whom indirect taxes were farmed out. The main source of tax revenue throughout Richelieu's regime remained four antiquated and unsound taxes, the *taille,* the *aides,* the *gabelle* and the *domaine.* Leaving aside the technicalities of these levies, one must note their uneven application. Some parts of France, like Languedoc, Burgundy and Brittany were largely exempt, as were several classes of persons, especially the nobility, the clergy and the officialdom to a large extent, as well as some of the professions. Perhaps one-fourth of the French population escaped, it is estimated, and the burden upon the rest, especially the peasantry, was correspondingly greater. From this frightful heritage the French monarchy never subsequently freed itself, and it has therefore been said with justice that by neglecting the govern-

[3] Hanotaux, *op. cit.,* IV, 368–69; *Cambridge Modern History,* p. 152, gives 160–180 millions, but without source.

ment's finances Richelieu undermined his work and "the Revolution of 1789 was of his making."

As the sale of offices suggests, Richelieu did not succeed in rationalizing the public services as much as he wanted to; indeed his improvements in general administration were few, unless one wishes to consider as such the extension of the use of royal commissioners, called *intendants,* who were indeed a potent factor in centralizing the state's administration. They proceeded ruthlessly, autocratically, unsystematically in competition with the officials who bought their jobs, often three holding one and the same post and serving in rotation; the tax exemption made it worth their while.

Bitter conflicts occurred throughout Richelieu's regime with the *parlements.* They, as was their duty, objected to his contempt for established law and procedure, especially in the case of political offenders. Time and again such persons, like Chalais and De Marillac, were tried by special commissions who did as the king and Richelieu bade them. Richelieu had little regard for law, in any case; neither his financial nor his other ordinances were in accord with established procedure. Under his imperious will, the absolutism of the French monarchy became blatant autocracy, in the end even "unrestrained by the fear of assassination," to use a famous phrase. The *intendants de justice, de police, et des finances* did what was necessary from the government's standpoint. In a sense they personified the practical working of the doctrine of *raison d'État:* disregard of established law and vested rights. At the point of the sword taxes were collected.

VII. RICHELIEU AND THE THIRTY YEARS' WAR

Such was the state of the France of Richelieu internally, in 1631, when the cardinal entered upon the most aggressive and successful foreign policy, which was to leave him arbiter of the fate of Europe. Like his own personal existence, France's position was maintained by the high *esprit* and indomitable will power of a nation glorying in its hegemony over Europe. It was an exciting, even an inspiring spectacle—the most brilliant baroque masterpiece of the age.

There can be little doubt that Richelieu, while at first relieved by the Swedish king's successes in 1631, struggled in vain to keep him under control. His endeavors to keep Gustavus at bay and to make him concentrate upon reducing the Austrian Hapsburgs, while leaving the

Catholic estates of the Empire at peace, foundered partly because of Maximilian of Bavaria's unwillingness to abandon Ferdinand. Maximilian's position was, in this regard, comparable to that of the elector of Saxony toward Gustavus Adolphus; both electoral leaders were disinclined to invite too active foreign participation in German internal affairs, and both failed. In any case, the news of Gustavus Adolphus' death at Lützen (November, 1632) cannot but have caused the cardinal to breathe a sigh of relief. Richelieu had just succeeded in crushing another of Gaston's rebellions and in the sequel the king had had the Duc de Montmorency, who had made common cause with the duke of Orléans, executed—an action which terrified the unruly French aristocracy, as Montmorency was a peer of France, in fact her greatest noble. November, 1632, thus marked the end of two of Richelieu's remaining rivals: the French high aristocracy and Gustavus Adolphus. For while Gustavus Adolphus had been sweeping all before him, the cardinal was confronted by "a vital force he could neither control nor predict." But after the great king had passed away, French diplomacy was more successful. By skillfully playing his Protestant associates against Oxenstierna Richelieu succeeded in keeping Sweden at war without himself openly entering the conflict.

It was only after the disaster of the battle of Nördlingen (1634) that Richelieu was forced by the Swedish chancellor to declare himself openly. In the meantime, partly as a result of Swedish weakness after the battle of Nördlingen, the French had acquired important forward positions at the expense of the Empire with which they were still formerly at peace, by conquering them from Spain. When taken together with those German territories placed under France's protection by their own ecclesiastical masters, like the bishoprics of Basle and Trier, the positions controlled by the French stretched all along the Rhine from Switzerland to the Rhineland, including Colmar, Schlettstadt, Zabern, Hagenau, Kaiserslautern, Speyer, Philippsburg, Mannheim, Ehrenbreitstein, and Coblenz. They held also the duchy of Lorraine, an imperial fief. When, in February and April, 1635, offensive and defensive alliances were concluded by Richelieu with the Netherlands and Sweden respectively, it seemed only natural that the allies of France should have insisted on an open break. Yet, at precisely this time the internal German conflicts were composed and the Treaty of Prague (May, 1635) [4] was concluded. From then on the war

[4] See above, pp. 187–8.

became less and less a war of religion, and more an open struggle between France and her allies against the Spanish and Austrian Hapsburgs, a war carried out on German soil and supported by such German princelings as were willing to let themselves be hired.[5]

Among these Bernhard of Weimar was the most brilliant military leader, but his career was cut short by his premature death at the age of thirty-five (July 11, 1639), after he had, the previous autumn, taken the fortress of Breisach on the Rhine above Basle—a crucial position for the control of communications. His death removed a man who might have proved as dangerous to Richelieu as Gustavus Adolphus had been: there were sharp disagreements between him and Richelieu over who was to control Breisach. After his death, the French made good their claim. But meanwhile the Spanish had taken Trier and, since the archbishop had accepted French protection, open war was declared against Spain on May 19, 1635. Against the Empire, the war was openly admitted only in 1638, but in the meantime Richelieu's military men and their allies carried on as if war was in fact in progress.

Although the conclusion of a general peace in 1648 lay quite a few years beyond the cardinal's death, its general framework was discernible in 1642 along lines which had been anticipated by the proposals of Gustavus Adolphus ten years earlier. In a very real sense it was Richelieu's work. The exclusion of Spain from the settlement, signifying the detachment of the imperial from the Spanish cause, constituted the triumph of Richelieu's diplomacy.

VIII. WAR WITH SPAIN

Open war with Spain involved, as Richelieu had realized all along, great military dangers along France's northern frontier, which was open and hard to defend, since Spain's great military strength was concentrated in the Low Countries. In the summer of 1636 a great invasion was launched by the cardinal infant from Flanders which gained rapid successes and soon threatened Paris. Among the generals, Johann von Werth, a reckless cavalryman, deserves to be remembered, for his daring exploits, including the seizure of Picardy and the crossing of the Somme, caused a veritable panic in Paris which Richelieu and the king countered by taking the field. Louis XIII had called for every nobleman of France

[5] *Lettres et Négociations du Marquis de Feuquières* (1753), *passim;* note, e.g., I, 9–10, 22, 144 and throughout.

who enjoyed tax privileges to join him, and had asked that the price of
arms be so regulated as to check profiteering.[6] Such an appeal seemed
essential, since the Spanish forces in this theater numbered reportedly
25,000 as against less than 10,000 French, and French forces could not be
withdrawn from Italy, Franche-Comté, or Germany. Everywhere the
French were outnumbered by their opponents. Soon it was decided to
raise 30,000 men to guard the Oise River, and a voluntary contribution
was asked of all Parisians. In an extraordinary scene, the leaders of the
guild artisans of Paris met with the king, received the royal kiss, and
proceeded to make large contributions to "the defense of the kingdom."
French historians have spoken of a "sacred union,"[7] and it was indeed
remarkable how national sentiment swept the people; everyone either
contributed or rushed to the colors.

Despite this great general rising, whether voluntary or compulsory, the
fortress of Corbie surrendered almost without a struggle, as had others
before it. Murmurs sprang up in Paris, and Richelieu became very
agitated. In this hour of peril, the faithful Père Joseph stood by him, as
usual, encouraging and indeed challenging him. It is reported that he told
the cardinal that only strong resolutions and complete confidence in
divine aid would help in such trials.[8] Popular hostility and strife were
rampant; Spanish hirelings were said to be abroad in Paris, and the
parlement undertook to make representations to the king about the
cardinal's administration. To these Louis XIII returned a striking reaffirmation of the absolutist conception of government which he represented: "It is none of your business to meddle in the affairs of my
state . . . and I forbid you to assume to be my tutors in so meddling
with the affairs of state."[9] My state! France was moving fast toward the
famous royal exclamation: "I am the state." Even if apocryphal, this
remark, attributed to Louis XIV, summed up perfectly the identification
of the monarch with the mysticism of the national body corporate, the

---

[6] *Mémoires du Cardinal de Richelieu*, I, 222 and 224.

[7] Gabriel Hanotaux, *Histoire du Cardinal de Richelieu*, V, 160.

[8] See Gustave Fagniez, *Le Père Joseph et Richelieu*, Vol. I (1894), 1577–1638, p. 398,
who bases his view upon Dupré Balain, a contemporary biography which remained unprinted; regarding this work see Fagniez, p. 15.

[9] Vicomte G. d'Avenel, *Lettres du Cardinal de Richelieu*, V, 541–42. This doctrine was
not new; Le Bret, one of Richelieu's official apologists in *De la Souveraineté du Roi* noted
that "since the Ordinance of Charles VIII, and since the kings who have come after him
have reserved to themselves cognizance of the affairs of their state, it is only they who
grant them [letters of marque]." P. 302 of 1632 edition.

state, *"l'État."* To this day Frenchmen write the word with a capital, the only French common noun so honored.

It is interesting that these proud assertions of monarchical absolutism were made at the very moment when many expected the French king to be defeated and soon to be obliged to sue for peace "on his knees." But in fact the king had, by the beginning of September, assembled a force almost the equal to that of the Spaniards, while at the same time French diplomacy had overcome Dutch hesitance, and Frederick Henry, Prince of Orange, was taking the field with twenty thousand men in the cardinal infant's rear. Soon the fortunes of war turned, Corbie was retaken on November 14, and the enemy cleared from most of the French soil he had invaded. At the same time, Prince Condé gained against the imperialists, as did Bernhard of Weimar. The crisis had been weathered.

No comparable cataclysm occurred in the war with Spain during the remainder of Richelieu's regime. The ups and downs of the various campaigns on the different battlefronts, while offering many fascinating details, were devoid of general interest; in the end they left the situation very much as before. Spain sought to take advantage of such internal dissensions as continued to arise. In 1637, the count of Soissons raised a force and again invaded Picardy. The campaign petered out when Richelieu advised the king to conclude a compromise settlement. However, the cardinal infant in Brussels remained a constant threat which the unhappy queen mother was prepared to exploit whenever opportunity offered.

The real significance of the war with Spain was that it served to reveal the hollowness of Spanish power. While possessed of the most remarkable professional army, the kingdom of Philip II had undergone a progressive decline since his death, and this decline deserves a brief analysis. But before turning to this, one might add here that within a few months two men died who had been central figures of the Counter Reformation, Richelieu's great antagonist, Emperor Ferdinand II (February 15, 1637),[10] and the cardinal's conscience and confidant, Père Joseph (December 18, 1638). To his very end, the Gray Eminence had remained true to his dream of the crusade against the Turk; on his deathbed he added some lines to his *Turciade*. It is a mistake to forget over the friar's political role his ardent religious spirit, which provided the driving force for all his actions. As Richelieu said of him whom he called his Ezekiel, *"pauvre*

---

[10] See above, pp. 188–9.

auprès de l'abondance, humble dans les honneurs, chaste auprès des délices, obéissant en tort, sobre auprès des festins, religieux dans le monde et Capuchin à la cour." There can be no doubt that Richelieu was saddened by the passing of his most devoted, perhaps his only true friend; whether he really missed his counsel any longer, may well be doubted.

IX. THE DECLINE OF SPAIN

The first part of the reign of Philip IV, which had brought the golden autumn of Spanish art and letters,[11] was dominated by the king's prime minister, Gaspar of Guzman, Count of Olivárez, known as the count-duke. Not a favorite in the strict sense, Olivárez occupied a position not dissimilar to Richelieu's. Hard-working and ruthless, he was devoted to the idea of monarchical absolutism and opposed to the surviving feudal independence of the great nobles and towns. The superior skill of his great antagonist has obscured the very real ability of this man who fostered Velasquez and the poets, restrained the Inquisition and sought to convert Spain from a government-by-estates into a centralized and absolute monarchy. Among all the medieval estate assemblies the Cortes of the several constituent kingdoms ruled by the crown of Spain had been among the proudest, most assertive, most fully endowed with legislative authority. A hundred years earlier, the Cortes of Castile had succumbed to the autocracy of Charles V. But those of Aragon, Catalonia and Valencia (as also those of Portugal) had maintained their position. From 1626 onward, perhaps in part inspired by what was happening in the Hapsburgs' Austrian lands and in France—but also in accord with the general trend of the times—Olivárez tried to reduce these Cortes to a position of subservience similar to that in Castile. The end result was the loss of Portugal (1640), a violent revolt in Catalonia (1641) leading to French occupation, and the overthrow of Olivárez himself (1643).

Olivárez's violent temper and overbearing conduct did not assist him in his efforts, but too much can be made of his personal faults. Really, the only way by which the count-duke could have succeeded would have been to curtail his ambitious foreign policy and to build up Spain's trade and internal economy, thereby making the Cortes unnecessary. But such a course the aggressive policy of Richelieu and his allies made virtually insupportable for the proud Spaniard. It must also be remembered that the builders of the modern state, Richelieu, Wallenstein, Olivárez and the

[11] See above, Chapter Two.

rest, depended upon the support and good will of the monarch whose authority they had to exalt. As the ruler became more absolute, the minister became more dependent upon him, a dependence which could be offset only by the minister making himself "irreplaceable." By flattering the prince's sense of pride and by involving him in pursuit of glory and conquest such a minister's position would be made more secure against domestic and foreign intrigue. Basically, the recipe of Olivárez was no different from that of the French cardinal. His difficulty sprang from the bigoted insistence of Philip IV that the king of Spain must be in the forefront of all efforts to spread the Roman Catholic faith and re-establish the unity of religion.

Behind this royal ambition deep indeed insatiable passions of the Spanish people were at work. Not only the Holy Inquisition but the *autos-da-fé* were intensely popular institutions. The gloomy fanaticism which they expressed was as much a manifestation of the spirit of the Spanish people as the tender devotion and fervent piety which filled the heart of high and low and led them to establish literally hundreds of new religious foundations and monasteries. This intense devoutness, which led the king publicly to attribute all the ills which befell his people and realm to his personal wickedness and sin, presented a strange contrast to the boldness and arrogance of Spain's soldiers, the cruel rapacity of her colonial officials, the calculating dexterity of her diplomatists, and the cold sexual passion of her Don Juans. A world which seems more truly akin to the spirit of the baroque than perhaps the life of any other nation of Europe, Spain characteristically had its most marvelous cultural flowering in this very period.[12] But the preoccupation with the Counter Reformation meant overextension in foreign affairs and war. The country could not stand the strain of such vast exertions, and decline became inevitable.

We have seen how badly Spain fared in the war of the Mantuan succession; her involvement was a natural result of her policy of close co-operation with the Empire and the Austrian house. While this may have seemed to some Spaniards like fighting for the imperial position, actually to many imperialists, especially Wallenstein and certainly to many German princes, it seemed exactly the reverse. This the composition at Regensburg (1630), bitterly fought by the Spanish ambassador,

---

[12] See above, pp. 50–8. In general, cf. Martin Hume, *The Court of Philip IV* (1907). See also Carl Justi, *Velasquez und sein Jahrhundert* (second edition, 1903, as republished with notes by Ludwig Justi, 1933).

showed; [13] Spain's control of the Rhine valley was vital to her position in the Low Countries, now that she no longer had dominion of the sea.

The situation after the battle of Nördlingen (1634) had been such that Spain might well have been content with the armed truce which the peace with France since 1631 had provided. But Richelieu, as shown above, could not resist the pressure of his Swedish and other allies, who were so hard-pressed that they insisted upon an open declaration of war. Further advances of the Spanish in the Rhineland provided the desired pretext (May, 1635). It is unfair to Olivárez and Philip to blame them for the resumption of hostilities; they were profoundly disturbed, but in the proud Spanish tradition could not but accept the challenge. The life-and-death struggle which ensued has already been sketched in its early phases.

By 1640, after five years of fighting on numerous battlefronts, in Flanders, Germany, Italy, and in the Pyrenees, two dramatic events showed that the Spanish were breaking under the impact of the protracted war. These were the rebellions in Catalonia and Portugal. While aided by the cardinal, who thus squared accounts with the Spaniards' support of various French opposition groups, notably the Huguenots and great nobles—it will be recalled that Marie de' Medici resided in Flanders and that the duchess of Chevreuse escaped into Spain and from thence to England and Flanders (1637)—the rise of the Catalonians at Barcelona, and the revolution in Portugal were more deeply motivated by passionate localism and by a determination to resist the centralizing efforts of Olivárez. Of the two, the action in Portugal had more lasting significance; never to this day has Portugal again been under Spanish rule. Since Olivárez had tried to crush Portuguese independence, a native great noble, the duke of Braganza, was made king in a *coup d'État* of extraordinary brevity; within four hours all was over (December, 1640) and the government of Olivárez was too weak to attempt an armed intervention.

The weakness of the count-duke stemmed in part from the revolt in Catalonia. Bordering France in the eastern Pyrenees, Catalonia had always been distinct in culture and tradition, more Provençal than Spanish, and animated by a strong sense of autonomy and freedom. In 1632, as in 1626, the Cortes of Barcelona had refused to be coerced. As the French gained in aggressive strength, they invaded Spanish territory proper. After having failed to invade the Basque country (1638), they

---

[13] See above, Chapter Five. p. 215.

proceeded against the eastern Catalan border (1639). At first they met serious reverses. The Catalans themselves mounted a stout and successful defense of Roussillon. But Olivárez, ill-advised by his local henchman, considered this a favorable time for subduing the Catalans. Ever since the earlier clashes, he had come to resent the Catalans violently as obstructing his efforts at centralization. In the report of a Venetian ambassador he is reported as "hating the constitutions and breaking into violent abuse" whenever he spoke of the Catalans.

Olivárez, instead of withdrawing the Castilian troops which had been sent to the aid of Catalonia, quartered them upon the province, where they pillaged and, being unpaid, conducted themselves generally in the fashion of the times. The inevitable followed. On May 12, 1640, Barcelona rose in revolt. The rebels broke open the prisons, and with the cry, "Vengeance and liberty!" went about slaughtering every Castilian soldier they could lay hands on, including the viceroy. Such open revolt was a terrifying sign to Philip IV of how far he had lost the loyalty of his subjects. Attempts at composing the difficulties failed. The leaders of the insurrection placed themselves under the protection of the king of France, and eventually took the oath of allegiance to him, while French armies occupied the country. At that point, the enemies of the count-duke at last took courage. Led by the queen, and by her son, Balthasar Carlos, the discontented united and, after acquainting the king with the background of the loss of Portugal which had occurred in the meantime, succeeded in overthrowing the hated autocrat, Olivárez. "This realm is perishing," cried a simple workman, throwing himself before the king, while the queen implored her husband to dismiss his minister before the entire inheritance was dismembered. On January 17, 1643, only a few months after his great antagonist, Richelieu, had died, Olivárez was dismissed. While his life was spared, he lost his estates and died two years later, having gone mad. The usual end of such *privados,* or favorites, was a favored theme of Spanish dramatists; in one of Calderón's plays the fallen says to the incoming one: *"Come tu te ves, me ví, veráste, come me miro."*

The striking parallel between Olivárez and Richelieu, and the equally striking contrast, has fascinated posterity. How often Richelieu came close to the same fate, and in similar crises! But apart from the difference in ability, which even weak masters like Louis and Philip could not fail to observe, there was the difference in the royal personalities. Philip was yielding, pleasure-loving, good-natured, mystically inclined; Louis stubborn, ascetic, vindictive and basically rational. But beyond these personalities, one must recognize as more permanently significant the solid national strength and resources of France, concentrated if greatly strained by Richelieu's ambitious policy. This powerful France could truly be compared to the windmills against which the gallant knight-errantry of impoverished and roving Spain tilted its outmoded weapons in vain. It did not help Spain's cause that Philip was in the habit of abasing himself *coram publico* in statements like that to the Cortes. That the king on such occasions expressed genuine feelings can be seen from his letters to the saintly nun, Sor Maria. On October 4, 1644, for example he wrote: "The greatest favor that I can receive from His holy hands is that the punishments He lays upon these realms may be laid upon me; for it is I, and not they, who really deserve the punishment, for they have always been true and firm Catholics." When later his beloved spouse and his equally adored and only son died, Philip wrote: "I know, Sor Maria, that I deserve heavy punishments, and that all that may come to me in this life will be insufficient to repay my sins" (October 7, 1646).[14] We shall see later how the score was finally settled in the peace of the Pyrenees.

X. RICHELIEU'S LAST YEARS

Not only in Spain, but elsewhere, considerable successes were scored by France and her allies during the last years of Richelieu's regime. For one, Spanish sea power, slowly rebuilt by Olivárez from the few ships left at the time he took over, was destroyed by the Dutch in the "scandal of the Downs" (1639). A Spanish fleet of more than seventy ships, carrying over twenty thousand men, about half of them troops destined for Flanders, was so savagely attacked by a small Dutch fleet under Admiral Marten H. Tromp that it sought refuge within English territorial waters, in the Downs. After rapidly gathering reinforcements and quite a few newly built ships, Tromp attacked again and virtually wiped out the Spaniards, ships and men. In vain did the British protest the violation of their territory;[15] the Dutch stood firm and Spanish naval power never recovered from the blow. From this time on, the key rivalry on the high seas was that between Dutch and British.

The war in Germany had likewise brought considerable returns. While French diplomatists continued to keep various princelings in line by

[14] Martin Hume, *The Court of Philip IV* (1907), 384, 400.
[15] See below, p. 321.

suitable money payments, French marshals, like the very able Guébriant, moved back and forth all over Germany, and their allies, the Swedes, supported by the Hessians, won various victories over the imperialists. The story is a depressing one, because no significant change resulted from the unspeakable sufferings inflicted upon the German common folk. Recurrent efforts to bring about peace did not succeed; [16] instead, Marshal Banér and after his death Marshal Lennart Torstensson intensified the war. The second battle of Breitenfeld (November 2, 1642), fought by the latter, all but wiped out the imperial forces.

Internally, intrigues continued in France, but with greatly reduced impact. At the center was the queen mother, Marie de' Medici, from Brussels making advances to some of the great French nobles. As already mentioned, in 1637 the count of Soissons entered into an agreement with the Spanish to invade France from Flanders. Richelieu persuaded the king to settle amicably. More dangerous were the attempts of the queen mother to overthrow Richelieu with the help of the queen, Anne of Austria. But Richelieu had many eyes, many ears. As Louis XIII once said, "The cardinal is a strange spirit, for he discovers everything. He has spies next to foreign princes, he learns of their designs, he has disguised men who surprise mail shipments and who plunder the couriers." But the queen did not appreciate this watchfulness and attention to the smallest detail. She corresponded with France's enemies, the Spanish ambassador, the queen of England, the cardinal infant in Brussels, the duke of Lorraine. The ever-alert Richelieu saw many of her messages; *"Les écritures on ait subodoré,"* he wrote to one of his helpers, warning him not to let on to it.[17] Master intelligencer that he was, Richelieu knew the value of not being suspected. But when he had all the evidence he needed, he struck. Seizing the queen's adjutant, M. de la Porte, as he was carrying a highly suspicious letter of the queen, he forced the queen to surrender (August, 1637).[18] Madame de Chevreuse, fearing for her life, escaped to Spain, never to return while the cardinal was alive, but stirring up trouble to the best of her ability. But the queen, in the sequel, received a *"visite"* from the king (December, 1637) and on September 5, 1638, a son was born to Anne of Austria who was to become the *Roi Soleil*, Louis XIV. With the succession thus assured, Richelieu's gravest appre-

---

[16] See above, pp. 190–1.

[17] Hanotaux, *op. cit.*, V, 214–15, where Louis XIII is quoted also.

[18] *Mémoires de M. de la Porte,* especially pp. 120 ff. See also Louis Batiffol, *La Duchesse de Chevreuse,* Ch. VI.

hension, lest the king should die and the weak and useless Gaston become king, was at long last banished.

However, rebellion raised its ugly head twice more. As always, Gaston was involved, but no one trusted him any longer. However, in 1641 the count of Soissons, in collaboration with the queen mother, Bouillon and Guise, ventured forth from his self-imposed exile at Sedan, a principality tenuously independent since the middle of the sixteenth century. The invasion went well at first, but when Soissons was murdered by a mysterious pistol shot, the campaign collapsed. However, Bouillon did not really abandon hope. The following year one of the cardinal's own helpers, Cinq-Mars, second son of a former finance minister, tried during an illness of the cardinal to take advantage of the king's favorable disposition toward him. Known as *Monsieur le Grand,* he allowed himself rather foolishly to enter into treasonable relations with Spain in the hope of securing the support of the Spanish party and the queen mother. But on July 3, 1642, Marie de' Medici died; Cinq-Mars was discovered, tried, and executed. Bouillon won a pardon by returning Sedan to French sovereignty. Soon afterward Richelieu fell ill again; this time the fever was too much and on December 4, 1642, he passed away, according to Hanotaux "the greatest public servant France ever had." His king, who had so heavily relied upon him, followed him within a few months on May 14, 1643.

Ruthless and without pity, either for himself or for others, Richelieu was a genius of the pure political type whose greatness is intuitively perceived by his contemporaries, even when they hate and oppose him. He was, at the same time, a striking illustration of the patent fact that the great men of politics are often evil men. Urban VIII, his witty, friendly rival, trenchantly commented upon Richelieu's death: "If God exists, he will probably have to atone; if not, he was a good man." He carried all the pathos of high ecclesiastical office into the new secular task which the religion of nationalism and its organization, the state, substituted for the former allegiance to Christianity and church. No doubt, like his great contemporary, Descartes, he considered himself a good son of the church; no doubt, either, that he built the instrumentality through which it could be superseded.

XI. MAZARIN—SUCCESSOR

Giulio Mazarini had entered the French public service, after serving as papal nuncio for a while and after ingratiating himself with Richelieu

(1630 and after). He had become a French subject in 1639 and a cardinal in 1641. Extraordinarily intelligent, suave and diplomatic, he was a child of Naples, where he was born in 1602. Naples being a Spanish possession, Mazarin had spent a good part of his youth in Spain and had acquired a thorough knowledge of that country as well as of Italy. Mazarin's fluent command of Spanish stood him in good stead in his relations with the queen regent, Anne of Austria, with whom he eventually entered into intimate relations, sometimes claimed to have been a clandestine marriage. Regardless of whether a spiritual or a carnal union, there can be no question that Mazarin·enjoyed the fullest support of his "sovereign" —a good fortune which contrasted strongly with the constant difficulties of his greater predecessor.[19]

But it was Richelieu himself who started Mazarin on his career and who insured for him the predominant position he occupied for nearly twenty years by persuading the ailing king to appoint him his successor in 1642. It was Richelieu's last great act of statesmanship, as he lay dying late that year. He also made great efforts to exclude Gaston of Orléans from the regency. The king subsequently tried to formalize his system of government by giving his council a share in the regency. Both these efforts were rendered nugatory by the queen, who a few days after the king's death was declared by formal *lit de justice* to be in possession of the absolute and unlimited royal authority during the minority of her son. Gaston became governor general of the kingdom, and Condé his deputy in the council. Thus in effect Anne and Gaston achieved the very position which Richelieu and the king had wished to withhold from them. Yet the disastrous consequences which they had feared were prevented by Mazarin's diplomacy, which soon gave him actual control of the affairs of the kingdom to an even greater extent than Richelieu had enjoyed during his most powerful periods. Thus the "system" continued, after all.

It was not long before a first cabal tried to displace Mazarin. The affair is known as the plot of the "Importants," because this group of vain men (Retz calls them *"tous morts fous"* [20]) thought they could supplant

---

[19] This is the conclusion arrived at by Comte de Saint Aulaire, *Mazarin* (1946). Note especially p. 71: *"Mystique ou non, platonique ou conjugale, leur union, dans la solitude peuplée de la Cour, sur ce sommet qui les isole et les expose, est leur forteresse et leur oasis. Ils s'y retranchent et s'y rafraîchissent au milieu des luttes terribles, pour la collaboration la plus confiante, la plus longue et surtout la plus féconde que l'histoire enregistre entre une souveraine et son premier ministre."*

[20] See *Mémoires du Cardinal de Retz* (1613–87), one of the most interesting sources for the period of Mazarin by one of his enemies. I have used the critical edition by Mon-

Mazarin by building on the queen's dislike for Richelieu. But Mazarin had already won over the regent by appealing to her sense of monarchical obligation and maternal concern for her son's inheritance. By September, 1643, Mazarin was in complete control.

The affair of the Importants, while strictly speaking a court intrigue, had its more general base in the universal discontent occasioned by the tax burdens resulting from the wars. Between 1609 and 1643 taxes had risen from 26 million *livres* to about 120, but due to the farming-out methods of tax collection, only a fraction of this huge sum reached the governmental treasury. Since current expenses were over 120 million *livres,* the government's debt continued to mount and had by this time reached perhaps 200 million *livres* at interest rates of around fifteen per cent. Mazarin never succeeded in coping with this frightful heritage of Richelieu's regime. The brilliant victories in war and diplomacy which he achieved were bought by the progressive impoverishment of the French people.

Another very serious complication confronted Mazarin upon the death of Pope Urban VIII (July 29, 1644). The cardinal sought to secure the election of a friendly pope, but instead his enemy, Cardinal Pamfilio, was elected and became Innocent X. In spite of protestations to the contrary, the Holy See during the next twelve years pursued policies that to Mazarin appeared hostile. What saved the French from serious damage was the lack of ability which this rather saturnine and disgruntled pope brought to his task.

We have had occasion elsewhere to tell the story of the negotiations leading up to the conclusion of the Treaty of Westphalia. In France these negotiations encountered much opposition from the pro-Spanish peace party. Mazarin, however, remained determined to split the Austrian from the Spanish Hapsburgs, and he succeeded in spite of a strong party at Court which, in the closest relation with Spain, tried to have a Spanish settlement included in the over-all treaty. Throughout the period preceding the final settlement, Mazarin was able to pursue a more steady course than Richelieu because of the queen regent's backing. His policy was reinforced by the abler military leadership which he secured from Condé (Enghien) and Turenne, from Guébriant and others, because he did not, like Richelieu, hesitate to employ men with military ambitions of their

grédien (undated) which follows, so the editor asserts, the text of the edition in *Grands écrivains de la France,* edited by Feillet, Gourdault and Chantelauze. The quoted remark occurs on p. 59 of Vol. I.

own. Turenne as the brother of Bouillon and Condé as the leading prince were both allied by family to the opposition elements; Mazarin refused to be guided by such political considerations. He achieved striking victories, as a result, but he eventually had to pay a heavy price for them in the civil dissensions of the Fronde after 1648.

It was part of his general policy that Mazarin, after the victory at Rocroy, pursued a definitely aggressive program in the war against Spain. Aided by the United Provinces, who made their dominant fleet under Tromp available for the blockading of any of the Channel ports, France's armies under Gaston, Gassion and Enghien conquered Gravelines and then Dunkerque, thus establishing French control of the coast of Flanders. Unluckily, these successes were too striking not to worry the cautious Netherlanders; the openly announced ambition of the French to occupy Antwerp made them reluctant to continue their vigorous support of France.

The French also pursued the war against Spain beyond the Alps and Pyrenees. Here, as elsewhere, the internal pacification caused a substantial amount of combative energy to flow into external aggression. French military leadership rapidly improved, especially after Rocroy. The same thing happened at sea. In the battle of Orbetello (1646) the French fleet, under the duke of Brézé, succeeded in stalemating the Spanish and soon thereafter the French took Elba and Piombino, whereupon the Italian allies of Spain began to shift their position. Tuscany became neutral, Modena turned toward France. Mazarin diplomatically declared that France had no territorial ambitions beyond securing the passages through the Alps, yet indicated a desire to free both Milan and Naples from Spanish overlordship.

In the light of these striking French successes and even more far-reaching ambitions, the Spanish negotiators offered very generous terms at Münster in 1646, but their failure to abandon the duke of Lorraine blocked agreement. In fact, Mazarin at this time hoped not only for Lorraine, but also for the Spanish Netherlands and Franche-Comté, as well as Alsace and Luxemburg. Mazarin was counting upon the civil war in England to enable him to achieve the acquisition of the Belgian territories; in exchange he was willing to return to Spain Catalonia and Roussillon, if not Navarre. But the Spaniards rallied; a French-inspired rebellion at Naples collapsed, and Lérida (in Catalonia) was retaken by Spanish arms. At the same time, Spanish diplomacy succeeded in reaching an agreement with the Dutch, and all efforts of Mazarin to prevent this treaty were in vain. The Dutch, delighted to find the Spaniard at last not only ready, but eager to bring the eighty-year-old war to a conclusion, settled the more readily as they had begun to worry about the aggressive ambitions of the French. But the most decisive change occurred within France itself. It was touched off by the failure of Mazarin to conclude the peace with Spain.[21]

XII. THE FRONDE AND AFTER

As the struggle against absolutism progressed in England, the French nobility, high and low, as well as the urban patriciate were once again stirred into resentment over the loss of their medieval constitutional rights. Because the *États Géneraux* had not been convened since 1614 and there was no constitutional way to force the monarch to call them, the *parlements* undertook to make themselves the spokesmen of the more vocal elements of the population. It is often said, by way of contrasting the French with the British situation, that the *parlement* was a court (in contrast to the estates). But this overlooks the fact that the English parliament was a high court of justice too. It was, in other words, the fact that the English parliament *combined* the functions of an estates' assembly with those of a high court, which made it unique among representative assemblies of the medieval type.[22] Be that as it may, it seems untenable to make the traditional constitutional function of the *parlement* responsible for its failure to play a role comparable to that of the English parliament. The reasons for this divergence must be sought in a number of basic differences between the two countries that provided the setting for their operation of the institutional machinery. Among these divergencies two loomed large: the fact that England had by Tudor efforts already become a well-consolidated and integrated kingdom with no such centrifugal forces as the religious interests and territorial ambitions of France's great noblemen; and the fact that England had no foreign challenge comparable to the Hapsburgs confronting it abroad. Add to this the further fact that the English (and Scottish) people were largely Protestant, with a very substantial following for the theocratic Presbyterians and the democratic nonconformist sects, and you have the

[21] The curiously one-sided study by Isabelle de Broglie, *Le Traité de Westphalie vu par les Contemporains* (1942), contains a good many bits of evidence for this French reaction.

[22] E. Gleason, *Le Parlement de Paris: son role politique depuis le regne de Charles VII jusqu'à la révolution* (1901), Vol. I, Ch. 3, pp. 115–75 and Ch. IV, pp. 177–395 (Mazarin), which includes a lengthy treatment of the Fronde.

real explanation for the divergence in institutional vigor that distinguished the *parlement* of Paris from the English parliament. It should be added that the *parlement* of Paris, though much the most important, was not the only one in France, for there existed seven other provincial parliaments in Normandy, Brittany, Provence, Languedoc, Guyenne, Burgundy, and Dauphiné. While these were less prominent, they, like the estates in their respective territories, played a separate and often independent role.

It was the *parlement* of Paris, though, which came to the forefront of political opposition in the year the peace of Westphalia was concluded. Since it contained in its upper chamber the great nobles of France, it could claim genuine representative character. Its presidents, like the venerable Mathieu Molé, belonged to the most respected personages of French political life. When Molé stood before the queen regent during the famous conference from September 25 to October 4, 1648, he spoke for all Frenchmen in protesting the people's desperate plight which led to the Declaration of October 22 (registered October 24). The terms of this temporary settlement corresponded to the program which the *parlement* of Paris, after uniting with the three high courts as the *Chambre Saint-Louis*[23] in June, had evolved during July. It was motivated by the desperate financial and administrative condition into which France had sunk; it claimed the "power of the purse," and sought to secure some measure of habeas corpus protection against the seventeenth-century equivalent of protective custody, the *lettres de cachet,* on the basis of which arbitrary arrests were continually being made.

The focal point of the crisis was the terrible suffering of the common people, for which the advocate general, Omar Talon, found touching words in a celebrated discourse before the young king. Among other moving passages we find him solemnly pronouncing this challenge:

For ten years now the country has been ruined, the peasants reduced to sleeping on straw, after their furniture has been sold to pay taxes which they cannot raise—to maintain the luxury of Paris, millions of innocent souls are forced to live on bread, bran and oats, and cannot hope for any protection except their impotence. These unfortunates do not possess anything but their souls, and them only because they cannot be auctioned off.[24]

Their plight now found an echo in the sentiments of the middle class and

[23] The interesting origin of this body is analyzed in A. Chéruel, *Histoire de France pendant la Minorité de Louis XIV,* II, 516 ff. Cf. his magistral treatment of this entire period *passim.*
[24] Translated from text as given by Chéruel, *op. cit.,* II, 501.

the nobility of the robe, because the crown in its bankrupt state had started to tax even those who were able to pay! Just as had been done in England, the finance authorities searched the books for long-forgotten sources of revenue. They discovered, for example, that more than a hundred years before, building had been forbidden in certain locations in the environs of Paris; they now proceeded to levy a heavy impost upon those who had in the meantime erected dwellings. Against all this, the *parlement* undertook determined opposition. It looked as if it would follow the British example and free the nation from despotic rule. But its protests were merely verbiage. As soon became apparent, talk of liberty and control of taxation meant merely what it had meant at the dawn of constitutional charters in the days of Magna Charta: special privileges for the upper classes. As Chéruel sarcastically, but justifiably, remarks: "These fathers of the fatherland cared little for the country." Devoid of those deep ideological concerns which animated the English revolutionaries, as we shall see, the *Frondeurs* were selfish men at heart.[25] Indeed, there prevailed a lighthearted frivolity among the leading figures which well justified giving the whole movement the name of a game the children played in the crowded streets of the Paris of that day. The entire Fronde was, as Mazarin very aptly remarked, comparable to a man trying to fight a fleet with a sailboat.

We cannot here trace the involved course of the plots and counterplots, the deeds of heroism and treachery that marked the movement's murky course. Suffice it to indicate a few highlights.

The central figures were the queen regent and Mazarin on the one side, Cardinal Retz, the dukes of Longueville, Beaufort, Chateauneuf and their friends, including La Rochefoucauld, on the other. Shifting back and forth between them were the duke of Orléans and the duke of Enghien, now Prince Condé. Gaston, whose weak, vacillating conduct as brother of King Louis XIII we have encountered before, was *Monsieur* and as governor general next to the queen regent the key source of authority during the regency. Condé, a brilliant, haughty, violent and emotional man, called simply "the Prince," supported the crown during the first period of the Fronde but then made common cause with the *Frondeurs,* and found himself imprisoned for a while. To understand fully the situation which developed, one must bear in mind that the great nobles, and more especially the princes of the blood, still ruled over enormous

[25] See Paul Doolin, *The Fronde* (1935), *passim.*

landed estates, including fortresses and walled cities, which they protected by armed forces under their immediate command. In other words,
there had not as yet come into existence that "monopoly of physical force"
which later political theorists fastened upon as the characteristic of the
modern state.[26] Consequently, not only such great lords as the Prince
Condé, but many another duke possessed his own military establishment.
They therefore had the means to enter into something resembling an
alliance for the joint defense of common interests.

The Fronde was essentially such an alliance. Besides the nobles, the
city of Paris played a vital part in it, and it was the ferment of rebellion
in Paris which led Mazarin to persuade the queen to leave the city in
early January, 1649, and to retire to St. Germain, while calling upon
Condé to lead the royal armies toward the reconquest and subordination
of the city. This task Condé undertook to accomplish by laying waste the
country about Paris and blocking the channels of supply. As a result, the
motley crowd of *Frondeurs,* after a few months of indecisive fighting,
were ready to give up. All through the period Mazarin's fine Italian
hand—to use a rather hackneyed figure of speech which fits him better
than perhaps anyone of the age—carried on negotiations. For Mazarin
did not believe in fighting, any more than in killing his enemies. The
"peace of Ruel," ratified by the *parlement* on April 1, granted concessions
to the noble lords who had fought the crown, and the declaration of
October 22-24, 1648, was reaffirmed, including the privileges for the
bourgeois patriciate. This "peace" was called "a farce to finish the serious
comedy we have lived through," by a thoughtful lady observer.[27] It was
a farce, indeed, but for the common folk, craftsmen and peasants whose
goods had been wasted and destroyed, whose women had been raped and
murdered, it was a bitter mockery, too. No one thought of recompensing
them for their losses.

Upon the conclusion of this peace, the prince of Condé became so
overbearing that Mazarin hesitated to grant him, or rather to advise Anne
of Austria to grant him all that he demanded, especially the key fortress

<hr>

[26] While pluralists might quarrel over the term "physical force," since surely no government, even the most totalitarian, ever possessed a genuine monopoly of every kind of
physical force, the monopoly of organized *military* forces surely is a characteristic feature
of the modern state, even when a constitution guarantees the "right to bear arms" to all
citizens, as does the American.

[27] Madame de Motteville, *Mémoires sur Anne d'Autriche et sa Cour* (ed. by F. Rieux, 4
vols., Paris, 1911), II, 372. An English edition of these *Mémoires* was published, as
translated by Katharine Prescott Wormley (1902).

of Pont de l'Arche in Normandy. Using the proposed marriage of one of Mazarin's nieces to a relative of his ancient enemy, Vendôme, as an excuse, Condé now made common cause with the Fronde. Yet a few days later, due to Mazarin's simulated surrender, he turned again and made a deal with the crown. This *volte-face* occasioned justifiable indignation among the *Frondeurs,* who were now set to take revenge upon so treacherous an ally. After incredibly baroque incidents, involving a staged murder and a simulated attempt upon the life of Condé, the Fronde party made a deal with Mazarin and the queen regent (early January, 1650), negotiated by Cardinal Retz, and a few days later (January 18) the princes of the blood, Condé, the Duc de Longueville and the brother of Condé, Prince Conti, were arrested and imprisoned. "A lion, a fox and a monkey caught in one net," was Gaston d'Orléans's witty if caustic comment.

The arrest of the princes precipitated the so-called second war of the Fronde; everywhere the supporters of the princes rose, as well as provincial *parlements* and other malcontents. For the war with Spain was continuing, and the financial situation was more desperate than ever. There followed a period of intermittent warfare, with Mazarin organizing a series of successful campaigns in the provinces. The crown was aided by loyal elements who responded with enthusiasm to the appearance of young Louis XIV, beautiful and spirited and "every inch a king." The rebels, who had been in constant touch with Spain, both in Brussels and Madrid, now brought Spanish forces into the fray. Once again some of the great ladies played their ever-ardent role in spinning intrigue and loosing combat: the beautiful duchess of Longueville, after fleeing Normandy before Mazarin's troops, set herself up at Stenay in Flanders and negotiated for Spanish aid. The joint troops were commanded by the great Turenne, also a *Frondeur* at this time. In the south, Condé's wife pleaded successfully with the *parlement* of Bordeaux to support her husband's cause.

All this goes to show that the second Fronde, even more than the first, was a revival of feudal notions of resistance by the landed aristocracy in support of their own privileges, rather than the constitutional revolution which was at the same time being fought out across the Channel. Yet, the words used in the war of pamphlets in support of the Fronde, many of them instigated and financed by Retz, were the same or nearly the same as those employed in England. The situation provides a striking illustration of the way in which political theory and action exemplify the

Latin proverb: *"Si duo faciunt idem, non est idem."* Contemporaries knew it well. When Mazarin once compared Retz and his friends to Cromwell and the parliament, he provoked a storm of indignation. Yet on several occasions the queen regent, when pressed to dismiss Mazarin, insisted that she would not repeat the error of Charles I in letting his minister go. As in England during the early phase of the Revolution, the Fronde protested that they were eager to serve the king and the crown, and maintained that they were only trying to free the monarchy of its evil councilors. Likewise, the argument was brought forward that only the king in conjunction with parliament could exercise supreme authority;[28] this was especially the theme of the Fronde's main theorist, Claude Joly (1607–1700).

As the pressure mounted—and the Spaniards were moving in from the north, recapturing Elba and Piombino, and laying siege to Barcelona— *Monsieur* became more and more hostile to Mazarin and eventually broke with him altogether, declaring that he would not sit in council with him. Once more the opposition against Mazarin took violent form in the *parlement,* as well as in gatherings of the nobility and the clergy in Paris. In fact, Mazarin's position was becoming very precarious. So, with the reluctant consent of Anne, Mazarin decided to escape. On February 6, 1651 the cardinal fled, told Condé on the way that he was being freed, and then proceeded to Brühl, the residence of the archbishop of Cologne, who was his friend. After his departure, chaos reigned in Paris. Had Condé wished, he could perhaps have seized effective control of the government until Louis XIV's assumption of it. But such was the curiously emotional personality of this remarkable soldier that he never really knew what he wanted. All he did was stand in the way of others, like Retz, who might have succeeded, although Retz, too, was not fully in earnest and lacked a clear sense of direction. So Mazarin, after communicating a long stream of able and devoted letters of advice to Anne, was able to return soon—as soon as the majority of Louis XIV, declared on his fourteenth birthday, on September 5, 1651, eliminated Orléans and Condé from key control.[29]

The prince was not inclined to accept this reversal quietly. He now

[28] *Les Véritables Maximes du Gouvernement de la France* (1652) in *Recueil de plusieurs pièces curieuses,* quoted by Ranke, *op. cit.,* III, 341. See also Guy H. Dodge, *The Political Theory of the Huguenots of the Dispersion* (1947), Ch. I, and Doolin, *op. cit.,* Chs. V and VI, especially pp. 123 ff.

[29] Note the nice description in Federn, *op. cit.,* 276 ff.

openly took up arms against the queen regent and her chief minister, in the second (and only real) war of the Fronde (1652). This war culminated in a remarkable battle in St. Antoine, a suburb of Paris, in which Turenne, once again fighting for the king, faced Condé. Due to the incredible energy and bravery of the prince and the *sang-froid* of Mademoiselle de Montpensier, the daughter of Gaston of Orléans,[30] the Fronde's forces were not annihilated. But the drive of the Fronde was broken. This did not at first become clear. Indeed, while Condé remained in the field, the Spaniards were winning striking successes against Mazarin's forces. They retook Dunkerque and Gravelines, and were admitted to Casale, while Don Juan of Austria laid siege to Barcelona (it fell to him toward the end of the year). At the same time Orléans was proclaimed independent governor general in Paris and the city seemed determined to maintain the Fronde. But soon dissensions arose; many of those who had consented to the *parlement's* insurrectionary acts under pressure of the mob, were beginning to wonder and urged peace overtures. When Mazarin, as a token of conciliation, departed from headquarters once more, this sentiment gained the upper hand. By the end of the year, the rebellion was pretty much at an end. On February 3, 1653, Mazarin re-entered Paris and was hailed as the victor and savior of the kingdom. Louis went to meet him three miles outside the city and escorted him back. But the cost to France of the two years' strife which Mazarin's departure and return had occasioned was enormous. Devastations comparable to those which the Thirty Years' War had brought to Germany were to be seen everywhere—a solemn reminder to the people as well as to the young king of the price of feudal anarchy.

Ranke remarked that "the Fronde was interwoven with intrigue, but it was not solely an intrigue." He suggested that its significance lay in the fact that the older institutions which were being suppressed by the absolute government, rose against it; *parlements,* clergy and nobility still hoped to return to medieval constitutionalism. Similarly, "on reading the opposition's statements, it becomes clear that the Fronde, to the members of the party, was a movement in defense of the constitution," the most competent student of the movement's political thought observed.[31] The Fronde's arguments were based upon law, and it was upon law that the authority of the *parlement* was based. But these formally accurate assess-

---

[30] See the very lively account of the day in the *Mémoires de Mademoiselle de Montpensier* (ed. by A. Chéruel) (1868), Vol. II, Ch. XIII, pp. 90 ff.

[31] Doolin, *op. cit.,* 157.

ments remain too much on the level of conscious discourse and manifest belief. More deeply rooted were the forces which Mazarin, like Richelieu before him, represented. National unity and the centralized secular government which are symbolized in the word *État,* the modern national state, were being obstructed by the *Frondeurs,* high and low. Unlike their English contemporaries, they did not accept this state and sought to constitutionalize it; they rejected it in the name of a law of a bygone society, and refused to listen to the reason which would refashion the law to make it suit an emerging new society. The *Frondeurs,* in that perspective, discredited sound modes of thought. They enthroned absolutism by their failure to reform constitutionalism.

XIII. CONCLUSION: THE PEACE OF THE PYRENEES AND MAZARIN'S END

After the defeat of the Fronde, one great enterprise remained for Mazarin to bring to an end: the Spanish war. The ups and downs of this conflict in the succeeding years need not be traced here; slowly French military and economic superiority wore down the Spaniards' will to fight, until in 1658 they initiated negotiations. They started in a rather odd setting. The queen regent and the king, as well as the cardinal and the entire court, had gone to Lyons to meet the dowager duchess of Savoy, Christine (sister of Louis XIII), and her daughter Margret. The intention presumably was to arrange the engagement of Louis XIV to his cousin. Curiously enough, the king's company included Marie Mancini, one of Mazarin's nieces, with whom Louis was deeply in love at the time. Still, the king seems to have responded to the young and attractive princess, only to be confronted the next day with the offer of the hand of the infanta of Spain, Maria Theresa. "This cannot be and shall not be," the king of Spain is reported to have exclaimed when he heard of the proposed engagement of Louis and the princess of Savoy. It seems indeed that all the elaborate preparations for the engagement were designed as a ruse to stir the jealousy of the court of Spain. Of course, elaborate negotiations had to be carried through before the royal pair could be married. In the meantime, Louis XIV became ever more deeply infatuated with Marie Mancini and, in the face of Mazarin's very outspoken opposition, demanded to marry her. He was dissuaded from this ill-considered match by dynastic considerations, but not without a bitter struggle. Mazarin had to exert himself to the point of threatening his resignation in order to win his point.

Besides the marriage of the infanta to Louis XIV, which fulfilled Anne of Austria's fondest wish, another event had helped clear the road to peace: the death of Cromwell. For while it was the help of the Lord Protector which had finally given France the decisive superiority over Spain, he had remained hostile to a settlement for a variety of reasons; these now disappeared. Hence the essential negotiations were carried on and the issue settled by Mazarin and Don Luys de Haro, the key minister of Philip IV. The setting was a truly baroque one. To avoid the necessity of either minister having to go to the country of the other, which might be interpreted as a confession of weakness, a temporary building was specially erected on an island, called Pheasants' Island, in the river Bidassoa, above San Sebastian. There the two ministers faced each other on tables so arranged that each sat in his own country; on either side of the river a large troop of armed guards stood watch in colorful costume.

The terms of the treaty, while falling short of Mazarin's most extended ambitions, were quite favorable to France. She returned Catalonia to her former master, but retained Roussillon, enlarged by Conflans and Cerdagne; thus the Pyrenees became the borderline between the two countries protecting Languedoc against Spanish invasion. France retained the fortress of Pinerolo, the gate to Italy, but abandoned all other territorial acquisitions in that country. As for Lorraine, the Spaniards now agreed to dismantle the fortress of Nancy, while France agreed to the return of the duke, Charles IV, to Lorraine proper; France annexed Barrois, Moyenvic, Clermont, and Stenay. Likewise, France acquired almost all of Artois, but returned Franche-Comté; she also took a number of harbors in Flanders, as well as Thionville, Landrecies and Avesnes. These were all important defensive positions the value of which Mazarin had come personally to appreciate in the course of his campaigns. Finally, Spain accepted the settlement of the Treaty of Westphalia, as far as Alsace was concerned.

It can be seen, then, that France had broken the stranglehold of the Hapsburgs on her eastern borders and had greatly reduced, if not eliminated, the threat to her eastern regions. In exchange, Mazarin made two important concessions: He abandoned the agreement with Portugal, "because," he pointed out, "the general peace of Christianity, which could not be achieved otherwise, is to be preferred to the special interests of Portugal." In point of fact, Portugal thereafter succeeded in maintaining her independence with English help. The other concession was to satisfy the prince of Condé, to whom Philip IV felt bound by obligations

of honor. Condé was therefore reinstated in his dignities and was given
the governorship of Burgundy. Condé, like his father, thereupon became
an obsequious subject of the king. When one considers the treaty as a
whole—and together with Westphalia and Oliva it settled the accounts
resulting from the fighting of the preceding two generations—it becomes
clear that its specific provisions were overshadowed by the striking change
in the relative position of the two powers: France took the place of Spain
as the foremost power in western Europe. This change proved in the
sequel to be of long duration. It was made palatable to the proud
Spaniards by the royal marriage which made the concessions appear
almost like a dowry. Don Luys fought long and hard to prevent the
marriage from implying a right of succession. But since the bar to it was
made conditional upon Spain's paying regularly for the dowry, and since
such payments were soon in default, the treaty actually laid the ground-
work for the extended wars of the next generation, known as the War of
the Spanish Succession.

The marriage was celebrated in the most stately fashion. First the
charming, apple-cheeked bride, so familiar from Velasquez's paintings,
was given away in marriage to Louis XIV by her father, with Don Luys
de Haro acting in Louis XIV's stead. Only Mademoiselle and a few of
her ladies-in-waiting attended incognito. Then, on June 5, 1660, the two
kings solemnly met and knelt down in the little building on Pheasants'
Island and swore to maintain the treaty and everlasting friendship. It was
a Sunday, and on the following day, the king of Spain gave his daughter
to Anne of Austria; on June 9 a brilliant marriage was once again
celebrated on French soil. The king and his bride returned to Paris at the
end of August in a triumphal procession. The end of one age and the
beginning of another were marked by these festive events.

Later that year peace was also established in the north (Treaty of
Oliva; see below, Chapter Nine). Mazarin, now at the height of his
political and personal power, did not long survive his striking achievement. He failed rapidly in the course of the winter, and by March 9, 1661,
he passed away. His enormous wealth, which he had offered to Louis
XIV, was disposed of in an elaborate will which contained striking
donations for public use, such as his magnificent library and his astounding art collections. There was, as we noted earlier, a marked business
impulse in Mazarin; to be sure, the fortune which he amassed was not
unrelated to his public functions, indeed he often spent lavishly for public
purposes. Still the fact remains that he became probably the richest man

of his time. And yet, after all is said and done, his two most important bequests to the generation following were the pacification of France and Europe, and the preparation and training of a king and minister capable of carrying on: Louis XIV and Colbert. As Ranke observed that "never has the great and the genuine been linked more closely with the mean, even the low, than in Mazarin," [32] so we may say that Mazarin was a telling embodiment of the modern state: the ordinary personal qualities of the man were submerged in the service to an impersonal institution. It was the greatness of the French state which somehow cast a sheen of superior genius upon its intrinsically unimpressive, selfishly selfless first servant. In his devout *History of the Popes,* Ludwig Pastor draws a contrast between Mazarin and his great and truly ecclesiastical contemporary, St. Vincent de Paul, who died a few months before Mazarin, on September 27, 1660. "Mazarin, caution and cunning personified, Vincent the embodiment of lovable simplicity and straightforwardness. . . . Mazarin's work did not last. It had been the Cardinal's determination to increase the royal power and he succeeded, but by so doing he roused the revolution which overturned the throne. On the other hand, the work of Vincent . . . will stand in time to come. It is not difficult to decide which of the two men was the greater benefactor of mankind." Such a judgment fails to perceive the deeper achievement of Richelieu and Mazarin. For better or worse, they acted as midwives to the modern state. It is still with us.

[32] *Französische Geschichte,* VIII, 329.

Chapter Eight

THE EASTERN DYNASTIES: HAPSBURG, ROMANOV, HOHENZOLLERN AND VASA, 1610–1660

I. THE GENERAL SETTING: DYNASTIC POLITICS

THROUGHOUT the preceding chapters casual reference has been made to Russia and Poland, and to the complex issues arising between them and Sweden, Brandenburg and Hapsburg. Here, as contrasted with western Europe, dynastic rivalries were the dominant factor of international politics. Whether crowned by glorious victory as in Sweden, reconstructive as in Russia, or utterly destructive of the nation's fortunes as in Poland, the ruling houses of Vasa, Hapsburg, Romanov and Hohenzollern looked upon their vast realms as did their unruly noblemen, large and small, upon their landed estates: great properties to be exploited, expanded if chance permit, fought for if need be, but rarely viewed (except to some extent in Sweden, Brandenburg and Austria) as the embodiment of abstract public office, surrounded by the pathos of *État* as Richelieu, Cromwell, or even Olivárez would view their states. A sense of majesty there was, especially in the hearts of Muscovy's tsars, but it was a sense born of a concept of divinely ordained personal rulership rather than of any such notion as that expressed in Frederick the Great's proud dictum: "I am the first servant of my state."

All this must be seen against the lurking threat of Turkish imperialism, injecting itself into the Thirty Years' War and not really subsiding until after the great siege of Vienna in 1683. Ever since the conquest of Constantinople at the beginning of the modern period,[1] Turkish power had been expanding, reaching by 1526 the Carpathians under Suleiman the Magnificent, whose fleets dominated the Mediterranean and thus came into conflict with Venice. This unique seafaring republic, together with Austria and Poland, had borne the brunt of the burden of resistance to the Turk, who suffered a major defeat at the battle of Lepanto (1571) By 1610 the Turks still held the line running from the Istrian coast o:

---

[1] See Edward P. Cheney, *The Dawn of a New Era* (1936), 325 ff.

CHART SHOWING HOW RULERS OF THE SEVERAL DYNASTIES
PARALLELED EACH OTHER, 1610-1660

	1610	1620	1630	1640	1650	1660
Russia	Time of Troubles	1613 Michael _____		1645 Alexis ____ →		
Poland	Sigismund III		1632 Wladyslaw VII	1648 John Casimir →		
Sweden	1611 Gustavus Adolphus		1632 Regency	1644 Christina	Charles X	
Turkey	Ahmed I	1617 Mustapha I / Osman II	1623 Murad IV	Ibrahim I	1649 Mohamed IV →	
Austria	1612 Rudolph / Mathias 1619		Ferdinand II	1637 Ferdinand III	1657 Leopold I	
Brandenburg	John Sigismund	George William _____		1640	Frederick William (Great Elector) →	
Hungary (Transylvania)	Stephen Boscay	Bethlen Gabor	1629 George Rákóczy		1648 George II Rákóczy	

the Adriatic to east of Pressburg (Bratislava)—including as dependent states Transylvania and Moldavia (the modern Rumania), where the restless and ambitious Bethlen Gabor ascended the throne in 1613. His alliance with the Bohemian revolutionaries, while troublesome, did not develop into the serious danger that might have arisen had the Turks themselves become really active. Though the diplomacy of Richelieu and Mazarin sought to bring Turkish military might into the struggle against the Hapsburgs, a Hapsburg policy of skillful appeasement, combined with internal Turkish weakness and the Turks' struggle against Persia in the east prevented all but intermittent interference on a limited scale. Ever since the Treaty of Zaitva-Torok (1606) they had enjoyed at least formal equality; during the long and turbulent reign of Murad IV peace was maintained, and only after his death (1640) did trouble develop with the Venetians, who eventually, in 1656, achieved a startling sea victory. It was only after the Kuprilis, father and son, had re-established order in

Turkey that the war against Austria was resumed, the Austrians having become less willing to compromise after the re-establishment of peace in the Empire. Thus during the entire period 1610–1660 the Turkish threat was latent, rather than actual. Wallenstein's recurrent projects for a crusade-like war against the Turks seem curiously fanciful; realistic appraisal of Turkish weakness was mingled with a lack of understanding for the realities of Richelieu's policy of weakening the Hapsburgs.

We said earlier that during the ten years after Henry IV's death the Hapsburgs, under weak Rudolf and Mathias, had played a rather minor role in eastern European politics. Mathias, as king of Hungary before his assumption of the imperial throne, had battled the Turks, but without going far afield. The marital ties which bound John Sigismund of Poland to the Hapsburgs enabled them to draw him into the conflict that initiated the Thirty Years' War, with the result that Turkish pressure remained light, except as it manifested itself in the restless activities of Bethlen Gabor. It was only under the pressure of Richelieu's policy in the west that the Austrian Hapsburgs turned eastward after the peace of Westphalia. With Russia, they had in the beginning of the seventeenth century hardly any concern at all. Though presumably the chief defenders and extenders of the Counter Reformation, they did not interest themselves in the issues between Catholicism and Greek Orthodoxy that were then playing such an important role in shaping the relation between Poland and Russia. (See below.)

II. THE BEGINNINGS OF THE ROMANOVS

Emerging from the "time of troubles," Russia in 1613 "elected" to the throne Michael Romanov (1613–45), the grand-nephew of Ivan the Terrible, after rejecting both Polish and Swedish candidates (the Polish crown prince had actually been chosen in 1611 by some of the boyars, but his father, King Sigismund, had prevented his accession). Michael's reign was a typical restoration regime; its second half was dominated by Michael's father, Philaret, who, after his return from Polish captivity in 1634 became head of the church and as such chief adviser of the tsar. Slowly but steadily the centralized control of former times re-emerged as local autonomy declined. A good part of the reign of Michael's son Alexis (1645–76) falls into a later period; its most dramatic events were connected with the career of Nikon, which are sketched below. Russia, during these two generations, came closer to the pattern of government with estates than at any period before or after. National representation was composed of two bodies, the duma of the boyars or nobles, and the *zemski sobor*. What this *zemski sobor* really was has been the subject of heated controversy.

The election of Michael had been effected by the *zemski sobor*. Whom did it represent and how? Let us look at the origins of the body. Ivan the Terrible had undoubtedly created it as a counterweight to the duma of the great nobles or boyars. At the same time, he had concentrated both political and economic power, and had established despotic rule of a type unknown in the west. It has been said that he made the state the master of society; it would be better to speak of government, since a state in the western sense did not exist.[2] This concentration of power broke down in the time of troubles, but was eventually recreated by the Romanovs. The strictly bureaucratic, nonrepresentative character of the *zemski sobor* under Ivan the Terrible did not at first reappear in the reign of Michael. The lower chamber was composed of representatives of the people[3] chosen on the basis of a combination of two different principles: representation of classes and professions, and geographical representation. The *zemski sobor* contained members of all classes of society, state employees, landowners, traders, craftsmen and peasants, and also delegates of the provinces of which the state of Muscovy (as Russia was then called) was composed. The franchise was given to house-owning heads of families. The period after 1613 seems to have been the heyday of this kind of governmental organization. It may be called the brief oligarchic period in Russian government, as contrasted with the popular "democracy" of the Cossacks, or the absolutist monarchical regime of the tsars after 1682.[4]

Among the *zemski sobor's* most notable acts must be reckoned the new code of laws, passed by the assembly in 1648–49, albeit under the pressure of a popular uprising in Moscow in June, 1648. It was printed in two thousand copies, and remained the basis of Russian law until 1832. Lithuanian and Byzantine law influenced this codification; it was, of

---

[2] Cf. B. H. Sumner, *A Short History of Russia* (1943), 84 ff. See also P. Milyukov in *Histoire de Russie*, Vol. I (1932). Most important, V. Kluchevsky, *A History of Russia*, Vol. III.

[3] See G. Vernadsky, *A History of Russia* (1929), Ch. V.

[4] M. N. Prokrovsky, *History of Russia* (1931), calls it "The Russia of the Nobles"; his Marxist approach makes him bring out more clearly the class aspect of politics. This seems also the view of James Mavor, *An Economic History of Russia* (first edition, 1914; second edition, 1924), who follows Kluchevsky, however, in his interpretation of the role of the *Sobors*.

course, formally attributed to Tsar Alexis. Its "aristocratic" flavor can be seen in the fact that it finally riveted serfdom upon Russian society as a legal institution.

The development of serfdom, converting a free peasantry into a species of slaves, tied to the soil, on penalty of death, exposed to cruel extortions and brutal treatment, generation after generation, was the most disastrous albeit most important event of this period. "Thus," as one leading historian has written, "in different ways, the bulk of the Russian people descended into a kind of abyss, of which there is no history." [5] While it readied the thin upper strata for "Europeanization," it kept the mass of the Russian people in complete isolation from the main currents of European culture and at the same time prevented it from developing a culture of its own. One might well be tempted to ask whether Russia is properly speaking a part of European history; certainly in the fifty years between 1610 and 1660 it was neither touched by Europe's intellectual and artistic enthusiasms nor affected by its catastrophes. Surely the destruction of the last remnants of the medieval order and the failure of the Counter Reformation were of as little moment to Russia as the discovery of the differential calculus or the vindication of Copernican astronomy. "Abhorred of God is any who loves geometry," exclaimed a Muscovite bishop.[6] There was a growing barbarism to be noted below the upper strata of the ruling groups. This growing barbarism found expression in the codification just mentioned. Society was tabulated according to various kinds of government service and divided into rigid classes with fixed obligations. "The clergy pray, the gentry serve at war, the merchants collect and supply money, the peasants plow the fields." [7] It was one great regimented society, organized for making war upon its neighbors. During the reign of these two tsars, intermittent war continued with Poland and there were also armed conflicts with Sweden and Turkey. With Sweden, a peace was concluded in 1617 at Stolbovo which returned Novgorod to Russia (but gave Sweden control of the Gulf of Finland). In 1634 a treaty with Poland was concluded at Polyanov; under its terms Michael was recognized as legitimate tsar, but Smolensk and other border towns were ceded to Poland. Some of these were reacquired during the war which was resumed in 1654 and not concluded until 1667.

---

[5] Sir Bernard Pares, *A History of Russia* (1926), 160.

[6] Pares, *ibid.,* 179.

[7] Pares, *ibid.,* 161. Here and elsewhere Pares employs the word *state* to indicate the government; it would be highly misleading to assume that anything like the modern state developing in Europe was to be found in Russia at this time.

But perhaps the most striking feature of Russian life in this period was the expansion southward and westward, carried forward by liberty-loving Cossacks who had contributed their share to the anarchy of the time of troubles. Three separate "hosts" of Cossacks, along the Don, the Ural and the Dnieper rivers, maintained themselves on a primitive popular basis, spreading Russian dominance in typical fashion. "We fight for the House of the Immaculate Virgin and the Miracle Workers of Moscow and for Thee . . . Sovereign Tsar and Grand Prince of Great and Little and White Russia, Autocrat and Sovereign and Possessor of many Hordes."[8] The fierce and ruthless aggressiveness of these crude barbarians was like a force of nature, unrelated to the policy of the tsar's government, involving them in controversies and eventually in war with Poland, Turkey and the Crimean Tartars. As Sumner says, they boasted their roving and independent life: "We serve for grass and water, not for land and estates . . . like young falcons . . . on Mother Volga . . . on the blue sea, the Caspian." They were really glorified robber bands, gangs of roving desperadoes who lived on booty, taking slaves, pillaging and burning as they went.[9] But they could not have done this, had they not received a certain amount of support from Muscovy, especially munitions. It was a lawless fringe element, pioneering its way. It established a pattern for the later conquest of Siberia by a mixed system of settlers and traders, partly voluntary, partly conscripted by the government for the purpose, partly sent into exile under penal sentence.

At times these Cossacks achieved extraordinary successes. In 1636 they wrested the fortress of Azov from the Turks and their Crimean allies, and defended it with incredible bravery against massed attacks by the great armies of Ibrahim I. Two hundred thousand men are said to have stormed the Cossack-held strongpoint. Realizing that they could not hold out by themselves, the Cossacks offered the fortress to the tsar, who had already been making apologies to the sultan to forestall war. Cautious, Michael called a *zemski sobor* which, instead of accepting so dangerous a gift, resounded with bitter complaints about taxes and spoliation of the people, as well as lawlessness. Thereupon Michael ordered the Cossacks to leave and they withdrew (Azov did not become Russian till the eighteenth century).

[8] Cited by Sumner, *op. cit.*, 42.

[9] Cf. the authoritative discussion in Kluchevsky, *op. cit.*, 106 ff., where he speaks of a "vagabond, homeless class," and explains that when someone "joined the Cossacks," it meant that he engaged temporarily in "roaming the steppes at will."

In the Ukraine, the Cossacks precipitated a long-drawn-out conflict with Poland which had its roots in religious and socio-economic issues. The region known variously as Little Russia and as the Ukraine, with Kiev as its ancient center, had fallen under Polish rule. The ruthless exploitation of the peasantry, characteristic of all of Poland and Russia throughout this period, served to reinforce a deep-seated concern over the maintenance of orthodoxy. As the Counter Reformation efforts of the Jesuits progressed in reconverting Poland to Catholicism, efforts had been initiated to destroy the Orthodox Greek church as well. To this pressure, some leading men had responded by sponsoring a union of Orthodox and Catholic churches under the Pope, preserving the essentials of ritual and belief. Known as the Unia, this movement aroused the bitter opposition of genuine Orthodox elements. Among these, the Cossacks of the Dnieper region were the most aggressive. Under their able leader, Bogdan Hmielnitsky, these Cossacks, supported by the Tartar Khan of the Crimea and reinforced by oppressed peasants from all over the Ukraine, waged a war of liberation against their Polish oppressors from 1647 until 1654. At first very successful, they were eventually reduced to desperate straits, due to the treachery of the Tartars of the Crimea. Thereupon, Hmielnitsky appealed to Tsar Alexis, offering him the allegiance of the Ukraine. Alexis, after securing representative support from a *zemski sobor* (October 1, 1653), came to the aid of Hmielnitsky. In a large gathering of the Cossacks (*Rada*) Hmielnitsky asked whom they wished to choose as sovereign, and they unanimously opted for the tsar of Russia and swore homage. In the ensuing war against Poland, the Russians at first won striking victories. Not only did they take Smolensk, but they conquered Vilna, Kovno, and Grodno, the key Lithuanian cities, as well as Lublin. But contemporaneous Swedish successes persuaded Tsar Alexis that he must make peace with the Poles and turn against this now more dangerous enemy (1656). But the peace did not last; war was renewed in 1660 not to be finally settled until the compromise of 1667 (peace of Andrusovo).

III. POLAND

The sudden weakness of Poland was the culminating effect of the internal development of that country. Nowhere in Europe were the notions of aristocratic feudalism carried to further extremes. The nobility looked upon themselves as the "nation"—they saw themselves as "the union of free souls" and as such formed the basis of the state, as one leading Polish interpreter has put it.[10] This great brotherhood of the nobility, the *szlachta*, may be compared to the citizenry of Athens in their freedom, their recklessness, which one may call a "democracy," if one is willing to forget the slaving masses under them.[11] During the period following a king's death, and before a new king could be elected, a regular interregnum would ensue, with a high church dignitary as interrex. Thus if the king's demise occurred at a crucial moment of war, as in 1648, virtual anarchy would leave the country at the mercy of its enemies. In that year, King Wladyslaw IV died, a noble and humane, albeit not a very strong ruler, and the best of the Vasa kings. The reigns of both his bigoted and weak predecessor, Sigismund III (1589–1632), and his incompetent successor, John Casimir (1648–67), had prepared and consummated the "deluge." Sigismund, preoccupied with dynastic ambitions—he was the cousin of Gustavus Adolphus and had been rejected by the Swedes—and misled into supporting ecclesiastical fanaticism, remained a stranger to his Polish subjects all his life. During the time, preceding our period, while the great Zamoyski was his chief minister, he did reasonably well, but Zamoyski's eventual successor, Zolkiewski, could not prevent the king's involvement in the Hapsburg cause after the outbreak of the Bohemian war, and hence the invasion of Poland by Turkey. It would be pointless to trace this incessant, if intermittent, warfare, even in outline. Suffice it to say that King Wladyslaw succeeded, where his father and his stepbrother had failed. His success was at least in part due to his tolerant religious policy. Not only did he grant the various "dissenters" a greater role in national life, but he harbored a dream, shared by so many of the finer spirits of this intolerant age, of reuniting the various Christian faiths. He eventually brought together at Toruń (Thorn) in 1644 representatives of the various groups for a religious conference. But instead of producing a measure of agreement and mutual accommodation, each faction returned with enhanced bitterness against its rivals. Nonetheless, the gathering at Toruń is illustrative of the vigorous and free spirit which characterized Polish life at this time; many "refugees" from the persecution of the Counter Reformation, such as the Bohemian Brethren, had found shelter within Poland at that time, including the great Comenius.[12]

---

[10] See Ladislas Konopczynski, *Le Liberum Veto—Étude sur le Développement du Principe Majoritaire* (1930), Ch. XI.

[11] See the beautiful illustrated work, published in 1927, by a group of scholars, *Polska Jej Dzieje i Kultura*. The second volume, dealing with 1572–1795, contains a great deal of value for our period, showing the life of the Polish people and its art.

[12] See above, p. 102.

Altogether, no greater contrast could be imagined than that between the governments of Poland and Russia. The latter had carried monarchical absolutism to a despotic extreme under Ivan the Terrible—and would do it again under Peter the Great—while at the same time pursuing a policy of rigid centralization, opposed to all local autonomy and self-government. By contrast, Poland became a republic of aristocratic land-owners, both large and small—really a federation of hundreds of small units, each represented in the national assemblies by delegates with fixed instructions. They were, in Burke's celebrated phrase, "a congress of ambassadors" representing different and hostile interests. This extraordinary exaggeration of the feudal heritage made Poland an attractive place for the landowning aristocracies of adjoining territories; the union with Lithuania (1569) had been built upon it; the estates of Prussia likewise favored adhesion to Poland on this ground. But it is misleading to speak of this system as "parliamentarism" as later liberal ideologues have been inclined to do. For the diet of Poland was no parliament in the sense of modern constitutionalism. Indeed, the term is as inappropriate as is the word state for designating the autocratic ruling groups of Muscovy. Rather than achieving the transformation to modern constitutionalism—an achievement intimately linked to the Protestant ethic of the Common-wealth-men, as we shall see—the Polish gentry and their Roman Catholic clergy carried the other horn of the dilemma of the medieval "govern-ment with estates" [13] to its radical, not to say senseless, *reductio ad absurdum.*

The Polish diet, while not assuming the responsibility for governing, prevented the king from doing so. It controlled the granting of money and the raising and maintenance of armed forces. Against it the king was helpless. As Bishop Piasecki wrote, in the period of Sigismund and Wladyslaw, with obvious satisfaction:

The King of Poland is in his public functions like a queenbee who merely furnishes honey to her subjects. He alone discharges all the many responsibili-ties of the Republic. So bountifully does he dispense of his treasure that in all his wide domains and among all the nations under his sceptre, there is no squire or soldier without his slave. The clerics receive rich abbeys from him, and all the royal authority is based on his power of purchasing by such means all who aspire to positions of dignity or wealth. . . . But the lives, the liberties,

<hr>

[13] See above, pp. 14–22.

and the estates of the nobility are altogether removed from the king's reach or rule.[14]

Since all these appointments were for life, the king's power was limited indeed. During our period it was further curtailed. The *sejm,* flanked by the senate of great nobles, was the exclusive preserve of the nobility (gentry) during our period. Hence, efforts on the part of the kings to secure measures that would strengthen the towns or alleviate the lot of the oppressed and enslaved peasantry were foredoomed to failure. Wherever else in Europe the royal power was consolidated and a modern state emerged, it coincided with a vigorous effort on behalf of the towns and a corollary assault upon the privileged position of the feudal nobility. Hence this failure of the Polish kings, inevitable perhaps under the circumstances, to broaden the economic, if not the political, role of the bourgeois element was as fraught with danger for the Polish people, as was the progressive enslavement of the peasantry.[15] It was part of the weakness of the executive power under the elective monarchy.

The results for the Polish people and the Polish state were in every way disastrous. Not only did the elective principle lead to the choice of a "foreigner," the Swedish Vasa crown prince, Sigismund (1589), but the power of the assemblies was highly noxious, because it did not carry with it any responsibility for effective governmental action. All these turbulent gatherings did was to say, "No." The extreme was reached, when, after the protracted war with the Cossacks under Hmielnitsky (in Polish the name is spelled Hmielnicki), the peace treaty which had been negotiated with difficulty to the advantage of Poland, was rejected because one delegate, Sicinski, cast his *"liberum veto."* The war continued.[16]

These exaggerations of an unworkable system of government invited the aggression of external foes. Sweden and Russia, and to a lesser extent Turkey, stood ever ready to invade Poland's wide-open lands. At the beginning of the period, Poland still seemed the powerful state that it had been in the sixteenth century. Through union with Lithuania it had

[14] Quoted in George Slocombe, *A History of Poland* (1939), 126. Its Chapter XII, "The Constitution of Poland," gives a good summary of the "constitution."

[15] Cf. the sage observations on this score by O. Halecki, *The History of Poland—An Essay in Historical Synthesis* (1942), 128 ff. .

[16] Michal Brobrzynski, *Dzieje Polski w Zarysie* (fourth edition, 1927), Chs. X–XIII, especially pp. 195 ff. Cf. also the discriminating discussion of this incident, its antecedents and consequences in Konopczynski, *op. cit.,* Chs. X–XIII, especially pp. 195 ff.

reached from the Baltic to the Black Sea. Although much of its hold was tenuous in the borderlands to the north and south, Poland actually had captured the Kremlin in 1610 and seemed in a position to become arbiter of Russia's future. By contrast, in 1656 almost all of Poland was occupied by either Sweden or Russia, and it was only the diplomatic intervention of Vienna and the heroic resistance of some ardent spirits kindled by religious enthusiasm which saved it.

The monastery of Czenstochowa was a national shrine, because it contained the picture of the Black Madonna. For the Protestant Swedish soldiery to defile this sacred image would have been a disaster, both national and religious, of unheard-of frightfulness. So the prior and his monks, with a few soldiers to help them, manned the turrets and fortress walls of the ancient monastery ready to lay down their lives in its defense. For forty days the Swedes stormed at the defiant strongpoint. But at last they withdrew, not realizing that this defeat would be greeted throughout Poland as a miracle and a sign from heaven that not all was lost. Freed of the Russian pressure, the nation rallied. The invader was driven back. Afterwards, the restored king announced that henceforth the Blessed Virgin should be adored as the "Queen of the Crown of Poland."

The defense of Czenstochowa Monastery by its little garrison of about seventy monks and two hundred soldiers under Prior Kordecki reminds one of the story of Joan of Arc. Here as there, a blending of national sentiment with religious ardor produced something of a miracle. As Hapsburg diplomacy turned the armies of Russia against the too victorious Swedes, the Poles took courage and drove the enemy from their land. By 1660 the peace of Oliva (see below) settled the first phase of this crisis; at the same time it revealed that the power of Poland was no more. Henceforth Poland was a pawn in the dynastic game of Hapsburg, Romanov and Hohenzollern.

We have already noted the significant word "deluge" which Polish historians have coined to characterize the series of catastrophes which from 1648 onward shook the foundations of the Polish state.[17] Halecki attributes the Polish disasters largely to outside aggression. This view, though more acceptable to national pride, seems questionable. It is true, however, that until 1648 Poland "stood in the rank of a great power which the whole of Europe regarded very seriously."[18] Deeply moving

[17] O. Halecki, *op. cit.*, 123.

[18] *Ibid.*, 113. Halecki's view represents that of the so-called Warsaw school of Polish

and eerie in its prophetic tone was the farewell address of John Casimir, as he relinquished the throne to return to friends in France:

> Believe me, ye Polish Cavaliers, without superior, except in Heaven, if your glorious republic continue to be managed in such manner [as hitherto] . . . the day will arrive, and the day is perhaps not far off, when this glorious republic will get torn to shreds hither and thither; be stuffed into the pockets of covetous neighbors, Brandenburg, Muscovy, Austria, and find itself reduced to zero, and abolished from the face of the world . . . farewell! [19]

The fate of Poland in this period in some ways resembled that of Spain, as did the pride and independence of her fighting, landowning nobility. The disappearance of both was part of the great transformation that took place between 1610 and 1660 in the European state system. Neither country succeeded in achieving the essential transition to the modern state; both became engulfed in essentially "romantic" notions about the restoration of the medieval system. The role of the Jesuits in both was great; their tendency to subordinate political to ecclesiastical considerations contributed its share to preventing the emergence of the modern state.[20]

IV. THE STRUGGLE FOR THE BALTIC: SWEDEN

The place of Poland as a major power was, at the end of our period, taken by Sweden. Her rapid rise to predominance in the Baltic was in part, no doubt, due to the combined genius of Gustavus Adolphus and his chancellor, Oxenstierna. They managed to turn a government with estates into a modern state[21] whose exploits profoundly affected the course of all European politics. Gustavus was able, as we have seen, to gain control of Russia's possessions on the Baltic in the peace of Stolbovo (1617), more especially of Ingria and Karelia, barring Russia from the Baltic. But no sooner was the war with Russia settled, than Gustavus Adolphus turned against Poland, and in the course of protracted warfare over twelve years he possessed himself of Livonia, as well as a number

---

historians, whereas the view of Brobrzynski is that of the leading voice of the Cracow school, which seems preferable. Halecki anyhow does not deny that the internal factors played their part, as did errors and vacillation in foreign policy.

[19] Quoted in Slocombe, *op. cit.*, 131.

[20] A third country with analogous problems and a similar fate was Ireland; see pp. 291–2.

[21] See above, Chapter Six.

of Prussian harbors. These, as well as the possession of Esthonia, were recognized in the truce of Altmark (1629), concluded with the aid of French and English diplomats, but basically the fruit of Richelieu's determination to bring the Swedes into the German war and to unsettle the triumph of Hapsburg, which was overreaching itself in the Restitution Edict. The war which followed has been described elsewhere; Gustavus Adolphus' intervention proved the decisive turning point in the Thirty Years' War.[22] Deep religious sentiment was involved. But the move also was part of the Swedish crown's struggle for supremacy in the Baltic, which was now being threatened by Wallenstein, on behalf of the Hapsburgs, rather than by Poland or Russia.

The striking ascendancy of Sweden in this period was closely related to that country's rapid advance in the direction of the modern state; indeed the Swedes came closer than any other European nation to working out the constitutional synthesis which England achieved in the course of her revolution.[23] In this respect Sweden contrasted strongly with Poland and Russia, her two main rivals for territorial control of the Baltic shores since the decline of the Teutonic Knights. The situation was different in her competition with Denmark and more especially with the Netherlands for maritime supremacy. Indeed, it is not too much to say that the Netherlands provided Sweden with the most important impetus toward and instruction about the techniques of modern statecraft. Not only did men like de Geer bring capitalistic mining and manufacturing to Sweden, but Gustavus Adolphus learned the military art from Maurice of Nassau, and naval craftsmanship from the great Dutch masters in this field. Thus Gustavus Adolphus, and with him many another Swede of distinction who served under him, acquired from the Dutch the essential knowledge for achieving the predominant position in the Baltic which was to be theirs throughout the seventeenth century.

Upon his accession in 1611, Gustavus Adolphus had been obliged to concede or rather to reconfirm Sweden's constitutional order of government with estates. His father's autocratic rule had stirred deep animosities among his freedom-loving people, and the estates had insisted upon a kind of coronation oath, the *konungsförsäkran,* or solemn declaration.

[22] See above, Chapter Six.

[23] For a competent general survey see Carl Hallendorf and Adolf Schück, *History of Sweden* (1929), especially the section entitled "The Rise of the Baltic Empire." On controversial issues, the authors lean, naturally, toward a Swedish viewpoint: this is especially notable in their account of Gustavus Adolphus.

According to this declaration, the king was to govern in consultation with the *Riksråd* or council of the realm. More especially, the council was to be consulted before any laws were introduced, new taxes levied, war and peace made, or alliances concluded. In more important instances, and at the judgment of the council, the *Riksdag* or estates of the realm was likewise to be consulted. These Swedish estates, unlike the English, French, or Polish, but like the estates in some German territories, included the peasants as a fourth estate along with the other three, and before Gustavus Adolphus embarked upon his great intervention in the German war, he addressed the peasants with special vigor.[24] However, the key estate was that of the nobility, and the position of the nobility had been strengthened by a charter issued at Gustavus Adolphus' coronation in 1617, and by the statutes of the nobility of 1626. In these solemn agreements, the nobility assumed the right and the duty of serving the country in the civil service and in the army.

Modeled in part upon German precedents of the period, the Swedish nobility was carefully organized, but remained open to all whom the king wished to reward for outstanding service to the country. Yet, the truly popular basis of the *Riksdag* remained, indeed was strengthened during Gustavus Adolphus' reign. To carry out his vast schemes of foreign policy, he needed to enlist the support of the entire people. For this purpose, the estates' assembly of the *Riksdag* served well. Truly representative, the *Riksdag* in this far northern kingdom presented a curiously modern picture as it heard and then approved the king's policy. It foreshadowed the great strength of a democratically constituted polity. In spite of occasional difficulties, the king succeeded with the able help of his chief minister, Axel Oxenstierna, in maintaining adequate popular support for his daring policy. Eventually, these practices were fully spelled out in the constitution drafted by Oxenstierna at the suggestion of the king, and adopted by the estates in 1634: they became known as *1634 Års Regeringsform*. By it, the *Riksråd* was transformed into a cabinet, in which the heads of the several administrative departments had a seat and voice. It was the great king's heritage to coming generations of Swedes. Under this constitution, Sweden for the time solved the basic problem of combining a strong executive with broad popular participation in basic policy decisions and law-making. To these general principles the Swedes returned in 1809, after an absolutist period

[24] See above, Chapter Six, pp. 178–9.

in the eighteenth century. The constitutional order enabled Sweden to weather the dangers of an extended regency, after the great king's early death (1632).

Internal development and external aggression bear here as elsewhere a close relationship to each other. In the case of Gustavus Adolphus, as generally with the Vasa kings, it is difficult not to seek the explanation in personal terms of greatness. But more general factors were undoubtedly involved.

There is an element of mysterious growth, as in the rise and fall of families, in this sudden outward projection of a hitherto self-contained people. The Swedish wars of the seventeenth century partook of this element of the unknown of history. The earlier wars, as well as Sweden's entry into the war in Germany, were at least in substantial part motivated by a determination to achieve *dominium maris baltici*. A brief war with Denmark, 1643-45, served the same purpose. Indeed, Swedish determination to continue the war in Germany after the peace of Prague (1635) had compromised the religious issues to the "satisfaction" of the German contestants can be understood only by reference to Sweden's determination to extend and secure her Baltic empire through the acquisition of Pomerania. After 1637 when the last Pomeranian duke, Bogislav XIV, died this territory became one of the most serious obstacles to peace, because by inheritance it was intended to go to Brandenburg and the Hohenzollerns proved very obdurate in maintaining their rights. Acquisition of Pomerania having become an essential condition of peace for Sweden, a compromise was eventually worked out by the French, in the Treaty of Westphalia, by dividing Pomerania between the two contestants and compensating them for their concessions by ecclesiastical lands further west.[25]

No sooner had this juicy Pomeranian morsel been added to Swedish territory, now already comprising half the Baltic shores, than the desperate straits into which Poland had drifted after the death of Wladyslaw in 1648 invited outright aggression on the part of Charles X Gustavus, who had succeeded Christina upon her abdication in 1654.[26] He declared war upon Poland in 1655 on the thin pretext that John Casimir refused to recognize him. In fact, the Swedish king wished to

[25] See above, Chapter Six, for background.

[26] Queen Christina's conversion to Catholicism is one of the most interesting events of this period, which only lack of space prevents us from dealing with. Ranke wrote a special study of it which he included in his *Die Römischen Päpste* (fifth edition, 1867), III, 77-103.

conquer the territories on the Baltic coast between Pomerania and Livonia, more especially Lithuania and Prussia. We have seen what extraordinary success this violent soldier had at first; in 1656 half of Poland was at his feet. Among those who shifted their allegiance was the elector of Brandenburg who, as duke of Prussia, was a vassal of the Polish king, but who secured an acknowledgment of his "sovereignty" in exchange. But the Swedish success was too great: Russia, Denmark and the Empire declared war upon Sweden, Poland rose to free herself, Brandenburg broke away, and all the Swedish king could do was to turn against the Danes, whom he twice invaded and all but annihilated. As a consequence, in the peace of Copenhagen, Denmark surrendered to Sweden what was left of her possessions at the southern end of the Scandinavian peninsula, thus giving Sweden joint control with Denmark of the straits through which she had formally enjoyed free passage since 1613 (Treaty of Knaered).

V. THE GREAT ELECTOR AND BRANDENBURG

In 1618 the house of Hohenzollern, electors of Brandenburg, inherited the Polish fief of Prussia, since the male line of the dukes of Prussia had died out. Nine years earlier they had established their claims on the Rhine as part of the Jülich succession.[27] Thus the east-west span of their dominions, which the next two hundred years were to see rounded out and eventually expanded into the German Empire that collapsed in 1918, was laid out. But during the generation immediately following these acquisitions, Brandenburg-Prussia, under her weak prince, George William (1619–40), played a largely passive role. No sooner had his gifted son Frederick William ascended the throne than the situation began to change. Though only twenty years of age, the young prince displayed remarkable sagacity in his dealings with an all-but-hopeless situation. A "beggar on horseback," his most recent biographer has called him.[28] His extended domains consisted largely of claims. But these claims, this great-grandson of William the Silent and nephew of Gustavus Adolphus of Sweden proposed to maintain with utmost vigor.

He decided to make haste slowly. Trained in the Netherlands, he would no doubt have liked to work in close co-operation with the house

---

[27] See above, Chapter Six, pp. 125–6.
[28] Ferdinand Schevill, *The Great Elector* (1947), a fine work of historical synthesis, Ch. 3.

of Orange. Frederick Henry of Orange was aging, yet when Frederick William asked for his daughter, Louise Henriette, he accepted him with alacrity (1646). This marriage followed several guarded efforts to win the hand of Queen Christina of Sweden, whom the great Gustavus Adolphus had when they were both children (1630) suggested in jest as a suitable wife. It would probably have been a bad match. Yet Frederick William's hopes for Dutch co-operation did not work out very well either. The failure of the Dutch merchant republic to ally itself with him, in its eyes an impoverished prince, turned the elector's eyes back to the east. That he gained much in the Treaty of Westphalia, we have seen elsewhere.[29] But the gains did not include all of Pomerania, which he considered rightly his lawful inheritance. A generation had to pass before he could seize by war what the peace had denied him.

In the meantime he was faced with another perplexing problem. Prussia he held as a fief of Poland. The Polish king, though a weak ruler, insisted upon the formalities. The proud young prince was obliged to proceed to Warsaw to render homage to his liege lord. He did so in 1641. "In his own eyes the spectacular event was a crushing humiliation . . . its bitterness grew with the passing of time." [30] The opportunity to escape from this dependence presented itself when Charles X Gustavus decided to attack Poland in 1655.

Frederick William had by that time come to the conclusion that he must provide himself with a standing army. His experiments with intermittent forces such as he raised in 1644 and again in 1651 to attempt an abortive forcing of the issue of his claims in the west, had shown him that such forces entailed a dependence upon the estates of his various dominions which threatened disaster. When, therefore, the clash between Sweden and Poland seemed imminent, he set about to establish the nucleus of a permanent organization to defend himself and his territories against his two more powerful neighbors. 1655 may properly be designated as the birth year of the Prussian army, which in course of time became the symbol of militarism and aggression.[31] But in the beginning the new force was clearly defensive. The great elector had come to recognize that "the conservation of his state and country would depend next to God upon arms," as he told the Prussian estates in 1662,[32] and a few years

[29] See above, Chapter Six, pp. 192–3.

[30] F. Schevill, op. cit., 109.

[31] C. Jany, Geschichte der königlich-preussischen Armee (5 vols., 1927–37), I, 115–92. Jany would select 1660 as the year, because the elector then decided to keep the army.

[32] Jany, op. cit., 192–93.

later in his testament to his son he added that "alliances are good, but one's own forces even better."

It was this determination of Frederick William to create a standing army, a *miles perpetuus,* as the times called it, which was at the heart of his protracted struggle with his estates, just as it had been in France a generation earlier. But whereas the estates were completely eliminated in the case of France, they remained functioning elements of the government in the Hohenzollern realm throughout the great elector's reign and later. What reduced their effectiveness, however, was their rigid insistence upon local patriotism. Thus there were separate estates in Prussia and Brandenburg, in Cleve-Mark and in Pomerania, as well as in the lesser component units of the great elector's dominions. With the estates in each of the three larger units, Brandenburg, Cleve-Mark and Prussia, a long-drawn-out controversy over whether their prince could permanently maintain an armed force ended with the victory of the elector. The perils of the war between Sweden and Poland as well as the renascent aggressiveness of France after 1660 served to convince the more recalcitrant representatives of the "people" of the monarch's argument. To a permanent threat there must correspond a permanent security force—an argument familiar again in our time. Nor should it be forgotten that the provincial estates in fact represented only the feudal landlords, now on the way to becoming agricultural capitalists (*Grundbesitzer*), and the burgher element of the towns, but not the peasants and more dependent workers. Indeed, Frederick William had to concede to the Brandenburg estates a reaffirmation of the right of the feudal lords to hold the peasants in virtual serfdom (1653).

Counterbalancing this gloomy side of growing absolutism, greeted by many as tyranny that should be resisted, Frederick William proved himself singularly enlightened in the field of religion. While himself an ardent Calvinist, he was ever ready to insist upon the basic similarity of the two Protestant faiths, and generally to pursue with unrelenting vigor a policy of broad-minded tolerance, in sharp contrast to most other European rulers, not excepting the more rabid revolutionaries in England. There is something Cromwellian in the character of Frederick William with its combination of religious piety, administrative skill, military ability and broad tolerance, as well as in the occasional outbursts of rage when encountering bigotry, disloyalty or wanton opposition.

The slowly advancing consolidation of Frederick William's dispersed possessions into a single modern state was put to a severe test by the war between Sweden and Poland, which Charles X Gustavus precipitated in 1655. The course of that war has been indicated elsewhere. It remains to sketch how the elector of Brandenburg exploited the varying fortunes of this war to wrest advantage for himself by a series of "treaties" culminating in the peace of Oliva (1660).

After concluding a treaty of mutual defense with the Dutch, in which he secured their naval protection for his Prussian ports in exchange for granting them maintenance of existing tariff rates, Frederick William nevertheless found himself in somewhat of a corner after the startling and overwhelming victories of Charles X, reinforced by the advance of Russia in the east. To be sure, he had anticipated a Swedish victory and had tried to negotiate an agreement beforehand, in spite of his feudal bond to the Polish king. But the Swedes had been too uncompromising and haughty. Now that within a matter of weeks the whole of Poland lay prostrate at their feet, the elector found himself obliged, in the Treaty of Königsberg (January 17, 1656) to acknowledge the suzerainty of Sweden, open the ports of Memel and Pillau to Sweden, and share their customs. For it had been the conquest of Prussia and its ports that had been the unavowed aim of Sweden, since the Prussian coast would all but complete Swedish control of the Baltic shores and make the Baltic a Swedish lake.

In December, 1655, Charles X had commenced to invade the duchy to force the elector's hand. The treaty was a clear case of duress, and the elector's determination to escape its onerous clauses was soon rewarded. For reverses, more especially the outburst of Polish national resistance, which we have recounted earlier, obliged the Swedish king to seek the support of Brandenburg-Prussia; at the same time the Polish king now offered Frederick William generous terms for returning to the fold of Poland. But since the Poles had little to offer but risks, the elector, although he kept them hoping, concluded a treaty with Sweden at Marienburg (June 25, 1656), which granted him large parts of western Poland between Prussia and Brandenburg, in exchange for armed support to Charles X. Frederick William had by this time assembled in Prussia a well-organized army of about 8,500 men. They won their spurs in the great battle of Warsaw (July 28–30), in which the Poles were decisively beaten a third time. But it proved a Pyrrhic victory for Charles, as we have seen, bringing Austria and Denmark into the fray and forcing him to turn west to meet the new threat. Even before that happened, Frederick William, unwilling to get lost in the vast reaches of eastern

Poland, had returned to Prussia to protect its borders against the Lithuanians who were attacking it. The elector had repeatedly, but vainly, urged his ally to conclude peace.[33]

After a futile attempt at seizing Danzig, which the Dutch helped to defend, Charles mounted a new assault upon Poland, but not without first being obliged to grant sovereign independence to the elector in the Treaty of Labiau (November 20, 1656): in the same treaty the Swedes also surrendered their share in the customs of the Prussian ports. Behind this development was the diplomacy of a remarkable Austrian diplomat, Franz von Lisola, who had urged the court at Vienna to make every effort to detach Brandenburg from Sweden. His first attempts to secure from Poland the relinquishment of its feudal claim to the Prussian duchy having miscarried—and the Treaty of Labiau as a result having been concluded—von Lisola tried again, after the Poles had been reduced a fourth time in the spring of 1657. Since in the meantime the Austrians and Danes had entered the war against Sweden, and Charles X had rushed west to defeat Denmark, Frederick William now entered into negotiations with Poland and its allies, helped by von Lisola who in the course of months of negotiation finally wrested from John Casimir the concession of Prussia's sovereignty, set down in the Treaty of Wehlau (September 19, 1657). In exchange for Prussian sovereignty, Frederick William gave up all claims to Polish territory outside the duchy that had been promised him by Sweden and had been occupied.[34]

In spite of startling successes scored by Charles X against Denmark, culminating in the Danish surrender at Copenhagen (1659), the Swedes finally quit, and the Treaty of Oliva, near Danzig, concluded the Polish-Swedish war which had threatened to engulf Brandenburg. Instead, due to the statesman-like skill and moderation of her ruler, this war had brought about not only the international recognition of Frederick William as sovereign of the Prussian duchy, but had left him with greatly enhanced prestige both at home and abroad. The Treaty of Oliva not only marked the turning of the tide against Sweden's Baltic empire, but the emergence of Brandenburg-Prussia as the effective rival of Sweden and Poland for predominance in northeast Europe. The elector's swift maneuvering has been denounced as an immoral disregard of all rules

---

[33] See A. Waddington's valuable *Le Grand Electeur Frédéric Guillaume—sa Politique Extérieure*, Vol. I (1905), 1640–1660. The views of Ranke, Droysen and others are discussed in the bibliography.

[34] Cf. the illuminating correspondence of von Lisola in *Archiv für österreichische Geschichte*, Vol. LXX.

of good faith, as it has been celebrated as a sign of true greatness. It was in fact neither. It was the steady and sober pursuit of his state's interests in the approved and prevailing fashion of the baroque age. The great Pufendorf was later to describe the activities of both Charles X and Frederick William in two highly significant histories. His bland portrayal of the diplomacy of the two able rulers remains a signal testimony to their historical role.[35]

The peace of Oliva was really negotiated at the insistence of Mazarin, who desired to prevent a Swedish collapse. Livonia was at last ceded to Sweden, whereas Brandenburg's claim to at least part of Swedish Pomerania was denied. This failure set the stage for the elector's later exploits. He had now become a European sovereign in his own right, and what remained, namely to link the scattered areas of the Hohenzollern domains, became the concern of this rising dynasty for the next two hundred years. In a memorable passage, Toynbee has used Brandenburg-Prussia as a prime illustration of his generalization about the bracing effect of an adverse challenge and man's victorious response to it. It was during the first twenty years of his reign that Frederick William shaped this response to the disasters which challenged him upon his arrival on the throne.

VI. HAPSBURG AND HUNGARY

The eventual rivalry with Austria which Brandenburg-Prussia's rapid rise was to precipitate was as yet a remote contingency. But apart from the Hapsburgs' position in Germany, which rested upon their various Austrian lands, as well as their somewhat divergent position in Bohemia,[36] they were also kings of Hungary and as such the sovereign princes of an independent foreign state with separate administration, army, and finance. It was through this independent kingdom that the Hapsburgs were fully and continually involved in eastern dynastic politics, just as Brandenburg was through Prussia, and Sweden through its Baltic possessions. Through most of the period with which we are concerned the Hapsburgs were, as we have seen, in a state of uneasy peace with the Turks; toward the end, after 1656, the Turks were on the march again. Hungary was a land of proud and in many ways unique traditions. As

---

[35] Cf. Ernest Salzer, *Der Übertritt des Grossen Kurfürsten* (1904), and the chapter on Pufendorf in Friedrich Meinecke, *Die Idee der Staatsräson in der Neueren Geschichte* (1925).

[36] Under the Golden Bull (1348), the king of Bohemia was an elector of the Holy Roman Empire, even though the kingdom did not constitute part of the German kingdom, which contained the bulk of the Empire's territory.

the name indicates, it traced its antecedents to the Huns, who spearheaded the great Mongolian invasions at the dawn of Western history. A proud and unruly nobility and squirearchy had gone far toward constitutionalizing the kingdom in the fashion of the later Middle Ages, and in many respects the government with estates in Hungary had been as far advanced as that of Spain or England. But then the torrents of Turkish hordes had flooded it, and had forced Hungary to seek what aid it could from the tottering Holy Empire at the turn from the fifteenth to the sixteenth century. What would be more natural than for the Hapsburgs to seek an extension of monarchical power and to weld Hungary more firmly into the unity of the Hapsburg Reich? The nobility on its part could not but sympathize with the straits of their Bohemian brethren, and perhaps even aspire to the kind of aristocratic predominance which the Polish nobility had achieved.

More important in our period than the small northern and western part of Hungary belonging to the Hapsburgs was the territory, known as Transylvania and ruled by two striking personalities, Bethlen Gabor (1613–29) and George Rákóczy I (1630–48). During their rule, Hungary achieved a measure of genuine independence, but this was lost again under the reckless George Rákóczy II (1648–60). Bethlen Gabor was the first Hungarian ruler who really knew and understood the Turks. Having fled to Turkey from the Hapsburgs' Counter Reformation, he returned after the murder of Bathory, soon to find himself elected to the throne. Under his stewardship, Transylvania became both economically and administratively consolidated; a measure of English influence can be traced at this time, largely due to the bond of Calvinism. We have seen [37] how Bethlen Gabor took advantage of the Thirty Years' War to press against the Hapsburgs' overlordship, especially with a view to religious autonomy; both in 1622 and 1626 he forced Ferdinand II to acknowledge the rights of Protestants.

Still, the Counter Reformation progressed largely due to the exertions of a remarkable Jesuit, Peter Pazmany. A great preacher, he believed in peaceful conversion, and between 1616, when he was made archbishop, and 1637, when he died, a decided majority had returned to Catholicism in western Hungary. Devoted to a western orientation, Pazmany linked the unity and future of Hungary to Hapsburg rule. Against such tendencies, Bethlen Gabor after 1626 resumed the fateful policy of trying to unite dynastically the kingdoms of Hungary and Poland. It was prema-

[37] See above, Chapter Six.

ture, since the first problem was how to reunite Hungary itself. But it is natural that in face of the great power of Russia, Turkey and the Hapsburgs, ambitious rulers should have sought to unite the two weaker kingdoms. His cautious successor, George Rákóczy I, avoided further adventures in this direction, but George Rákóczy II entered, as we have seen, into a full-scale alliance with Charles X Gustavus, and in 1657 attempted to win the crown of Poland by aggressive war. Not only did the campaign fail, but it brought on a Turkish invasion and the dismemberment of Transylvania after the death of the king (1660). With this disaster the independent role of Transylvania came to an end. The freeing of the country from the Turk from then on depended upon the Austrian Hapsburgs, who throughout this period had, through their governors or palatines, like Count Esterházy, sought to reunite Hungary around the western part, which had remained under their rule. This they did not succeed in doing without first bringing their Reich to the very brink of disaster.

VII. THE EASTERN AND WESTERN CHURCH AND THE GREAT SCHISM [38]

Western influence had long been suspect in Muscovy. "Forbear thou to study the Latin tongue, in that it is evil," seems to have been one way of expressing the sentiment of the prevailing orthodoxy. During the first generation of our period, as indeed ever since the days of Ivan the Terrible, western science and art, as well as western religious and political views had been filtering into Moscow. Against them a fierce reaction arose; this reaction in its train became associated with what is known as the great schism which split the Orthodox Christians into Old Believers and regular churchmen. The break was precipitated by certain innovations brought about by the Patriarch Nikon (born 1605, died 1681) in the years 1652–58.

Nikon was in many ways the most striking personality Russia produced in this period. Of peasant ancestry, he became the foremost exponent of the "reform" of the Russian church which aimed at bringing it into line with the older Greek tradition. This reform was linked to the conception of a "church universal" but it raised the deepest passions, because it touched the sacred ritual which had been developing in the

[38] We are following Kluchevsky, op. cit., Chs. XIV and XV, implemented by Wladimir Solovyev, Russia and the Universal Church (1948), Pt. I, Chs. IV–VII, and Hans von Eckhardt, Russisches Christentum (1947).

Russian congregations. In his thoughtful discussion of the background of the great schism (*raskol*) which resulted from the Nikonian reforms, Kluchevsky suggests that "the religious outlook and attitude of every community is inseparably bound up with the texts and the rites by which that attitude is nourished." [39] In earlier times, the Russian church had been guided by the church of Byzantium, but after the conquest of Constantinople by the Turks (1453) the links had become tenuous. It stands to reason also that the vast extension of the Russian realm, the anarchy of the "time of troubles" and the Polish invasions had done their share in loosening the older ties and allowing local variations to develop. At the same time there had developed the conception of Moscow as the "third Rome," and it was only natural that once the Russian government became stabilized, the problem should present itself in a new form. The problem was complicated by the fact that some considerable portion of the Greek clergy, after the conquest of Constantinople, had established a definite bond with the Church of Rome, just prior to the outbreak of the Reformation. When, therefore, the Jesuits in the course of the Counter Reformation fostered the Uniat movement in the Ukraine (see above), which sought to compromise the conflict between Eastern Orthodoxy and the Roman Church, the urgency of a reform that would reassert genuine Greek Orthodoxy became pressing. In short, the effort of the Patriarch Nikon must be seen in its political and historical perspective, in order to be fully appreciated. For during the second quarter of the seventeenth century, the Russian church was filled with a self-confidence born of the consolidation of Great Rus and of the success of the masters of Russian politics, which contrasted strikingly with the sorry state of the Greek Orthodoxy. "In all the world, Orthodox Rus was now the sole cherisher and defender of genuine Christian truth." [40]

On the other hand, it is difficult for the western mind to realize how completely the Russian church, intimately related as it was to all phases of Russian life, was subordinate to the secular government. Rarely did a church dignitary criticize the tsar. The caesaropapist tradition of Byzantium prevailed. Indeed, even the idea, so familiar in the west, that the clergy might assume an independent position, was wholly alien to Greek Orthodoxy and its Russian successor. The church was seen as the servant of the state, and since the jurisdictional area of tsar and patriarch were

[39] Kluchevsky, *op. cit.*, III, 299. Note also Arthur D. Nock's value emphasis upon ritual in his *Conversion* (1933).

[40] Kluchevsky, *op. cit.*, 304.

the same, namely Russia, there was no possible way in which the latter could play politics by favoring one ruler against another, as in the west. It was, in a sense, the system envisaged by James I and Archbishop Laud—as indeed there are a number of interesting parallels between these two ardent ritualistic reformers. Both sought to force a return to older *forms,* and both encountered violent opposition which they sought to meet by every kind of coercive means. Both were strikingly courageous and animated by a deep love of spiritual power and a corresponding readiness for sacrifice. But whereas Laud enjoyed the support of his prince and fell, a victim to the forces of popular discontent which he had helped to fan, Nikon went down because of his own prince's disfavor. It was Nikon's inclination to assume a position of equality with the tsar, comparable to that which had been occupied by his predecessor, Philaret (1619-33). But Philaret owed a good part of his position to the fact that he was the father of the reigning tsar. If he enjoyed the honor of being called great lord (*gossudar*) and of sharing the government with his son, it was a personal rather than an institutional situation. Nikon tried to recreate this situation, even kept troops and police forces of his own, and gave the appearance of intending to develop the church into a "state within the state." This tendency even a mild tsar like Alexis could not tolerate. So when Nikon tried to force his hand by "resigning" and withdrawing into retirement, the tsar did not call him back, but instead had him confined. Nikon never regained his freedom.

Looking at it in broad political perspective, one is obliged to conclude that the great Nikon, domineering, passionate, restless and imaginative, might have succeeded had he undertaken either the great reforms or the political revolution which his ecclesiastical pretensions foreshadowed. By undertaking both, he multiplied his enemies and they banded together and overwhelmed him. Nevertheless, even after his fall, the reforms went forward. For a short while, Tsar Alexis hoped he might succeed in patching up the situation and healing the *raskol,* but the uncompromising attitude of the Old Believers, led by such striking personalities as Abbakoum,[41] made this impossible.

The struggle of the Old Believers against the Nikonian reforms was

---

[41] Abbakoum was a great preacher who died a martyr in 1681—the same year that Nikon, also a prisoner, passed away. "Strange," Abbakoum once wrote, "in what error they are caught. With fire, knout and gallows they want to strengthen the faith. Which apostles ever taught that?" Quoted in V. Gitermann, *Geschichte Russlands* (1944), I, 311, after a Russian source, and translated by C. J. F.

intimately bound up with antiwestern sentiment. Thus both reformers and antireformers were emotionally conditioned by the same antagonism. "Alas, what needs hast thou, O miserable Rus, of Latin customs and German fashions?" one of their leaders exclaimed. It has been suggested that the great schism had three roots: Russian nationalism, Latinophobia and fear of bilingual ritualism; but it would seem that these were different manifestations of the same basic nationalism. Greek and Latin were, to be sure, both "foreign" influences. But whereas the Latin language, its study and the reading of its literature, connoted "free teachings" and free inquiry, the Greek language opened the road to sacred philosophy and the studies related to it by which a man is enabled to understand God's word. "It need hardly be said that the Hellenists won the day," Kluchevsky dryly remarks.[42] It seems incredible that men of good will and Christian sentiment could have persecuted each other, after insulting and reviling each other, over such matters as whether to call Jesus "Issus" or not, or whether to make the sign of the cross with two fingers as had become habitual in Russia, or with three as was done in the Greek churches (as well as the west). But when one reflects that these symbols were national in character, and that they somehow stood for the deeply felt need of preserving Russia from Polish, Swedish, and other foreign influences, the violence of the passions aroused by these issues becomes perceivable. By a strange inversion, the insistence upon ancient custom and upon the ever greater antiquity of the Greek tradition paved the way for the wave of western reforms which Peter the Great was to initiate in times to come.

[42] Kluchevsky, *op. cit.*, 327.

Chapter Nine

THE MODERN STATE LIMITED: THE PARLIAMENT, CIVIL WAR, COMMONWEALTH AND PROTECTORATE

I. THE BEGINNINGS OF CHARLES' REIGN

RICHELIEU's rule made the triumph of the modern state secure on the continent by converting France into an autocratic monarchy. Its authoritarianism and its nationalism were given almost unlimited sway in the realm of His Most Christian Majesty. But the fulfillment of the modern state, and in a certain sense its overcoming were provided by constitutionalism, with its subjection of all authority to law, and the division of governmental authority by constitutional law. This vital achievement of the modern west, without which the flowering of science, technology, industry and agriculture in the last two hundred years is inconceivable, was fought for and in its essentials largely accomplished by the Puritans in England during the fateful years from the accession of Charles I to the end of the Protectorate. And again, it is highly significant that the driving force of human inspiration for this valiant struggle was religious. By "religious" we mean the broad convictional pattern of belief in values of a higher order, not merely the narrow theological doctrine which is too often identified with religion. These doctrinal aspects were not unimportant, but they gained their significance for Englishmen in this period, because the forms of ritual[1] and of the church government were closely identified with an entire style of living. Constitutional, economic and social factors played their roles, of course, but they were all animated and, as it were, brought to incandescence by the heat which the religious fire generated.

The liberal historians of the nineteenth century, with their antiroyalist sympathies, held the first two Stuarts responsible to a considerable extent for the course of events which led to the revolution in England. Conservatives and royalists from Clarendon and Hume to Hilaire Belloc have countered this view by stressing the antitraditional radicalism of

---

[1] For a study showing the importance of ritual in religion that corrects established preconceived notions, see A. D. Nock, *Conversion* (1933), Ch. I.

272

the Puritans and their allies and laying upon them the blame for the sanguinary conflict. But can the great revolutions of history, with their world-wide implications, be so readily disposed of in terms of human frailties? Are not these great dramas, in which entirely new forces struggle to be set free, likely to be better understood if it is recognized that there was much virtue and righteous good sense on both sides, as well as much passion and downright knavery? After all, the issues were fought over in many different places. Constitutionalism, democracy, even socialism have since become established as major constituents of western society, and accepted ingredients of men's everyday thoughts. On the other side, Charles and his several ministers and aides surely were more nearly in line with prevailing patterns of thought and action throughout Europe. What they attempted to do and what they in fact did surely was neither startling nor extreme, considering the actions of a Richelieu, a Mazarin, of the two Philips in Spain, of the princes of Germany, even of a Gustavus Adolphus.[2]

When Charles ascended the throne of England, he was looked upon by many as the hope of Protestantism. He was seconded by his friend, George Villiers, recently made duke of Buckingham, who had already become firmly established as his father's favorite. Charles had been deeply angered by the treatment he had received in Spain; he presently (May 1) married a French princess, Henriette, the sister of Louis XIII. Henriette was Catholic, but it was hoped that she might share her husband's animus against Spain, the center of Catholic reaction. After all, her brother, the French king, harbored strong anti-Spanish and anti-Hapsburg sentiments, which were already being reinforced by the great Richelieu's statecraft. Charles had all along been sympathetic to the plight of his sister Elizabeth of the Palatinate and inclined to exert himself on her behalf. Propriety and moderation, intelligence and gallantry combined to make Charles a young man of exceptional "virtue." Genuinely religious and filled with a deep sense of the dignity of his royal office, Charles was very reserved to most men, and out of melancholy given to only a few intimate friendships. As he looks at us out of van Dyck's superb portrait, he appears a noble, but not a strong man, a resigned and somewhat morose aristocrat; yet a man capable of arousing deep affection and devotion. One of the more generous tributes to Charles was included

[2] A fairly balanced judgment has been sketched by Sir Charles Petrie, *The Stuarts* (1937), 78 ff.

by Andrew Marvell, Milton's friend, in his "An Horatian Ode upon Cromwell's Return from Ireland" (1650):

> He nothing common did or mean
> Upon that memorable scene,
> But with a keener eye
> The axe's edge did try;
>
> Nor call'd the gods, with vulgar spite,
> To vindicate his helpless right;
> But bowed his comely head
> Down, as upon a bed.

The inherent nobility of the man bore out an earlier resolution Charles had made that "if I cannot live as a king, I shall die like a gentleman," and he thereby probably aided the Restoration and made the monarchy in England secure as a worthy symbol of national unity.

The heritage which James had left Charles was not a cheering one. The treasury perpetually empty, English prestige abroad brought to a low ebb by isolation and vacillation, tempers in the country irritable on account of James's steady extension of the royal prerogative—these were some of the grave aspects of Charles' task at the start of his reign. In calling his first parliament, he stressed the need of war against Spain; indeed, he suggested that the anti-Spanish policy was of its own making, and that it therefore should support him. But parliament, while indeed in favor of such a policy, felt that the king should in turn recognize other difficulties and respond to their complaints in regard to domestic issues. As one member put it:

[The king] did not only become a continual advocate to his deceased father for the favourable granting of our petitions, but also did interpose his mediation for the pacifying and removing of all misunderstandings. God having now added the *posse* to the *velle,* the kingly power to the willing mind, enabled him to execute what before he could but will.[3]

Unfortunately, as happens so readily in the course of dynastic succession, the words of the crown prince were a far cry from the deeds of the king. In many ways Charles was deeply imbued with the sense of a king's divine calling; his very religiosity fed this inspired sentiment. In

---

[3] Sir Thomas Edwards, as quoted by Ranke, *A History of England* (1875), 540.

feeling thus, he was only giving expression in England to a prevailing mood throughout Europe. What Charles had seen in Spain and knew of France and the rest of the continent was a general sentiment supporting the sanctity of kings as the personification of communities no longer held together by a common religion. He was a true son of his age, the baroque. He failed to sense the unique and distinctive elements of the situation in his country in which national feeling had alrady progressed to the point where it could take the place of religion. Everywhere such impulses were gaining in vigor and were skillfully put to the support of absolute monarchy in France and elsewhere. But in England the consolidation of the nation had progressed to the point where national representatives had become meaningful and conscious of their mission.

II. PARLIAMENT AND KING, 1625–1629

The membership of the first three parliaments of Charles' reign was of unusually high quality. Besides some remarkable men, like Sir Edward Coke, Sir John Eliot, Prynne and Selden, many members of the Commons were Puritan squires of high motivation and independent mind. They were eager to serve their country and the Protestant cause to the best of their ability, which was limited only by their lack of knowledge of the world beyond the Channel. Many speeches of remarkable literary quality were made in the course of these sessions and there was little that was petty or mean.[4] Clarendon was certainly right when in his distinctly anti-Puritan *History of the Rebellion and Civil Wars in England* (1721) he wrote in retrospect:

I do not know any formed act of either House (for neither the Remonstrance, nor Votes of the last day were such) that was not agreeable to the Wisdom, and Justice of Great Courts upon such extraordinary occasions.

Clarendon therefore felt justified in attributing much of the ensuing difficulties and dissensions to the crown's failure to work with the parliaments:

And here I cannot let myself loose to say, that no Man can show me a source, from whence those waters of bitterness, we now taste, have more probably flowed, than from these unreasonable, unskillful, and precipitate Dissolutions of Parliaments.[5]

[4] See Rushworth, *Historical Collections,* I.
[5] Pp. 4–5.

Certainly, the idea that parliament without the king should be supreme in England was not entertained by these men, who were determined to resist the king's efforts to assume such supremacy himself. Rather, under the leadership of men like Sir Edward Coke and Sir John Eliot, they were anxious to maintain that balance between crown and parliament which had been the traditional pattern of the polity throughout the Middle Ages and which the Tudors had left formally intact. In any case, the Tudor kings had the support of the middle classes in their work of national unification; that work had now been consummated and the nation unified. It forthwith demanded to be heard.

Of the three parliaments the third, meeting in 1628, was the most memorable because it resolved upon the Petition of Right. Under its terms, the royal prerogative—for this, as we have seen, was the term under which absolutism's claims were advanced in England—was to be excluded from two basic spheres of the national life: an Englishman's person and property. For by insisting that no "gift, loan, benevolence, tax or such like charge" could be levied and demanded of a man "without common consent by Act of Parliament," and that no freeman may be "called to make answer, or to take such oath, or to give attendance, or be confined or otherwise molested or disquieted, nor more especially be imprisoned or detained," [6] the Petition of Right vindicated that freedom under law which Sir Edward Coke and his lawyer friends believed to have been the "law of the land" since Magna Charta and other ancient statutes. The background for the abuses which the Petition was intended to set right lay in the "forced loan" as well as in "poundage and tonnage," the first a tax and the latter customs duties which the government had felt obliged to collect without parliamentary sanction in order to support its far-flung and unsuccessful policy of foreign intervention. This policy was largely the work of the duke of Buckingham, whom the commons had "named" in 1625 and sought to impeach in 1626, in both cases provoking the wrath of the king who felt that no one must question the choice of his ministers. For this royal attitude there was plenty of precedent from Tudor times, yet in earlier days the "estates" had certainly concerned themselves with this issue of personnel.

Essentially, Buckingham's foreign relations were highly personal and lacked both clarity of vision and steadiness of purpose. Launched upon the perilous course of war with Spain, which James had for twenty long

[6] See R. S. Gardiner, *Constitutional Documents*, 66 ff.

years sought to avoid, Buckingham had at first proceeded in co-operation with the Netherlands, France and the German Protestants. But instead of supporting the latter, hard-pressed as they were soon to be in spite of Christian of Denmark's intervention, Buckingham squandered his scanty resources in a vain attack upon Spain's homeland, which surely he should have known he had no resources to occupy or even seriously to invade (1625). Having missed the opportunity really to change the balance of armed strength by his failure to provide Mansfeld with the pay his mercenaries required, Buckingham could be held responsible for the Protestants' crushing defeat at Lutter (1626). In the meantime the vain courtier, provoked by the French unwillingness to have him come to negotiate—a matter we have seen to be connected with his silly dalliance with the French queen on one side, with the cardinal's weak position after the peace with Spain on the other—allowed himself to be pushed into war with France by the very passions which his support of Richelieu against the French Protestants had aroused. Thereupon Buckingham plunged into the support of La Rochelle,[7] and again suffered ignominious defeat (1627).

A detailed analysis of these various disasters reveals Buckingham as incapable of a realistic appraisal of his resources; his speculative imagination induced him to multiply commitments and compound errors of judgment. When, in the summer of 1628, he was once again getting ready to redress his fortunes by an overseas expedition for the relief of La Rochelle, he was murdered by one Felton, "an honorable man" as Felton described himself, who afterward explained that the Remonstrance of parliament had induced him: "Nought he did in hate, but all in honour."[8] How largely Felton's deed expressed the general sentiment was shown by the widespread rejoicings that took place all over England. The people's joy caused bitter sorrow to the king, who never forgot that it had been parliament which had inspired the murderer of his friend. But, instead of learning the lesson, Charles became hardened against the opinion of his people.

When, after some months, parliament reassembled, the religious issue was to the fore. But the important Resolutions on Religion drawn up by a subcommittee and finalized on February 24, 1629, were never put to a vote. For in the meantime tension between the king and the parlia-

---

[7] See above, pp. 210–3.

[8] See R. S. Gardiner, *History of England from the Accession of James I to the Outbreak of the Civil War* (1884), VI, 349, for the whole story.

ment had mounted to the point where it eventually burst forth in three resolutions foreshadowing parliament's claim to supremacy. These resolutions, not formally carried beyond the commons, which were forthwith dissolved on March 2, declared anyone an enemy of the commonwealth who either brought forward religious innovation along the lines of popism or Arminianism or advised the levying of duties without consent of parliament or who paid such duties. In short, anyone who sided with the king on these issues was a traitor to his country, according to these angry freemen. The king had their parliamentary leaders, after a hearing before the council, committed to the Tower, including their greatest, Sir John Eliot. Charles at the same time announced his intention of being done with parliaments.[9] Insisting that the calling of parliaments was part of the royal prerogative, he proclaimed it a "presumption for any to prescribe any time" for the holding of such parliaments; at the same time Charles indicated that he would wait until his people "saw more clearly into his intent and actions," and until the leaders of the resistance had been punished and their followers "shall come to a better understanding." The stage was set for Charles' attempt to emulate the example of his brother-in-law, Louis XIII, who had governed France without the estates-general since 1614. But there was no Cardinal Richelieu to aid the king; instead he had Archbishop William Laud (1573–1645), a well-intentioned and pedantic bureaucrat, in love with "order" and the formalities of ritual worship. The brilliant assistance of Wentworth was to come into play too late and was too ill-supported to change the outcome.

III. CHARLES' PERSONAL GOVERNMENT, 1629–1640

The years during which Charles made the fateful attempt to develop an absolute monarchy in the continental sense, misapprehending the traditional English meaning of the concept of monarchy, appear drab in retrospect. Neither his futile diplomacy[10] nor his efforts at domestic pacification through repression occasioned a dramatic culmination, unless the two Bishops' Wars at the end be so considered. His three most important collaborators and advisers, Lord Treasurer Weston (till 1635), Archbishop Laud, and Thomas Wentworth, created earl of Stafford only in 1640, became symbols of the royal usurpation of power. Yet they were

---

[9] Gardiner, op. cit., 83 ff.

[10] Its futility is attested by Chapters Five and Six above; see also R. S. Gardiner's History, VII, Ch. LXX, and Ranke, op. cit., II, Bk. I, Chs. I, II, and Bk. II, Chs. II, III.

able men; the latter two were courageous, uncorruptible and forceful. But unlike their counterparts on the continent, they could not plead a convincing case of foreign danger or domestic civil war. What they had in common was a lack of understanding and sympathy for the deep religious feelings of their fellow Englishmen, rooted in a spirited sense of self.

The challenge of the Three Resolutions, which the parliament had issued before being dissolved, lay in the claim to parliamentary supremacy, now for the first time taken in the modern sense to mean the commons without lords or king. They were revolutionary in implication; many of the members who had been swept into supporting them backed away soon after. The king could not be blamed for trying to punish the ringleaders of this revolt. Anyhow, among the eight arrested, only Sir John Eliot, Valentine and Strode stood firm. Taking their stand upon parliamentary privilege, they refused to make submission. Cheerful and convinced of the righteousness of his cause, Sir John Eliot in 1632 died a martyr to constitutional freedom and to puritanical Christendom. While Eliot was fighting for the privileges of a parliament that was presumably in eclipse, the merchants of London in the summer of 1629 tried to sabotage the tonnage and poundage by resolving not to pay them, and declaring anyone who did so "a betrayer of the liberty of England." But while their general resolution faltered in the course of one short summer, a representative merchant named Chambers refused to the end, and lay in prison for six years rather than yield. Martyrdom is the lot of individuals, while whole classes follow the path of expediency; yet the martyrs attest to the vitality of a group and its capacity for survival.

The necessity of getting along without parliament drove the king to many weird expedients; to avoid open breaches of the law, his officials searched the ancient statutes for forgotten sources of revenue and came up with a strange kettle of fish: feudal land title burdens, forest laws and the like. These arbitrary, albeit formally legal impositions alienated many who had no previous sympathy with the parliamentary party. But perhaps the most ingenious and at the same time important device was the revival of monopolies which, since parliament had outlawed them for individuals, were now awarded to corporations. These monopolies affected the price of articles of general use, and therefore provoked widespread anger. Slogans, like the "popish soap," lent color to the popular feelings; pamphleteers cried out against the general abuse:

It is a nest of wasps, or swarm of vermin, which have overcrept the land, I mean the monopolers and polers of the people . . . they sip in our cup, they dip in our dish, they sit by our fire; we find them in the dye-vat, wash-bowl and powdering tub . . . they have marked and sealed us from head to foot.[11]

For abuse it *was* to carry the licensing of particular corporations to this length, and the contributions exacted were a form of indirect taxation not sanctioned by parliament. Yet this system of licensing corporations also provided an opportunity to such religious dissenters as founded and developed the Massachusetts Bay Company. When this corporation became an autonomous government it really reverted to the medieval corporate concept. The East India Company similarly developed into a "state within the state." But most of these corporations remained strictly dependent—co-ordinated, as the twentieth century would say—and served merely to provide a smoke screen for the government's desire to collect fiscal revenues without sanction of the people's representatives.

But these usurpations might have passed into acquiesced-in "precedents," as had comparable innovations in earlier periods, had they not been accompanied by thoroughgoing efforts of the government to "force the conscience" of the more ardent Puritan spirits by an elaborately detailed ritual. As previously mentioned, the king's guide and "evil genius" in these undertakings was Archbishop Laud. Basically a "good" man, though of limited wisdom, he was courageous, self-righteous, hard-working and of high integrity; he believed in order as the essential condition of peace, and intensely disliked doctrinal and philosophical dogmatism. It seems strange that a man with so many fine qualities should have aroused so deeply the anger of his countrymen that they, though themselves by nature inclined toward moderation, should have insisted upon his execution as a traitor to his people. The explanation lies in part in his particular shortcomings—faults which might under other conditions have been overlooked as the foibles of a fine and strong personality. But the deeper cause must be sought in the revolutionary passions with which their religious convictions filled Englishmen of that generation. Laud did not understand, much less sympathize with, the deep, inwardly felt glow of Puritan religiosity, which struggled for a direct relationship between each person and his God, without the intermediaries of ecclesiastical organiza-

[11] *Parliamentary History,* II, 656.

tion and ritual.[12] To him, religion *was* ritual and ritual demanded conformity. Thus uniformity and unity were closely linked in church and state. Laud was ready to back the royal prerogative and the sacerdotal sanctification of the king's office, because he realized the need, so he thought, of effective enforcement of the detailed regulations. The passion which such a view aroused in the most ardent spirits of the age was expressed by many, but no one did it more dramatically than John Milton in his three treatises, *Of Reformation in England, Of Prelatical Episcopacy,* and *The Reason of Church Government,* all published in 1641. In the first of these, Milton,

amidst those deep and retired thoughts, which, with every Man Christianly instructed, ought to be most frequent of God, and of his miraculous ways and works amongst men, and of our religion and works, to be performed by him . . .

declared that he did not know

of anything more worthy to take up the whole passion of pity on one side, and joy on the other, than to consider first the foul and sudden corruption, and then, after many a tedious age, the long deferred, but much more wonderful and happy reformation of the church in these latter days. Sad it is to think how that doctrine of the gospel planted by teachers divinely inspired, and by them winnowed and sifted from the chaff of over-dated ceremonies, and refined to such a spiritual height and temper of purity, and knowledge of the Creator, that the body . . . were purified by the affections of a regenerate soul, and nothing left impure but sin; faith needing not the weak and fallible office of the senses, to be either the ushers or the interpreters of heavenly mysteries . . . that such a doctrine should, through the grossness and blindness of her professors . . . stumble forward another way into the new-vomited paganism of sensual idolatry . . . as if they could make God earthly and fleshly . . . they began to drag down all the divine intercourse betwixt God and the soul, yea the very shape of God himself into an exterior and bodily form.

It was against these and such-like passionate feelings that William Laud sought to build dams of carefully elaborated church discipline. Is it not the recurrent fate of those who would avert an oncoming revolution to seek by rigorous enforcement of outward conformity to provide the revolutionary leadership with that emotional ferment without which their rational doctrines would never arouse mass support? Laud certainly

[12] See Perry Miller, *The New England Mind—The Seventeenth Century* (1939), *passim*.

possessed all the required characteristics for such an undertaking: the fussy concern with detail and lack of vision for the whole, the industrious attention to preventing violations of rules and the indifference to the creative values without which rules are meaningless, the rigidity in unessentials and obtuseness on the basic issues. Animated by those finer qualities which alone would provide the vigor and élan required for the execution of such a program, William Laud was indeed a tragic figure upon the stage of revolutionary England. One does him and his adversaries less than justice, if one treats the conflict as accidental and readily avoidable. Once the problem raised by the Reformation as to the church and its government had reached the point where it must, in England as elsewhere throughout western society, be decided one way or the other, the right to have the last word [13] became decisive. Not only decisive in the ordinary political sense, but desperately decisive as it involved a man's soul and its salvation. Either the king or the people as represented in parliament must have that last word; they might agree, as they did in Sweden, but such a fortunate coincidence merely postponed the evil day of reckoning. Gustavus Adolphus' daughter abdicated and went into exile soon after Charles I met his fate. In this perspective, the three great developments of the first half of the seventeenth century were all of one pattern: the same issue was fought over on the battlefields of Germany, France and England, and it was settled in favor of the proposition that some one governmental authority must have the last word. Here, in this proposition, emerged the modern state.

It was Archbishop Laud's misfortune that he did not understand this issue fully, though in opting for the royal prerogative he seemed to understand it in part. What he missed was the realization that the "last word" is spoken by him and by them who have the *power* to speak it. He deemed a question of law what turned out to be a question of fact, and a fact shaped by the deepest creative impulses of the English people.[14]

The tragedy of Thomas Wentworth (1593–1641) was of a different order. Though long denounced as a traitor to the parliamentary cause, a more careful examination of the record has since shown that Wentworth remained true to his deeper instincts; basically interested in government and power, he shared with Laud the concern for peace and order.

---

[13] This most simple way of stating the issue highlighted by the doctrine of sovereignty is suggested by R. S. Gardiner, *op. cit.*, VI, 248.

[14] J. Trevor-Roper, *Archbishop Laud* (1940). George M. Trevelyan, *op. cit.*, and to a lesser degree R. S. Gardiner also have assessed Laud in these more balanced terms.

But through his participation in parliamentary politics and the drafting of the Petition of Right, Wentworth clearly understood the crucial issues involved politically in the struggle for parliamentary supremacy. Yet since he was unsympathetic to if not uncomprehending of the deeper religious ferment, he opted for royal authority. Like Bacon, he stated the issue succinctly: "Whoever ravels forth into questions the right of a king and of a people, shall never be able to wrap them up again into the comeliness and order he found them." That surely is the voice of conservatism. It matters little whether Wentworth did so out of a sense of constitutional balance (though, all things considered, it must be admitted that the royalists had the better of the argument, since there was precedent for the prerogative, but not for parliamentary supremacy), or out of other more personal ambitions. In the high game of politics, such abstract and personal elements are inevitably intermingled; they jointly determine the motivation of men of action.

But long before Thomas Wentworth became the central figure in the privy councils of the king, the conduct of the government had irreparably damaged the king's position. A less high-minded and more self-seeking man than Wentworth would have avoided the task of rescuing what was so palpably a lost cause by 1639. For until that fateful year Wentworth was employed first as President of the North (1629–32) and afterward as Lord Deputy of Ireland. In these two posts he had shown extraordinary ability and vigor. His policy of "thorough" was of the more aggressive mercantilist pattern; he promoted industry and commerce—customs more than doubled in Ireland in three years—he raised an army, checked piracy, reformed ecclesiastical corruption and curbed the exploitation of the poor peasant by the great nobles. Yet, in putting through these beneficial policies, Wentworth acted arbitrarily and at times despotically, seeking always the advantage of the crown. It is generally held that he became more highhanded as a result of his success in Ireland. But when first consulted by the king, in 1637, he counseled moderation until the military power of the king should have become superior. In short, here was the pattern which Wallenstein had advocated unsuccessfully, which Richelieu had turned to triumph in France, and which Olivárez was trying to practice in Spain. It certainly looked like the "wave of the future" in 1638; what ruined its chances in Britain was religion.

The Court of High Commission was, in this perspective, more noxious than the Court of Star Chamber. A later secular age was inclined to emphasize the injustice of the latter's secular political trials. Actually, both bodies went back in all essentials to Tudor times, and their work aroused indignation in Charles' reign not so much because of the procedures employed as because of the order in church and state which these actions were employed to enforce. As a court of equity, the Court of Star Chamber did useful work till its end, and nine-tenths of it was of this sort. Its share in enforcing the ecclesiastical order is what destroyed its authority. What was the exception with Star Chamber, was the rule with the Court of High Commission. Writers and printers, lecturers and clergymen, congregations and conventicles were punished for "deviation," as latter-day regimenters would say. Through "metropolitical visitation," Laud unearthed such deviations far and wide and brought them into court. A revival of a medieval method of church discipline, which had not been forgotten by Luther and Calvin, these visitations were Laud's instrument for acquiring personal power and control. He tried to stop all avenues of escape: many dissident congregations had tried to evade the heavy hand of prescribed ritual by engaging lecturers, while wealthy nobles employed private chaplains of the more orthodox Calvinist faith. These Laud outlawed, as he persecuted the smaller gatherings, known as conventicles. It is easy to mistake these developments as meaning "reaction" in the strict sense. In point of fact, Laud was an Arminian, a believer in free will, as against the orthodox predestination doctrine. He believed in state enforcement of religious rules, known as Erastianism then,[15] as against the theocratic dogma of orthodox Calvinism. The more ardent believers in orthodoxy, some twenty thousand of them, whether opposed to ritualism or to Erastian and Arminian "heresies," emigrated to America, but the vast majority remained and chafed under the episcopal yoke. This yoke was becoming more onerous as clergymen attained to high office in government, and Laud himself vigorously participated in secular administration; it was as if England were to return to the medieval pattern, when clerics shared in government. To this general trend must be added the tolerance shown the Catholics. A Catholic queen beloved by her husband, and a victorious forward march of the Counter Reformation on the continent combined to arouse the deep-seated suspicion that Laud's policy of ritualism and sacramentalism was directed

---

[15] Thomas Erastus (1524–83) had held that the sins of professing Christians are to be punished by the secular government and not by the withholding of sacraments. "Erastianism" came to mean the broader doctrine that the secular government (state) has the last word in matters concerning church government.

toward re-establishing Catholicism. Nor were Englishmen alone in this sentiment. When Laud became archbishop in 1633, Urban VIII offered him a cardinal's hat.

The visit of Charles I to Oxford in 1636, celebrated in grand style, with feasts and shows and all the pomp and circumstance of baroque art and letters, may be considered the high point of his reign. Trevelyan has said that this autumn festival was "the last careless hour of the old English monarchy." Really careless it probably was not; for the baroque fulfillment lay in more somber display. But it may well be compared with the Spanish king's great festival in 1636, described by Sir Walter Aston in a letter to Secretary Coke.[16] Here, too, the sense of doom was an essential ingredient of the atmosphere.

The following year, 1637, marked the beginning of revolutionary ferment in earnest. Not only William Prynne, but John Lilburne and others were put in the pillory that year, but the crowds cheered them and groaned when their ears were cut off. More important yet was the ship money case, highlighted by the resistance of John Hampden. For while many knuckled under and paid the unauthorized impositions, John Hampden refused and chose imprisonment, a martyr to the cause of popular participation in government.

But the most dangerous conflict arose in Scotland. Where King James had shrewdly compromised and left undisturbed the orthodox Calvinist doctrine and ritual, as established by John Knox in his Book of Common Order, Charles allowed Laud to try to set up a uniformity in doctrine and discipline with Anglican practice. In 1637 the Prayer Book was suddenly imposed upon the Scots, without any consultation of the Scottish people or their representaives. A storm broke loose immediately. A covenant was drawn up, making full use of the existing democratic government in the village kirks to unite the entire people behind this "resistance." Thereupon King Charles resolved to use force. He would conquer Scotland by arms and repress rebellion, he thought. Unfortunately, he had altogether inadequate military resources at his disposal to accomplish so ambitious a project. In two "wars," known as the first and second Bishops' Wars, the proud king did not even dare fight a single battle. The Treaty of Ripon, concluded in October, 1640, conceded complete defeat, acknowledged the Scots' religious and political claims, and agreed to an indemnity. This last concession proved fatal; for in order to raise the needed funds, the king had to call parliament once again,

16 See Martin Hume, *The Court of Philip IV*, 311–12.

having already tried unsuccessfully to get the Short Parliament to finance the conquest of Scotland. The new parliament's first act was to order the arrest of the king's chief councilor, Thomas Wentworth, earl of Strafford. When he fell on his knees before the lords, November 11, 1640, the king's cause was lost. But it took Charles eight long, bloody years to realize this fact. To start with, the king weakly assented to a bill of attainder, which led to the execution of Strafford on May 12. He died with the words on his lips, "Put not your trust in princes,"—a belated champion of the armed administrative state in a country which was getting ready to work out a constitutional system. A striking figure, he resembled Wallenstein in his ability, ruthlessness and curious mixture of realism and visionary aspiration. He had tried to reconcile the irreconcilable.

IV. NEW ENGLAND: PURITAN COMMONWEALTH

The ritualism and sacramentalism of Archbishop Laud drove thousands of Englishmen, gentlemen and commoners, across the seas, as we have noted. Led by such splendid men as John Winthrop and Thomas Dudley, the first two governors of Massachusetts Bay Colony, they were little noted by the chroniclers of the great events of the time. Who among those compiling the *Theatrum Europaeum* should have thought it would prove of more lasting significance that thousands of simple Puritans should go into the wilderness to found a true and godly commonwealth than that the great Gustavus Adolphus should land in Germany in 1630? Yet, the United States' destiny was molded by these settlers, reinforcing as they did the struggling colony of Plymouth under Governor Bradford. Rooted in the same tradition of constitutional liberty, their action was as revolutionary as Sir John Eliot's, Hampden's, and Cromwell's. And their motivation was as deeply religious as anyone's in that age.[17]

Before John Winthrop and his followers arrived in Massachusetts Bay they had agreed among themselves that the government of the company should be transferred to the colony, and that they would thereafter remain—"continue in New England." Their agreement was accepted by the "general court" of the company, meaning the meeting of stockholders. This momentous decision enabled them to convert the corpora-

[17] See Samuel Eliot Morison, *Builders of the Bay Colony* (1930), especially Ch. III. Cf. also Robert C. Winthrop, *Life and Letters of John Winthrop* (2 vols., 1867). See also the discussion above, Chapter Five, pp. 154 ff.

tion into a commonwealth, especially since the settlers had raised almost the entire capital among themselves. "The Massachusetts migration was an event entirely without precedent in the modern world," a leading English historian of colonization has written. "Sober, well-to-do men of middle age, to whom the spirit of adventure was entirely foreign, were contemplating a transfer of themselves, their families, their goods to new homes across the seas, there to found not a colony, but a commonwealth."

The last generation took great delight in belittling these Puritans. Brooks Adams painted a most revolting picture of the bigoted parsons and clerks who ran the would-be theocracy of New England.[18] Actually they were deeply convinced that it was their God-appointed task to found the new Jerusalem as God's chosen instruments. "We are a company," John Winthrop told his people on the way over, "professing ourselves fellow members of Christ." Hence, he thought, "the care of the publique must oversway all private respects. . . . The end is to improve our lives to do more service to the Lord . . . that ourselves and posterity may be better preserved from the common corruptions of the world." Often since, the public life of the commonwealth they founded has fallen far below this lofty standard; yet it remains as a beacon light, an undercurrent of American constitutional tradition.

During the years of Charles' personal government in England, the colonists worked out their program of mixed government. Between the aristocratic, which John Winthrop believed in, and the upsurge of more popular forces, led by Richard Saltonstall and dramatized by Thomas Dudley, who was the first to preside over a partly elected legislature, a governmental pattern sprang up which has long since become the typical American system. Reinforced later by the speculations of Locke and Montesquieu, the separation of powers between several sets of representatives had already become established by the time the commonwealth men began to struggle over it in England. Indeed, the problem which the several constitutions of Cromwell undertook to solve had already been settled: annual elections of a chief executive and of his deputy, using secret ballots, along with an election of the executive council and superior court of justice as well as that of a representative legislature. "By 1644," Morison observes, "the transition of the Massachusetts Bay government from trading company to commonwealth was complete." All this came

---

[18] Brooks Adams, *The Emancipation of Massachusetts* (1887), who wrote about Puritan intolerance with all the disdain of nineteenth-century liberalism. The view in Perry Miller, *op. cit.*, seems today more just and historically sound. See also Chapter Five.

to pass not in the name of democracy, but of godliness; for the franchise was granted to those who were members of the church in good standing. But there was implied an element of basic equality just the same; when in 1635 some noblemen had wanted to come only on condition that the Bay recognize a hereditary house of lords in the colony, they were told that it could not be, for "if God should not delight to furnish some of their posterity with gifts fit for magistracy" it would not do to "call them forth, when God hath not, to public authority." Their lordships did not come.

In the generous conception of John Winthrop it had originally been all of New England that was to be united in one Puritan commonwealth. However, he had to content himself with the organizing of the New England Confederation—a league for the common defense. Through it was given institutional form, for the first time in the new world, that federal principle which was going to play such a vital part in the constitutional development of America. Though based upon different readings of the Bible, the several commonwealths were united in their desire for godliness and independence. The New England Confederation helped them strengthen both.

Both against Charles and the parliament, New England stoutly maintained its self-government. The king could not secure the Bay's charter in 1634, and the parliament was not allowed to bestow favors upon them, foreshadowing the revolutionary conflict a century and a half later.

Of all the creations of the period, the Puritan commonwealths of New England seem most remote from the predominant features of baroque style. Indeed, the outlook of their founders was in many respects explicitly set against the baroque formalism of the court as against the picaresque naturalism of folk life on theater and stage. Yet, as we have seen, there was another side to the baroque medal: the intense spiritualism of Spanish and German mysticism, the passionate otherworldliness of Port Royal found their political counterpart in the Puritan commonwealth. Yet these Puritans are especially significant in the perspective provided by the emergence of the modern state, because they provided the "democratic" ingredient which the Levelers sought in vain to realize in England. In spite of the opposition of such leaders as Winthrop, the essential basis for democratic development was laid in the New England township with its fairly popularly elected selectmen, its town meeting and the other paraphernalia of a free, democratic society.

Trevelyan has suggested that the formation of parties was the most striking development of 1640-42; the "reign of King Pym" [19] ushered in this startling new political weapon. If so, it certainly did not last very long, for the following of Pym fell apart shortly after his death (December, 1643). Certainly Pym and Hampden, while employing some of the methods which have become familiar in party politics since, did not build a permanent organization; their opponents even less so. The Long Parliament was so named because it sat from November, 1640, "formally" till March 16, 1660, though actually only till December 6, 1648.[20]

The Long Parliament's first move was, as has been noted, the impeachment of the earl of Strafford, followed by that of Archbishop Laud and other servants of the king. But long before the execution of Black Tom Bryant, as the London folk had dubbed Thomas Wentworth on May 12, 1641 (a state murder which had to be sanctioned by a bill of attainder, since the Lords refused to find for impeachment on high treason), the parliament had turned to the basic issues of the government in church and state which were at the root of all the troubles. Of these, the role of the bishops was perhaps the hottest. Pym, sure of the support of the masses of the city of London, permitted a novel petition demanding the abolition of episcopacy to be presented directly on December 11 by the "people" to parliament. The fifteen thousand petitioners recited the "manifold evils, pressures and grievances" which the prelates had brought on, including "the great increase of idle, lewd and dissolute, ignorant and erroneous men in the ministry which swarm like the locusts of Egypt over the whole kingdom" and "the swarming of lascivious, idle, and unprofitable books and pamphlets, play-books and ballads; as namely, Ovid's 'Fits of Love,' 'The Parliament of Women' . . . withdrawing the people from reading, studying, and hearing the Word of God," [21] as well as

---

[19] See J. H. Hexter's *The Reign of King Pym* (1941) for a penetrating analysis of party politics. The Grand Remonstrance identifies the king's councilors as a "party," it should be noted.

[20] On that date some forty members were forcibly excluded by "Pride's Purge." The further exclusion of over one hundred on February 2, 1649, turned the remaining body into the "Rump Parliament," which contained less than a hundred "Independents." This revolutionary rump was eventually supplanted by the body appointed by Cromwell, and known as the Barebones Parliament (July 4, 1653). To maintain in face of all this that the Long Parliament continued to exist is the grossest sort of legal formalism. Cf. W. C. Abbott: *Writings and Speeches of Oliver Cromwell*, I, 705 ff.

[21] Gardiner, *Constitutional Documents*, 138 ff. See also the next quote.

monopolies, patents, toleration of popery, turning of communion tables, ritualism, benefices, profanation of the Lord's Day, frequency of whoredoms and adulteries, abuse of excommunication, imposition of oaths, and more especially the "oath *ex officio*," which was likened to the inquisition "reaching over into men's thoughts." These evils, city folks asked, should be "redressed," and more especially that the government of archbishops, lord bishops, deans and archdeacons, etc., "be abolished, with all its dependencies, roots and branches." This became a battle cry of the revolutionary elements, while the more conservative elements soon backed away, but not until a bill had been framed and put before the lords in July, 1641.

In the meantime parliament had pushed through and gotten Charles to consent to an act providing for regular meetings of parliament (the Triennial Act, February 15)[22] which also took from the king discretion to dissolve a parliament during the first fifty days without the consent of both houses, and for appointing their speakers. This act was reinforced by a special one, forbidding altogether the dissolving of the Long Parliament (May 10). Having thus entrenched themselves and their majority, Pym and Hampden proceeded to tear down the edifice of autocratic government which had been fashioned by the Tudor and Stuart kings. The Court of Star Chamber and that of High Commission went on July 5, Ship Money August 7, Limitation of Forests the same day, Knighthood Fines August 10, and ecclesiastical innovations September 1.[23] But the most crucial issue was undoubtedly that of church government; the Root and Branch Petition, if enacted, proposed to tear down one of the pillars of the English constitution. "This scheme," Ranke observes, "appeared totally subversive of both Church and State in England." It was therefore natural that more moderate elements should have suggested a compromise by which the episcopal system would have been reformed rather than destroyed. But before this story another must be told, that of the king's visit to Scotland.

It should be obvious that Charles could have consented to Strafford's attainder only under the greatest pressure. Trevelyan has told the story with superb vividness:

During the night after Strafford's Attainder has been accepted by the Upper House, a mob surrounded Whitehall. The voice of wrath terrible in num-

---

[22] In doing so, Parliament revived ancient articles of Edward III, calling for annual parliaments. Were they still "law," seeing that they had not been followed for 150 years?

[23] For all these acts see Gardiner, *op. cit.*, 179–98.

bers . . . shook the frail walls of the old timbered palace. The courtiers confessed themselves to the Queen's priests and marked on staircases and at
passage-turnings where men could make a stand. But the outlook from the
windows took away all desire of a battle, from those who thought how many
women were in the upper chambers. Far away in houses along Strand and
Holborn, Lords and Commons lay with uneasy consciences, listening through
bedroom windows to the rise and fall of the distant roar. Dawn broke upon
the pitiless siege, and all day long fresh congregations came up hot from Sabbath
gospellings in the City churches. Charles was in agony; he consulted the
Judges and Bishops, who were divided in opinion. At nine on Sunday evening
he gave way. Noise had conquered.[24]

A hypersensitive man, Charles' actions after that day, often reviled as
"double-dealing," would appear rather as those of a shell-shocked man
who had a nervous breakdown. It is very usual for such persons to be
seized with the one all-dominating desire to go away. Charles' visit to
Scotland seems to have been such an escape. To the aroused parliamentarians it seemed an acknowledgment of weakness, if not of guilt. It
made no sense, considering the role the Scots had played in precipitating the crisis, and one wonders that Charles suffered no worse disaster
than that of having to surrender control over Scottish affairs to the Presbyterians, led by the earl of Argyle. A strange and romanesque "plot"
of Argyle's rival, the marquis of Montrose, in which Charles was believed
to have been involved, added the baroque touch without which things
could not be settled.

In the meanwhile, "hell broke loose" in another quarter. The Irish
people, confronted with a return of the oppression which Wentworth had
barely been able to curb, rose and massacred several thousand Protestants
and drove into starvation several thousand more. Tales of horror made
the rounds in England, laying the emotional basis for the later atrocities
of Cromwell and his armies. At this very time, in early November, 1641,
the news sufficed to stir up enough indignation to give a majority to the
Grand Remonstrance and to heal sufficiently the breach which the Root
and Branch agitation had opened up between the more radical elements,
among the Presbyterians, Independents and the moderate groups.[25] For
while the parliamentarians knew better, it was widely bruited about that
the king and queen were responsible for this slaughter, and the Grand

---

[24] *Op. cit.,* 212.
[25] The Grand Remonstrance is reprinted in Gardiner's *Constitutional Documents,* 202 ff.
See for its background John Forster's authoritative, although partial *The Debates on the
Grand Remonstrance* (1860).

Remonstrance was framed to appeal to parliament against the monarch. Yet the weeks before adjournment had witnessed a bitter clash over the Prayer Book. The more radical Root and Branch men, proceeding from the relatively broad agreement on the evils of episcopal government, if not of episcopacy as such, had turned to ritualism and the communion tables. They then began to attack the prayers, but not without immediately encountering bitter opposition. A hornets' nest was stirred up by these implications of Pym's "godly thorough reformation" of the church, and deep fears were aroused. When parliament reassembled, many of the moderates were unwilling to vote with Pym's and Hampden's men, and an actual "party" for the king might have formed right then and there but for the feelings aroused by the Irish rebellion. The fear, agitation and bitterness aroused by this uprising did not suffice, however, to provide for smooth passage. The Grand Remonstrance passed with only twelve votes to spare, and has been called "the most bitterly fought and most momentous argument in the history of the English Parliament." [26] Like the American Declaration of Independence which it inspired, it was an "appeal to the people." Without reference to the lords, it was, upon John Hampden's motion, printed immediately.

The Grand Remonstrance was a curiously redundant document. A preamble, including a petition, was followed by a long recital of grievances consisting of 103 articles which in turn—without any warning— were followed by a self-satisfied review of the Long Parliament's achievements in 39 articles. Then the Remonstrance suggested remaining obstructions and answered "slanders" of the obstructing elements; these answers constituted a repetitive survey of the parliament's work in another 22 articles, implemented by a more specific accusation against the king's councilors, especially in the matter of the Irish rebellion, which they were accused of having conceived as a "design" that would be a "prologue" for a similar one in England. Turning against the prelates, who pervert the "Lords," the Remonstrance asked for a general synod, then proposed to "reform and purge" the universities, and asked the king to agree to a standing commission for the supervision of the ecclesiastical establishment, to be named by parliament itself. This was the core of the policy of the Root and Branch men, as was noted. It meant a decisive change in the fundamental law of the land. Finally, though not as an afterthought as is sometimes claimed, Articles 197–204 ask that the king choose councilors whom the parliament "may have cause to confide in,"

[26] W. C. Abbott, op. cit., I, 143.

and that he have such men swear to observe the constitution, "those which concern the subject in his liberty." It was not an afterthought any more than the Remonstrance's demands regarding the bishops' secular power, since the two constitute the quintessence of the petition with which the Remonstrance opens.

This famous manifesto, so cumbersome and argumentative in its phrasing, seemed as much addressed by its authors to their fellow members of parliament and the people at large as to the king. Charles responded to it in two proclamations, one issued December 10, 1641, agreeing to enforce the true religion, in other words reassuring the people against "popery," the other published December 23 and answering the petition proper. The king, after expressing annoyance at the "disrespect" shown by parliament's allowing the Remonstrance to become known, rejected the preamble's allegations regarding a "malignant party prevalent in the government," and "in no wise admits" these premises. Nevertheless, he was "pleased to answer" and pointed out first that he would agree to any measures for preserving the kingdom against the designs of the popish party, but then continues that the bishops' right to vote in parliament was "grounded upon the fundamental law of the kingdom." He felt that the abolition of the Court of High Commission had "moderated" the inordinate power of the clergy. Further, he once more agreed to remove "innovations" in religion, and to take into consideration the calling of a national synod, but at the same time protested on his conscience "that no church can be found upon the earth that professes the true religion with more purity of doctrine than the Church of England," and urged that schismatics and separatists, as well as "popery," must be curbed. Second, as for the choice of councilors, he rejected the implications of the Remonstrance, and said, "We wish you to forbear such general aspersions," and proclaimed it to be the undoubted right of the crown, as of every free man, to choose its own helpers, the ministers of state. (As for the alienation of estates in Ireland, Charles said he might well agree, but only after the rebellion had been put down would he enter upon the subject.) In short, the two central demands of the Remonstrance, the elimination of the prelates from parliament and the sharing by parliament in the choice of ministers, the king rejected on the ground of the existing constitution. Is it not always true that the law is pleaded against the revolutionary forces at work in a society faced with breakdown? [27]

[27] See George S. Pettee, *The Process of Revolution* (1938), especially Ch. II.

VI. THE CIVIL WARS, 1642–1648

The Grand Remonstrance was in effect, and presumably in intention, an ultimatum. The king's proclamations rejected the ultimatum. War was bound to follow. The fact that Cromwell declared that "if the Remonstrance had been rejected he would have sold all he had the next morning, and never have seen England more," [28] shows the depth of feeling involved; he believed that "many other honest men" were resolved to do the same. In their minds the revolution had occurred; it was a fact even then, though it took some hard years of fighting to convince them and the traditionalists. It is of vital importance to bear this in mind in assessing what followed. Historians have been unduly harsh in condemning Charles' conduct in the succeeding weeks. He was, by his position, the defender of the established order of things; it seems unreasonable to expect him to have yielded to the revolutionaries. Nor does there seem too much to be gained by speculating upon the consequences which a royal victory might have brought with it.

It has been customary to speak of the war party and the peace party, of the Puritans and the Royalists, and to declare that "there was indeed no middle party." [29] More searching inquiry has shown that there *was* such a party and that it was the party of "King Pym." Praised or blamed for precipitating the civil war, Pym actually pursued a course of moderation between the war party and the peace party in parliament. It is clear that he was the cautious champion of security for parliamentary privileges and civil liberties who realized that "preparedness and unremitting wariness" were called for as long as the king refused to grant that security.[30] Perhaps it is not too much to say that the death of Pym really dealt the death blow to this middle way; certainly as the war went on, most people were forced to take sides and declare themselves. "Before the end of the war all the gentry and most of the yeomen and merchants had declared themselves, each on the side which he most favored or most feared." [31]

And yet, the English civil war was not a class war; all classes were divided in accordance with religious convictions, locale and other lesser

[28] Clarendon, *op. cit.*, II, 43–44, who adds: "So near was the poor kingdom at that time to its deliverance."

[29] Trevelyan, *op. cit.*, 226, following Gardiner, *Civil War*, I, 61–62.

[30] See J. H. Hexter, *op. cit.*, especially Ch. III. The quote is from p. 56.

[31] Trevelyan, *op. cit.*, 227.

considerations. In a very real sense, the civil war was, like the Thirty Years' War, a war of religion; like its larger counterpart, it broke out over a "constitutional" issue involving the disturbed balance of estates and king, and it led to a basic alteration in the traditional constitution come down from the Middle Ages. The laborers apart, men of every class were engaged on both sides. Gentlemen, farmers, craftsmen and merchants were engaged for king and parliament.

There was, however, a marked difference in regional prevalence: North and west favored the king, east and south parliament. This did not mean an actual struggle for predominance of one region over another. Rather it followed the distribution of religious sentiment and of traditionalism. Generally speaking, the war was mild compared with the brutal outrages on the continent, in France, Germany and elsewhere. This is no doubt attributable to its relatively short duration, to the fact that most of the fighting elements were English or Scottish (the king's employment of Irish troops later in the war caused great and general indignation), and to the religious and moral convictions of Oliver Cromwell, who insisted upon iron discipline of his troops. It may be argued also that after all the religious differences were mostly within Protestantism, and that the fanaticism of the Counter Reformation did not appear till afterward, in Cromwell's Irish campaigns.

The course of the war itself was rather confused. It is usually divided into two distinct wars, the first lasting till June, 1646, and the second from May till August, 1648. In both, the decisive battles were won by Oliver Cromwell. Starting as a minor officer when hostilities began, Cromwell rose to the position of second in command under Fairfax. It was through his superior achievement as a soldier and organizer that Cromwell reached his pre-eminence; truly in his case "the battle was the payoff."

Space does not permit a detailed recital of the tortuous course of the fighting, interspersed with negotiations that remained inconclusive, and were bound to, since both sides simply reasserted their established position. After the initial military advantage of the Royalists, largely due to their cavalry, led by the gallant Prince Rupert, son of the Elector Palatine and the king's sister Elizabeth, the balance slowly shifted to the parliamentary side. This shift was basically the result of Cromwell's success in building a semiprofessional army, the famous Ironsides. Rupert himself dubbed them that after the battle of Marston Moor, July 2, 1644—

the first, decisive battle of the war.[32] Cromwell, like Gustavus Adolphus some twelve years earlier, and the princes of Orange a generation earlier, concluded that the spirit of the troops—what nowadays is called morale— was of crucial importance. The hard spiritual core of the Ironsides pro- vided a foundation for a conception of duty to serve, as contrasted with the personal bond of feudal loyalty. The contrast was even greater, of course, when the fear of the impressed or the greed of the hired mer- cenary was the motive for enlisting in the king's forces. The Protestant and more especially Calvinist idea of one's calling as the testing grounds for divine favor found vigorous expression in the Ironsides' indomitable spirit. It is striking to read again and again, in the strictly military and practical reports of Cromwell to his superiors, such sentiments as these:

Sir, this is none other but the hand of God; and to Him alone belongs the glory, wherein none are to share with Him.

Or again:

God does terrify them (the enemy). It's good to take the season; and surely God delights that you have endeavored to reform your armies and I beg it may be done more and more. Bad men and discontented say it's faction. I wish to be of the faction that desires to avoid the oppression of the poor people of this miserable nation, upon whom one can (*sic*) look with a bleed- ing heart.[33]

It is the sense of a divine calling, indeed, that throbs in such lines. And it gives the lie to such cynical remarks as Frederick the Great's "God is with the largest battalions." Cromwell's forces did, eventually, become the larger, and toward the end, in 1646, numbered sixty to seventy thou- sand, while the king's had melted away to twenty or thirty; but it was the victories that swelled the battalions.

Against this deep sense of conviction of Cromwell's Ironsides, there stood a waning "instinct of loyalty" toward the king as God's anointed. Whether "inbred" or not, this traditional feeling was bound up with religious sentiments, whether Catholic or Anglican, centering upon the

---

[32] The battles of Edgehill, October 23, 1642, of Newbury, September 20, 1643, and Nantwich, January 25, 1644 were indecisive; especially the first convinced Cromwell that a more efficient organization would have to be created than the volunteer units who were hard to direct in battle, and loath to leave their home counties. The second battle, of Newbury October 27, 1644, was also indecisive.

[33] W. C. Abbott, *Writings and Speeches of Oliver Cromwell,* Vol. I (1937), pp. 344 and 360. Many similar phrasings throughout his communications to parliamentary leaders; less so to Fairfax and other army men.

priestly authority of king and bishop. This feeling was strong enough in many of the Cavaliers to overcome their sympathy with parliamentary and constitutional freedom. To them it was all epitomized in what they considered their "honor." Thus Sir Edmund Verney, so Clarendon tells posterity, declared:

I have eaten the King's bread, and served him nearly thirty years, and will not do so base a thing as to forsake him; and choose rather to lose my life— which I am sure I shall do—to preserve and defend those things which are against my conscience to preserve and defend; for . . . I have no reverence for Bishops, for whom this quarrel subsists.[34]

There were, of course, others aplenty to whom the cause as such was dear; convinced authoritarians and absolutists, believers in episcopacy and in the divine right of kings, as well as stout traditionalists who feared the revolutionary potential of the parliamentary cause.

Behind the fighting forces of both sides dissension was constantly at work. In Oxford, the king's headquarters, political intrigues were rife, both in personal terms, and between the Protestant episcopalians and the Catholic elements clustering around Queen Henrietta and her friends. More important, in the long run, was the sharp conflict which arose on the parliamentary side between the Presbyterians and the Independents. Throughout the first civil war, the Presbyterians were in control, while the Independents slowly extended their influence in the army, not so much by design as because Cromwell's and Fairfax's units offered them an opportunity to work for the cause in which they believed. The Presbyterians dominated the Westminster Assembly of Divines which sat from July, 1643, till 1649. It was believed necessary to settle the differences which had arisen between Pym and his friends who were in favor of secular, parliamentary control of the ecclesiastical establishment [35] and the more rigorous Presbyterians, led by men like Samuel Rutherford. The latter shaped the thought embodied in the Solemn League and Covenant, adopted by the commons on September 25, 1643, as a necessary concession to the Scots, whose alliance Pym sought and secured thereby. Its key article agreed to reform the religion, its doctrine, wor-

---

[34] *The Life of Clarendon,* Bk. II, Part II, p. 954.
[35] This position was Erastian, just as much as that of Laud; see above, footnote 13. It gradually evolved toward two sharply opposed views: (1) the parliamentary Presbyterian position which sought to "force the conscience" of all into a new uniformity, and aroused the ire of men like Milton, and (2) the Independent position of the Cromwellian group who maintained that the government should protect freedom of conscience.

ship, discipline and government, "according to the Word of God, and the example of the best reformed Churches," which the preceding phrase had already suggested was "the reformed religion in the Church of Scotland." [36] By this Covenant, the parliament was morally bound, in other words, to establish the Presbyterian system, i.e. the clerical synods. That the majority of parliament ever became true Presbyterians in this Scottish sense may well be doubted, in spite of the fact that they have traditionally been so called.

The theological controversy which evidently revolved around the issue of church government, just as did the quarrel with the king, shows that the control of the church was the heart of the English revolution. The eventual shift of the Presbyterians to the side of the king was intimately bound up with this problem of ecclesiastical authority. If modern constitutionalism received its first tentative formulations under the Commonwealth and Protectorate, it did so because the logic of an inalienable right to liberty of conscience led to the right of free religious association and autonomy in the government of such associations. These associations emerged as the vital minorities who must be protected against majority tyranny, as much as against royal and episcopal despotism; how could this be done, except by organizing effective restraints upon the exercise of governmental power under the constitution as the fundamental law of the land? These issues remained throughout the revolutionary period; they first clearly emerged in the fighting forces of parliament. For the Presbyterians wanted to select officers and men on the basis of their belief; Cromwell vigorously resisted such efforts. At his instigation, St. John put forward, after the battle of Marston Moor, a motion in the commons which sought "to endeavour the finding of some way, how far tender consciences, who cannot in all things submit to the common rule [in points of church government] . . . may be borne with according to the Word." [37] A bitter conflict arose between Cromwell and his commander, the earl of Manchester. Again and again, we read of efforts of Cromwell to retain or have reinstated a man of "independent judgment."

I will not deny but that I desire to have none in my army but such as are of the Independent Judgment . . . that in case there should be propositions for peace or any other conclusion of peace, such as might not stand with the ends that honest men should aim at, this army might prevent such mischief. [38]

[36] Gardiner, *Documents,* 268. See also above pp. 147–9, re Synod of Dordrecht.

[37] Abbott, *op. cit.,* I, 294. As Abbott noted, "With it there began the struggle between the rigid Presbyterian system and the looser bond of Independency."

[38] Abbott, *ibid.,* 290.

To rid the parliamentary forces of these influences, Cromwell eventually joined forces with Sir Harry Vane, the skillful politician who with St. John and others took over the control which Pym's untimely death had left unsettled. They secured the adoption of the Self-Denying Ordinance, under which no one could serve both in parliament and in the army, except by special dispensation. This special dispensation was, however, granted by the Commons to Oliver Cromwell, when he was appointed lieutenant general under Fairfax on June 10, on the very eve of the decisive battle of Naseby (June 14, 1645). As Fairfax and his council declared, agreeing with a petition from the City:

The general esteem and affection which he [Cromwell] hath both with the officers and the soldiers of the whole army, his own personal worth and ability for the employment, his great care, diligence and courage, and faithfulness in the service . . . with the constant blessing of God . . . make us look upon it as a duty we owe you and the public to make the suit.

So Cromwell became formally head of the horse just in time to win the battle of Naseby, in the course of which Ireton, Skippon and Fairfax were all beaten by the Royalists under Rupert, while Cromwell displayed his usual *sang-froid* and extraordinary staying capacity as he reconquered a battlefield which had been all but lost to the parliamentary armies.[39] Of the king's 7,500 men, 5,000 fell prisoners, as well as 12 guns, the whole train and baggage, much ammunition, and 112 colors. But worst of all, in the baggage were found the secret papers of the king showing that he was seeking to bring foreign powers into England to help him suppress the rebellion.[40] This discovery, widely publicized, outraged the English public, testifying to the rising national sentiment. How different from Germany, where foreign armies were hailed alternately as liberators and allies, with only timid protests by a few princes, like the elector of Saxony.

Cromwell, in reporting Naseby to the speaker of the Commons, once again "calls God to record" and sounds the theme of the impending struggle between the victorious New Model Army and the parliament:

---

[39] See for this battle the able account in Abbott, *op. cit.*, I, 358, based upon Gardiner, *Civil War*, Ch. XXXI. Cf. also C. H. Firth, *Cromwell's Army* (1902). Gardiner's comment is worth quoting: "Whichever leader could bring a preponderant force of horse to bear upon the confused struggle of foot-men in the centre would have England at his feet." That leader was Cromwell.

[40] This is Hobbes' view; *Behemoth* (Molesworth ed.), 132.

Sir, this is none than the hand of God; and to Him alone belongs the glory, wherein none are to share with Him. The General served you with all faithfulness and honour; and the best commendations I can give him is, that I dare say, he attributes all to God, and would rather perish than assume to himself. Which is an honest and a thriving way. . . . Honest men served you faithfully in this action. Sir, they are trusty; I beseech you in the name of God, not to discourage them. . . . He that ventures his life for the liberty of his country, I wish he trust God for the liberty of his conscience, and you for the liberty he fights for.[41]

The king's defeat was annihilating all hopes remaining for the royal party. Before long, the forces of Montrose, who had thus far been successful in Scotland, were defeated at Philiphaugh (September 13, 1645) and Montrose fled. Likewise, town after town surrendered, and the many fortified places of the nobility were taken and destroyed. On May 5, 1646, Charles surrendered to the Scots, and parliament put forward to him the proposals of Newcastle, which Charles rejected, hoping for a break between the Scots and the parliament. Instead, the Scots delivered the king into the hands of parliament on January 30, 1647, in exchange for their back pay; he was held at Holmby House until the army captured him (June 4) to prevent an agreement on Presbyterian lines. A last effort of the king, after war had broken out between Scotland and England (and between the Presbyterians and Independents, too) to gain the upper hand by force, collapsed at Preston (August 17-20) when Cromwell and his Ironsides in a three-day-running battle utterly defeated and destroyed an invading Scottish army under the duke of Hamilton. But behind this second civil war and defeat lies the revolution of the army against parliament which was born of the civil war.

VII. THE REVOLUTION, 1647–1649

It is the characteristic of revolutions to move from the less to the more radical position. Indeed, at the outset those appealing to force against a disintegrating political order usually argue that they "must reestablish the ancient or traditional order of things" which has been violated by those who in trying to save it have overstepped the bounds. It is only in the course of such vain attempts to recapture the past that the radically new becomes apparent and eventually seeks to impose itself.

Such was the course of events in England after 1646. With the king no

[41] Abbott, *op. cit.*, 360.

longer in the field, although not reconciled to the victory of the parliamentary forces, a bitter controversy arose between the majority in parliament and the majority in the New Model Army. The first group was prepared to set up a Calvinist church government and discipline under parliamentary control and supervision; the latter desired genuine liberty of conscience and the separation of all churches from the government, which many thought should be republican. This set of issues had, as we have seen, been brewing ever since Cromwell first perceived the morale-building potential of the ardent religious feeling of the sectaries. It now flared forth in the dual form of intense debates within the army [42] and a sharp conflict between the army and the parliament. The radicalism of the army majority found its most striking expression in the Agreement of the People, presented to the council of the army on October 28, 1647. This constitutional proposal represents in one sense the high watermark of revolutionary sentiment; for the later Agreement of the People, presented to the house of commons by the army on January 20, 1649, was a much modified and attenuated version. The earlier agreement was essentially the work of the group who became known as the Levelers, due to their strong democratic bent. It voiced the sentiments of the elements who were behind, but were not satisfied with, the Heads of the Proposals. These the army had put forward on August 1, 1647, as an alternative to the parliament's Propositions of Newcastle of July 4, 1646, which had been largely identical with those of Uxbridge of 1645. Since the king had already made reasonable counterproposals—counterproposals which were in line with the eventual settlement of 1660—there was not much sense to these proposals for a Presbyterian settlement.

However, the significant thing about all these proposals and counterproposals was that they still were conceived as within the constitution, which was treated as an established frame of reference. If the king wanted to return to the status of 1641, and the parliament wished to have the king agree to a different scheme of Calvinist church government, it could still be said that their several aims were reform either moderately framed or reluctantly conceded. But the army's Heads of Proposals and very much more so the Agreement of the People of 1647 were truly revolutionary in spirit, if not in wording. One might readily agree with Gardiner's judgment that the Heads of Proposals were vastly

---

[42] See *The Clarke Papers* (ed. by C. H. Firth), 4 vols., 1891–1901 and A. S. P. Woodhouse, *Puritanism and Liberty, Being the Army Debates* (1938), with an excellent introduction.

superior from a constitutional viewpoint to the Presbyterian plan of "waiting upon events." Still, they "contained too much that was new, too much in advance of the general intelligence of the times," and there was the further fact that as proposals of the army they were in themselves and as such revolutionary. For it was the army's taking the lead politically that constituted the second revolutionary breakthrough, parliament's claim for supremacy having been the first. Apart from transitional provisions to liquidate the civil war, the proposals of the army aimed at two central objects: (1) regular rotations and a more popular basis for parliaments, and (2) religious liberty. The king, naturally enough, seems to have been more favorably inclined toward these proposals; they permitted the continuation of the episcopal system, and restricted the scope of parliamentary power.[43] Without going into the devious history of the negotiations between the king, the army and the parliament—negotiations which were telescoped by the king's flight from the custody of the army to Carisbrooke Castle on the Isle of Wight—it is clear that the grounds for genuine settlement between the several parties, including the Scots, no longer existed. The revolution had in fact occurred.

This primordial fact the Agreement of the People of the Levelers proved beyond the peradventure of a doubt. It contained the outline of a constitution for a republican commonwealth, conceived in terms of protecting the individual citizen against the arbitrary acts of the majority, the fundamental idea of modern constitutionalism. The people were proclaimed the court of last resort, they "of course, choose themselves a Parliament," and the power of these future "Representatives of this Nation is inferior only to those who choose them." Finally "matters of religion and of the ways of God's worship are not at all entrusted by us to any human power," for "in all laws every person [is] bound alike," that is to say, freedom of religion and equality before the law are proclaimed "native rights" and the authors of the agreement said they were "agreed and resolved to maintain them . . . against all opposition whatsoever." Here spoke the voice of the revolution. The king knew it and parliament knew it, and they thereupon decided to compose their differences to put it down. But in vain. The army seized the king, and proceeded to try him, after having, through Pride's Purge (December 6, 1648), succeeded in subjecting parliament to its dominance. To the

---

[43] For the several documents see Gardiner, *Constitutional Documents*, 275 ff. The quotes are from Gardiner's Introduction to the volume.

Presbyterian members who had been detained, the army's officer is said to have replied when they asked by what authority he was holding them: "By the law of the sword." This law Ireton had derived from "necessity," a necessity of which Milton was to say in *Paradise Lost* that it was "the tyrant's plea."

With parliament purged, only about two hundred members remaining in the commons and a handful in the lords who were subservient to the army leadership, an "act" was passed in the commons, though with many abstentions, erecting a high court of justice for the king's trial on January 6, 1649. Accused in this act of high and treasonable offenses designed to enslave and destroy the English nation, the said Charles Stuart was to be heard, tried and judged by a commission of over 150, including the earls of Kent, Nottingham, Pembroke and Denbigh, the Lords Chief Justice of King's Bench (Rolle) and of Common Pleas (St. John), as well as Fairfax, and Cromwell. The charge was brought on January 20, the king declined the jurisdiction of the court the next day, stating that neither divine nor municipal law allowed such a proceeding. He insisted that "the king can do no wrong," and indicated that the popular sanction could not be claimed: "You wrong even the poorest plowman." In other words, Charles with dignity asserted that he spoke not only for his own right but for the true liberty of all his subjects. This liberty, he said, consisted not in the power of government, but in living under such government as secured them their lives and property; the arms he had taken up "were only to defend the fundamental laws of this kingdom." It was the past pleading against the future, and judgment was consequently pronounced on January 27, 1649. After reciting all the king's "treasons and crimes," the court adjudged "that he, the said Charles Stuart, as a tyrant, traitor, murderer, and public enemy to the good people of this nation, shall be put to death by the severing of his head from his body." Two days later, the death warrant was issued over the signature of Oliver Cromwell and the rest. The victorious revolutionary leader had convinced himself that nothing short of death for the king would do.

VIII. THE COMMONWEALTH FREE

The beheading of the king aroused the indignation of all Europe. It also stirred an immediate and lasting controversy which has not subsided to this day. In February, 1649, Bishop Gauden's *Eikon Basilike,* or the

King's Image (as Milton translates it), pretending to be a "True Portraiture of his Sacred Majesty in his Solitudes and Sufferings," appeared and swept the country. It crystallized much latent sympathy. The great Milton's stalwart justification of this "tyrannicide" in *The Tenure of Kings and Magistrates* (1649) was followed a few months later by his more impassioned *Eikonoklastes* or "Breaker of the Image" in which the harsh self-righteousness of the Puritan celebrated the victory with not a little slanderous invective. For surely the proposition that Charles' life had been "without care or thought, as if to be a king had been nothing else in his apprehension but to eat, and drink, and have his will, and take his pleasure," [44] is mean and unjust. But this personal aspect apart— and it was vitally related to the main point of the argument—both works expounded the traditional distinction between a king and a tyrant which is found in conventional medieval and "monarchomachical" political thought. Charles was throughout depicted as a tyrant. In answer to the king's supposed admonition to his son that "he keep to the true principles of piety, virtue, and honour, and he shall never want a kingdom," Milton exclaimed: "And I say, people of England, keep ye to those principles, and ye shall never want a king." These principles were those of a government under law, that is a constitutional government. "Those oaths of allegiance and supremacy we swore, not to his person, but as it was invested with his authority; and his authority was by the people first given him conditionally, in law, and under law, and under oath also for the kingdom's good."

The controversy has continued ever since, and it is often alleged that by executing the king, Cromwell and the Independents erected an insurmountable barrier between themselves and the majority of the English people; the revolution carried forward in the name of the people could not achieve a democratic political order. This is probably true enough; but is the premise correct that the revolutionary impulse was democratic? Is not such an interpretation the result of projecting backward the value judgments of a later period? Certainly, the outlook and viewpoint which Milton presented in *Eikonoklastes* was not preoccupied with democracy, but with constitutionalism, not with majority rule, but with the rule of law, not with man's right to vote and elect, but with his right to a free conscience, unrestrained by ecclesiastical regimentation. And the great, the everlasting struggle of Oliver Cromwell throughout the

---

[44] *Eikonoklastes* is found in Vol. I of *The Prose Works of John Milton* (Bohn's Library), pp. 301 ff. *The Tenure of Kings and Magistrates* is given *op. cit.*, II, 1 ff.

Commonwealth and Protectorate was to find a *constitutional* legitimacy, not a popular majority.

The role of the Levelers, and more especially of John Lilburne, "Freeborn John," was indeed equalitarian. His Agreement of the People (1647), which has been called the first modern constitution, certainly proclaimed the supremacy of the people.[45] But it asserted at the same time "that matters of religion and the ways of God's worship are not at all entrusted by us to any human power." To call it a constitution is certainly rather farfetched; for, beyond the proposition that there should be elected a parliament every two years on a certain day, virtually no provisions for the government of the nation are contained in this document. Rather, the Agreement of the People of 1647 resembles the American Declaration of Independence in being a broad proclamation of basic principles: freedom of religion, freedom from compulsory military service, equality before the law—these were proclaimed as "native rights."

Much more detailed in its constitutional provisions was the Agreement of the People of January 20, 1649, which the council of officers of the Model Army presented to the Rump Parliament. Not only did its first four articles contain very specific provisions for the election and holding of parliaments, but an executive "council of state" was envisaged in the fifth article, and emergency powers and incompatibilities outlined in the sixth and seventh. But again, parliamentary (and popular) supremacy was limited by a set of natural rights, now considerably expanded to include the right of private property and the principle of *nulla poena sine lege*. Religious freedom is more fully stated, but at the same time limited to the "Christian religion," and furthermore "it is not intended to be hereby provided that this liberty shall necessarily extend to Popery or Prelacy." This more conservative Agreement of the officers of Cromwell's army clearly revealed the core of the revolutionary position: a government of elected representatives under a constitution protecting freedom of religion and conscience. The Rump declined, as Cromwell had foreseen, to act upon the army's urgent recommendation. But on May 19, 1649, it did declare England to be a Commonwealth, after having appointed a council of state, abolished the office of king, and the house of lords. Such Commonwealth or Free State was described as embodying: "the supreme authority of this nation . . . without any king

---

[45] The term *sovereignty* does not appear in this or the later document, which should caution one against speaking of popular sovereignty—a term properly belonging to the age of Rousseau.

or House of Lords." On January 2, 1650, all men over eighteen were obliged to take an oath to this Commonwealth.

In the meantime, the new king set about energetically to reconquer his lost dominions. His viceroy in Ireland, the duke of Ormond, James Butler (1610–88), who had already proved his mettle in the days of Buckingham and during the civil war, at first succeeded in uniting all the Irish factions behind the royal cause, but after Cromwell landed (August 15, 1649) and put the best of Ormond's army to the sword at Drogheda, the Protestants went over to Cromwell and the Catholics were reduced by cruel conquest. Nonetheless, in the spring of 1650 the king's most gallant Scottish follower, Montrose, raised the royal standard in the north and challenged the Presbyterian leadership. Charles thereupon abandoned Montrose to his fate and made a deal with the Covenanters; the latter captured Montrose and beheaded him as a traitor. Upon so foul a deal was the pretender's support by the Scots based. No wonder it collapsed under the hammer blows of Cromwell's Ironsides. In vain did Cromwell plead with the Scots that they were betraying their own cause: "I beseech you, in the bowels of Christ, think it possible you may be mistaken." [46] Having appealed to the Scots in two remarkable declarations, Cromwell castigated the ministers for trying to conceal these appeals from their people, "who might see and understand the bowels of our affections to them, especially such among them as fear the Lord." He, Cromwell, was not afraid of such propaganda. "Send as many papers as you please amongst ours; they have a free passage." [47]

It was all to no avail; the Scots' response was as righteous as Cromwell's appeal: "You would have us to think that there is a possibility that we may be mistaken. Would you have us to be skepticks in our religion?" They looked upon Cromwell as "a greeting devil," and continued to believe that the Lord was on their side. But if battles prove anything, they were mistaken. Though hampered by extraordinary difficulties, Cromwell completely routed the Scots under Leslie at Dunbar (September 1–3, 1650). "Oliver carried on as with a divine impulse . . . his eyes sparkled with spirits," according to Aubrey's *Miscellanies*. The victory of Dunbar has rightly been called Cromwell's crowning achieve-

---

[46] This extraordinary passage occurs in Cromwell's adjuration to the Scottish ministers, in which he calls God to record repeatedly: "There may be a Covenant made with death and hell. I will not say yours was so." Cromwell begged the ministers to read Isaiah 25: 5–15, and suggested "that you or we, in these great transactions, answer the will and mind of God, it is only from His grace and mercy to us." See Abbott, *op. cit.*, II, 302–3.

[47] Abbott, *loc. cit.* The Declarations are also printed there in full, pp. 283–88 and 290–91.

ment in arms. He himself considered it a miracle of divine intervention; yet, as Professor Abbott remarks, "Cromwell had no choice but to fight; the stroke of genius was to attack." The inevitable followed: Scotland was brought nearer submission by the capture of Edinburgh, and though another campaign during the spring and summer of 1651 had to be waged, the king's Scottish support collapsed after the battle of Worcester, which was fought and won on the anniversary of Dunbar. To Cromwell it was the "crowning mercy" and he felt that "the dimensions of this mercy are above my thoughts." [48] And well he might, for Worcester made the king-pretender a fugitive and eliminated the last remaining danger of foreign invasion.

But was the Commonwealth to be free? Had the people been able to elect responsible representatives in accordance with their preferences? Unfortunately no such happy issue resulted from Cromwell's striking victories in the field. Indeed, the necessity for these military exertions set the Commonwealth upon the path of dictatorship from which it found itself unable to turn for the remainder of its duration. The army, which had been the arbiter at the time of the king's death, now raised to the formidable size of thirty thousand men, rivaled the great professional armies of the continent. But instead of royal absolutism, a military despotism became its political concomitant in England. It was the peculiar destiny of England that Cromwell, like Washington but unlike Napoleon, would not be crowned a "king," but continued to search for some sort of constitutional legitimacy. Paradoxically, it was his insistence upon such a constitution that forced him to exercise unconstitutional powers; throughout the remainder of his career he retained the "last word" in all vital matters of the Commonwealth. It was thus that the Commonwealth turned into the Protectorate.

The crucial issue of constitutionalizing the revolutionary power was, as the Agreement of the People had emphasized, the election of a new parliament. It was precisely this aspect of the Agreement which the Rump had neglected to act upon. Now, after the victory in the field, Cromwell once again put forward the dissolution issue; when his bill passed into committee (October 14, 1651), it was generally expected that "a dissolution was immediately impending." [49] Yet eventually the date was fixed, on November 18, 1651, for November 3, 1654! The Rump then proceeded

---

[48] Abbott, op. cit., II, 463.
[49] See S. R. Gardiner, History of the Commonwealth and the Protectorate 1649–1656, I, 472.

to elect Cromwell to the council of state. Did they remember that Oliver, in the words of Gardiner, "long suffering as he was, had more than once . . . been swept away by strong emotion to dash to the ground the institutions or the men whose guardian in all honesty he had professed himself to be?"

The question of parliament was only the most prominent among a number of issues around which the problem of a permanent settlement, both civil and ecclesiastical, revolved. How to organize a national church, yet leave freedom to the sects, was brought nearer a solution in the months following Worcester; so was the unification of Ireland and Scotland with England and Wales in a true Commonwealth. The overseas empire was made secure through the reorganization of the fleet. A large part of the navy had gone over to parliament early in the civil war, but the predominant army element was slow in taking control of the naval establishment.[50] When Robert Blake (1599-1657) took over the navy in February, 1649, the situation changed radically for the better. The size of the navy was doubled from 1649 to 1651. As "general of the sea," Blake pursued Prince Rupert, who had fitted out a small navy and was harassing the trade of England, and eventually chased him from the Mediterranean. These successes put the Commonwealth in position to challenge Dutch commerce, which it did by the Navigation Act of 1651. Whether this act, providing, as mercantilism taught, that all goods shipped into and out of England must be carried in British bottoms or those of the country of origin, really assisted England's mercantile development may be doubted;[51] that it precipitated the war by the immediate hurt it inflicted upon the Dutch is certain. Yet Clarendon's view that Cromwell and his party deliberately precipitated the conflict in order to have "a state of war" continue seems biased and partisan.[52] Why then did they do it? While the occasion was provided by the truculence of Blake and Tromp (the Dutch admiral) as well as some others, "the causes of that conflict ran deep into the past; they were as wide as the commerce of the world and as deep as the long-enduring rivalry between the two chief mercantile and naval powers of Europe."[53] Until then England

---

[50] See Sir W. I. Clowes, *The Royal Navy, a History*, Vol. II (1898).

[51] That it did not do so is the view of W. Cunningham, *Growth of English Industry and Commerce* (fifth edition, 1912).

[52] Abbott, *op. cit.*, II, 547. It is interesting that only ten years had passed, since the Dutch had destroyed Spanish predominance; Tromp was the hero of that victory. See above, pp. 229 and 234.

[53] Firth, *Cromwell*, p. 314, considers that "nothing could have been more unwelcome

and Holland had been helping each other as the two leading Protestant powers: lately, however, due to the dynastic link between the Stuarts and the Oranges—Charles I's daughter was married to William II—the Dutch had provided refuge for the Cavaliers, and the fleet of Prince Rupert had been fitted out in Holland.

The cards were stacked heavily against the Dutch. Their large merchant marine, carrying goods all over the world, was supported by a rather small navy, which suffered from a divided command. By contrast, the British merchant marine was small, and the navy large; furthermore the British controlled the sea lanes leading from and to Holland. Yet, after initial successes, the war for a while went against the British, until they recovered. Blake and Monk in a three-day battle off Portland in February, 1653, utterly defeated Tromp. While the negotiations for peace went forward, presumably inspired by Cromwell, the war went more and more against the Netherlands. By the spring of 1654, the British had achieved complete mastery of the "narrow seas." They had captured over 1,400 ships from the Dutch, including 120 men-of-war, and their navy was larger and better than ever before. But it was a costly war, and England was straining under the burden. The army cost a million and a half, the navy nearly a million pounds sterling. There was a deficit of nearly half a million per year, and the indiscriminate confiscations which parliament levied to meet the situation had aroused widespread indignation; Cromwell himself was quite angered by them.[54] So the protector took the negotiations in hand "for the preservation of freedom and the outspreading of the kingdom of Christ." After protracted efforts, which did not yield the alliance of which Cromwell had dreamed, peace was concluded at last on April 5, 1654. The Dutch admitted the supremacy of the British flag in the British seas, accepted the Navigation Act as it stood, promised to pay damages, and secretly agreed to exclude the princes of Orange from command by land or sea. The hope, however, of a permanent settlement proved illusory; trade rivalry was too intense between the two nations.[55]

[to Cromwell] than this war with the Dutch . . . the war threatened to frustrate the scheme of a league of Protestant powers." Abbott is more reserved and believes that the evidence regarding Cromwell's attitude is inconclusive, but that some members of the council, like St. John and Haselrig, certainly favored the war, *op. cit.*, II, 551. "It seems inconceivable that England could have gone to war had he been strongly opposed to it," Abbott sagely remarks.

[54] See Firth, *op. cit.*, 305.

[55] Abbott, *op. cit.*, II, 541 ff., and III, 182 ff.

In the meantime, and long before the conclusion of the Dutch war, the internal developments in England had come to a head. Cromwell and his officers were increasingly troubled by the conduct of affairs in the Rump Parliament. Corruption and nepotism were rife, and the leadership lacking in revolutionary fervor. Presbyterians and indifferents played a role which ill-accorded with the chiliastic hopes of the latter-day saints for a new order—a new Jerusalem. All through 1652 efforts were made to bring the issue of parliamentary dissolution to an auspicious conclusion; but in the spring of 1653 there was still no sign of parliament yielding. A compromise fostered by Sir Henry Vane, as ever subtle and inscrutable in his devious maneuvers, was moving toward adoption by the Rump. Confronted with this "betrayal," Cromwell and the army resolved upon force. On the crucial day of April 20, 1653, when the house of commons was approaching a vote on a new election law, Cromwell went there himself with some musketeers, broke in upon the proceedings, and, in his words: "Upon this, the House was dissolved even when the Speaker was putting the last question." It was a violent scene that preceded it. Cromwell having come into parliament had sat for a while silently, with his hat on, but had then risen, taken off his hat, and begun speaking. As he did so, his temper rose, typically as in battle, and he commenced railing at the members in mounting anger, "charging them not to have a heart to do anything for the publick good, to have espoused the corrupt interest of Presbytery and the lawyers, who were the supporters of tyranny and oppressions, accusing them of an intention to perpetuate themselves in power . . . that the Lord had done with them and had chosen other instruments for the carrying on of his work." [56]

When challenged by Sir Peter Wentworth, whom by a nod he had accused of being a whoremaster, Cromwell went to the center aisle, put his hat back on, and striding up and down "like a madman" and kicking the ground with his boots, cried out: "You are no parliament, I say you are no parliament; I will put an end to your sitting: call them in, call them in!" Two files of musketeers marched in to clear the house, while Cromwell shouted at the protesting Vane: "O Sir Henry Vane, Sir Henry Vane, the Lord deliver me from Sir Henry Vane." While he went on accusing others of being drunkards, whoremasters, corrupt and impious, the speaker was forced off his chair and the members cleared out of the house. As one reads these proceedings, the mind wanders back to that earlier scene, when King Charles had broken in upon parlia-

[56] Ludlow, *Memoirs* (Firth ed.), I, 351 ff.

ment only to see himself weakened further as the enemy of the fundamental law of the land. But now parliament had by its own doings lost its footing in ancient tradition. The constitution upon which it once stood so firmly was no more, and its protests in terms of parliamentary privilege remained empty words. "What shall we do with this bauble, take it away," said Cromwell, when confronted with the mace, venerated symbol of parliamentary privilege.[57] Cromwell himself told some of his officers immediately afterward: "When I went there, I did not think to have done this. But perceiving the spirit of God so strong upon me, I would not consult flesh and blood." And since the council of state tried to continue in office, Cromwell the next day went to their meeting, and likewise dissolved it, but not without having been told by Sergeant Bradshaw: "Sir, you are mistaken to think that the parliament is dissolved, for no power under heaven can dissolve them but themselves"—a uniquely forceful expression of the traditional English belief in the transcendency of law.

Nevertheless, the Commonwealth was at an end. What had been true in fact for some time, that the "Commonwealth Free" had turned into a military dictatorship was now apparent to all.[58] The next five years were filled with Cromwell's efforts to mend the breach he had made, and to establish by deliberate effort a constitution such as would perpetuate forever the commonwealth of the "Saints." It seems rather difficult to explain the extraordinary inclination of many historians to doubt Cromwell's "sincerity" in these efforts. For they were born of the very essence of the revolutionary concern with the fundamental right of man for freedom of religion. To differentiate between Cromwell's ecclesiastical policy and these governmental concerns is to miss the "spirit" of the revolution of the Puritan Saints.

IX. THE PROTECTORATE

A military dictatorship seeking to constitutionalize itself in face of a hostile general public—that was the paradox of Cromwell's Protectorate.

[57] Somewhat differing accounts of this scene have come down to us from Sir Algernon Sidney and Whitelocke. See Abbott, *op. cit.*, II, 641 ff.

[58] Compare Professor Abbott's conclusion: "The circle had come round at last to arbitrary power again, more arbitrary than before. Louis XVI to Napoleon, Louis Philippe to Napoleon III, Nicholas II to Stalin, Charles I to Oliver Cromwell, the tale is always the same. The dissolution of Parliament broke down the last pretense that England was a free Commonwealth," *op. cit.*, II, 654. Note also the moving, if discriminating assessment of Cromwell in the concluding paragraphs of that section of Abbott's great work.

Somehow, the Lord failed his "Saints" by not enlightening the majority of Englishmen about the benefits to be derived from their rule. Theoretically, Cromwell and his army officers would have liked to secure popular support by general elections; for that was clearly the basis of legitimacy implied in their general outlook. Unfortunately, they knew only too well that the majority of Englishmen were either disaffected, indifferent or increasingly inclined to return to the old constitutional order. Hence the only way out was a restrictive electoral system. In the name of Cromwell, letters were dispatched to the Congregational churches inviting them to nominate representatives; these nominations the council of the army sifted and presently writs were issued in the name of Cromwell as commander-in-chief for those who had been selected to gather at Westminster. In the meantime, a self-appointed council, consisting of three civilians and seven army men, had assumed executive responsibility; this was superseded by a new council of state which the "nominated" parliament appointed, after Cromwell had formally surrendered his power to it.

Dominated by an ardently religious spirit, symbolized by men such as Praise-God Barebone, a member from London, this parliament was probably unique in the annals of constitutionalism for the purity of intentions and lack of common sense of most of its members. Endless prayer meetings alternated with protracted discussions of utopian schemes of social betterment. There was alive in many of these proposals a visionary anticipation of much later developments, but somehow these earnest seekers after perfection seemed unable to stay on this earth; after some months of debate, which at times waxed acrimonious, they humbly returned their commission to the practical master of the situation, Oliver Cromwell—presumably impelled to do so by the army officers. For among this decisive revolutionary group sentiment had been growing for a renewal of efforts to establish a written constitution, such as the Heads of the Proposals (1647) and the Agreement of the People (1647, 1649) had sketched earlier. Immediately upon the Barebones' resignation, the army came forward with an Instrument of Government, which Cromwell after some debate accepted.[59] Under its terms, Cromwell personally became Protector of the Commonwealth of England, Scotland and Ireland, and was to share supreme legislative power with an elected, triennial parliament, while sharing executive power (the chief magistracy) with

[59] For the text. see Gardiner, *Documents*, 405–17.

a council of from thirteen to twenty-one members. Foreign affairs were placed in his hands, except for the declaring of war and peace, which was to require the consent of the council; with a similar consent, the Lord Protector was to exercise emergency powers. Parliamentary consent was required in all matters of legislation and taxation, and no adjournment or dissolution was permitted during the first five months of parliament's sittings. There were detailed provisions for electoral representation: four hundred from England and Wales, thirty from Scotland and thirty from Ireland. All those who had fought against the parliamentary side—"aided, advised, assisted, or abetted in any war," was the broad formula employed—were excluded from the next four elections, and Irish and Catholic "rebels" were excluded altogether. Also a two hundred pound property qualification was set up. Special parliaments were provided for, notably in case of war. A standing army of thirty thousand was established in perpetuity, unless the need for it should disappear. The Lord Protector's office, while for life, was not made hereditary under the Instrument, but remained elective (the royal family excluded), the council serving as electors, while other high officers of state, including the chancellor and treasurer, were likewise made elective by parliament.

In addition to these organizational features, the Instrument included strongly worded articles protecting the freedom of religion (excepting however popery and prelacy!). It has been rightly said that the Instrument of Government was the first fully elaborated modern constitution, based upon the division and balance of governmental authority, and the recognition of at least *one* fundamental right. Among the great creations of this highly creative age, the Instrument of Government ranks with Rembrandt's paintings, Descartes's philosophy, and the other works of superlative and lasting value. Like the greatest of these in other fields, it was appreciated only by a small minority in England, and few if any on the continent. Yet in essentials it anticipated the constitutions of Europe and America which the American and French revolutions were to bring forth in such an avalanche. Begot by the bitter experience of despotism of either monarch or representative, the Instrument sought a balance as the basis of a permanent settlement. While lacking proper provisions for its own amendment, its greatest weakness was the lack of support of either tradition or popular enthusiasm. The latter defect Cromwell sought to remedy by securing from all voters an acknowledgment that "the persons elected shall not have power to alter the government as it is hereby settled in one single person and a parliament."

Although this amounted to a plebiscitary referendum on the new constitution by all qualified voters, the element of compulsion deprived it of its sanctioning effects. There was much other dissatisfaction, and efforts by the parliament elected under the Instrument to change it were eventually embodied in a constitutional bill. The Protector's body argued that the parliament was not called upon, or even authorized to consider the form of government; in a famous speech in the painted chamber of Parliament House on September 12, 1654, Cromwell made it clear that though the parliament was free *under* the constitution as outlined in the "Instrument," it was not free to alter it:

In every government there must be somewhat fundamental, somewhat like a *Magna Charta,* that should be standing and be unalterable. . . . That Parliaments should not make themselves perpetual is a fundamental. . . . Of what assurance is a law to prevent so great an evil, if it lie in one or the same legislator to unlaw it again? . . . Is not Liberty of Conscience in religion a fundamental? . . . Indeed, that has been one of the vanities of our contests. Every sect saith, Oh! Give me liberty. But give him it, and to his power he will not yield it to anybody else. . . . The magistrate has his supremacy, and he may settle religion according to his conscience. . . . This I say is a fundamental. It ought to be so: it is for us and the generations to come. . . . There are many circumstantial things which are not like the laws of the Medes and Persians. But the things which shall be necessary to deliver over to posterity, these should be unalterable, else every succeeding Parliament will be disputing to change and alter the government. . . . You have been called thither together to save a nation,—nations. . . . The [Instrument of] Government doth declare that you have a legislative power without a negative from me. . . . You may make any laws . . . and . . . they are *ipso facto* laws, whether I consent or not, if not contrary to the [Instrument of] Government. You have an absolute legislative power in all things that can possibly concern the good and interest of the public. I think you may make these nations happy by this settlement.[60]

So Cromwell had each member sign a statement or "test" by which he would recognize the government; nearly 150 signed then and there, and enough more later to make a majority. They did not all agree; but they realized that the "last word" was theirs who had drawn up the Instrument. Nevertheless, the commons proceeded to raise the constitutional issues again, and eventually came forward with a constitutional bill.[61]

[60] Abbott, *op. cit.,* III, 451–62. See also Carlyle, *Cromwell,* III 416 ff., including Carlyle's pointed annotations and intercalations.
[61] For the text see Gardiner, *Documents,* 427–47.

This deeply angered Cromwell and persuaded him to dissolve this parliament also. He thereupon turned increasingly to his major generals. His efforts to create a constitutional government upon a stable basis were failing fast.

The question may well be asked: what was behind these stresses and strains? Was there any basic conflict from which the contrasting position can be explained? There was the persistent antagonism of army and parliament, intimately linked to the clash between the more radical elements of Independency and the successive attempts at "ordering" the religious life of the nation according to an orthodoxy which commanded a majority in the house. In the light of the prevailing temper of the age, as well as the mass of contemporary evidence, this issue suggests the core of the conflict; but the influence of commercial and other economic interests cannot be gainsaid. Nor should the flowering of an ardent nationalism in the age of Cromwell be overlooked,[62] which readily expressed itself even in rather aggressive imperialism. Indeed, conventional "estimates" of Cromwell's career as a statesman usually list his strengthening of the empire as one of the high points. Uneasy apologies for his brutal policy in Ireland are combined with frank enthusiasm for his Caribbean adventures; yet all this activity does not seem to touch the core of the revolution, nor the heart of its leader. These were more significantly expressed in his deep emotional response to George Fox who, having come to exhort him to protect the Friends against persecution, was told by Oliver "with tears in his eyes," "Come again to my house, for if thou and I were but an hour of a day together, we should be nearer one to the other." [63] For it was the intensity of his belief in the inner light of faith which, in combination with his extraordinary practical sense, made Cromwell the leader he was; his was a leadership at once inspirational and successful. Among the many remarkable speeches Cromwell addressed to successive parliaments, none perhaps expresses the quintessence of this leadership more strikingly than the opening speech to the first parliament of the Protectorate, on September 4, 1654:

You are met here on the greatest occasion that, I believe, England ever saw, having upon your shoulders the interest of three great nations, with the territories belonging to them. And truly I believe I may say it without an hyper-

---

[62] See Abbott's bibliography on this significant item, as well as the (as yet unprinted) dissertation by George A. Lanyi, *Oliver Cromwell and His Age—a Study in Nationalism* (1949).

[63] Abbott, *op. cit.*, III, 639. Cf. also the similar case of Naylor, *ibid.*

bole. You have upon your shoulders the interest of all the Christian people in the world.[64]

It was Cromwell's willingness to have his first parliament consider the ratification of the Instrument which precipitated these more conservative Puritans into attempting a new constitutional proposal. As we have seen, it proved abortive, being based upon what looked to Cromwell and the army like a conspiracy with the enemies of the new order—Cavaliers, Levelers, and the like. Upon the dissolution of parliament, several risings occurred, notably that of Penruddock (April, 1655). In the sequel and for the sake of security, Cromwell and the council of state organized the military emergency administration of the major generals. During the remainder of 1655 and part of 1656, the country was administered by these plenipotentiaries of the Lord Protector, each major general in charge of one district. By their Puritan rigor, their arbitrariness and their exactions they became thoroughly hated. By a curious inversion of public sentiment, the people and the parliament elected by them turned to Cromwell to help them against these "swordsmen." The Humble Petition and Advice, formulated in the winter of 1656–57, sought to make Cromwell king, but he rejected this as not in keeping with his reading of God's will, which seems also to have been the will of the generals. In any case, he accepted the strengthening of the Lord Protector's authority beyond the Instrument of Government's provisions.[65]

Neither in the army nor in the people's representatives could Cromwell secure a solid backing for his broad conception of tolerance. To be sure, he too excluded popery and prelacy, and eventually even "blasphemy," from the faith to be tolerated. His was, in Professor Abbott's formulation, an "intolerant tolerance." He confronted a problem which we have once again come to appreciate: how far can you tolerate the intolerant? This question had been relatively easy to answer when the intolerant was a Laud, or even a Presbyter. But what of his own army? Yet the rule of major generals with its closing of theaters, forbidding of sports, arbitrary arrests, imprisonments and banishments, in short what Trevelyan has nicely called "the ubiquity of the soldier and saint," was likewise

---

[64] For the full text see Abbott, *op. cit.,* III, 434–43.

[65] After he had refused the title, it was passed and presently amended. It enlarged the authority of parliament at the expense of the council of state. It also gave the Protector the right to name his own successor and the life members of another house. When a quarrel developed between the two, Cromwell dissolved the house of commons again early in 1658.

oppressive and angered Cromwell beyond words. So eventually Cromwell found himself alone, inspired and inspiring but unable to stabilize a liberal order.[66]

No sooner had the war with the Dutch been ended than England was plunged into a new conflict with Spain. There can be little doubt that it was of Cromwell's own making. "He had apparently made up his mind that war with Spain was his most profitable adventure," Professor Abbott has written, but in the light of all the evidence, "no suspicion of that seems to have leaked out."[67] His speeches clearly show however that this decision was motivated by other considerations than profit and adventure. There were constant plots against the dictator and his rule—resistance movements or fifth columns they would be called nowadays—and these plots were being supported from the Spanish Netherlands (Brussels) as well as France. In the peace treaty with the Dutch, it had been explicitly stipulated that no assistance was to be given to the Cavaliers or their royal masters; it is clear that an agreement with France to do likewise would be facilitated by England making war against Spain, with which France too was still at war.[68] Furthermore, roving pirates were continually harassing British trade from the port of Dunkerque, and the conquest and seizure of that place became a major objective of Cromwell's policy, to which the French acceded very reluctantly. There was finally the Elizabethan conception of the Spaniard as the archenemy:

. . . For it is certain they [the Spaniards] have the same mind, and the very same desires, which they had in the year 1588, when they endeavoured to subdue this whole island; nay, it is certain their hatred is more inflamed and their jealousies and suspicions more increased by this change in the state of our affairs, and the form of our republic.[69]

[66] For the issue of toleration, see W. K. Jordan's magistral work, *The Development of Religious Toleration in England* (3 vols., 1936 and later), especially Vol. II: "From the Convention of the Long Parliament to the Restoration." Cf. also for Abbott's views, *op. cit.,* especially III, 437 (Protector's speech), 527; see also the discussion at I, 277–79, for his earlier position.

[67] Abbott, *op. cit.,* III, 852 ff., and IV, 1 ff. (Chs. XVII and XVIII) contain much the best documented and balanced account of the Protector's complex and devious policy in this matter. Abbott notes the tendency of all dictatorships eventually to engage in foreign wars of conquest in order to escape from domestic pressure; he seems to consider this an unfailing law.

[68] See above, Chapter Seven, pp. 234–5 and 242.

[69] See *Manifesto of the Lord Protector* adopted in late October, 1655. It is believed to be, at least in Latin, the work of John Milton. See Abbott, *op. cit.,* III, 878–91. (The

As is usual in such cases, the Spanish crown had as many complaints against the British. There was enough excuse on each side for such a conflict, and each side made the most of its case. But it did not do either of them much good; the real issue was France.

It has been suggested that in all this, Cromwell was engaged in the politics of the past, in the Spanish Armada, the Gunpowder Plot and the Thirty Years' War, and that he did not represent the spirit of his time, nor that of the people he ruled. The rising power was France, and the dangers of French hegemony, under Louis XIV, were just around the corner. This view, however, overlooks the fact that a revolutionary regime has peculiarly intense problems of survival, and must address itself to the immediate problems it faces even more than governments generally. All sound foreign policy bears the stamp of the past; continuity in foreign affairs is vital to their successful conduct. The war with Spain hurt British trade, it did not produce fiscal relief—on the contrary, it further increased the public debt—but it enabled the Protectorate to continue its building up of the naval power of Britain, it yielded some additions to the colonial empire, "the Empire of England," as it was then called, and finally brought the conquest of Dunkirk and its acquisition by England. Symbol of the Lord Protector's Protestant leadership, the war with Spain gave Cromwell precisely that national stature which the Stuarts' foreign policy had failed to yield them in their hour of need.

It was a striking feature of weakness, contributing greatly to the downfall of the Protectorate after Cromwell had passed away, that Cromwell's administrative ability did not extend to the field of public finance. Indeed, the chaotic condition of the treasury under the Stuarts was worsened under the Commonwealth and Protectorate. A great variety of *ad hoc* devices, including confiscations and special levies, administered by parliamentary committees and special commissioners, never succeeded in balancing the budget. Between 1654 and 1660, in spite of a total average annual revenue of almost 1.5 million pounds, the average deficit amounted to half a million pounds.[70] Hence the recurrent demands for the reduction of the army and navy, and the substitution of a militia.

---

quote is from p. 890.) This Declaration reviews all the complaints Englishmen had against Spain, the seizure of ships, the violence and cruelty against settlers, the persecution of Protestants, the Inquisition, and the harboring of "priests and Jesuits nestling under the protection of the Spaniards."

[70] See Dr. W. A. Shaw's estimates in "The Commonwealth and the Protectorate 1649–1660" in *Cambridge Modern History*, III, 457–58.

X. THE UNITED NETHERLANDS

In defending the war with Spain, Cromwell had stressed the peace with the United Netherlands, and the common dangers of the two Protestant sister republics. Contrary to quite a few of his associates, the Lord Protector was unwilling to recognize trade rivalry as sufficient cause for war. Before we conclude the story of the Protectorate, it seems well to sketch, even though briefly, some key aspects of the United Netherlands' story since the accession of Charles I.

The naval and mercantile rivalry between Britain and the Netherlands was only one aspect of the unbelievable vitality and creativity which lifted the United Provinces, and especially Holland, to a position of unique leadership and prominence during the two generations with which we are concerned in these pages. Their marvelous productivity in arts and letters is dealt with elsewhere, as is the story until 1625, but a few further comments on the political life of the Dutch Republic are needed to provide background for its activity, not only in fighting Cromwellian England, but also in destroying Spanish sea power and in checking the French ascendancy on the continent.

It will be remembered that the United Netherlands had passed through a severe crisis from which Maurice of Nassau as the leader of the popular forces of orthodox Calvinism had emerged victorious over the aristocratic and urban enlightenment.[71] Soon afterward, the United Netherlands found themselves again at war with Spain, the Ten-Year Truce having lapsed. The extraordinary military skill of Maurice, both in the field and in the building and besieging of fortresses, had provided the Dutch with a measure of security. But the genius of Maurice was matched by that of the great Spanish general, Marquis de Spinola, who eventually laid siege to the key fortress of Breda. Worry over his inability to break this siege is believed to have hastened the great stadholder's death, on April 23, 1625. On Maurice's death, the stadholdership passed to his brother, Frederick Henry of Orange (1584-1647). Though still formally treated as a republican office, the stadholder's position increasingly resembled that of other crowned heads. This was in part due to the fact that the stadholder provided some element of common government for the otherwise loosely federated republics of Holland, Zeeland, Utrecht, Overijssel, and Gelders.[72] In a sense, the stadholders of the house of Nassau-Orange

---

[71] See above, Chapter Five, pp. 147-50.
[72] Besides the provinces just mentioned, the United Netherlands included Friesland and

acted as guardians of this constitutional equality, and thereby sought to restrain the proud republicans of Holland. Oldenbarneveld, as we have seen, fell a victim to this rivalry.[73]

Frederick Henry was elected captain general and admiral general almost immediately upon his brother's death. Statesman-like in his tolerance and tact, he wielded his great powers with a skill and common sense which made the United Provinces secure against great odds, and gave the Dutch people their "Golden Age." Frederick Henry, ably supported by his clever and ambitious wife, Amalia von Solms, who during his long absences in the field carried on the government for him, succeeded in raising the stadholder's position to that of a virtual sovereign. Indeed, so brilliantly successful was his stewardship, that the estates of the United Provinces passed, in 1631, the Act of Survivorship, by which they bestowed succession upon Frederick Henry's son.

The extraordinary war, fought by Frederick Henry with superb generalship throughout most of his reign, was essentially a war of position. While he could not prevent the surrender of Breda (1625), he profited from the Spaniards' exhaustion to conclude an agreement with Richelieu, through his able diplomatic helper, Francis Aerssens, for whom Richelieu had the highest regard. The critical situation confronting Holland was the "reason of state" for conceding to Richelieu the naval help against La Rochelle, mentioned earlier,[74] in exchange for financial assistance against Spain. On this basis, Frederick Henry was able to resume the initiative and in 1627 and 1629 conquer the fortresses of Groll and Hertogenbosch (Bois-le-Duc)—both superb feats of engineering. This was followed in 1632 by the brilliant siege and capture of Maastricht, which Pappenheim tried to relieve, but in vain. During these seven years of striking achievement and growing strength, the resources of Holland were being increasingly depleted. The capture of Maastricht raised understandable hopes of peace, and but for the death of Gustavus Adolphus on the battlefield of Lützen, peace might well have been achieved in spite of the diplomacy of Richelieu. It was not to be.[75]

Groningen, which were under another stadholder, a cousin of Frederick Henry from the House of Nassau-Dietz, who also headed Drenthe, which thereby became associated with the United Netherlands in a fashion similar to the lands along the southern border, known as those of the "Generality" and including parts of Brabant, Breda and Maastricht and administered by the United Provinces jointly.

[73] See above, Chapter Five.

[74] See above, Chapter Seven, p. 211.

[75] Dutch historians, notably D. C. Nijhoff, *Staatkundige Geschiedenis van Nederland* (1893) are inclined to divide the reign of Frederick Henry into an earlier, happy period,

During the second half of his reign, down to the peace of Westphalia, Frederick Henry fought essentially a holding action. He recaptured Breda in 1637, but although the alliance with France, concluded in 1635, opened up the prospect of recapturing at least half of the southern Netherlands (Belgium), Frederick Henry became increasingly wary of French ambitions, and inclined to hold back. Thereupon, in 1639 Olivárez decided upon an all-out effort to defeat the Dutch. But it was too late. The grand fleet of Spain, like the Armada in 1588, suffered utter defeat at the hands of Martin H. Tromp at the Downs. The incredible energy with which the Dutch people rose to meet the approaching danger testified to their unbroken spirit and vitality, as did the reckless courage with which Tromp attacked, when greatly inferior in ships, at the Spaniards' first approach. This destruction of Spanish sea power was followed, as we saw earlier, by the French victory at Rocroy (1643), which broke forever the myth of invincibility of the Spanish infantry. At the same time it raised the specter of a French threat against the Netherlands' southern border, and induced the Dutch to press for peace. Spain's loss of Portugal in 1640 had removed what was perhaps the most important source of conflict: Dutch colonial rivalry, and more especially the prosperous Dutch settlements in Brazil and in Indonesia were in formerly Portuguese territory.

Dutch colonial expansion, it will be recalled, had been fostered by two great chartered companies, the East India and the West India companies. These were tightly controlled monopolies of trade. Oldenbarneveld's control of the former had been a fertile source of conflict in earlier days. Its hold in the spice islands had slowly expanded, and under a number of great governors, especially J. P. Koen and A. van Diemen, had gradually come to include Java, Sumatra and some of the lesser isles, as well as Malacca. In addition, the Dutch gained entry to, and a virtual monopoly of, trade with Japan, after the forcible suppression of the Christians (1637–42). The West India Company was less successful. Its great scoop, yielding fifty per cent on the company's capital that year, was the capture of the Mexican silver fleet (1628) by Piet Hein, perhaps the

---

1625–32, and a later more somber one. See Vol. I, pp. 482–514. Not so P. J. Blok, *History of the People of the Netherlands*, Vol. IV, Chs. I–VI. Edmondson's chapter in the *Cambridge Modern History* is based upon too favorable an estimate of F. Aerssens' diplomacy. Following Groen van Prinsterer's research, he uncritically accepts the technique of power politics. Nijhoff feels that Aerssens' estimate of Richelieu was *"zoo afgodish vereerend"* that one is tempted to accuse him of hypocrisy. In any case, he considers him responsible for the "ill-famed" alliance of 1635.

most dauntless of Holland's many daring sea devils. The wonderfully romantic tale of Dutch exploits and Spanish counterexploits in the struggle for the colonial booty of America cannot be told within this short compass; the seizure of San Salvador (1625–27) and of Pernambuco (1628–54) did not prove lasting. All in all, the West India Company was not a financial success; the cost of maintaining the military and naval forces required proved too high. For the Dutch, as for the British, it was a matter of "freedom of trade"—a principle which later led to the wars between the two rivals. This principle was accepted by Spain in the peace of Westphalia; it would have been well had they never challenged it.

The slowly progressing negotiations for a peace settlement were interrupted by the death of Frederick Henry and the accession of his son, William II. Against the peace policy of Holland and its burgher leadership, William, brilliant, ambitious, restless as a youth of only twenty-two well might be, tried to revive the war; to strengthen the unity of the state, he inclined toward France, which was continuing its war against Spain. Although he could not prevail against the general peace sentiment, William scored a striking success in asserting his authority against the hostile trading elements of Holland, and it is certain that he would have further promoted the monarchical position in the Netherlands, or even have changed the course of events in England, since he was married to the sister of his friend, Charles II. But he died of smallpox late in 1649. Since his potential successor was as yet not even born—he was to become William III and unite the two rival Protestant powers against French aggression—the defenders of local autonomy and burgher interests, the so-called Loevestein party, seized the opportunity. A great assembly was held in 1651 and re-established and extended the ancient provincial autonomy to the point where the United Netherlands reverted into a confederacy rather than continue a federal state under a common government. Had not Holland held such a predominant position, this decision might have had disastrous consequences; as it was, the chief executive (grand pensioner) of Holland became once more, as in the days of Oldenbarneveld, the chief Dutchman.

The man who was put into this crucial position, Jan de Witt, though only twenty-eight in 1653, was a statesman of extraordinary skill and resourcefulness; assisted by a brilliant admiralty, he succeeded in guiding Dutch fortunes successfully out of the war with Cromwellian England. He has at times been reproached for being willing to concede to Cromwell a secret article barring the return of the house of Orange to the stadholder's position; but this can readily be justified by the paramount advantage of peace, especially as the young William was only four years old, and there was therefore plenty of time for a turn in the "wheel of fortune." This came with the restoration of Charles II; the secret article was at once revoked. But most of de Witt's striking successes lie beyond the scope of this volume. At first, in the years after the conclusion of the peace of Westminster (1654), de Witt devoted himself primarily to restoring the Dutch economy by ordering the finances and the like.[76] To be sure, he carried on a limited colonial war with Portugal (1657–60) and successfully took a hand in the Swedish-Danish war (1657–60) in order to keep the straits into the Baltic open. But these were relatively small efforts involving great mercantile interests. All in all, the Dutch Republic was as rich and powerful in 1660, as it had been in 1625, but now fully recognized as an independent and sovereign unit, and at peace with most of Europe.

XI. COLLAPSE OF THE PROTECTORATE AND RESTORATION OF THE MONARCHY

The weakness of England in the concluding years of the Protectorate, including its war with Spain, undoubtedly helped the Dutch to remain "on top." For behind a façade of power and glory, Cromwell's dictatorship was being undermined by the same corrosive forces which seem invariably to attack such regimes. The two Napoleons, Hitler and Mussolini, have all suffered a similar fate. The mounting repression in time generates nonco-operation and sabotage to a lethal extent. In the summer of 1658 the Spanish envoy, Giavarina, was apparently unable to make up his mind whether constant plots were actually taking place, or were being put forward by the Protector to justify his repression. That a growing majority of the English people were weary of the military despotism seems clear enough.[77] Not even the striking successes of the English against Dunkerque, in co-operation with the French, made much difference in this. Just as Germans came to welcome the squadrons of enemy airforce raining destruction upon their cities, since their one hope was to be rid of Hitler and his regime, so many Englishmen had come to look upon Cromwell's latter-day "Saints" and all their work. The depth of the fury may be appreciated from the fact that after the Restoration a London mob dug up Cromwell's bones and strung them to a gallows.

[76] Nijhoff, *op. cit.*, II, 48 ff., containing also a sane assessment of Jan de Witt's statesmanship.
[77] Abbott, *op. cit.*, Ch. XV.

The vast and highly ornate, typically baroque state funeral which the government provided for the Protector stood in strange contrast to the inherent simplicity of the man. It was also out of keeping with his last hours, completely devoted as they seem to have been to religious reflections. Just before he passed away, having said to those around him that his design was to make what haste he could to be gone, he spoke a prayer:

Lord, though I am a miserable and wretched creature, I am in Covenant with Thee through grace. And I may, I will, come to Thee, for Thy people. Thou hast made me, though very unworthy, a mean instrument to do them some good, and Thee service; and many of them have set too high a value upon me, though others wish and would be glad of my death; Lord, however Thou do dispose of me, continue and go on to do good for them. Give them consistency of judgment, one heart and mutual love; and go on and deliver them, and with the work of reformation; and make the Name of Christ glorious in the world. Teach those who look too much on Thy instruments, to depend more upon Thyself. Pardon such as desire to trample upon the dust of a poor worm, for they are Thy people too. And pardon the folly of this short Prayer;—Even for Jesus Christ's sake. And give us a good night, if it be Thy pleasure. Amen.[78]

This was on September 3, 1658—the anniversary of Dunbar and Worcester. As he died, a terrific storm broke over England, striking awe into the hearts of friend and foe.

Rather than attempt an estimate of Cromwell in the conventional fashion, I suggest that the Protector was the greatest single individual of the two generations between 1610 and 1660. This Mahomet of the North, this Promethean challenger of tradition and its Gods, brought the revolutionary political fulfillment of the spiritual ferment of the Reformation. In Andrew Marvell's "Ode" we find a balanced view:

> And well he therefore does, and well had guessed,
> Who in his age has always forward pressed;
> And knowing not where Heaven's choice may light,
> Girds yet his sword, and ready stands to fight.

How I see him should be apparent from what has been sketched as the essence of his great career; neither siding with his apologists nor with his detractors, recognizing that his image, if any man's, depends upon one's view of man and history, I feel him to have been an intensely human being, and a true embodiment of that practical idealism which

[78] Abbott, *op. cit.*, IV, 872.

represents the genius of his people.[79] No other political leader but Abraham Lincoln ever approached the depth of his religious feeling, yet retained a firm grasp of common sense realities. That the Levelers and Diggers hated him even more than the Royalists—Winstanley in his *Loyal Martyriology* called him "the English Monster . . . a pattern for Tyrannie, Murther and Hypocrisie"—is clearest testimony of his moderation. How civilized, generous, even magnanimous was his dictatorship, compared to the totalitarian molochs of our time!

The confused and depressing disorder which soon overtook the Protectorate as Oliver's mediocre son Richard struggled with tasks he could not handle, has tended to make people forget that, in Professor Abbott's words, "barring some miracle, its [the Protectorate's] days were numbered . . . it seems apparent that the English state was nearly at its last gasp when Cromwell died." Yet, when the restored monarchy, a few years later, suffered grievous defeat at the hands of the Dutch, Pepys ruminated: "It is strange how everybody do nowadays reflect upon Oliver and commend him, what brave things he did, and made all the neighbours fear him."

There is little of interest in this rapid disintegration of a rule which even its architect and master could not have succeeded in perpetuating. Within a few months, Richard Cromwell was "Tumbledown Dick," and the generals who took over fell to quarreling among themselves. The developing chaos was cut short by one of Cromwell's most able and level-headed generals, George Monk (1608–69). Throwing in his lot with the civilians, he called for a parliamentary election; the people's representatives called back Charles II. For a restoration of the historical constitution was the line of least resistance; hurried plans for constitutional reform such as those outlined in John Milton's *Ready and Easy Way* had no chance because Englishmen were tired of innovation. Yet, in a sense, this very restoration reaffirmed a key tenet of the Puritan opposition to Charles I's government of church and state: the value of constitutionalism. It was a lasting achievement. When the king entered London, amidst the delighted acclaim of his people, he is said to have turned to one of his companions and remarked: "I never knew that I was so popular in England." The spirit of comedy was to succeed the heroic

[79] On this see R. S. Gardiner, *Cromwell's Place in History* (1897) pp. 114–6, and the masterly survey of the entire body of literature in Abbott, *op. cit.,* Vol. IV, Ch. XVI, a restatement of his earlier essay in *The Yale Review* (1913), which appeared in a revised version in *Conflicts with Oblivion* (1924).

tragedy of Cromwellian dictatorship. Nevertheless, though unappreciated by many at the time, a great lesson had been learned, the lesson of constitutionalism. This lesson in the importance of organizing the government according to and under a basic law, dividing and defining its powers, has been the lasting heritage of England's revolution. It was the fulfillment of the emergence of the modern state.

Chapter Ten

THE LEARNED AX—A BIBLIOGRAPHICAL ESSAY

I SHALL resist the temptation of engaging in philosophizing about the nature of history. Compounded of scholarship and art in varying proportions, "history is many things to many men." The great works of historians dealing with the two generations from 1610 to 1660 are so numerous, and the more detailed studies of special aspects of the history of politics, economics, art and thought so rich and varied that anyone who would undertake a synthesis of so abundant a harvest must needs become an eclectic. Gardiner and Firth, Ranke and Droysen, Hanotaux and Trevelyan among others have made this period the focal point of their life work. Spengler may be wrong in thinking of the baroque as the high tide of western European culture, but these fifty years were certainly among the most dramatic in the national histories of England, France and Germany, probably the most decisive in the history of science, mathematics and philosophy, and among the most productive in the history of literature, art and music. No wonder that the great historians of the several fields and nations have concentrated their efforts on evaluating and re-evaluating this extraordinary age and the incredibly vital, powerful personalities in all fields of human endeavor that crowded its stage. It was truly the age of the giants.

Under these circumstances, and in the very nature of things, it is impossible to do more than indicate the range of possible further reading and to hint at the vast stores of additional learning that lie readily at hand for him who would probe deeper. Nor do I, only a "part-time historian," wish for one moment to seem to pretend that I have read anywhere near as much of this extensive material as I should have liked to do during the twenty years since work on this book was first begun, work which was frequently interrupted by other professional duties and the distractions of the Second World War with its demands upon one's time and emotional resources.

Among the general works covering this period, first mention might be made of Volume IV of the *Cambridge Modern History,* entitled *The*

Thirty Years' War, including special studies on various separate aspects, in the tradition of this great synthesis. No special reference is made below to particular studies in this work. It contains a fairly elaborate bibliography, based upon F. C. Dahlmann and G. Waitz, *Quellenkunde der deutschen Geschichte* (but not its ninth edition, 2 vols., 1931–32). Cf. also E. M. Coulter and M. Gerstenfeld, *Historical Bibliographies* (1935). In the 1930's, E. Saulnier and A. Martin published *Bibliographie des Travaux Publiés de 1866 à 1897 sur l'Histoire de France de 1500 à 1789* (1932–38), which supplemented G. Brière and P. Caron, *Répertoire Méthodique de l'Histoire Moderne et Contemporaine de la France* (nine volumes, 1899–1924) and P. Caron and H. Stein, *Répertoire Bibliographique de l'Histoire de France* (1923–38). For the bibliography of British history see G. Davies, *Bibliography of British History, Stuart Period, 1603–1714* (1928); for more recent work, the annual studies by A. T. Milne should be consulted. (Reference is omitted here to the bibliographies on the other nations; they are given in Coulter and Gerstenfeld.)

Among studies covering the entire period of the seventeenth century, Professor G. N. Clark's *The Seventeenth Century* (1929) is important. To it may be compared Basil Willey, *The Seventeenth Century Background* (1934). Clark does not, however, concern himself to any extent with the problems raised by the baroque style. Equally unique is Eberhard Gothein's *Staat und Gesellschaft des Zeitalters der Gegenreformation* (in *Die Kultur der Gegenwart*) II, V, 1 pp. 137–230 (1908). However, Gothein roughly takes the century from 1550 to 1650 as his special period. Very different from either of these is Eugen Friedell's *Baroque and Rococo* (1928; English edition, 1931) which is preoccupied with the problems of its title. It suffers from the lack of a clear conception of the baroque and treats its material with some poetic license. (It constitutes Book II of *A Cultural History of the Modern Age.*)

Besides these works, it does not seem necessary to compile a list of general surveys of European history which incidentally happen to cover this period. An exception is the work of Leopold von Ranke. It is well known that Ranke made the history of the sixteenth and seventeenth centuries peculiarly his own. As a result, we have from his pen an English history, a French history, a history of the Ottomans and Spain, a history of the papacy—all with main emphasis upon the sixteenth and seventeenth centuries. Of course, these works are "old-fashioned" and "out-of-date," yet they still constitute the most comprehensive historical synthesis in the grand style for this period. I agree with George Trevelyan when he notes regarding Ranke's *History of England* (English edition, 1875) that it is "one of the great histories of our country, too much neglected." He adds: "The cause and growth of English parties in their wider aspects are luminously exposed, as are also foreign relations." Something quite similar can be said about the other works, and taking it all in all, we are obliged to conclude that no other historian before or since has so much to offer to the student of all Europe in the years 1610 to 1660. Ranke was still inspired by the cosmopolitan idea of a unity of Europe, even though it is clear enough that what he narrates is the establishment of the several nation states, especially their embodiments par excellence: France and England. His extraordinary conception of the "concert of powers" is contained in an essay justly celebrated for its sweep: *"Die Grossen Mächte"* in *Werke,* Volume 24 (1877).

The other national histories are mentioned below under the appropriate chapters, as are the specialized studies on culture and intellectual history. It is, however, essential to call attention to the *Histoire Générale* edited by Ernest Lavisse and Alfred Rambaud, of which Volume V, entitled *Les Guerres de Religion, 1559–1648,* and Volume VI, entitled *Louis XIV— 1643–1715,* are germane to this period.

It remains to comment briefly on some general economic histories. J. Kulischer, *Allgemeine Wirtschaftsgeschichte des Mittelalters und der Neuzeit* (two volumes, 1928–29) and F. L. Nussbaum, *History of the Economic Institutions of Modern Europe* (1933), which is based on Sombart, quoted below, and H. Heaton, *Economic History of Europe* (1936), are good general works.

CHAPTER ONE. THE PATTERN OF POLITICS AND ECONOMICS

The general background of thought and institutions in any age is so much part and parcel of general history that what has been said above concerning general works of reference applies to this chapter as well. But there are certain works of a more specialized kind which deal particularly with thought and institutions of a period which deserve to be added here. On the governmental and political side, the general tendency has been to center attention upon thought and refer back to institutions; the opposite is the case in the field of economics.

There is no general work, however, addressing itself to the political thought of the seventeenth century which could be compared with, e.g., Pierre Mesnard's *Trésor de la Philosophie Politique du Seizième Siècle.*

The general treatises of George H. Sabine, *A History of Political Theory* (1937; new edition, 1950) Chapters XXI–XXVI, and Paul Janet, *Histoire de la Science Politique dans ses Rapports avec la Morale* (1858), Volume II, are perhaps the best, along with A. Franck, *Reformateurs et Publicistes, XVIIe Siècle* (1864). The older W. A. Dunning, *A History of Political Theories from Luther to Montesquieu* (1905), Chapters IV to X, has been unduly neglected. Of more specialized interest, but of basic importance regarding interpretation is Friedrich Meinecke, *Die Idee der Staatsraison in der Neueren Geschichte* (1925), which unfortunately is still unavailable in English. The several papers in F. J. C. Hearnshaw's *Social and Political Ideas of the Sixteenth and Seventeenth Centuries* (1926, 1949) while interesting, are not adequately connected and fail to bring out the baroque setting. I recommend J. W. Allen, *English Political Thought* (1938), of which unfortunately only the first volume, reaching from 1603 to 1644, has appeared; for the remainder, the work by G. P. Gooch, amplified by Harold Laski, *English Democratic Theories of the Seventeenth Century* (1927), may be consulted, though it lacks depth and perspective. For France, Henry Sée's *Les Idées Politiques en France au XVIIe Siècle* (1923) is the best, though not very good. For Italy, Germany and Spain no good special studies are available.

Population studies for this period are rather deficient. Beloch's "Die Bevölkerung Europas zur Zeit der Renaissance" (*Zeitschrift für Sozialwissenschaft,* Vol. III, pp. 765 ff.) is basic.

On the economic side, Eli Heckscher's masterly all-European treatment of *Mercantilism* (English edition, 1935) supersedes all earlier works, although it has been attacked as too continental in outlook by no less an authority than Jacob Viner. But these criticisms, given in several articles, are on a matter of emphasis, rather than substance and they apply more to the eighteenth than the seventeenth century. Besides Heckscher, Werner Sombart's *Der moderne Kapitalismus* (fifth edition, 1922), though unreliable in detail, provides a comprehensive treatment of the seventeenth-century phase of economic development in Volume II (though by no means confined to our period). Both these writers have rightly stressed the importance of power rather than wealth as a central goal of mercantilism. I believe there was a shift in emphasis, the earlier mercantilists having been more concerned with power through trade, and the later with wealth through trade. For England, see more especially W. Cunningham, *The Progress of Capitalism in England* (1916), and the same author's *The Growth of English Industry and Commerce* (fifth edition, 1910–12), which rightly stresses the governmental aspect of early mercantilism. The more specifically political aspect has been more fully developed by Philip W. Buck, *The Politics of Mercantilism* (1942), but his study is restricted to England.

The controversy on the *Ständestaat* may be studied in the writings of Georg von Below, Tezner and Rachfahl. Of the first, *Territorium und Stadt* (1900) is basic, but Below's *Landständische Verfassung von Jülich und Berg* (1885), as well as his editions of *Akten,* are perhaps the most searching inquiries into this turgid subject, apart from the penetrating research of British scholars on parliamentary history.

On Althusius, see the author's Introduction to his edition, *Johannes Althusius' Politica Methodice Digesta* (1932) and the interesting discussion by Mesnard, *op. cit.* On Grotius, see Basdevant's magistral *Hugo Grotius* (1904), J. Huizinga, *Hugo de Groot en sijn eeuw* (1925), W. S. M. Knight, *The Life and Works of Hugo Grotius* (1925), Johannes Schlüter, *Die Theologie des Hugo Grotius* (1919), V. van Vollenhoven, *On the Genesis of the De Jure Belli ac Pacis* (1924), the same author's *The Framework of Grotius' Book, De Jure Belli ac Pacis* (1931), Erik Wolf, *Grotius, Pufendorf, Thomasius* (1927) and the same author's chapter on Grotius in *Grosse Rechtsdenker der Deutschen Geistesgeschichte* (1939; second edition, 1944) (also contains an interesting chapter on Althusius and Conring). The vast bibliography on Grotius is surveyed in J. ter Meulen, *Concise Bibliography of Hugo Grotius* (1925). On Hobbes, the basic work is by Ferdinand Tönnies, *Thomas Hobbes, Leben and Lehre* (1896; third edition, 1925) which superseded the previous standard work by G. Croom Robertson, *Hobbes* (1886), and Leslie Stephen's *Hobbes* (1904). Tönnies contains a short, selected bibliography. Since he wrote, Leo Strauss has offered a penetrating analysis of *The Political Philosophy of Hobbes—Its Basis and Genesis* (1936) in which the bourgeois aspect of Hobbes' thought is well brought out. John W. Gough has subjected the contractual problems to special analysis in *The Social Contract; a Critical Study of Its Development* (1936), but his inquiry does not carry to the point developed here. The mechanistic aspect of Hobbes' position is most fully developed by F. Brandt in *Thomas Hobbes' Mechanical Conception of Nature* (1928, translated from the Danish original of 1921), but the baroque quality of Hobbes has not been stressed, except in general works.

On constitutional ideas in England, Charles H. McIlwain's *The Political Works of James I* (1922) as well as the same author's *The High Court of Parliament and Its Supremacy* (1910) are of basic importance. More recently, Francis D. Wormuth has, in *The Origins of Modern Constitutionalism* (1949), brought out a study which seeks to adumbrate how the ideas of a separation of powers, bicameralism, the written constitution and judicial review crystallized in the course of the English Revolution. J. W. Allen, *English Political Thought 1603-1660* (Vol. I, 1603-1644, 1938) is also important.

CHAPTER TWO. BAROQUE IN LIFE AND LETTERS

Among the general discussions of baroque as a style in relation to the general history of culture, one is obliged to mention mostly German works. It seems almost as if the Germans had discovered a peculiar affinity to the baroque style, although its greatest creations were not German until a later period. A good sketch of the changes in approach to the problem is given by Heinrich Lützeler, "Der Wandel der Barockauffassung," *Deutsche Vierteljahrschrift für Literaturwissenschaft und Geistesgeschichte,* Vol. XI (1933), pp. 618-33. The same journal has published two other important studies: W. Weisbach, "Barock als Stilphänomen," Vol. II (1924) pp. 225-56, and Willi Fleming, "Die Auffassung des Menschen im siebzehnten Jahrhundert," Vol. VI, pp. 403-46. Other basic contributions are contained in Wilhelm Hausenstein, *Vom Geist des Barock* (1921), and Hans Rose, *Spätbarock* (1922), besides those mentioned under the next chapter because primarily concerned with the fine arts or music. Among specifically literary appraisals, Karl Vietor's *Probleme der Deutschen Barockliteratur* (1928) and Ludwig Pfandl's *Geschichte der Spanischen Nationalliteratur in ihrer Blütezeit* (1929), pp. 215-52, stand out. Both give admirably balanced accounts, but lean toward the courtly interpretation. Very interesting also is W. Stammler, *Von der Mystik zum Barock 1400-1600* (1927), though not expressly concerned with our period. He stresses the Spanish and French influence in bringing baroque into German letters. Finally two older general studies ought to be mentioned here: Wilhelm Dilthey, *Weltanschauung und Analyse des Menschen seit Renaissance und Reformation* in *Gesammelte Schriften,* II, and E. Gothein, *Staat und Gesellschaft des Zeitalters der Gegenreformation* in *Die Kultur der Gegenwart* (1908).

The vast literature on Milton is digested in D. H. Stevens, *Reference Guide to Milton from 1800 to the Present Day* (1930). For his life, the magistral work by D. Masson, *The Life of John Milton* (1859-94) is basic. Among the estimates, I have found, besides Macaulay's famous essay, the following three suggestive, though for different reasons: F. E. Hutchinson, *Milton and the English Mind* (1948), and James H. Hanford, *John Milton, Englishman* (1949). Both seek to evaluate Milton as the "representative Englishman"; the unique significance of Milton as the Dante of the Baroque is thereby somewhat obscured. L. P. Smith's *Milton and his Modern Critics* (1941) comes to the rescue against Ezra Pound, T. S. Eliot, *et al.* On English drama, A. Nicoll, *A History of Restoration Drama, 1600–1700* (1923), proved helpful.

Regarding the great writers of Spain, general reference should be made to Pfandl, quoted above. I noted also Emil Lucka, *Inbrunst und Düsternis —Ein Bild des alten Spaniens* (1927), and Carl Justi, *Velasquez und sein Jahrhundert* (1888; English edition, 1889; new edition, 1933). I have indicated in the footnotes the works of Vossler, Schevill, Kane, and Rennert on Lope and Góngora. Unfortunately, no comparable work on Calderón is available; M. V. Depta's study is rather pedestrian. S. D. Madariaga's brief essay, *Shelley and Calderón* (1920), is highly suggestive for the relation of the romantics to Spain. I should also like to mention Ernest Merrimée, *Essai sur la Vie et les Oeuvres de Francesco de Quevedo* (1886).

Corneille has brought forth as vast a mass of commentary as Milton. See E. Picot, *Bibliographie Cornélienne* (1875) and P. Le Verdier et E. Pelay, *Additions à la Bibliographie Cornélienne* (1908). The outstanding biography is by G. Lanson (1898; fifth edition, 1919); a more recent one by A. Dorchain, *Pierre Corneille* (1921). An interesting contrast is drawn between Shakespeare and Corneille by B. Croce, *Ariost, Shakespeare, Corneille*. The baroque aspect of Corneille is fully developed by J. E. Hiller, *Lessing und Corneille—Rokoko und Barock* in *Romanische Forschungen*, Vol. 47 (1933), pp. 159 ff. Striking remarks about French baroque style are found in Carl Burckhardt's *Richelieu—Der Aufstieg zur Macht* (1935), pp. 499 ff.

For Vondel and his time we have the fine monograph by A. J. Barnouw, *Vondel* (1925). Interesting also is J. Huizinga's sketch *Holländische Kultur des siebzehnten Jahrhunderts* (1933); however, after arguing that Dutch culture does not belong to the baroque, Huizinga proceeds to interpret Vondel, the key figure (as well as Grotius) as "the perfect Baroque poet" (p. 43). The impact of this baroque poet upon German literature has been the subject of a very illuminating study by H. Härten, *Vondel und der deutsche Barock* (1934).

German baroque literature of this period constitutes, according to Karl Vietor, a "problem" as analyzed in the study quoted above. He indicates some broader considerations in "Das Zeitalter des Barock" in *Aufriss der deutschen Literaturgeschichte nach neueren Gesichtspunkten* (1930) in which he asserts that Jakob Böhme "certainly is the most creative man of the German baroque." This view, very interesting in itself, seems somewhat at variance with Vietor's inclination to interpret the baroque as a court culture; Böhme, like Bunyan, Le Nain, *et al.,* represented the other pole. Another important, earlier contribution was made by Fritz Strich in "Der lyrische Stil des 17. Jahrhunderts," *Festschrift für Franz Muncker* (1916). The special problems which Gryphius presents form the subject of a striking study by F. Gundolf, *Andreas Gryphius* (1927). This followed an earlier study on *Martin Opitz* (1923); both are fully cognizant of the baroque problem. The same is true of Walter Jockisch, *Andreas Gryphius und das literarische Barock* (1930); cf. also W. Flemming, *Andreas Gryphius und die Bühne* (1921). For Grimmelshausen, we mention W. Burkard, *Grimmelshausens Erlösung und barocker Geist* (1929), and A. Bechtold, *H. J. Ch. von Grimmelshausen und seine Zeit* (1919). For Böhme see *Jacob Boehme: Studies in his Life and Teaching by Hans L. Martensen,* new and revised edition with notes and appendices by Stephen Hobhouse; it gives a good general introduction to the literature on this remarkable writer. Along with him the work of Angelus Silesius should be considered; the introductions by G. Ellinger and L. H. Held to their respective editions are valuable.

CHAPTER THREE. BAROQUE IN ART AND MUSIC

The literature on baroque architecture, art and music has been rapidly increasing. Among the most important early challenges, special mention must be made of Heinrich Wölfflin, *Renaissance und Barock,* fourth edition by Rose (1926). The pathfinding work of Alois Riegl, *Die Entstehung der Barockkunst in Rom* (1908) concentrates upon early architectural forms, as compared with Wölfflin's emphasis upon painting. Of course, the general works mentioned in the previous chapter, such as Spengler, Hausenstein and Wilhelm Dilthey, should also be consulted.

For architecture, A. E. Brinckmann's *Die Baukunst des 17. und 18. Jahrhunderts in den romanischen Ländern* (1915), in the *Handbuch der Kunstwissenschaft* (ed. by Fritz Burger and A. E. Brinckmann), is of basic importance; his interpretation avoids risky sociological generalization. The same author's *Barockskulptur* (1917) is likewise built upon the author's preoccupation with strictly esthetic aspects, more especially the idea that baroque art was concerned with the problems of increasing inter-penetration (*Durchdringung*) of plastic and spatial elements in terms of a specific "rhythm"; Brinckmann sees this interpenetration, melting and in-tertwining of the two as the core of baroque art.

Rather different is the approach of Werner Weisback who, a friend of Ernest Troeltsch, boldly asserted the political and social pattern of the great courts of the Counter Reformation to have been the life setting of baroque art. First in a brilliant article, "Barock als Stilphänomen," *Deutsche Vierteljahrschrift für Literaturwissenschaft und Geistesgeschichte*, Vol. II, pp. 225 ff. (1924), then in a larger volume, entitled *Der Barock als Kunst der Gegenreformation* (1921), as well as in *Die Kunst des Barock* (1924), of which an enlarged Spanish edition appeared in 1934 under the title *Arte barocco en Italia, Francia, Alemania, España*, Weisbach developed his thesis, which certainly constitutes part of the truth. He became involved in controversies with others, especially Nikolaus Pevsner, who took the position that no such coordination worked, especially in two articles "Gegenreformation und Manierismus," *Repertorium für Kunstwissenschaft*, Vol. 46, pp. 243–62 (1925), and "Beiträge zur Stilgeschichte des Früh- und Hochbarock," *ibid.*, Vol. 49, pp. 225–46 (1928). Pevsner insists upon the worldly aspect of Baroque; on page 226 an interesting passage asserts the kinship between Bernini, Poussin, Rembrandt and Velasquez.

A very curious, almost Don Quixote-like attack upon the idea of baroque art, let alone baroque spirit, was mounted by Benedetto Croce, who in 1925 returned to the views of the most doctrinaire classicists in asserting that "baroque" and "art" were contradictions in terms, and that therefore "art is never baroque and the baroque is never art," in a little essay entitled *Der Begriff des Barock*.

The paucity of writings on the general aspects of baroque in English is extraordinary. There is M. S. Briggs's pedestrian, but well-illustrated account *Baroque Architecture* (1914), S. Sitwell's rather impressionistic *Southern Baroque Art—a Study in Painting, Architecture and Music in Italy and Spain of the Seventeenth and Eighteenth Centuries* (1924; third edition, 1931), T. H. Fokker's *Roman Baroque Art—The History of a Style* (1938), and G. F. Webb's *Baroque Art* (1950) which last in a few pages highlights three interesting points of impact of baroque art upon England, of which only the first, namely John Webb's efforts in the fifties, of the seventeenth century, falls within our period.

There are, on the other hand, of course numerous and important works on individual artists. We can only mention a few. On Bernini, the standard work is Stanislao Franschetti, *Il Bernini—la sua vita, la sua opera, il suo tempo* (1900). More modern in approach is Ernst Benkard's engaging brief *Giovanni Lorenzo Bernini* (1926), which deserves to be translated. Very illuminating for the outlook on art of Bernini who, in Benkard's words, "determined the artistic expression of the seventeenth century" is the diary of the man who was assigned to Bernini during his stay in France, De Chantelou, *Journal en France du Cavalier Bernin par Chantelou,* ed. by Charensol (1930); cf. also the good German edition prepared by Hans Rose, *Tagebuch des Herrn von Chantelou über die Reise des Cavaliere Bernini nach Frankreich* (1919). Together with Filippo Baldinucci's *Vita di Giovanni Lorenzo Bernini* (I used the attractive edition, with translation and commentary by Alois Riegl—1912), it gives a vivid insight into the esthetic inspiration of the great baroque artist and dispels the notion that baroque and Renaissance can be considered mutually exclusive.

It is a great help that Jacob Burckhardt's *Erinnerungen an Rubens* (1898) have recently become available in English under the title *Rubens* (1950). For his corpus and an able introduction see A. Rosenberg, *P. P. Rubens* (1905), as well as the Phaidon volume of more recent date with an introduction by B. A. M. Stevenson (1939). Rubens' life and manifold political activities have been sketched in lively fashion by W. Cammaerts, *Rubens, Painter and Diplomat* (1932). For van Dyck, the basic work is by Lionel Cust, *Anthony van Dyck* (1900); more recently, this painter has been discussed competently by Gustav Glück, *van Dyck* (1931; second edition, 1935).

Besides Carl Justi's classic *Velasquez und sein Jahrhundert* (1888; new edition, 1933; English edition, 1889), Don A. de Beruete, *Velasquez* (1906) is the standard work. See also C. B. Curtis, *Velasquez and Murillo* (1883).

On Poussin, the leading studies are Walter Friedländer, *Poussin* (1914), and Otto Grautoff, *Nicolas Poussin* (1914) in two volumes. On Claude Lorrain Walter Friedländer also wrote a decisive work (1921). See also Pierre Courthion's (1932). The general story of French painting is competently, if rather too eulogistically set forth by Alfred Leroy, *Histoire de la Peinture Française au XVIIe Siècle* (1935),[1] which may be contrasted with Werner Weisbach's *Französische Malerei des XVII. Jahrhunderts im*

---

[1] This work contains a selective bibliography on individual French painters.

Rahmen von Kultur und Gesellschaft (1932) in which Weisbach, somewhat at variance with his earlier views, stresses the fluidity of all art styles and the concept of "classicism" as applied to the work of Poussin. A recent French work of quality is by Pierre du Colombier (1932). On the brothers Le Nain, Paul Jamot's enthusiastic *Les Le Nain* (1927) is good.

From the enormous literature on Dutch painting in this period we select as a general study W. Bode, *Great Masters of Dutch and Flemish Painting* (1909). Besides him, Max J. Friedländer's *Die niederländische Malerei des 17. Jahrhunderts* (1923) is outstanding for presenting the more modern viewpoint. A. B. de Vries has published the most up-to-date study on *Jan van Meer van Delft* (new edition, 1948). The modern viewpoint on Vermeer is given by E. V. Lucas, *Vermeer, the Magical* (1929). W. R. Valentiner's richly illustrated *Franz Hals* (1923) and the Phaidon volume on that painter (though colors here are "off") offer the best guidance for further study of Hals.

Jacob Rosenberg's *Rembrandt* (two volumes, 1948) has superseded all previous general treatments as rightly suggested in a review by Francis Taylor, the director of the Metropolitan Museum. But such a statement is not intended to deprecate the high order of the many fine studies, including C. Vosmaer, W. Bode, Carl Neumann, C. J. Holmes, W. Weisbach and A. M. Hinds, all of which, as well as numerous more specialized works, are given in Rosenberg's bibliography.

Baroque music has at last found an able analyst in English in the work of Manfred F. Bukofzer, *Music in the Baroque Era* (1947), which contains a very ably selected bibliography. Along with it, Robert Haas, *Die Musik des Barock* (1934) in *Handbuch der Musikgeschichte,* which is beautifully illustrated, deserves special mention. On the relation of baroque music to the general ideas of the period, H. Leichtentritt, *Music, History and Ideas* (1938), Chapter VI, is very helpful; it opens with a nicely balanced general discussion of baroque art, as defined by the earlier continental interpreters. On Heinrich Schütz the works of Spitta are authoritative.

Another general account of considerable merit is found in Paul Henry Láng, *Music in Western Civilization* (1941), Chapter 10. The impact of music, especially Italian music, upon poetry is interestingly analyzed in W. Stammler, *Von der Mystik zum Barock* (1941). Leonardo Olschki's *The Genius of Italy* (1949), chapter XVI, provides interesting background for this aspect of baroque music.

CHAPTER FOUR. RELIGION, PHILOSOPHY AND THE SCIENCES

The first half of the seventeenth century has rightly been called the cradle of modern science and philosophy. A. N. Whitehead has offered an illuminating sketch in *Science and the Modern World* (1925). The basic work on the period is Wilhelm Dilthey's *Weltanschauung und Analyse des Menschen seit Renaissance und Reformation* (1914), in which he showed that the seventeenth century shaped modern man, a view popularized by Oswald Spengler's *Untergang des Abendlandes* (1920), who distorted it, of course, to suit his pessimistic philosophy. Along with it, the later sections, especially IV (pp. 351 ff.), of Dilthey's *Einleitung in die Geisteswissenschaften,* Vol. I (1883); (new edition by Groethuisen 1922) are important, because here Dilthey shows how the metaphysical attitude of man toward reality was dissolving in the seventeenth century under the impact of empirical science. The thesis has in more recent years become pretty generally accepted; but neither Dilthey nor his followers have seen the link of this change with the feeling for power, and hence the baroque.

On Catholicism, the richest general treatment, linking the institutional and the spiritual side, is found in L. V. Pastor's *The History of the Popes,* Vols. XXV–XXXI (1938–40), from the German *Geschichte der Päpste,* Vols. XII–XIV (1927–29). It contains very extensive reference material, but is, of course, written from the Catholic standpoint. For Protestantism in this period, Ernst Troeltsch's *Die Bedeutung des Protestantismus für die Entstehung der modernen Welt* (second revised edition, 1911; English edition by W. Montgomery, 1912) and the same author's *Die Soziallehren der christlichen Kirchen und Gruppen* (1911; third edition, 1923), Part III, are basic. Of the latter work, there is also an English edition, by Olive Wyon (1931). Equally important is Max Weber's *Die protestantische Ethik und der Geist des Kapitalismus* (1904–05), reprinted in *Gesammelte Aufsätze zur Religionssoziologie* (fourth edition, 1947), which has been published in English by Talcott Parsons (1930). Weber himself did not live to deal with the extensive criticism which his studies provoked in English, though he rejected Rachfahl, Sombart and Brentano. Among these critiques, the most widely known is R. H. Tawney, *Religion and the Rise of Capitalism* (1926); sharper and less sympathetic is H. M. Robertson, *The Rise of Economic Individualism* (1933), who would actually reverse the relation of cause and effect, as far as Protestantism and capitalism are concerned. The whole controversy is rather comprehensively reviewed and sensibly summed up in A. Fanfani, *Catholicism,*

Protestantism and Capitalism (1935), who concludes that since capitalism existed before Protestantism, its essence or spirit, as Weber would call it, could not very well have come into existence after it itself was well established. The most important research along these lines was done by J. B. Kraus, S.J., who in *Scholastik, Puritanismus und Kapitalismus* (1930) shows pretty conclusively that not only capitalism, but its spirit were characteristically present in the *Hochscholastik;* Kraus's methodological observations are very sane. Important also for the understanding of Protestantism in this period are the writings of R. Niebuhr, especially *Faith and History—A Comparison of Christian and Modern Views of History* (1949), *passim,* and *The Nature and Destiny of Man,* II (1943) especially Chapters VII, VIII, X.

On the Jesuits, the literature is extensive. H. Boehmer's *The Jesuits* (1928, as translated and enlarged from the German work, *Die Jesuiten,* 1904; second edition, 1907) is a good general survey, not markedly pro or contra, with a brief selective bibliography. The older extended history of the order, written apologetically, is by Jacques Cretineau-Joly, *Histoire Réligieuse, Politique et Littéraire de la Compagnie de Jesus* (1845–46), six volumes. The moral issues which were controversial between the Jesuits and Jansenists are doctrinally treated by J. J. Ignaz Döllinger, *Geschichte der Moralstreitigkeiten* (1889), two volumes. Chapter II deals with probabilism. R. Fülöp Miller has in his *Macht und Geheimnis der Jesuiten* (1929; English edition, 1930) treated the subject with this well-known author's familiar sense for the dramatic; the subtitle calls it a study in cultural history. Recently, for the four hundredth anniversary of the founding of the order, M. P. Hearney, S.J., has written a brief general history, *The Jesuits in History* (1941) of which Chapters VIII–XI are pertinent. The popular leftist idea that Catholicism and more especially Jesuitism and Fascism may readily be identified is expounded with considerable passion by F. A. Ridley, *The Jesuits—A Study in Counter-revolution* (1938). To this may be compared, for the sake of perspective, the picture of the first century of Jesuit History, published in Antwerp in 1640. Among the source materials, *Monumenta Historica Societatis Jesu* (since 1898) are basic. For the Capuchins compare Father Cuthbert, *The Capuchins* (1928), in two volumes.

On Jansenism, the work by C. A. Sainte-Beuve, *Port-Royal,* in five volumes, is still of great importance. Volumes 3 and 4 deal specifically with Pascal. Leon Brunschvicg, however, made Pascal peculiarly his own; his *Le Génie de Pascal* (1924) and *Pascal* (1932), as well as his

Descartes et Pascal, Lecteurs de Montaigne (1944), are worthy fruits of his long devotion, as is his edition of the works of Pascal, *Oeuvres Complètes* (*avec la collaboration de Pierre Boutroux et de Felix Gazier*) in fourteen volumes. Boutroux himself provided a monograph which was offered in English in 1902. Mention might also be made of Jacques Chevalier's *Pascal* (1930) and of L. F. Jaccard, *Saint Cyran, Précurseur de Pascal* (1945).

On the "inner light" see Rufus M. Jones's *Mysticism and Democracy in the English Commonwealth* (1932) for a most perceptive study. Böhme's work has been increasingly recognized not only by students of religion, but of literature. So high an authority as Karl Vietor calls him the most outstanding literary figure in Germany in this period. Hans L. Martensen's *Jakob Böhme—Theosophische Studien* (1882) has lately been made available in English by Stephen Hobhouse under the title *Jacob Boehme: Studies in his Life and Teaching*. Outstanding is the recent work by A. Koyré, *La philosophie de Jacob Boehme* (1929). Of course, Troeltsch, cited above, is also very relevant. The same is true for Calvinism, though on its relation to Anglicanism the work of Roland G. Usher, *The Reconstruction of the English Church,* 2 vols. (1910), is basic.

For the history of science, René Pintard's *Le Libertinage Érudit dans la Première Moitié du XVIIᵉ Siècle* (1943), in two volumes, establishes the setting. The pertinent sections in W. T. Sedgwick and H. W. Tyler, *A Short History of Science* (revised by Tyler and R. P. Bigelow, 1939), and W. C. D. Dampier-Whetham, *A History of Science in Its Relations with Philosophy and Religion* (1942), later part of III, are good surveys. Important is the special study of E. A. Burtt, *The Metaphysical Foundations of Modern Physical Science* (1925). A. P. Usher's *A History of Mechanical Inventions* (1929) shows the relative unproductivity of the period in this field. C. A. Crommelin, *Physics and the Art of Instrument Making at Leyden in the Seventeenth and Eighteenth Centuries* (1928), is authoritative for the invention of the telescope, etc. On Galileo the best work is perhaps C. C. Fahey, *Galileo Galilei* (1903); there are three recent studies by A. Koyré, *Études Galiléennes* (part of *Histoire de la pensée*) (1939). Of the earlier works, Emil Wohlwill's *Galilei und sein Kampf um das Kopernikanische System* (vol. I, 1909; vol. II, 1926) is of basic importance. The literary side of Galileo's work is engagingly developed by L. Olschki, *Galilei und seine Zeit* (1927). He sharply rejects the views of Adolph Müller, S.J., who in *Galilei und das Kopernikanische Weltsystem* (1909) had attributed Galileo's use of Italian to his propagandistic tendencies, as part of his ambitious and egocentric personality. The older literature on the trial is reviewed in F. S. Taylor, *Galileo and Freedom of Thought* (1938). On Kepler, Ch. Frisch's biography in the last voume of his *Joannis Kepleri Opera Omnia* (1858–71) was best, until Max Casper's *Johannes Kepler* (1948) appeared. Kepler's cosmology is analyzed in its relation to astrology by H. A. Strauss, *Die Astrologie Johann Keplers* (1926). For William Harvey, Archibald Malloch, *William Harvey* (1929), and Charles Singer, *The Discovery of the Circulation of the Blood* (1922), are highly regarded.

On witchcraft in this period, Alice M. Murray's *The Witch Cult in Western Europe* (1921) and George L. Kittredge's *Witchcraft in Old and New England* (1928) seem very good; for the record, see also C. L'Estrange Ewen's *Indictments for Witchcraft, 1559–1736* (1929).

Having above indicated the literature on Pascal and the Hobbes material in section I earlier, it remains to add a few essential titles on Bacon and Descartes, since Spinoza really belongs to the next period.

For Bacon, the "definitive" work is J. Spedding, *The Letters and Life of Francis Bacon* (1861–74) in seven volumes. A new interpretative biography by Ed. Kemler will be published soon. On Descartes, *op. cit.,* pp. 452–92, is very important. The work by Gilson, Maritain and Koyré has significantly contributed to our understanding of the relations of Descartes with scholasticism; A. Koyré, *Descartes und die Scholastik* (1923), and Etienne Gilson, *La Liberté chez Descartes* (1913), L. Brunschvicg, *Descartes et Pascal* (1944), and J. Chevalier, *Descartes* (1921), are standard brief interpretations; Maxime Leroy, *Descartes, la Philosophie au Masque* (1929), brings out the baroque aspect. The interrelations with other thinkers are well developed in F. C. Bouillier, *Histoire de la Philosophie Cartésienne* (1868). More recently, Leon Roth has offered a penetrating new interpretation, *Descartes's Discourse on Method* (1937), where he shows that "the formulae of Descartes, like the trumpet calls of Bacon, suggest problems which go beyond themselves." Finally, the ties of Descartes to religion are subjected to detailed analysis in Henri Gouhier, *La Pensée Religieuse de Descartes* (1924).

CHAPTER FIVE. THE SULTRY YEARS OF PRECARIOUS BALANCE: THE DUTCH ASCENDANCY

The general literature on these confused years is very thin. Besides the works dealing with the seventeenth century as a whole, some of the works on the Counter Reformation are important. In addition to those mentioned in the general introductory remarks, the *Histoire Générale* edited by Lavisse and Rambaud, volume V, gives good general estimates for the several regions, as well as arts and letters. As a portrait of one of the leading spirits of the Counter Reformation, who was active in the period after 1610, L. Battifol's *Marie de' Medicis* (undated; from the French original published we do not know when) is very stimulating.

The Jülich-Cleves succession is given considerable space in the work of Ritter cited below. On it, we have a remarkable analysis in Oldenbarneveld's memorandum published by Janssen in *Geschichte des Deutschen Volkes seit dem Ausgang des Mittelalters* (1883-86), four volumes. E. von Schaumburg, *Der Jülich-Clevische Erfolgestreit* (1859), was written before it became established that the key memorandum (by Strahlendorf) was spurious. On this aspect see F. Meinecke, *Das Strahlendorfische Gutachten und der Jülicher Erfolgestreit* (1886), which follows earlier studies by Droysen and Stieve.

On the Grand Design, besides the *Mémoires* of Sully himself as quoted in the text, the findings of modern historians against the authenticity of this plan, as far as Henry IV is concerned, are stated authoritatively by Jean H. Mariéjol, but they seem nonetheless inconclusive to this writer. P. F. Willert, *Henry of Navarre* (1893; new edition, 1924), who gives a readable history of Henry IV's reign, treats it as settled that the design was an "invention" of Sully, paying no attention to the difficulties which such a conclusion raises regarding the known character of Sully.

Much learning has been expended upon whether the Grand Design was truly Henry's or rather an invention of Sully's, or yet developed by Sully on the basis of a casual thought expressed by Henry. While interesting, this controversy in no wise affects the Design's general significance: a federation of states to perpetuate the universal order of the passing medieval system. Christian Pfister, some years ago, summed up the extended controversy in "Les économies royales de Sully et le Grand Dessein de Henry IV," in *Revue Historique* (1894). Jean H. Mariéjol has summed up the record, as stated, without regard to the symbolic value of the *dessein* in his *Henry IV et Louis XIII* (*1598-1643*), which constitutes Volume VI, Part II of Ernest Lavisse, *Histoire de France* (1905), pp. 123 ff.

For the England of James I, George Trevelyan's *England Under the Stuarts* (1904)is much the most readable general account. For a broader treatment, S. R. Gardiner's *History of England, 1603–1642* (1883) in ten volumes is the classic.[2] Godfrey Davies' *The Early Stuarts* (1938) is based largely on his scholarship. On the special constitutional issues, Chapters II and III of J. R. Tanner, *English Constitutional Conflicts 1603–89* (1928), are very good; his is really more than a technical analysis, setting the problems in broad historical perspective. On the clash between Coke and Bacon in terms of law, Hastings Lyon and Herman Block, *Sir Edward Coke, Oracle of the Law* (1929), is very readable, but the standard histories of Pollock and Maitland and Holdsworth should not be neglected. The key documents are conveniently assembled in G. W. Prothero, *Select Statutes and Other Constitutional Documents Illustrative of the Reigns of Elizabeth and James I.* R. G. Usher's *The Institutional History of the House of Commons* (1924) contains a valuable discussion of this material.

On the Union, besides the general work of Ritter cited above, we would want to mention the same author's monograph, *Politik und Geschichte der Union zur Zeit des Ausganges Rudolfs II, und der Anfänge des Kaisers Mathias* (1880); for the Liga, similarly F. von Bezold, *Kaiser Rudolf II und die heilige Liga* (1886). For the special situation of Donauwörth, see F. Stieve's *Der Kampf um Donauwörth* (1875). Ranke also contributed a special monograph on this period, "Zur Reichsgeschichte von der Wahl Rudolfs II bis zur Wahl Ferdinands II, 1575–1619," in *Zur Deutschen Geschichte—Vom Religionsfrieden bis zum 30 jährigen Krieg* (1869).

For Dutch history, there is now H. Brugmans, *Geschiedenis van Nederland* (1935–36), in eight volumes, done in the newer style, of this Volumes IV and V are pertinent here. P. J. Blok's *History of the People of the Netherlands* (1898–1912), in five volumes (from the Dutch), remains very useful, however. It contains an extensive annotated bibliography. The end of volume III carries the story to the end of the truce (Chapters XI–XVI). He, in accordance with Motley and Fruin, calls the death of Oldenbarneveld a "judicial murder"—but on the whole gives a balanced presentation of the great crisis. The radical position in favor of Maurice of Nassau was put forward by Groen van Prinsterer many years ago in a rather disjointed, but interesting book entitled *Maurice et Barneveld* (1875).

The literature on the Puritans and Pilgrim Fathers is given below,

---

[2] See, however, R. G. Usher's sharply critical evaluation, *The Historical Method of Samuel Rawson Gardiner* (1915).

under that for Chapter Nine. Likewise, what is said above under Chapter One on mercantilism and colonialism applies here as well. On colonial rivalry, the theoretical side is carefully treated for England by Klaus E. Knorr, *British Colonial Theories,* 1570–1850 (1944), Ch. II.

CHAPTER SIX. THE THIRTY YEARS' WAR AND THE LIQUIDATION OF THE MEDIEVAL EMPIRE

An elaborate bibliography of the writings on the Thirty Years' War is contained in *Cambridge Modern History,* Vol. IV (1906), pp. 801–70 and in Dahlmann-Waitz, *Quellenkunde der Deutschen Geschichte* (new edition, 1931), pp. 667–707. The third volume of Moritz Ritter's *Deutsche Geschichte im Zeitalter der Gegenreformation und des Dreissigjährigen Krieges* (1908) is the most authoritative general German account; it is based upon the archival material. By far the most interesting recent general treatment in English (or any other language) is Miss C. V. Wedgwood's *The Thirty Years War* (1939); she gives a bibliography of materials published since Dahlmann-Waitz. Among these, I should like to recommend Karl Brandi, *Die Deutsche Reformation und Gegenreformation* (1927–30), and Hans Delbrück, *Geschichte der Kriegskunst im Rahmen der Politischen Geschichte,* Part IV (1920), containing able analyses of the main battles. Finally, R. S. Gardiner's *The Thirty Years War* (1874), though out of date, deserves a place in any general bibliography, in spite of its liberal and Protestant bias, as does Leopold von Ranke's *Geschichte der Päpste* (1874). Miss Wedgwood's splendid general treatment is a bit twisted at times by her insistence upon standards of conduct derived from the nationalism and pacifism of a later age.

On the Bohemian war, Anton Gindely's *Geschichte des Böhmischen Aufstandes,* in three volumes (1869), which is part of his *Geschichte des Dreissigjährigen Krieges,* is still well worth reading. R. Stanka, *Die Böhmische Confederationsakte von 1619* (1932), und Helmuth Weigel, *Franken, Kurpfalz, und der Böhmische Aufstand* (1932), are helpful in bringing out the constitutional issues. The strictly Czech national aspect is stressed in a number of general histories of that country.

For the Danish phase, Dietrich Schäfer's *Geschichte Dänemarks,* Volume V, 1559–1648 (1902) brings out the Danish position more clearly than other treatments. The background of the peace of Lübeck of 1629 is given in Ernest Wilmans, *Der Lübecker Friede 1629* (1904). Very valuable also, Hermann Hallwich, *Fünf Bücher Geschichte Wallensteins,*

Volume I (1910), Books II and III. The reasons for Swedish nonco-operation are unfolded in M. G. Schybergson, *Unterhandlingarna om en evangelisk allians aren 1624-25* (1880). Cf. also the literature on Gustavus Adolphus below. For the defense of Stralsund Fritz Adler's biography of Lambert Steinwich, *Bürgermeister von Stralsund* (1936), may be consulted.

On the Edict of Restitution, the chapter in Ritter, *op. cit.,* is specially recommended. Since F. V. Hurter wrote his *Geschichte Kaiser Ferdinands II und seiner Eltern,* Volume III, the role of Ferdinand has undergone some re-evaluation, but it is still the most exhaustive study on the imperial side. On the Mantuan War, Romolo Quazza has published a monograph, *La Guerra per la Successione di Mantova e del Monferrato 1628-1631* (1926). Concerning Père Joseph see the literature given in the next chapter.

On Wallenstein, the voluminous earlier literature has in recent years been augmented by several important studies. H. Ritter von Srbik once again considered *Wallenstein's Ende* (1920) in terms favorable to the duke. The contrary position was developed with much skill by Josef Pekař, *Wallenstein—1630-34 Die Tragödie einer Verschwörung* (1937). This is the German version of an earlier Czech work, *Valdsteyn 1630-34.* Its appendix contains an elaborate set of notes. Pekař has the advantage over Srbik that the important report of Ottavio Piccolomini had by that time been published: Hubert Jedin, "Die Relation Ottavio Piccoliminis über Wallensteins Schuld und Ende," *Zeitschrift für die Geschichte Schlesiens* (1931), pp. 328-358.

On Gustavus II Adolphus, both Swedes and Germans produced interesting new studies at the time of the anniversary. Georg Wittrock's patriotic *Gustav Adolf* (1930, German edition of a Swedish one published in 1927), devotes a good deal of attention to Sweden's internal development. Johannes Paul's *Gustaf Adolf* (1927-32), three volumes, challenges Droysen's classic *Gustaf Adolf* and its antireligious, strictly political interpretation; I believe rightly so. Nils Ahnlund offered a fine biography (1932); more recently, Max Hein supported its conclusions in a study on Gustavus Adolphus in *Historische Vierteljahrschrift* XXXI (1937), pp. 73-106, in which he showed that Gustavus Adolphus truly wished to be *protector* not *proditor Germaniae* and that his policy was ultimately constructive, K. Weibull explored the relations between Gustavus Adolphus and Richelieu in *Revue Historique* (1934). See also W. Tham, *Axel Oxenstierna* (1935).

The peace of Westphalia has never received the definitive treatment which it would seem to deserve. The text is readily available in Karl Zeumer's *Quellensammlung zur Geschichte der Deutschen Reichsverfassung in Mittelalter und Neuzeit* (second edition, 1913), pp. 395 ff. and 434 ff. (Osnabrück and Münster respectively). A handy translation into German was published by F. A. Six, *Der Westfälische Friede von 1648* (1942). The Dutch-Spanish Treaty has recently been analyzed by C. Smit, *Het Vredesvertrag van Munster 30 Januari 1648* (1948).

CHAPTER SEVEN. THE MODERN STATE ABSOLUTE: FRANCE UNDER RICHELIEU AND
MAZARIN

Since the period of Richelieu and Mazarin is, next to the Revolution, the most dramatic of modern French history, the student is confronted with a wealth of broad as well as more specialized works. Besides, the time produced a rich crop of memoirs, among them the very important *Mémoires* of Richelieu himself, those of the Duc de Rohan, of Cardinal Retz, of Mademoiselle de Montpensier and Madame de Motteville, to mention only a few of the most striking. To these should be added such collections of letters as those of Madame de Sévigné and of Elisabeth Charlotte von der Pfalz, in many volumes. *The Life of Edward Lord Herbert of Cherbury,* giving an account of his embassy at Paris, is revealing for the period of Mazarin; the reports of the Venetian ambassadors, of which Ranke made such skillful use, remain a most instructive source, as do of course the great state collections of documents, such as J. L. M. Avenel's *Lettres, Instructions Diplomatiques, et Papiers d'État, du Cardinal de Richelieu* (1853 and after) in *Collection des Documents Inédits d'Histoire de France;* finally the invaluable *Carnets* of Mazarin must be mentioned here, as well as Richelieu's *Testament Politique* (recently edited by Louis André, 1947).

There is, of course, first of all, the comprehensive treatment in Lavisse, *Histoire de France,* Volumes VI, II, "Henry IV et Louis XIII" by Jean H. Mariéjol (1905); and VII, I, "Louis XIV. La Fronde. Le Roi. Colbert (1643-1685)" by E. Lavisse himself. Among the more extended general works, Gabriel Hanotaux's and the Duc de la Force's *Histoire du Cardinal de Richelieu* (1896 and later) (now in six volumes) is basic, though uneven in value, the earlier parts being superior to the later; in Volume I, pp. 16-17, is found a basic documentary bibliography. Hanotaux's work is a general history, whereas the establishment of absolute monarchy, its role and influence, and its administrative system are the topic of the special work of Vicomte G. d'Avenel, *Richelieu et la Monarchie Absolue* (1884–90). To these must be added Comte de Beauchamp's *Louis XIII d'après sa Correspondance avec le Cardinal Richelieu* (1902) and G. Fagniez's stimulating, if somewhat partial *Le Père Joseph et Richelieu* (1894) in two volumes. Of comparable basic importance are A. Chéruel's works on the Mazarin period: *Histoire de France pendant la Minorité de Louis XIV* (1879–80, in four vols.) and *Histoire de France sous le Ministère de Mazarin—1651–1661* (1882, in three vols.). Chéruel's treatment, too, is done from a national French viewpoint, but with superior scholarship.

As contrasted with these leading French works, all inspired by national pride and an acceptance of the political achievement of Richelieu, two rather challenging literary works, marked by hostility toward the state-building activities of the cardinal and his faithful helper, Père Joseph, have come from English pens: Hilaire Belloc's *Richelieu* (1929) and Aldous Huxley's *Grey Eminence* (1941). Neither of them is scholarly, critical history, but they provide stimulating perspectives.

It is a curious fact that French historians are disinclined to give much attention to the views of foreigners. Yet Leopold von Ranke's *Geschichte Frankreichs vornehmlich im sechzehnten und siebzehnten Jahrhundert* (1850–51) remains most valuable, since he worked upon and wrote the histories not only of England and Germany as well, but also special studies of the papacy and of the Ottomans and hence provides a broad European perspective. More recently, a brilliant and profound study of Richelieu's rise to power has been offered by Carl Burckhardt, *Richelieu, der Aufstieg zur Macht* (1935); likewise a very striking and culturally broad study of Mazarin's reign was given by Karl Federn, *Mazarin* (1922), which contains a selective bibliography. As compared with these works, James B. Perkins' *France under Mazarin—with a Review of the Administration of Richelieu* (1886) and his *Richelieu* (1900) have little merit beyond the fact that they are written in English.

Among special studies, I should like to mention Louis Battifol's lively *La Duchesse de Chevreuse* (1920), which handles its discriminating scholarship nimbly; the same author's *Le Cardinal de Retz* (1927) again proves his skill in dealing felicitously with the intricacies of seventeenth-century intrigue. Auguste Leman has addressed himself to two very important aspects of Richelieu's foreign policy; in one, *Richelieu et Olivárez —Leurs Négotiations secrètes de 1636 à 1642 pour le rétablissement de paix* (1938), he undertakes to show that these negotiations were not merely carried on to negotiate, but were genuinely intended to secure peace; in the other, *Urbain VIII et la Rivalité de la France et de la Maison d'Autriche de 1631 à 1635* (1920), he is concerned likewise with the duel between Richelieu and Olivárez and shows Urban as Pope playing a skillful balance of power game to keep them both at bay. On the complex issues of the Valtelline, and more especially the extraordinary figure of George Jenatsch, we have a new and superior critical study by Alexander Pfister, *Georg Jenatsch—sein Leben und seine Zeit* (1938).

On the administrative and governmental problems of the time of Richelieu, two remarkably exact studies have been produced in recent years by R. Mousnier, *La Venalité des Offices sous Henry IV et Louis XIII* (without date) and *Le Conseil du Roi de la Mort de Henry IV au Gouvernement Personnel de Louis XIV* (in *Études d'Histoire Moderne et Contemporaine,* 1947-48). These searching inquiries have shed a flood of light upon the actual practice of government in the period of the emerging modern state; they tend to confirm our major thesis that this is the period when it actually *did* emerge in France. There is no really adequate study of the French *parlements,* unfortunately; E. Gleason's *Le Parlement de Paris: son Rôle Politique depuis le Règne de Charles VII jusqu'à la Révolution* (Vol. I, Ch. 3, pp. 115-75, dealing with Richelieu, and Ch. 4, pp. 177-395, dealing with Mazarin, including a lengthy treatment of the Fronde) is the standard work, but it is limited to one *parlement* and not very adequate for that. On the constitutional theory, Paul R. Doolin, *The Fronde* (1935), is recommended. Finally, on the subject of French economic life and policy, H. Hauser, *La pensée et l'action économiques du Cardinal de Richelieu* (1944), is highly regarded; I like C. W. Cole, *Colbert and a Century of French Mercantilism* (1939), of which Chapter 4 deals with Richelieu and 5 with Mazarin, while 3 is concerned with what Cole calls "Interlude—1610–1624."

On Spain, the most readable and scholarly general account is Martin Hume's *The Court of Philip IV* (1907), which addresses itself not only to the political, but to social and cultural history as well. Curiously enough, Hume does not mention Justi's remarkable classic, *Velasquez und sein Jahrhundert* (new edition, 1933, but first published in 1888) of which an English edition by A. H. Keane was published in 1889. We shall abstain from mentioning the general histories of Spain (see above notes for Chapter Two), except for the beautifully illustrated Volume IV of D. Antonio Ballesteros y Beretta, *Historia de España y su Influencia en la Historia Universal* (1927).

CHAPTER EIGHT. THE EASTERN DYNASTIES

There does not exist, to my knowledge, a general treatment of the Eastern dynastic world, and this perhaps in part accounts for the lack of cohesion in the total picture. It is with some regret that we finally decided to follow the prevailing pattern and examine, even if ever so briefly, the several national communities, sketching in developments as they unfolded, but inevitably disrupting the narrative. For the Ottoman Empire which might have dominated this situation, as it did a hundred years earlier, we have two older works which are basic, Josef von Hammer-Purgstall, *Geschichte des Osmanischen Reiches,* four volumes, 4 and 5 (1829), and J. W. Zinkeisen, *Geschichte des Osmanischen Reiches in Europa,* seven volumes, 3 and 4 (1855-56). What they lack in historical synthesis is supplied by Leopold von Ranke's sketchy, but interesting *Die Osmanen und die Spanische Monarchie* (third edition, 1857). This is not a work dealing with the relations between Spain and the Ottoman Empire, but contains two separate studies. Pages 1-124 deal with the Turks; an English edition appeared in 1843. Ranke prefaced these two studies by asking the question: how did it happen that these two great powers lost their predominance between the middle of the sixteenth century and our period? And he believes that the *relazioni* of the Venetian ambassadors are more likely to provide an answer than other material. More recently, Max Ritter von Sax specifically addressed himself to this problem in *Geschichte des Machtverfalls der Türkei* (second edition, 1913) but since this study extends to the end of the nineteenth century, only the third section, especially pp. 47-67, is concerned with our problems.

For Russia, the basic history is V. O. Kluchevsky, *A History of Russia* (English edition, 1911-31), of which the third volume deals with our period. The organization of his material is often rather bewildering. His treatment may be compared with S. F. Platonov, *History of Russia* (1929), considered the greatest authority on the seventeenth century. The collaborative history by Paul Milyukov, Charles Seignobos and Louis Eisenmann, *Histoire de Russie* (1932-33), in three volumes, is written from the standpoint of Russian liberalism, while M. N. Prokrovsky's *History of Russia* (1928) gives the Marxist slant; it was official.

until the author was "excommunicated." Finally, Sir Bernard Pares' *A History of Russia* (1926) gives a rather diffuse account of the seventeenth century. It is even more difficult to gather the main trends from H. B. Sumner's *A Short History of Russia* (1943), but the book throws much light upon the long-range perspectives of Russian history. G. Vernadsky's *A History of Russia* (1929), on the other hand, offers, in chs. 16 to 18, a clear and concise survey of political, economic and cultural developments in our period. More recently, Valentin Gitermann has, in his *Geschichte Russlands*, Volume I (1944), Part IV, likewise given a good general portrait of the beginning of the period. A more comprehensive German history of Russia of considerable merit is Karl Stählin, *Geschichte Russlands von den Anfängen bis zur Gegenwart* (1923-39), in four volumes. Parts of Volume 1 deal with our period. Older, but still very good is R. N. Bain, *The First Romanovs* (1905).

For Poland, material in English is not very satisfactory. Indeed, there is no full-length history of this important nation in any language except Polish. A readable general account is George Slocombe, *A History of Poland* (1939). Two main schools of Polish historians have argued the issue of Poland's decline and fall, the Cracow school and the Warsaw school. The former, perhaps best represented by Michal Brobrzynski, *Dzieje Polski w Zarysie* (fourth edition, 1927), argues that internal factors were primarily to blame, whereas the Warsaw school argues that external aggression was mainly at fault. This viewpoint is succinctly set forth by O. Halecki in his *The History of Poland—An Essay in Historical Synthesis* (1942). On the relations of Poland and Russia, see R. N. Bain, *Slavonic Europe 1447-1796* (1908). The institutional side of the issue is developed in broad European perspective by Ladislas Konopszynski, *Le Liberum Veto—Étude sur le Développement du Principe Majoritaire* (1930). No pretense is made here to fathom the depth of Polish historical scholarship; but Volume II of the beautiful illustrated work *Polska Jej Dzieje i Kultura*, published in 1927 by a group of scholars, certainly deserves mention.

Carl Hallendorf and Adolf Schück published (1929) a rather sketchy *History of Sweden*, but the high scholarship of its authors saved it from superficiality. One of its sections deals with the rise of the Baltic Empire. The standard full-length history in Swedish is by E. Hildebrandt (ed.), *Sveriges Historia till Våra Dagar* (1919-26). The seventeenth century is dealt with in Volumes VI and VII, by Georg Wittrock and Gustav Jacobson, respectively; these are of a high order (in the earlier edition, published in 1906, the period 1611–1660 called "stormaktstiden" by the Swedes, was done by Martin Weibull). The new edition now has, in Volume XV, an up-to-date bibliography on all phases of Swedish history by S. E. Bring (1945). A beautifully illustrated history of the Swedish people's culture in many volumes has been brought out under the editorship of Ewert Wrangel, A. Gierow and B. Olsson. The anniversary years of Gustavus Adolphus' reign have brought two remarkably comprehensive works of great interest, done by outstanding scholars: *Sveriges Riksdag* (since 1926), of which the third volume, *Standsriksdagens Utdaning 1592–1672* (1933) by Nils Ahnlund, deals very thoroughly with the Swedish parliament as a typical "government with estates." The other is a publication of the Swedish general staff entitled *Sveriges Krig 1611–1632* (1936–39), in six volumes, which effectively pulls together all previous work on these great Swedish campaigns, reinforced by much unpublished documentary material.

On the great elector and Brandenburg, we now have Ferdinand Schevill's *The Great Elector* (1947), a fine work of historical synthesis which is comprehensive and vivid: it contains a good selective bibliography. There are of course the two German classics: Leopold von Ranke, *Zwölf Bücher preussischer Geschichte* (first published as *Neun Bücher* in 1847) of which Volumes I and II are pertinent; the other is J. G. Droysen, *Geschichte der Preussischen Politik* (second edition, 1870) of which Part III deals with *Der Staat des Grossen Kurfürsten* and takes a sharply Prussian line (in contrast to Ranke). More recently, Hermann von Petersdorff, in *Der Grosse Kurfürst* (1939), reviewed much new evidence, but without arriving at very novel conclusions: the patriotic *Motif* predominates. For the foreign policy of Frederick William, A. Waddington's *Le Grand Electeur—Frédéric Guillaume de Brandebourg—sa Politique extérieur* (1905) is careful, if pedestrian, though naturally critical in the French tradition. The first volume deals with 1640–1660. On the strictly military side, C. Jany, *Geschichte der Königlich-preussischen Armee* (1927–37) in five volumes, is authoritative. The first volume deals with our period.

The history of the Austrian Hapsburgs and their realms is treated most satisfactorily in K. and M. Uhlirz, *Handbuch der Geschichte Osterreichs und seiner Nachbarländer Böhmen und Ungarn* (1927–39), in three volumes. The constitutional and administrative aspects are conveniently assembled in A. Luschin von Ebengreuth, *Osterreichische Reichsgeschichte* (1896). In English, of the somewhat old-fashioned, but detailed work by

William Coxe, *History of the House of Austria* (1889), in four volumes, Volume II is still useful as a reference. On the cultural side, the recent collaborative work by F. M. Mayer, R. F. Kaindl, and H. Pirchegger, *Geschichte und Kulturleben Deutschösterreichs* (1929-37), in three volumes, Volume I is very helpful.

The standard Russian histories given above all concern themselves at some length with the Great Schism and its relationship to the conflict between the eastern and western churches. Among special studies published in recent years, Wladimir Solovyev, *Russia and the Universal Church* (1948), Part I, Chapters IV-VII, and Hans von Eckhardt, *Russisches Christentum* (1947), deserve special mention. F. C. Conybeare, *Russian Dissenters* (1921), and Robert Stupperich, *Staatsgedanke und Religionspolitik Peters des Grossen* (1936), Introduction, are also very valuable. Finally, *The Life of Archpriest Avakum* (English edition, 1924) while mostly concerned with the later crisis, is rewarding.

CHAPTER NINE. THE MODERN STATE LIMITED

In spite of the criticism which has been leveled at it from time to time, S. R. Gardiner's three great works, *History of England, 1603-1642*, in ten volumes (1883-84); *History of the Great Civil War, 1642-1649*, in four volumes (1893); and *History of the Commonwealth and Protectorate, 1649-1656*, in four volumes (1909), together with C. H. Firth's *The Last Years of the Protectorate, 1656-1658*, in two volumes (1909), have remained basic and become classics. Maybe Professor Gardiner's judgments are considerably less consistent than they ought to be, as Professor Roland G. Usher argued in his study of Gardiner's methods; still no work of equally concise and profound scholarship has come to take the place of these many volumes as far as the general history of the period is concerned. But a number of very valuable works with more specialized focus have enriched our understanding of this heroic age of English history. Foremost among these I would place W. C. Abbott's *The Writings and Speeches of Oliver Cromwell*, in four volumes (1937-47), with an admirable bibliography. Outstanding also is the study by J. R. Tanner, *English Constitutional Conflicts in the Seventeenth Century 1603-1689* (1928), which gives more than the title suggests. Godfrey Davies' *The Early Stuarts, 1603-1660* (1938) builds upon the scholarship of Gardiner and Firth to arrive at different conclusions, as does likewise the charmingly written and comprehensive study by George Trevelyan, *England under the Stuarts* (1924), previously mentioned. J. W. Allen's *English Political Thought (1603-1644)* (1938) is the mature fruit of the author's exacting scholarship, but limited by the overemphasis upon verbal interpretation.

On Cromwell, besides Abbott's work, C. H. Firth's is probably still the best straight biography. His nationalism has been skillfully analyzed by George Lanyi in an as yet unprinted dissertation (Harvard), entitled *Oliver Cromwell and His Age—a Study in Nationalism* (1949). *Cromwell's Army* (1902) is the subject of a remarkable study by Firth. The recent biography of *Archbishop Laud* by J. Trevor-Roper (1940, 1949) is in a class by itself, as far as perspective and objective detachment is concerned; we badly need a comparably penetrating study of Thomas Wentworth, earl of Strafford, and of Charles I; H. D. Traill's *Lord Strafford* (1889) is old-fashioned. The specific institutional issues are the subject of Roland G. Usher's magistral *The Rise and Fall of the High Commission* (1913), especially Chapters IX-XII, and of Charles H. McIlwain's classic, *The High Court of Parliament and Its Supremacy* (1910). The general background of religious history may most authoritatively be gathered from J. Stoughton, *History of Religion in England,* in eight volumes (1881). When taken together with W. K. Jordan's exhaustive *The Development of Religious Toleration in England,* in four volumes (1932-40), especially Volumes II and III, the primary focal points of English intellectual and political concern ought to be well established. Regarding the controversial writings on the relation between Protestantism and the capitalist spirit, the more important titles are given above.

Besides Cromwell's *Writings and Speeches* there are of course a great many other contemporary accounts. Among these, the so-called *Clarke Papers* (edited by Firth; 1891-1901, in four volumes) are outstanding. A selection was made from them, together with some supplementary documents, by A. S. P. Woodhouse, who added a thoughtful introduction, under the title, *Puritanism and Liberty* (1938). Very illuminating, from the Royalist standpoint, is the earl of Clarendon's celebrated *History of the Great Rebellion and Civil Wars in England,* first published in 1702-4 in three volumes; W. D. Macray offered a new edition in six volumes in 1888. By contrast, John Thurloe's *State Papers* (seven volumes, 1742) is important as a source, but without the dramatic human interest of Clarendon. Anti-Cromwellian, yet republican are the *Memoirs* of Edmund Ludlow (1892). Very illuminating also the memoirs of the *Life of Colonel Hutchinson* (1806), by his widow, Mrs. Lucy Hutchinson, as showing the outlook of the Independents of the "better" class.

Margret James' *Social Problems and Policy during the Puritan Revolution—1640–1660* (1930) was the first in a series of significant writings on the social and economic ferment of the period, stimulated by the revolutionary issues of our time. I would especially note D. Petegorsky, *Left-Wing Democracy in the English Civil War; a Study of the Social Philosophy of Gerrard Winstanley* (1940), and G. H. Sabine, *The Works of Gerrard Winstanley* (1941), as well as Arthur Barker's *Milton and the Puritan Dilemma, 1641–1660* (1942). W. Haller, Godfrey Davies and D. M. Wolfe have published the Levelers Tracts and Manifestoes.

One special monograph on the preceding phase of the revolution deserves mention: J. H. Hexter's *The Reign of King Pym* (1941), which offers a new and interesting interpretation of party politics.

In conclusion, we might add to this brief note that Godfrey Davies brought out a full and highly meritorious *Bibliography of British History, Stuart Period, 1603–1714* (1928), to which reference may readily be had by the studious.

INDEX

355